WILDERNESS AND PARADISE

IN CHRISTIAN THOUGHT

From left to right: Jim Smith, George Williams, Timothy George

Foreword to the 2016 Reprint Edition

by Timothy George

A scholar of international renown, George Huntston Williams (1914-2000) was one of the great church historians of the twentieth century. A native of Ohio, he joined the faculty of Harvard Divinity School in 1947 and served successively as Winn Professor of Ecclesiastical History (1956-63) and, in the oldest academic chair in the United States, as Hollis Professor of Divinity (1963-80). A person of vast erudition and wide-ranging intellectual interests, Williams determined to be a *generalist* in the field of church history. Calvin Pater, one of Williams's students, once exclaimed, "Only Williams could decide to specialize in everything; thus clasping to his breast *both* and *and*, with *either* and *or* together, a state of affairs that would have scandalized a Kierkegaard." His doctoral studies, completed under John T. McNeill, focused on medieval political theology, but he also wrote and taught with great insight and wisdom on the whole range of the Christian story from its biblical and patristic grounding to its contemporary expressions and challenges.

Williams's long and interesting life cut a wide swath across the landscape of the twentieth century. Among those he encountered along the way were Eugene V. Debbs and W. E. B. Dubois, both visitors in Williams's boyhood home; Adolf Hitler, whom Williams once encountered in Munich's Carlton Café during his student days in Germany; Reinhold Niebuhr, who recommended Williams to Harvard and Paul Tillich, who was his colleague there; Martin Luther King Jr., who once audited his courses in church history and with whom he marched in Alabama in support of racial equality and civil rights; and St. Pope John Paul II, whom he met at the Second Vatican Council and about whom he wrote a major intellectual biography, *The Mind of John Paul II* (1981). Williams felt deeply his calling as both scholar and minister. He labored under the burden of a holy and risky calling to keep alive the truth, the truth that sets men and women free. He liked to quote the words of Adolf von Harnack: "We study history in order to intervene in the course of history and we have a right and duty to do so; for without historical insight we either permit ourselves to be mere objects of the historical process or tend to mislead people in an irresponsible way."

Williams is best remembered for his magisterial study, *The Radical Reformation*, first published in 1962, a book that appeared in three editions and was subsequently translated into several languages. Nineteen sixty-two also saw the publication of *Wilderness and Paradise in Christian Thought*. This volume illustrates as well as anything Williams ever wrote what I have elsewhere called his principle of "luminous particularity." Williams traces the wilderness theme through myriads of turns and permutations in the history of ideas, never forgetting the subtle and complex interconnectedness of the events and concepts he portrayed. He understood such construals not as isolated, opaque moments in the history of religion but rather as translucent windows onto a whole pattern of Christian experience.

As one reviewer said of *Wilderness and Paradise* soon after its publication, this "study grapples with the full scope of biblical thought and its various applications to concrete human situations, starting from the Garden of Eden to the Kindergartens of our modern secular educational system." Throughout this long history, Williams knew that "wilderness" could be both savage and benign, a scene of isolation and demonic infestation on the one hand, and a reservoir of renewal and retreat—a sacred encampment—on the other. The same awareness is also evident in the second part of the volume where Williams traces the development of five interrelated themes present in "the theological idea of the university." For a much fuller account of how Williams saw this motif unfolded in the history of Harvard itself, we have now his posthumously published study, complete in three volumes, *Divinings: Religion at Harvard from its Origins in New England Ecclesiastical History to the 175th Anniversary of the Harvard Divinity School, 1636-1992* (Göttingen, Germany: Vandenhoeck & Ruprecht, 2014).

Wilderness and Paradise was published in the same year as Rachel Carson's best-selling *Silent Spring*. It was a time when many were beginning to recognize the acute ecological crisis confronting the world and its inhabitants. In tracing the many mythic and theological meanings of wilderness and paradise throughout the Christian story, Williams dared to see the implications of his study for the fragile world God created and gave to men and women with a charge of stewardship to keep. His words were prophetic and are still relevant today.

Unless some believers in every generation can, through that poverty by which we divest ourselves of all lordliness, join St. Francis in his canticle addressed to the sun and to the bears as brethren, to the snow and to the swallows as sisters, then in the present stage of mankind's awesome capacity for enforcing lordship over nature—whether in ruthless urbanization of the countryside, or in exploitation of natural resources heedless of generations to come, or in any careless experimentation in the realm of life, disease, and death—we shall presently find that we can no longer address even one another as brother and sister and that a utilitarian view of nature will have blasted our human nature. We shall find that the garden of culture, like the garden which is the Church, will wither or bewilder when it is by artifice fenced off from the ground of our creatureliness.

Timothy George is the founding dean of Beeson Divinity School of Samford University and general editor of the *Reformation Commentary on Scripture.*

Foreword

Wilderness and Paradise in Christian Thought is divided in two parts.
Part One has grown out of the Menno Simons Lectures delivered in
1958 at Bethel College in North Newton, Kansas. The Introduction
and selected parts of the work constituted the Presidential Address before the American Society of Church History on December 29, 1958,
in Washington, D.C. The Introduction and some of the material on
American Christianity were published as "The Wilderness and Paradise in the History of the Church," *Church History,* XXVIII (1959),
3–24. The essay in its present version deals with the way in which the
biblical understanding of the religious and ethical significance of the
desert passed into and influenced Christian history and Western culture.
It is divided into four chapters: (1) the three meanings of the desert in
the Bible itself, (2) the ancient and medieval permutations of the
wilderness complex, (3) the perpetuation of the wilderness impulses in
the Reformation era and into modern times, and (4) the distinctively
American developments of the eschatology of the garden (paradise)
and wilderness.

In Part Two, a closely related essay, the evolution of the idea of the
university as a paradise of learning is traced from the earlier idea of
the whole Church as a provisional paradise, through the claim of the
more disciplined monastery to be a paradise, to the incorporation of the
paradisic motif in the emerging clerical university of the Middle Ages.
The elaboration of this and kindred motifs, and allied themes, is traced
with special reference to Harvard College, whose founders in the seventeenth century preserved the medieval conception of the *translatio
studii,* and were conscious of the assignment laid upon them in transferring to the New World the disciplines of learning, in a tradition that stretched, by way of old Cambridge, Paris, and Athens to Jerusalem; from the schools of the prophets in the Israelite desert to the
wilderness of America. This essay first appeared as an excursus to *The
Harvard Divinity School* (Boston, 1954) and was subsequently printed
in slightly amplified form by the Commission on Higher Education
of the National Council of Churches under its present title, *The Theological Idea of the University* (New York, 1958).

In preparing the revision of this second essay, and in working on
the several versions of that on the wilderness, I have been helped in
various ways by the following colleagues, students, and associates:

Professor Cornelius Krahn and Edward G. Kaufman of Bethel
College; the late Professor Alexander Miller of Stanford University;

the Reverend Hubert C. Noble of the National Council of Churches; Professor Horton Davies of Princeton University; Dr. Ernst Kantorowicz of the Institute for Advanced Studies; Professor Ernst Benz of the University of Marburg; Professor Leonard Miller of the Connecticut College for Women; Professor John Edward Dirks of Yale University; Miss Elizabeth Abbot Smith of the Arlington Historical Society, Miss Dorothy Rounds of Arlington High School, and Miss Edith Lovejoy Pierce of Evanston; Professor Richard Cameron of Boston University; Professor Raymond Albright of the Episcopal Theological School in Cambridge; Professor Robert Darwin Crouse of Bishop's College in Quebec; Dr. James Vendettuoli, Jr., of Groton School; Professors James Luther Adams, Frank Cross, Christopher Dawson, Georges Florovsky, Joachim Gaehde, Helmut Koester, Henry A. Murray, George Smith, Krister Stendahl, Amos Wilder, and G. Ernest Wright, and Messrs. George McCandlish, Paul Lee, Alvin Beachy, Ernest Lashlee, Harold Worthley, and Joseph Brown of Harvard University; Professors Étienne Trocmé, Rodolphe Peter, and Stanislas Giet of the University of Strasbourg; and Professor Augusto Armando Hugon of Torre Pellice.

The author would like to add that, though the book is an essay limited in scope to ecclesiastical and educational history, he is very much interested in real gardens and especially the unspoiled wilderness. Indeed he hopes that by dealing historically with the humanistic as distinguished from the humane and the naturalistic meanings of the wilderness he will have indirectly encouraged other writers to reconceive the urgent problem of conserving wilderness areas and of extending wildlife refuges all over the world for the perpetuation of threatened species. The naturalist in the ecclesiastical historian will, however, apart from this bit of foreword, have almost no occasion to express himself in the book that follows. For the time being he will content himself with the mere statement of his underlying conviction as a "Christian naturalist" that man cannot remain truly man if he coninues to bulldoze and slaughter away so much of his natural environment that he will have lost all sense of interrelatedness with his fellow creatures of earth and sky. As Justice William O. Douglas in *My Wilderness* has said recently: "Man sometimes seems to try to crowd everything but himself out of the universe. Yet he cannot live a full life with the products of his own creation." In the same book he writes: "A civilization can be built around the machine. But it is doubtful that a meaningful life can be produced by it. . . . The wilderness stands as the true 'control' plot for all experimentation. . . . Only through knowledge of the norm can an appraisal of the abnormal or diseased be made. . . . With [wilderness areas] intact man need not become an automaton. . . . He needs a measure of the wilderness. . . ." A similar thought is echoed on the other side of the Atlantic by Samivel at the conclusion of *Grand Paradis,* a description of the magnificent Italian national wilderness reservation: "With their calculators, their automation, their cunning transformation of the powers of perception, the progeny of Adam are henceforth too powerful to refuse the role of protectors. . . . It is incumbent upon them to assume custody for the destiny of the woods and the beasts that can no longer hold their own. Otherwise all will be lost and the earth will be sad."

The devoted conservationist, who surely needs as many allies as he can muster in the increasingly difficult task of safeguarding our heritage of nature, may along with the readers for whom the following book is primarily intended find unexpected sanction and warrant for his efforts in the biblical and ecclesiastical testimony that man is but one of God's creations. Man was placed in the midst of Paradise as a steward to give names to and bewonder the teeming multitudes of forms that had before him issued from the hand of the Creator. Noah was instructed by God to preserve from universal destruction two or seven of every kind of beast and bird, both clean and unclean, that is, without undue regard to their eventual utility to man. After the Flood and the legitimation of the eating of meat, the prophets could still look forward to the restitution of peace within the animal kingdom and of harmony between man and beast. One of them, Hosea (2:20), even foresaw God entering into a covenant with the beasts of the field, the birds of the air, and the reptiles on the ground in order to secure the peace of the elect. Job (40:15) in his understandably self-centered wretchedness was reminded by God of the comfort to be gained from perspective: "Behold now the hippopotamus which I made with thee." Jesus said that the heavenly Father regards the lily of the field and the sparrow that falls. Paul (Romans 8:22) thought of the whole of creation as in some obscure way groaning together with man in pain until the redemption. The newly discovered *Gospel according to Thomas* preserves a gospel *of* all creatures (1–4; 77–79) alongside the familiar gospel *to* all creatures (Mark 16:15). And all through the history of Christianity, as we shall show in selected detail, the wilderness, as beloved and beckoning, as punitive and purifying, has been a haunting vision.

The quest for the wilderness, physical and metaphysical, is a theme of unexpected variation, which brings together in one perspective many disparate aspects of Christian civilization.

Introduction to the 2016 Reprint Edition

GEORGE HUNTSTON WILLIAMS' (GHW) *Wilderness and Paradise in Christian Thought* (1962) remains a classic expression of Christian reverence for Creator, creation and enlightened human vocation.

Williams' distinguished career as a Harvard church historian (1947-80) inspired two festschrifts: *Continuity and Discontinuity in Church History* (1979) at his 65th birthday and retirement from classroom teaching and *The Contentious Triangle: Church, State and University* (1999) at his 85th birthday on the eve of a new millennium. A selection from each volume serves to introduce George Williams' two foremost reflections on Nature.

Williams' student Timothy George, in his 1999 essay "A Historian for All Seasons," noted GHW's lifelong interest (both personal and scholarly) in "creation care." As a self-identified "Christian naturalist," *Wilderness and Paradise* was written to encourage "other writers to re-conceive the urgent problem of conserving wilderness areas and of extending wildlife refuges all over the world for perpetuation of endangered species" (ix). As Dr. George observes, "Fully cognizant that elements within the Judaeo-Christian tradition have been called upon to sanction the exploitation of nature, he finds ample resources within that same tradition for rethinking the ecological unity of humankind with the cosmos, for the elaboration of an "earth ethic," for a vision of the human as steward rather than manipulator of creation, as carers for our fellow creatures...rather than conquerors of the cosmos." (28)

Williams' teacher (and later Harvard Divinity School colleague) James Luther Adams, in his 1979 essay "George Huntston Williams: A Portrait," offers further insight. "In his elaborate history of attitudes toward nature in Western history (1971), he traces the antimonies suggested by seven sets of scriptural passages. The great achievement of the covenantal religion of Israel was to disengage itself from the cults of fertility of the Caananites and to think of man as in this sense overcoming nature... Williams has not been willing to put to one side the theological concern for the cosmos, and for the earth and its diversified world in which all creatures have a precious place in God's eyes. There is grace from below as well as grace from above." (16)

In this earlier *fest* another iconic church historian, Jaroslav Pelikan, praised his friend's range of thought in "Hundred-handed, Argus-eyed: The Historical Scholarship of George H. Williams." There, he cited the succinct assessment of Williams' valuing of nature by Yale president A. Bartlett Giamatti in *The Earthly Paradise and the Renaissance Epic* (1966): "brilliant discussion."

George Williams' heart for Nature, as he observed during my days as Harvard doctoral student and minister, was rooted in childhood experiences in rural Ohio, the witness of Scripture and subsequent studies in both history and the sciences. His appreciation of Harvard Divinity School (which he chronicled and helped rescue as Acting Dean in the 1950s), was deepened by that school's historic "errand into the wilderness." As Lynn White, Jr's 1967 *Science* essay "Historical Roots of the Ecological Crisis" inspired a swell of critical examination re Christianity and the impact of theology on environmental domination, so George Huntston Williams' works here provide both a redemptive voice from that era and continued resources for ecotheology (see bibliography) and creation care across generations. As he was fond of saying, we are "creatures of a Creator and subjects of a Kingdom."

James D. Smith III
The Feast of St. Francis of Assisi
Centennial of George Williams' birth
October, 2014

Rev. James D. Smith III (Th.D., Harvard) is professor of church history at Bethel Seminary San Diego, Visiting professor at Richmont Graduate University (Atlanta), and associate pastor of La Jolla Christian Fellowship.

Part One # THE WILDERNESS THEME

*Permutations of the Biblical Experience of
the Desert in the History of Christianity*

FORTY DAYS
(Mark 1:13)

For forty days with creatures of the wild—
God and the world of nature reconciled—
For forty days he brings the golden age.
Perhaps his hunger calms their hungry rage.
They will not try this shepherd of the sheep
But, quieted, in his shadow drop to sleep.
His prayer beneath the moon forestalls their growl,
Imposes silence on the midnight howl.
And, while he prays beside his watching post,
Four-footed guardians form a dusky host.
Not only wind and wave obey his will;
The wild beasts understand his "Peace, be still."
Mastered, the desert creatures soon are tame.
In forty days the wolves have learned his name.

EDITH LOVEJOY PIERCE
Printed in *The Christian Century*,
LXXVI (February 18, 1959), 195.

Introduction

In his now classic "The Significance of the Frontier in American History," read before the American Historical Association in 1893,[1] Frederick Jackson Turner quoted from *A New Guide for Emigrants* [to the West] (2nd ed., Boston, 1837), written by the pioneer Baptist misisonary and founder of seminaries John Mason Peck, who died just a century ago.[2] Peck had distinguished three types of Westerners: the pioneers, the settlers, and "the men of capital and enterprise." Turner found this typology useful and adapted it in his succession of studies, which has helped to shape our understanding of American history.

William Warren Sweet applied Turner's frontier concept as a basic category in the interpretation of Christianity in America in a series of studies of religion on the frontier, a specialized aspect of which he presented a quarter of a century ago in his presidential address before the American Society of Church History.[3] Sweet too mentioned Peck, in passing; for the founder of Rock Spring Seminary (1827), which was a forerunner of Shurtleff College in Alton, Illinois,[4] was an important figure in the history of the Baptists and a representative builder of the Middle West.

In the present essay on the significance of wilderness and paradise in Christian thought it is appropriate to allude once again, by way of introduction, to John Mason Peck.

A certain Presbyterian minister, who had come recently into Illinois, later recalled the following incident. Making his way over the lonely prairies, interspersed here and there with patches of timber, he was arrested by the sound of an ax. Upon observing a woodman near by, he called to him, "What are you doing here, stranger?" "I am building a theological seminary," was the reply. "What, in these barrens?"

[1] Most accessible in the collection of earlier essays under the title *The Frontier in American History* (New York, 1920), pp. 19–21.

[2] On his life we have the account in *Dictionary of American Biography;* Coe Hayne, *Vanguard of the Caravans* (Philadelphia, 1931); Matthew Lawrence, *John Mason Peck: The Pioneer Missionary: A Biographical Sketch* (New York, 1940); and the earlier and theologically fuller *Memoir of John Mason Peck,* edited from his journals and correspondence by Rufus Babcock (Philadelphia, 1864).

[3] "The Churches as Moral Courts of the Frontier," *Church History,* II (1933), 3 ff.

[4] Peck's role as educator is taken up by Austin K. DeBlois in *The Pioneer School: A History of Shurtleff College, the Oldest Educational Institution in the West* (Chicago, 1900).

"Yes," responded the woodman, "I am planting the seed." The planter in the wilderness was John M. Peck.[5]

A seminary is a seedbed or garden for the nurture of the clergy.

There are three millennia of biblical and ecclesiastical history behind the impulse to plant a seminary in the barrens, a garden in the wilderness, a paradise in the desert. It is indeed so basic a concept in Christian history that the wilderness motif might be said to exceed in significance the frontier as a category in the interpretation not only of American history but of Church history in general; for, like the frontier, the wilderness is not only geographical but psychological. It can be a state of mind as well as a state of nature. It can betoken alternatively either a state of bewilderment or a place of protective refuge and disciplined contemplation, as well as literally the wilds.

When the emigrants from the eastern seaboard of America moved into the West, they passed through a real wilderness haunted by wolves and savages, but the millennial tutelage of Scripture had charged that wilderness with epic significance and theological meaning. The wilderness had become, in fact, a complex symbol of significance both for the corporate and for the personal expressions of the Christian life.

As in the history of America, so in the much longer history of ancient Israel, upon which, through their Bible, the American settlers and pioneers were drawing for inspiration and guidance, the wilderness as desert in its geophysical sense was continuously surcharged with the added meanings provided by the religious experience of the race.

In ancient Palestine the wilderness meant, in terms of physical geography, the steppe beyond the land which could be cultivated with the help of seasonal rains, and the dry wastes even farther from the beneficent effects of occasional rains. In terms of religion it meant for the settled Hebrews, as for the surrounding peoples, the realm of desiccation which could encroach even upon their gardens, orchards, and pastures if the annual cultic renewals were not observed. It was, however, the distinctive character of the Hebraic cultus and myth to break away from the purely cyclical conception of seasonal dryness and renewal and to correlate the shift of the seasons with the moral behavior of the nation. In the variations over the years appeared a purposeful direction, until at length the vision extended from the Garden of Eden, through the wanderings in the wilderness of Sinai, to the prospect of a new Eden.

[5] The episode was recounted by the Rev. John M. Ellis, a graduate of the Andover Theological Seminary, and preserved by Samuel Baker in his "Historical Address" in *Jubilee Memorial of Shurtleff College, Upper Alton, Ill.* (Alton, Mo., 1877), p. 85.

It was, in fact, the formative wilderness experience of the people of Israel at Sinai that gave the term *wilderness* a historically and ethically positive meaning as well as the negative meaning which the Hebrews shared with the other peoples on the edge of the desert, preoccupied as they all were with the annual agricultural renewal and the cultic assurance of seasonal fertility. It is the persistent recollection of this historic experience of the Sinai desert amid the annual festival enactment of the conversion of dryness into fertility that has given the scriptural texts the extraordinary complexity and potency which was to survive in varied impulses into Christian history.

The *wilderness state* has indeed become almost a technical theological term in certain Christian traditions. It is one of the most useful images supplied by Scripture to designate the recurrent fact that even in the life of the redeemed there are periods or phases of partial failure, depression, uncertainty, and even defection. The children of Israel had been saved from bondage to this world, slavery in Egypt, by their miraculous passage through the Red Sea; they wandered in a wilderness for forty years before reaching the Promised Land; and many of them died murmuring against God and Moses and the new commandments. Even Jesus after his baptism in the waters of Jordan faced a comparable period of forty days in the wilderness, tempted by Satan. It is recorded that the very Spirit which had appeared as a dove at his baptism led him into that wilderness. Throughout the history of Christianity the parallel of the forty years and the forty days after the redemptive event of symbolic or exemplary baptism in the Red Sea and the Jordan River has been held up for typological contemplation as to the meaning of the believer's temptations or aimless wanderings, the dryness and murmurings, that seem to be the chronic blemishes of the Christian life.

The quest for the wilderness as a place of refuge prepared for the true Church persecuted by the world, the quest again for that wilderness which may through spiritual and moral subjugation and cultivation even more than physical conquest, tilling, and seeding become a garden or Eden of the Lord—this is a basic impulse in the history of many branches and institutions of Christianity.

We shall find that in the positive sense the wilderness or desert will be interpreted variously as a place of protection, a place of contemplative retreat, again as one's inner nature or ground of being, and at length as the ground itself of the divine being. We shall find that in its negative sense the wilderness will be interpreted as the world of the unredeemed, as the wasteland, and as the realm or phase of punitive or purgative preparation for salvation. The corresponding term *garden* or *paradise,* in the sense of the Garden of the Great King of the universe, will in due course be applied provisionally to the Church, then more exclusively to the disciplined monastery alone, then to the school growing out of the Church and monastery, namely, the medieval university, and at length in the New World to the theological seminary as a seedbed of missionaries and ministers. Concurrent with this institutional extension of the term *paradise* will be its interiorization as the enlightened mind and its externalization and geographical relocation as the terrestrial paradise at the antipodes, and at length the reconception of the primordial wilderness, contemplated as Nature and as a revelation of Nature's God.

The account which follows is not, of course, a retracing of the pilgrimage of God's people through history or even the idea of pilgrimage and wandering, except indirectly. It is not an account of successive interpretations of the Fall from the Garden, although it will touch upon this. Nor is it a pursuit of a specialized aspect of millennialism, although the eschatological mood is prominent. It is not primarily a history of one particular myth and the survivals of its cultic remnants, for the original Semitic cultic myth had itself been partly broken or demythologized in an ethical direction by the Hebrew prophets. In any event, through the two millennia of Christian history which constitute the bulk of our account of the wilderness and garden texts, Christians who employed them in diverse and fresh contexts were unaware of any setting in the liturgy of the Temple or sanctuary which they may once have had. Nor is the essay primarily a philological study. Moreover, it covers too much synoptically to constitute a close and careful analysis of the historic or psychological processes whereby the ancient texts were combined and assimilated to become personally or institutionally significant.

It is rather a sketch of successive, representative types of the interpretation of the wilderness and the garden as expressions of both the grace and the wrath of God, of his protective and his punitive providence. It is in fact a survey of the persistence of the ambiguity of the Hebraic experience of the wilderness and the equally distinctive prophetic understanding of the precariousness of the garden. This precariousness of the sown land, or, by theological extension, the garden (the vineyard of the Lord, Eden, Paradise), that can during a moral shift or deficiency in the changing seasons of the spirit be blasted by the breath of God and turned into a desert, and at the same time the miraculous convertibility of the wilderness into a refuge and a realm of purification, has made of the paradise-wilderness motif a powerful religio-psychological force and scriptural resource in the never-ending to-and-fro of Christian history, in many reforming or restitutional movements, in many heretical, sectarian, and monastic formations, and in many mystical, educational, and missionary formulations and impulses. The concept of the wilderness and wasteland has at length become a major theme also in American literature and art.

Apologizing in advance to the specialists for the brevity of my expositions in each of the many and disparate areas and eras to be traversed, I nevertheless hope that they (along with the more general readers) will feel that one may validly evoke a feeling for the whole by attention to selected parts. The sketch should be of interest to the student of mythology, the philologist, the historian, the psychologist, the literary critic, the naturalist, and the conservationist, because nowhere else have the permutations been traced and distinguished in one consecutive account of the idea of the wilderness, which has ever and anew been redefined against the constancy of the biblical texts and the variability of the climes, both environmental and spiritual, in which successive Christian generations have wrought out their lives.

Although allegorization and typological extravagance, tendentious misappropriation, and outright misconception of the original meaning of the wilderness in Scripture are part of the account, the most interesting feature is the fact that generation after generation the Christian transcripts and applications of the garden and wilderness passages have, with impressive frequency and inner cunning, despite all their variety and imprecision, faithfully reproduced the fascinatingly ambivalent character of the primordial desert motif in the Old Testament itself.

Of almost equal interest is the fact that the wilderness texts of the Bible have been variously combined in the long course of Christian history, until at length certain conflations have become, as it were, stable compounds in the building up of increasingly complex exegetical syntheses with their own peculiar affinities, motion, and vitality more or less independent of the scriptural matrix from which they were derived.

Since the Scriptures of both Covenants have in the course of time been looked back upon by Christians as a unit, I have, instead of treating the New Testament material as part of the early Christian elaboration of the Hebraic themes, brought the principal motifs of both the Old and the New Testament together as the first movement. The classical symphony with its four movements, its variations on two or more themes, has, indeed, suggested the basic structure of the following composition as an artistic unity. In tracing the two motifs of wilderness and garden through (Chapter I) the Bible, (Chapter II) the ancient and the medieval Church, (Chapter III) the Reformation and modern times, and in (Chapter IV) American Christianity, may the underlying expectation be fulfilled that we shall thereby better understand the Church, its missions and its seminaries, its schisms and dissensions, and also Christian lives with all their darkness and temptations, their luminosity and achievement, their contemplative depth and, alas, also their corporate bigotry.

One might, to be sure, ask at the outset of our excursion whether the biblical theology of the desert and the accumulative interpretations thereof actually induced the movements or whether, to explain their inner experience, the mystics simply resorted to the imaginative language of Scripture; and whether, to justify mass migrations and sectarian secessions, their leaders did not simply appeal to plausible scriptural sanctions.

The motives of the children of Adam, even when they are Christians, perhaps especially when they are Christians, are mixed; but the author traces the evolution and transmutation of the desert experience, convinced that these theological ideas have moved history, that behind these movements, even when occasionally destructive or futile, we may hear the Creator walking in the Garden in the cool of the day or descry the Lord of hosts either punishing or protecting his people in the wilderness of the world, as also the biblical prophets themselves perceived when they observed how the desert can through faith and the showers of the Spirit be made to blossom as the rose, and conversely, how even the enclosed gardens with their shrine and sanctuary can be blasted by the wrathful breath of God.

The churches of our day have surely felt the withering blasts from without, and from within have been impoverished by erosion or encumbered by the woody growths of competitive institutionalism. But the Christian scholar or poet still lives in an enclosed and fertile part of that garden, sustained by the grace mediated through the fellowship of research, prayer, and kindled imagination. Disciplined by his Christian duty and opportunity to come face to face with the many before him in the vast *communio sanctorum* of the centuries, he may strengthen others who find themselves planted where the soil is exhausted and join with them in the never ending task of holding back the moral and spiritual wilderness on the frontier of which man precariously maintains his hold upon the life that God created and called good.

Connecticut-born John Mason Peck, who was discovered chopping in the barrens of Illinois in 1827, showed himself heir to this great tradition when he answered that he was building a theological seminary in the wilderness. When later, as a Baptist missionary and recruiter of immigrants, Peck prepared the foreword of his *Guide to the West,* he quoted Isaiah 66:8 in exhilarated confidence that a new nation was indeed being "born at once." Another prophecy from the same book, Isaiah 51:3, may be appropriately taken as the motto of the following essay because of its perennial influence:

> For the Lord will comfort you;
>   he will comfort all her waste places,
> And make her wilderness like Eden,
>   her desert like the garden of the Lord. . . .

We shall, at the end of this book, be able to paraphrase Frederick Jackson Turner: Up almost to our own day, many major and minor movements in Christian history have been in a substantial degree the history of the interpretations of the biblical and post-biblical meanings of wilderness and paradise in the experience of God's ongoing Israel.

Chapter 1. Wilderness and Desert: Garden and Paradise in the Bible

Palestine, progressively drier as one moves south from the forests of Lebanon to the wilderness of Judea, is a land where the same caves and grottoes from time immemorial have served successively or interchangeably as cisterns and places of sepulchre, as shelters from heat and cold, as shrines for chthonic deities and for biblical worthies and saints. It is a land where slight variations in the seasonal or subterranean supply of water has made the difference between life and death, between fruitfulness and desert; and where the Hebrews, whose formative experience had been in the desert of Sinai, were ever and anew obliged to rethink the relationship of their God of the wilderness Law to the needs of a settled agricultural and urban society.

The whole of biblical history has, in fact, been interpreted in terms of the wilderness motif; of the struggle between the religion of the desert and the religion of the city;[1] or again, of the fall from the garden (paradise) devastated by sin, the wandering in the wilderness, and the vision of a second Eden.[2]

[1] The most recent major work on the sociological significance of the desert in the history of Israel is Samuel Nyström, *Beduinentum und Jahwismus: Eine soziologisch-religionsgeschichtliche Untersuchung zum Alten Testament* (Lund, 1946). In briefer form is the doctoral essay of John Flight, "The Nomadic Idea and Ideal," *Journal of Biblical Literature*, XLII (1942), 158–226. An earlier work by Elias Auerbach, *Die Wüste und Gelobtes Land*, 2 vols. (Berlin, 1932–1936), does not bring out the motif suggested by the title. The perpetual meteorological and related ethnic conflict between the Sown and the Unsown as distinguished from the recurrent conflict between the civilization of Egypt and Mesopotamia in the formation of Israel is the theme of James A. Montgomery's *Arabia and the Bible* (Philadelphia, 1934). See also Nelson Glueck, *Rivers in the Desert: A History of the Negev* (New York, 1959).

[2] The pioneer and now classic work here, with its lapidary formula "Endzeit gleicht Urzeit," is Hermann Gunkel's *Schöpfung und Chaos: Eine religionsgeschichtliche Untersuchung über Gen. 1 und Ap. Joh. 12* (Göttingen, 1896). Gunkel modified his theory in subsequent researches. Johannes Pedersen significantly added to the mythico-cultural interpretation and located it in a much larger Semitic context in *Israel: Its Life and Culture*, 4 vols. (Danish: Copenhagen, 1920; English: London, 1926), notably in the chapter "The World of Life and Death," II, 453–496. Alfred Haldar carries the study further in his monograph which systematically locates Hebraic concepts in a larger cultural context, *The Notion of Desert in Sumero-Accadian and West-Semitic Religions*, Uppsala Universitets Arsskrift, 1950, No. 3. Haldar had previously worked out his theme in his analysis of Nahum. Gerhard von Rad in his section on "Die Wüstenwanderung" in *Theologie des Alten Testaments* (Munich, 1957), I, 279, recognizes the opposing view of the desert experience within the biblical record, contrasting Jeremiah 2 and Ezekiel 20.

For the Bible as a whole the theme is dealt with briefly by Jacques Guillet, *Thèmes Bibliques* (Paris, 1951), *cap.* i; M.-E. Boismard, "Le Dieu des Exodes," *Lumière et Vie*,

The word *paradise,* of course, is a Greek adaptation of a Persian word for a magnificent garden. In the Bible this Greek-Persian word appears in a theological sense only in the New Testament. In its three appearances in (late parts of) the Old Testament it simply means park. The cosmological term in the Old Testament is Eden ("delight") and Garden of Eden. From this Garden of Paradise the first man and woman were driven into the wilderness of the uncultivated world, which they had to subdue and till by the sweat of the brow. Except as the Garden helps define one of the non-literal meanings of the wilderness in the Old Testament, it will not be directly under discussion in the present essay.[3] Our attention is instead drawn to the opposite of the garden, namely, the wilderness.

1. The Desert, the Deep, and Death in the Old Testament

The Bible abounds in references to the desert and the wilderness in both the geophysical and the non-literal sense in varying degrees of spiritual differentiation.

Avril, 1952, pp. 107–128; J. B. Soucek, "Pilgrims and Sojourners (An Essay in Biblical Theology)," *Communio Viatorum* (Prague), I (1958), 1 ff.

For the New Testament items see below, nn. 19 and 20.

[3] The literature on Adam and the Fall is much more extensive than that on the wilderness. Among the most recent writers on the Paradise of Genesis, Ivan Engnell in " 'Knowledge' and 'Life' in the Creation Story," *Wisdom in Israel and in the Ancient Near East: Presented to Professor Harold Henry Rowley,* ed. M. Noth and D. Winton Thomas (Leiden, 1955), pp. 103–119, explores what he considers the Hebraic adaptation of the divine marriage enacted in the annual festival of the royal enthronement. Adam in this view is a royal personage, transmuted by Hebraic theology into the prototype of mankind. Brevard S. Childs in *Myth and Reality in the Old Testament* (London, 1960) takes up the myth of Paradise and the Fall on pp. 42 ff. and stresses the extent to which the cultic and mythical materials have been demythologized; then he analyzes the theological tension of the purposefully broken myth. Mircea Eliade has dealt with the biblical myth in the much larger setting of "The Yearning for Paradise in Primitive Tradition," *Diogenes,* Summer, 1953; reprinted in *Daedalus,* Spring, 1959. Herbert Weisinger in *Tragedy and the Paradox of the Fortunate Fall* (London, 1953) has done for one aspect of the paradisic motif in the history of literature, with special reference to tragedy, what is being done on a lesser scale in the present survey for a related aspect of the garden and wilderness motifs in the history of the Church. The concept of *felix culpa,* which he traces back from John Milton's *Paradise Lost* to its roots in primitive religions, transmuted by the Hebrews, is for Weisinger the generic term for "one of the most tenaciously held faiths which man has ever grasped" in his effort to overcome the forces of chaos and disorder. *Felix culpa* writ large and in English means for Weisinger man's provisionally hopeful observation that "The sun rises after the night; the grain sprouts after the winter; the waters run after the drought; the dead god lives again; and man falls, but not in vain." After reaching the paradox of the fortunate fall in Hebrew thought by Chap. V, he traces the motif in its Christianized form in Chap. VI, and in a concluding chapter suggests that it has been the sublimation of the motif which has transferred to tragedy the power of religion.

i. The Desert as the Realm of the Demons and Death

The Hebraic words for *wilderness* in the Old Testament are numerous. Although in their literal sense they designated different kinds of terrain —sandy and rocky desert, steppe, and forest[4]—there appears to have been no significant difference among them in their successive non-literal or theological applications. Generally speaking, the wilderness was the Unsown as distinguished from the Sown (land). The latter included the green pastures, orchards, vineyards, fields, oases, and gardens surrounding the villages and towns. The Sown Land in the Scriptures was also felt to be precariously maintained, subject to the blasts of dry wind from the desert. Often the desert encroached upon the Sown Land when the seasonal rains were withheld and the cultivated lands were parched.

Among the peoples surrounding the ancient Hebrews an elaborate seasonal ritual had grown up to secure the fertilizing rains. This was the widespread Tammuz cult and its Canaanite and Aramaean analogues, the cult of the dying and rising storm god Baal Haddad, traces of which can still be seen lurking behind certain phrases in the Old Testament.[5]

Thus the prophet Joel (2:3) speaks of Yahweh in reference to a wicked people: "Fire devours before them, and behind them a flame burns. The land is like the garden of Eden before them, but after them a desolate wilderness, and nothing escapes them."

The Hebrew prophets also sought to interpret the blasting of the cultivated lands of their own people as Yahweh's punishment for national sinfulness. Jeremiah (25:38) writes: "Their lands became a wilderness . . . because of the glow of his [Yahweh's] wrath."[6] Thus Yahweh might, like Baal Haddad or Tammuz, be the cause of the wasting of Israel's orchards and gardens, deserting them in his wrath to descend to the nether region during a period of punitive drought. The desert or wilderness became, then, almost a moral term. Even

---

[4] A desolate, dry, lonely place (*midbar, arabah, tsiyyah, tohu, chorbah, yeshimon; eremia, eremos*).

[5] The Tammuz cultus would have been directly influential in Palestine only in Assyrian times. Of this cultus Haldar, *op. cit.*, p. 19, writes: ". . . it is during Tammuz' sojourn in the Nether World that his 'word' caused destruction. This is naturally a consequence of the fact that, when the god has been taken down to the Nether World, the state of chaos supervenes, *i.e.*, the enemies enter into the *edin*, which is turned into a desert by the hurricane, and then also the abode of man, people and cattle become the objects of Tammuz' destruction, in point of fact they become his enemies. Further, it is of importance to state that Ishtar, too, is to be reckoned among the enemies of Tammuz."

[6] This is Haldar's emendation connecting it with the Tammuz cultus; *op. cit.*, pp. 47 f.

Jerusalem could be thought of in this metaphysical or theological sense as a patch or outcropping of the desert (i.e. Jeremiah 6:7 f. and 7:34) because of its spiritual dryness.[7]

The desert, moreover, was often associated with death and darkness by the peoples surrounding the Hebrews. In Egypt, for example, the dead were not buried in the valuable cultivable land outside the villages and towns, but rather in remote and unwatered places. Hence gloomy Sheol, the collective term for all the graves, came in the later stages of the Old Testament to be linked with primordial disorder and the withered wilderness.

The trackless wastes of the desert out beyond the cemeteries were thought of as frequented by evil spirits akin to the (later) Arabic ghouls and jinn. For the indigenous Canaanites the desert was peopled with dragons, demons, and monsters of the night. And the Hebrews, settled in their midst, inevitably assimilated some of the native mythology and cultus, no doubt reinforcing their own wilderness lore about the dreadful denizens of the desert night. There were the hairy satyr (*sair*), the storm devil (*shed*), the howling dragon and monster (*tan*, *tannin*), the winged female night monster (*lilith*), which entered Hebrew demonology during the Babylonian Exile, and the collective figure for all the desert spirits, Azazel.

Isaiah (34:13 f.) vividly describes the demon and beast-infested wilderness in reference to Moab which God would soon blast: "Thorns shall grow over its strongholds, nettles and thistles in its fortresses. It shall be the haunt of *tannim*, an abode for ostriches. And wild beasts shall meet with hyenas, the *sair* shall cry to his fellow; yea, there shall *lilith* alight, and find for herself a resting place." In the Song of Moses (Deuteronomy 37:17) there is admonitory testimony as to the temptation faced by the Hebrews to appease the storm demons in the approved Canaanite manner: "They sacrificed to *shedhim* which were no gods, to new gods they had never known, to new gods that have come in of late, whom your fathers had never dreaded." Yet in the same Pentateuch is preserved something of the Hebraic liturgy of an annual appeasement of some of the wilderness spirits in the collective figure of Azazel. Aaron takes two goats, one for God and one for the demon of the desert: "But the goat on which the lot fell for Azazel

[7] Pedersen, *op. cit.*, II, 457 and 460, presents the Hebraic view: "Outside the world of man is the wilderness, and yet so close to it that man must constantly strive to keep it away. This means that the desert still lies as a threatening possibility in the very land of man. If sin and curse got such a hold of man that the blessing was reduced to nothing, then the wilderness would be there at once. . . . The wilderness is wherever the curse lies; therefore there is no distinct borderline between that and the land of man."

shall be presented alive before the Lord to make atonement over it, that it may be sent away into the wilderness to Azazel."

In time the Canaanite-Babylonian demonology was to be further reinforced by Persian dualism.

Here then stretches the remote religio-physical background of the later identification of the desert as the realm beyond God's presence and somewhat beyond his control, the sphere for the exploits of the devil and his demonic hosts, the designated arena of mortal combat with the temptations of the spurious deities of necromancy, of fertility, and of uncovenantal forces (cf. Jesus' Mount of Temptation) outside the central shrine of Yahweh in Zion.

To the two realms of the demonic desert and death were gradually joined a third, the immense deep, the ocean which lies provisionally curbed under the earth. For the Hebrews it was a still awesome reminder of the primordial chaos, the trackless waste (*tohu*) of Genesis 1:2 and Job 26:7, which lies lurking under the world of man and which like the desert is the haunt of serpents and dragons.

Thus the wilderness, caused by the summer drought and seemingly extended in seasons of moral defection on the part of Israel by the breath of God's wrath, could become a symbol of the uncreated order and a surrogate in the poetry of the prophet and psalmist for the primordial abyss at the beginning of creation and for death at the end.[8] Common to the three interrelated realms of the deep, of the desert, and of death was darkness. Over it all God would one day prevail.

Some of the most moving passages in the Old Testament deal with the resurrection of the valley of dry bones into corporate life (Ezekiel 37) and the conversion of the disorder of the wilderness into a garden.[9]

Isaiah (41:18 f.) looked to a time when God would transform the physical and also the spiritual wilderness of Israel into something like the beauty and perfection of Paradise: "I will make the wilderness a pool of water, and the dry land springs of water. I will put in the wilderness the cedar, the acacia, the myrtle, and the olive; I will set in the desert the cypress, the plane and the pine together."

Elsewhere in Isaiah (35:1 ff.) we have formulated the doctrine of a second exodus. Israel in bondage to a new Egypt will pass through a

---

[8] Pedersen, *op. cit.*, II, 463 f. In Genesis 1:2 *tohu* is translated as "without form," obscuring its literal sense of "trackless waste" or "howling wilderness."

Among neighboring peoples the evil spirit of the desert was akin to the monster of the deeps, Leviathan, and akin to the serpent that emerged destructively within the Garden of Eden.

[9] The parallel in the realm of the sea is the dividing of it, made dry or held within its bounds.

new desert to a new land of promise: "The wilderness and the dry land shall be glad, the desert shall rejoice and blossom: . . . then the eyes of the blind shall be opened, and the ears of the deaf unstopped; then shall the lame leap like a hart, and the tongue of the dumb sing for joy. For waters shall break forth in the wilderness and streams in the desert; . . . and a highway shall be there, and it shall be called the Holy Way." Ezekiel (notably in chaps. 34 and 47) thought of God treating with the wild beasts to enable the elect to dwell safely in the desert and to rest in the forest and he looked forward to a day when, after the return of the elect to wasted Zion, the healing waters would issue out of the sanctuary in Jerusalem itself and flow down into the desert of Judea and form a kind of paradise in which trees of unfading medicinal leafage would flourish.

We have reached the second exodus in our sorting out the biblical texts which deal with the wilderness, before taking up the desert of the first Exodus. But such a presentation is not so disorderly as might appear. It has seemed important to stress in the first place the character of the desert in Hebraic thinking quite apart from the unique place of one particular desert, namely, that of Sinai.

ii. The Desert as the Place of the Covenant

To be sure, the redemptive significance of the Sinai wastes is inextricably interwoven in the Bible (as it has come down to us) with the competing conception of the desert as symbol of death, disorder, and darkness now briefly illustrated from Scripture and common to all peoples inhabiting the Fertile Crescent. And as with this cultic-seasonal-eschatological thought about the wilderness, so here in the interpretation of the historic experience of the children of Israel escaped from bondage to Egypt through a desert there is a double meaning suggested: (a) the wilderness as a place of redemptive, covenantal bliss, and (b) the wilderness as the place of testing and tutelage.

The pre-exilic prophets for the most part interpreted the forty years as a period when God was particularly close to Israel, when he loved his chosen people as the bridegroom his bride, feeding her with special food from heaven. Jeremiah (2:2), speaking in the name of Yahweh, declared: "I remember the devotion of your youth, your love as a bride, how you followed me in the wilderness, in a land not sown." Hosea (2:14 f.), recalling the nuptial period in the wilderness of Sinai, prophesied that God would again draw Israel into that more intimate relationship, even though she had, like an adulteress, transgressed the commandments: "Therefore, behold, I will allure her, and bring her into the wilderness, and speak tenderly to her. . . . And there she shall answer as in the days of her youth, as at the time when she came out of the land of Egypt." The Deuteronomist (32:10 f.) recalled that God "found him [Jacob or Israel] in a desert land, and in the howling waste of the wilderness; he encircled him, he cared for him, he kept him as the apple of his eye."

Such expressions as these may be taken as representative of the idyllic or even, in view of the bridal language used, the nuptial conception of the wilderness in which God covenanted with Israel in a kind of betrothal that linked them indissolubly for the duration of history. The Song of Solomon (Canticle of Canticles) fits well into the bridal conception of the relationship of God and Israel, betrothed in the wilderness (3:6; 8:5) and likened to a garden enclosed (4:12). However we account for the origin of the Canticle, with its Egyptian and Babylonian-Canaanite antecedents and analogues,[10] we know that it ultimately became a major resource for the wilderness-garden theme and the betrothal imagery in the history of the Church.[11] Even in the Old Testament God was thought of as the Bridegroom of a people who were coming up into history out of the anonymity of the wilderness of the peoples (Canticles 8:5).

But the idyllic or nuptial conception of the sojourn in the Sinai Peninsula, as already indicated, was not the only interpretation. The other was that of those in Israel who looked back upon the forty years as a time of temptation, of testing, and of sifting; of those who warned their wayward generation not to falter and murmur and backslide and perish like the six thousand who had died because of defection (Deuteronomy 8:2 f.): "And you shall remember all the way which the Lord your God has led you those forty years in the wilderness, that he might humble you, testing you to know what was in your heart, whether you would keep his commandments or not." The Psalmist (78:40 f.) in the same mood recalled: "How often they rebelled against him in the wilderness and grieved him in the desert! They tested him

[10] See particularly Theophile James Meek, "The Song of Songs and the Fertility Cult," and several other essays in *The Song of Songs: A Symposium,* ed. Wilfred H. Schoff (Philadelphia, 1924).

[11] It is well to draw attention at this point to the specific wilderness and garden passages, namely, 3:6: "What is that coming up from the wilderness like a column of smoke?"; 8:5: "Who is that coming up from the wilderness, leaning upon her beloved?"; 4:12: "A garden enclosed is my sister, my spouse."

The Septuagint has "clothed in white" instead of "out of the wilderness." As a consequence the wilderness and nuptial imagery are never so close in the Byzantine as in the Latin development of our theme. See Johannes Leonard Miller, "The Interpretation of the Song of Songs: The Ancient Versions," Harvard Th.D. thesis, Cambridge, 1957.

again and again, and provoked the Holy one of Israel." Israelites (106:13 f.) "soon forgot his [God's] works; they did not wait for his counsel. But they had a wanton craving in the wilderness, and put God to the test in the desert." The memory of the golden calf-goddess set up willfully in the wilderness would for all generations to come continuously reinforce the counsel we have already noted above to beware in the desert way of salvation the most diabolical of religious and moral temptations.

iii. A Desert as the Place of Refuge, Purgation, and Consecration

Besides the wilderness as an encroaching desert, besides the specific wilderness of Sinai traversed as a formative historic event, understood both as an experience of temptation and as a period of covenantal bliss, the Old Testament has a third conception, that of any wilderness which may serve either as (a) a place of refuge and contemplation, or more commonly (b) any place where the Chosen are scattered for a season of discipline or purgation.

Certain of the prophets completely idealized the wilderness or nomadic stage in Israel's history, when, in the simplicities of tribal justice, God's righteousness presumably prevailed, as no longer after Israel settled down to agricultural and urban life. The best-known group to organize a return to the desert and to the nomadic ideal were the Rechabites (Jeremiah 35:6 f.). The Rechabites and the prophets Elijah and Elisha were later to be looked back upon by the Christian Fathers of the desert as proto-monks. As to a place of refuge, Elijah withdrew to the wilderness and cave on Mount Horeb (I Kings 19:48), and Elisha and his school of prophets withdrew to the wilderness of Jordan (II Kings 4:38 ff.), protected by God after they had struggled against the forces of Baalism in the cities. It was, moreover, precisely by way of the wilderness of Damascus (I Kings 19:16) that Elijah was bidden by the Lord to anoint a new king of Israel (Jehu) and the new prophet (Elisha). The Rechabite Jonadab supported the "wilderness" king Jehu after his anointment (II Kings 10:15, 23); and Jeremiah, a later sympathizer of the Rechabites, longed for the wilderness (9:2) that he might regain his spiritual bearing.

The more somber sense of the flight to the desert is struck by the Psalmist (106:26 f.), who declares: "Therefore he [Yahweh] raised his hand and swore to them that he could make them fall in the wilderness, and would disperse their descendants among the nations, scattering them over the lands." To the wilderness the whole of Israel was directed by Hosea more for the purpose of therapeutic punishment than for protection from outward foes. He (12:9 f.) spoke for Yahweh, warning: "I am the Lord your God from the land of Egypt; I will again make you dwell in tents, as in the days [of old commemorated in] the appointed feast."

Amos (5:26 f.) excoriated his people for turning to other deities and declared that God would take them "into exile beyond Damascus." Ezekiel (20:33-36) promised a return from exile after the strewing of God's people for a season among the nations: "I will bring you out from the peoples and gather you out of the countries where you are scattered, with a mighty hand, an outstretched arm, and with wrath poured out, and I will bring you into the *wilderness of the peoples,* and there I will enter into judgment with you face to face."

We have now sampled the Scriptures of the Old Testament and found three meanings of the wilderness so surcharged with historic, cultic, and mythical connotations, and so accented theologically and ethically, as to yield in a more generalized or abstracted fashion the following four concepts or motifs, which we shall find recurring in various combinations throughout post-biblical history: (a) the wilderness as a moral waste but a potential paradise, (b) the wilderness as a place of testing or even punishment, (c) the wilderness as the experience or occasion of nuptial (covenantal) bliss, and (d) the wilderness as a place of refuge (protection) or contemplation (renewal).[12]

Before going on to the New Testament and Church historical

---

[12] Eric Voegelin has admirably summarized the composite biblical meanings of the desert in his *Order and History*, I, *Israel and Revelation* (Baton Rouge, La., 1956), pp. 113 f.:
"The Events of the Exodus, the sojourn at Kadesh, and the Conquest of Canaan became symbols because they were animated by a new spirit. Through the illumination by the spirit the house of institutional bondage became a house of spiritual death. Egypt was the realm of the dead, the Sheol, in more than one sense. From death and its cult man had to wrest the life of the spirit. And this adventure was hazardous, for the Exodus from Sheol at first led nowhere but into the desert of indecision, between equally unpalatable forms of nomad existence and life in a high civilization. Hence, to Sheol and Exodus must be added the Desert as the symbol of the historical impasse. It was not a specific but the eternal impasse of historical existence in the 'world,' that is, in the cosmos in which empires rise and fall with no more meaning than a tree growing and dying, as waves in the stream of eternal recurrence. By attunement with cosmic order the fugitives from the house of bondage could not find the life that they sought. When the spirit bloweth, society in cosmological form becomes Sheol, the realm of death; but when we undertake the Exodus and wander into the world, in order to found a new society elsewhere, we discover the world as the Desert. The flight leads nowhere, until we stop in order to find our bearings beyond the world. When the world has become Desert, man is at last in the solitude in which he can hear thunderingly the voice of the spirit that with its urgent whispering has already driven and rescued him from Sheol. In the Desert God spoke to the leader and his tribes; in the Desert, by listening to the voice, by accepting its offer, and by submitting to its command, they at last reached life and became the chosen people of God."

elaboration of these motifs, let us glance at the way in which sectarian Judaism first appropriated the biblical texts, notably the community in the wilderness of Qumran.

2. The Essenes and the Jewish Apocalyptists: A Coherent Theology of Wandering, Warfare, and Water

The Essenes of the Dead Sea caves were an apocalyptic community that imitated the ancient sojourn in the wilderness of Sinai. They were priestly legitimists and apocalptists. In the end they foresaw, after the persistent failings of Israel long since returned from the Babylonian Exile, still a third exodus, as it were, and a third conquest of the promised land. This time the conquest was thought of as concurrent with, and instrumental in, the ushering in of the Kingdom of God. Theirs was thus at once a spiritual and an inherently bloody warfare.

Under a high-priestly teacher who fled from Jerusalem when a decree under a rival high priest sought to stamp out all opposition, the puritanical Essene schismatics withdrew into the wilderness of Judah to await the divinely appointed opportunity to return in vengeance. The Essenes applied to themselves the prophecies cited above of Amos 5:25-27 and Ezekiel 20:35, and thought of their encampment (*yahad*) as an eschatological sojourning in "the land of Damascus" or alternatively as their habitation in "the desert of the peoples."[13]

The *Zadokite Documents,* well known before the discovery of the Qumran caves, are replete with references to the desert of Damascus; but the documents are now regarded as Damascan only in the eschatological sense of Amos, in some such way as "Babylon" in the New Testament was later to designate "Rome." The *Zadokite Documents* and the recently discovered *Manual of Discipline* among the Dead Sea Scrolls are major sources for our understanding of how the ancient Essenes interpreted theologically their flight, or exodus, into the wilderness.

The Essenes isolated themselves in their well irrigated and fortified desert retreats to achieve a form of perfection and to shun all contact with the temptation of city and village, living in rigorous simplicity. By study, prayer, and communal discipline they hoped to prepare a way in the wilderness for the coming of the Messiah(s). The *Manual* says:

These are the provisions whereby they [the righteous] are to be kept apart from consort with forward men, to the end that they may indeed "go into the wilderness to prepare the way," i.e., do what Scripture enjoins when it

---

[13] Frank Cross, *The Library of Qumran* (New York, 1958), esp. pp. 56 and 59, n. 46.

says [Isaiah 40:3], "Prepare in the wilderness the way." (The reference is to the study of the Law which God commanded through Moses to the end that, as occasion arises, all things may be done in accordance with what is revealed through God's Holy Spirit.)[14]

Scattered in the wilderness for a season, the Essenes sought to be born again as the true Israel inwardly prepared to enter into the New Covenant in the last days. They were convinced that by group discipline and self-restraint they might undo the effects of the Fall from Paradise. Their conception of truth was eschatologically grounded.[15] The two Messiahs whom they awaited, the priestly and the royal, would lead the Essenes in a return to Paradise and enable the saints to feed upon the tree of life. The enigmatic figure called the Teacher of Righteousness, who first led the Essenes into the protective wilderness from the tyranny of a worldly high priest, laid the foundation for their esoteric truth and their life of study. Hence the great concentration on collecting, editing, and interpreting the biblical scrolls. They studied the methods of spiritual and ethical warfare that they might discipline themselves by the ancient treatise on *The Wars of Yahweh* (referred to in our canonical Old Testament) to be ready to fight the final war of God and repossess Zion. Here are the words from their own *The War of the Sons of Light and the Sons of Darkness*:

When the Sons of Light who are now in exile return from the "desert of the nations" [cf. Ezekiel 20:34 f.] to pitch camp in the desert of Judah, the children of Levi, Judah and Benjamin who are now among those exiles, shall wage war against these peoples.[16]

The Essenes were not proto-Christians. They expected two Messiahs and they expected to fight in the final war of God. But their ideas about baptismal cleansing and sacramental fellowship meals in the expectation of the coming of the Kingdom, their rigorous exercise of the ban (excommunication), their eschatological conviction about the purity of their paradisic truth recovered within the fellowship of a disciplined wilderness encampment sustained by the Spirit, point to the Christian dispensation and the primitive Christian Church, which in its turn would look upon itself as the true Israel not under a new Moses but under a suffering Messiah whose sword was to be exclusively of the spirit and whose highway had been prepared in the desert by the preaching of John the Baptist.

[14] *Manual of Discipline,* viii, 13–19. The sentence in parentheses is part of the original Essene commentary.
[15] Cross, *op. cit.,* p. 166.
[16] Theodore H. Gaster, *The Dead Sea Scriptures* (New York, 1956), p. 281.

The Essene community shows to what extent the imagery or symbol-ism of warfare, water, and wandering had already become inextricably interwoven in the theology of the wilderness before John the Baptist came preaching repentance in the wilderness of Jordan (or Samaria).

The Essenes were not the only apocalyptists who espoused the escha-tology of the wilderness. The "seekers of righteousness" in Maccabean times (I Maccabees 2:29-35) sought out the wilderness whence to launch the assault upon the enemy of Israel, and Judas Maccabeus (d. 161 B.C.) took shelter in the wilderness of Judea (II Maccabees 5:27). In the early days of the Church an Egyptian (Jew), temporarily con-fined by the Roman governor with Paul, led four thousand revolution-ary-apocalyptic zealots into the wilderness.[17]

More directly influential than the Essenes or the Maccabeans in the Christian development of the wilderness-paradise theme were certain other Jewish apocalyptists upon whose inspiration Christians were to draw, and out of whose visionary company several converts to Chris-tianity were to come.

First and Second Enoch, the *Vita Adae et Evae* and its variant, the Apocalypse of Moses, are filled with the expectation in the tradition of Isaiah 45:17-24 and Ezekiel 47:1-12 (and in anticipation of, or in parallel to, "the new earth" of Revelation 21:1-6) that the desolation round about Jerusalem would one day be converted into a paradise. Let the seer of the beautiful and moving Apocalypse of Baruch, contempo-raneous with the chief writings of the New Testament, speak for all his kinsmen:

For the shepherds of Israel have perished, and the lamps which gave light are extinguished, and the fountains have withheld their stream whence we used to drink. And we are left in the darkness, and amid the briers of the forest, and the thirst of the wilderness.

But the earth will be transformed into paradise in the age of the Messiah:

And it will come to pass at that self-same time that the treasury of manna will again descend from on high, and they [who have persevered in righteousness] will eat of it in those years. . . .

And wild beasts will come from the forest and minister unto men, and asps and dragons will come forth from their holes and submit themselves to a little child.[18]

---

[17] Acts 21:38 (= Josephus, *Jewish Antiquities*, xx, 167; *Jewish War*, ii, 622).
[18] The Apocalypse of Baruch, ed. and tr. R. H. Charles (London, 1896), 77:13 f.; 29:8; 73:6. On the wilderness speculation rampant among the apocalyptic sects, see Werner Schmauch, *Orte des Offenbarung und der Offenbarungsort im Neuem Testa-ment* (Göttingen, 1956).

3. The Wilderness Theology of a Fourth Exodus as Recorded in the New Testament

If the return from the Babylonian Exile was the fulfillment of the prophecy of a second exodus, and if the flight of the Essenes into the wilderness of the Dead Sea may be reckoned for our purposes a third exodus, then the emergence of the primitive Christian Church from bondage to old Israel and the flight of Christian converts from bewilderment in the Greco-Roman world of cults and monstrous webs of theosophy may be put down as a fourth exodus.[19]

It was precisely in the wilderness that John the Baptist, an Essene-like figure, discharged the role of the eschatological Messenger (Malachi 3:1) or of Elijah *redivivus* (4:5), the restorer of the convenant and all things, preparing the Way (Malachi 3:1) in the wilderness (Isaiah 40:3) for the Lord, who was to come with the Spirit and with fire (Matthew 3:11). It is quite possible, indeed, that John thought of himself as having been summoned to create a "pure and purifying remnant," qualified to prepare by baptismal repentance for the advent of the Messiah or for the fiery judgment of the Lord.[20]

Although Jesus in the end dissociated himself from the wilderness eschatology of John's followers, reconceiving his role presumably in terms of the Suffering Servant, the fact that he had been baptized by John in the wilderness obliged the Evangelists to come to terms with the whole cycle of wilderness theology, notably in their reworking of the Temptation scene. From the waters of the Jordan, Jesus was portrayed by the Synoptists as driven by the Spirit into the wilderness for forty days. His fasting and praying were thought of as analogous to the forty days of Moses in the clefts of the rocks of Sinai (Exodus 24:18), also to the forty years of Moses in the wilderness of Midan (Acts 7:29 f.), and to the forty years of the elect people as a whole, as Jesus' replies to Satan suggest (cf. Deuteronomy 8:2 f.). But even this interpretation and the subsequent reinterpretation of the baptismal rite as also the epiphany of the Father, of the Spirit, and of the anointed, only begotten Son, indicate the extent of the widespread expectation in sec-

---

[19] Jean Steinmann, *St. Jean-Baptiste et la spiritualité du désert* (Paris, 1955, New York, 1958); Pierre Bonnard, "La signification du désert selon le Nouveau Testament," *Hommage et Reconnaissance, Karl Barth* (Neuchâtel, Paris, 1946), pp. 11–18; Robert Funk, "The Wilderness," *Journal of Biblical Literature*, LXXVIII (1959), 205–214; Jean Daniélou, *Les Manuscrits de la Mer Morte et les origines du Christianisme* (Paris, 1957); Matthew Black, *The Scrolls and Christian Origins* (New York, 1961).

[20] C. H. Kraeling, *John the Baptist* (New York, 1951); W. H. Brownlee, "John the Baptist," *The Scrolls and the New Testament*, ed. Krister Stendahl (New York, 1957), pp. 33–53; J. A. T. Robinson, "The Temptation," *Theology*, L (1947), 43–48; *idem*, "The Baptism of John and the Qumran Community," *Harvard Theological Review*, L (1957), 175–191; *idem*, "Elijah, John and Jesus," *New Testament Studies*, IV (1957/58), 263–281.

tarian Judaism of a miraculous renewal of the people of the covenant to take place after a new exodus into the desert, after a new royal and prophetic unction in the wilderness (cf. I Kings 19:16). This wilderness theology survived in various permutations among the New People of the Way. And baptism by the water rite of John the Baptist would become the means whereby the exodus from this world would be sacramentally effected. Christian reflection will not only find in Jesus' temptation in the wilderness of Jordan a redemptive recapitulation of that of the elect people in the wilderness of Sinai. It will also have shaped the transmission of this episode in consonance with the conviction that the second Adam in the wilderness had reversed the consequences of Adam's temptation in Paradise, in conformity perhaps also with the ideal of the steadfast martyr surrounded in the sands of the arena by hostile beasts.

It is of special interest that Mark, who opens his Gospel with the Isaianic prophecy of the voice in the Jordanian wilderness, is alone among the Evangelists to express, albeit in subdued and merely implicit phrasing, the conviction that the baptized and therewith symbolically anointed Messiah was in the wilderness surrounded by *friendly* beasts, presumably as the new Adam in Paradise. Unlike the scene portrayed in Matthew and Luke, Jesus in Mark 1:13, "was with the wild beasts; and the angels ministered to him." Mark's complete phrasing at this point echoes not only Psalm 91:4-13 (as with the other Synoptists) but also Isaiah 11:6-8. It is, to be sure, by no means certain that the animals in the Marcan version betoken for the Evangelist himself Jesus' provisional conversion of the wilderness into Paradise,[21] but Mark has preserved an interesting fragment from that cycle of thought. There are parallels to the paradisic interpretation of the wilderness of temptation in the Jewish pseudepigraphic literature, e.g., the Syriac Apocalypse of Baruch, 58:6, and especially in *Vita Adae et Evae* (6:1-8:3), wherein the penitent Adam fasts forty days while standing up to his neck in the Jordan to summon all swimming creatures to assemble about him and mourn in company with him. Of considerable interest is the fact that the (later) Monarchian, Latin prologue to Mark makes

---

[21] With Joachim Jeremias' article, "Paradeisos," in G. Kittel, *Theologisches Wörterbuch zum Neuen Testament*, V, 763-771, esp. 770 f. Further literature is brought together by Urban Holzmeister, S.J., "'Jesus lebte mit den wilden Tieren': Mk 1, 13," *Vom Wort des Lebens: Festschrift für Max Meinertz* (Münster, 1951), pp. 85-92; W. A. Schuze, "Der Heilige und die wilden Tiere, *"Zeitschrift für neutestamentliche Wissenschaft*, XLVI (1955), 280-283, and J. Levie, *Les évangiles synoptiques* (2nd ed., Louvain, 1953), p. 85. Frederick Grant holds that the animals are embodiments of the demonic and, as the minions of Satan, attack Jesus the martyr, like beasts of the Roman arena. The most recent interpretation in the literature is to be found in Rudolf Bultmann, *Die Geschichte der synoptischen Tradition* (3rd ed., Göttingen, 1957), Beiheft, p. 35.

explicit the friendly character of the animals' company ("congregationem bestiarum et ministerium . . . angelorum").[22]

Although Mark himself may have attached no special significance to the paradisic motif in the materials which he happened to preserve, it is evident that he, of all the Synoptists, was the most interested in the wilderness, not only in the unlocalized eschatological sense,[23] but also in the literal sense of hilltop, lake, and desert. The latter interest, in character socio-religious, may well have stemmed from Mark's hostility toward the cultus of the Temple and the synagogue, a hostility reflecting perhaps that of the original community for which his Gospel was written.[24] His circumstantial recounting of two miraculous feedings of the multitude in desert places may also reflect the missionary practice of the young Galilean Church, which, in contrast to the more conservative Jerusalemite Church, was conceivably unwilling to work within the framework of established Judaism, breaking away from the synagogue and village authorities to assemble prospective converts in large outdoor meetings in the hills and plains between the villages and even in desert retreats further removed from the local defenders of established religion. Mark's description of the throngs during the ministry of Jesus makes it possible to conjecture that the evangelists of the Galilean mission, consolidating a tradition going back to Jesus' own ministry in the region, conducted extended meetings in the open in the course of which bread was shared, possibly in programmatic anticipation of the Messianic Banquet. In this case the evangelical repasts at preaching stations in out-of-the-way places in northern Palestine would correspond to the enclosed agapes held in the intimacy of the communitarian Church of Jerusalem.

Besides the desert repasts, besides the wilderness-paradise motif in Mark's version of Jesus' temptation and also the howling desert of John the Baptist, there were in the New Testament writings several other allusions to the wilderness experience and here and there tentative onsets of a theology of the wilderness, every such passage destined, of course, to have an abiding influence in the history of the Church.

Paul, for example (I Corinthians 10:1 ff.), understood burial and

---

[22] John Wadsworth and Henry White, *Novum Testamentum . . . secundum editionem sancti Hieronymi* (Oxford, 1889–1898), I, 172. On the Monarchian and Priscillianist (Spanish) elements and the earlier literature, see Donatien de Bruyne, "Les plus anciens prologues latins des évangiles," *Revue Bénédictine*, XL (1928), 193–214.

[23] James M. Robinson stresses the eschatological significance of the unlocalized wilderness particularly in connection with John the Baptist as the returned Elijah. *Das Geschichtsverständnis des Markus-Evangeliums* (Zurich, 1956), pp. 15 ff.

[24] So, for example, in the most recent work on Mark, that of Étienne Trocmé, *La formation de l'évangile selon Marc* (in press), which stresses the Galilean sources of Mark and then carries further the distinction made since Ernst Lohmeyer between the Galilean and Jerusalemite sources and missions.

resuscitation with Christ through faith and baptism as the divinely instituted means whereby Jews and believing Gentiles might successfully pass through a new Red Sea. He considered the sea and the cloud by day as types of Christian baptism. The Christian eucharist was for him the New Covenantal counterpart of the manna from heaven; and he interpreted the life of Christians between their conversion and the coming of the Kingdom in power as a wilderness experience in which they would be tempted as were the Israelites of the Old Covenant in the desert but would be sustained to the end by the eucharistic bread of heaven.

The author of the Epistle to the Hebrews had a different conception of the exodus and the wilderness experience (3:7-18). The traditional reading of its references to the wilderness finds no essential difference, but the careful scrutiny of recent New Testament scholarship[25] suggests that the author of the Epistle had, in adjusting to and yet rejecting the Gnostic perversion of Christian theology, interpreted the trials and stages of the wanderings in the wilderness after the baptismal exodus from the world as the successive steps upward on the spiritual ladder of the believing Christian, or that he may, indeed, have been appealing to Essenes (the legitimist Hebrews) to recognize in the people of the New Way the authentic Israel in the desert.

Quite different from the Epistle to the Hebrews and much more Judaic than I Corinthians is the Book of Revelation. Herein we have a conflation of the Mosaic and Christian exodus (15:2-4), while, in the traditional imagery of apocalyptic, the Church of Jesus Christ is thought of as a woman with a male child who, having fled into the wilderness to escape the clutches of the red dragon, must remain there 1260 days. It is quite possible that the Apocalyptist, close as he was to the torment of Jewry in the throes of the war with Rome beginning in 66 A.D., was here interpreting that conflict in the light of Christian redemption and that he was identifying the woman in travail (12:1 f.), clothed with the sun and crowned with stars—the symbol of Zion or of Israel (cf. Genesis 37:9)—as the woman and man child (12:6), in effect the new Jewish-Christian Israel. In any event, the Christian Jews of Zion early took refuge in the region of Pella and conceivably held out in the wilderness for the (Danielic duration of) three and a half years of the Jewish war (roughly 1260 days).[26] Whatever the authentically

[25] Cf. Ernst Käsemann, *Das Wandernde Gottesvolk* (Göttingen, 1939) and H. Kosmala, *Hebräer-Essener-Christen* (Brill, 1959).

[26] For the flight of the Jewish Christians to Pella in the wilderness of Damascus (Amos 5:26 f.; cf. Matthew 24:16), see Eusebius, *Ecclesiastical History*, iii, 5. For the historic identification of the woman, see Stanislas Giet, *L'Apocalypse et l'Histoire* (Paris, 1957), pp. 110-112.

prophetic or the retrospectively historic sense of the enigmatic feminine figure, she was destined to exercise an extraordinary influence over the imaginations of seers and sectarians throughout Christian history. It is of interest, therefore, to note in passing that the sectarians of Qumran had already appropriated and identified themselves with the cosmic woman crowned with stars, the true Zion. The extensive Mariological development of this text will not become a part of our account because here precisely the desert element drops from view.[27]

Besides escaping persecution, the Seer of Revelation suggests also another reason for retiring to the wilderness (1:9; 17:3), and that is to enable a contemplative Christian to see the divine more clearly, unencumbered by the world. The Seer's own retreat in Patmos was as a model or norm to be frequently appealed to in the history of Christian spirituality by all wishing to withdraw even from their fellow Christians the better to perceive and hearken to the will of God.

In rounding out our sketch of the principal texts, we should say a further word about Paradise in the New Testament. Apart from the possible paradisic implications in the Marcan version of Jesus' temptation in the desert, where the word *paradise* is, in any event, absent, we have only three instances of the word, and as it happens in all three cases, in a transcendent sense (Luke 23:43; II Corinthians 12:4; Revelation 2:7). More, however, than this spare use of the word would indicate, the theological meaning of paradise was swiftly amplified and differentiated by the first generation in the Christian era, in part in dependence upon Jewish apocalyptic speculation about Paradise and the renewal of the Promised Land, and in part as a consequence of the Pauline stress upon man's primordial state, Adam's fall, and Christ's redeeming work as the second (the last) Adam (I Corinthians 15:45). Although these extensions of the meaning of paradise will not be pursued in their permutations and combinations in the present essay except as they bear on the evolution of our wilderness motif, we should have them schematically before us.

We may first of all distinguish in the New Testament epoch the primordial from the eschatological-experiential concepts of paradise. By the primordial sense we mean not only the original Garden of Eden but also those remnants of it which were thought to have survived somewhere beyond the headwaters of the Tigris and the Euphrates. The first Christians shared with Jews this conception but the word in this terrestrial sense does not happen to have been used in the canonical New Testament writings, though it appears in the same

[27] For the beginnings, see R. P. Braun, "La femme vêtue du soleil," *Revue Thomiste*, 1955, pp. 639–669.

sense in allied and subsequent Christian literature. In any event it is
the three eschatological-experiential meanings of the term as used by
chance in the New Testament which bear most directly on, and inter-
act with, the wilderness theme.

In its transcendental meaning, the term *paradise* designated in the
New Testament (a) a level or zone in heaven thought of as a realm
which might be occasionally reached in ecstasy (II Corinthians
12:2 ff.), or as a forecourt of the Kingdom, to which the souls of *only*
the martyrs had access prior to the resurrection (or exceptionally, as
in the case of the good thief at the crucifixion; Luke 23:42 f.); (b) the
whole of God's Kingdom thought of indistinctly as both above in
space and ahead in time, and as at once Zion the Golden and Paradise
with the tree of life planted in its midst (Revelation 2:7; 22:2); and
(c) the disciplined community of faith, the Church. For this third
metaphysical sense of *paradise* there is actually no New Testament
documentation; but the conception of the Church as at once the true
Promised Land and as such a provisional Paradise is so important in
the earliest history of the Church that it seems proper to include it here
in rounding out the New Testament usage as we turn now to the development of the themes in the history of the Church. According to
this third schema, paradisic peace began to appear in the wilderness of
the world, when the Saviour was born in a manger. The paradisic
interest becomes especially prominent in the apocryphal gospels, for
example, the Latin Pseudo-Matthew, which, inspired by the Isaianic
vision of the harmony of nature, pictures not only such domestic
animals as the ox and ass surrounding Jesus in the crib in the nativity
narrative (cap. 14) but also the dragons, lions, and leopards worship-
ing the infant during the flight through the desert to Egypt (caps. 18,
19, 35).

In the Church so conceived, as the community in covenant with the
second Adam, Paradise could be thought of as provisionally regained,
the approaching millennium could be thought of as experienced by
anticipation, and the age of gold could be glimpsed. Notably was this
true of the apostolic community in Jerusalem (cf. the later Pseudo-
Clementine literature) living in the common possession of goods and
sustained by the continuous presence of the Holy Spirit poured out
upon the young and the old. It is with this paradisic conception of the
Church that we begin the next chapter, to pursue at the end of the
apostolic age the development of our themes as the Church expanded
into the Mediterranean world and beyond, continuously and selectively
reworking and allegorizing the scriptural formulations of the desert
experience of the people of the Old Covenant.

Chapter II. Wilderness and Paradise in the Baptismal Theology of the Church of the Martyrs, in Monasticism, and in Mysticism

1. The Church of the Martyrs as a Provisional Paradise[1]

The millenialist yearnings of the Seer of Revelation persisted in force through the pre-Constantinian era and therewith the expectation of the transformation of the world into an earthly paradise ("a new heaven and a new earth"). The Montanists of Asia Minor and beyond, in the mood of the Apocalypse, sought to meet the Bridegroom with Jerusalem descending in the remoteness of Pepuza.[2]

John, the Lord's disciple, is reported on the authority of Bishop Papias of Hierapolis (d. 130) to have looked forward, like the roughly contemporaneous Jewish seer of the Syriac Apocalypse of Baruch, not only to paradisic abundance but also to paradisic harmony, when "all animals using those foods which are got from the earth shall be peaceable and in concord one with another, subject unto men with all obedience."[3]

Important as the millennial hope must have been, however, the major stress in the extant documentation of the pre-Constantinian age is the joy of the "new people" in having been led from the weary "wilderness of the world" toward the "promised land," and in being permitted to participate, through the sacraments, in the purity of the provisional paradise in the midst of the redeemed community. Outside the New Testament writings it was Pseudo-Barnabas (6:8-19) who first identified Christ and his Church with Paradise and the Promised Land attained by baptism. According to this apostolic Father—generally conceded to have been more acerb than mellifluous—Palestine, after having been laid waste by generations of apostasy, gave rise in the fullness of time and through the work of the second Adam to a new

---

[1] The most recent accounts of paradise and similar themes in the early Church are those of Ildefonse Ayer, "Où Plaça-t-on le Paradis Terrestre?," *Études Franciscaines*, XXXVI (1924), 117–140: XXXVII (1925), 113–145; Jean Daniélou, "Terre et Paradis chez les Pères de l'Église," *Eranos-Jahrbuch*, XXII (1953), 433–472; and Gerhart B. Ladner's comprehensive *The Idea of Reform: Its Impact on Christian Thought and Action in the Age of the Fathers* (Cambridge, 1959).

[2] Epiphanius, *Panarion*, xlviii, 14; xlix, 1. The Montanist use of cheese instead of wine in their observance of the Supper may be a primitivist note.

[3] Irenaeus, *Against Heresies*, V, xxxiii, 3, in Alexander Roberts and James Donaldson, eds., *The Ante-Nicene Fathers* (henceforth *ANF*) (Buffalo, 1885), I, 563. Cf. Baruch 24:5 f.; 71:4–7.

realm flowing with milk and honey, namely, the Church with its sacrament of baptismal rebirth. The sustained metaphor of Barnabas was based upon the practice of his time and locality of giving each newborn infant a drop of honey before it was put to its mother's breast. In effect, the partaking of milk and honey by the neophytes in the earliest extant liturgies impressed upon the participants their double status as at once sucklings in being reborn in Christ and victors in their attainment in the Church of the Promised Land.[4]

The baptismal theology and practice of the ancient Church was everywhere based upon the identification of[5] the new Christian Israel with the people of the Old Covenant, who passed through the Red Sea and the wilderness of Sinai to the Promised Land. In some traditions the long period of catechetical instruction and ritual exorcism before baptism was likened in the church orders to the wanderings of the people from bondage to this world symbolized by Egypt. The sign of baptism was commonly understood as the Christian equivalent of the sanguinary sign of the first Passover as well as being the forehead seal of the new recruits for the *militia Christi*.

The baptismal phrasings of the liturgy go back even beyond the episode of the Red Sea. Noah's ark was, in its turn, taken as the type of Christ's cross which, floating above the cataclysmic abyss of the primeval flood, saved men from the wilderness of many waters, while Satan was imagined as the Serpent of the deep who first came up out of the subterranean abyss to tempt Adam and who finally, like a sea monster, had been caught on the hook of the cross. In the language of the liturgy of baptism much of the ancient Semitic feeling for the interconnection of the desert, death, and the deep survived in new Christian meanings attached to the uniquely redemptive sacrament of baptismal death to the world and resuscitation in Christ.

After passing through the new flood, the new Red Sea, the new Jordan of baptism, the neophytes not only entered the Promised Land but also participated in the partial restoration of Paradise. The baptismal waters and the fragrance of the ointments were likened to the rivers of Paradise and the perfumes of odoriferous trees therein, while

[4] N. H. Dahl, "La terre où coulent le lait et le miel selon Barnabé," *Aux Sources de la Tradition Chrétienne: Mélanges offerts à Maurice Goguel* (Neuchâtel, Paris, 1950), pp. 62–70. For a later version see Tertullian, *Against Marcion*, III, 16: "For [Joshua was a type of Jesus], inasmuch as Jesus Christ was to lead a *new* people—because we are born in the wilderness of this world (*in saeculi desertis*)—into the Promised Land which flows with milk and honey, that is into the possession of eternal life, than which nothing can be sweeter. . . ."

[5] See Per Lundberg, "La typologie baptismale dans l'ancienne Église," *Acta Seminarii Neotestamentici Upsaliensis* (Uppsala, 1942), and A. Salles, "Trois Antiques Rituels du Baptême," *Sources chrétiennes*, Paris, 1958, No. 59.

the octagonal shape of the baptistry symbolized the return of the eighth day, the paradisic and golden first age of mankind in innocence.[6]

Within the disciplined Church what reason had lost by the Fall could be regained by the Holy Spirit; what the soul and body had lost by disobedience could be regained by the sacramental "medicine of immortality," "the bread of heaven." Analogous to the view of the Essenes there prevailed the conviction that Christ the incarnate Word, through the commissioning of the Spirit's work within the Church, had made possible the restitution of the knowledge of good and evil distorted by the willfulness of the first Adam.

Irenaeus of Lyons (c. 130–c. 200), in defending the Church against the Gnostics, who claimed to have a higher or deeper esoteric knowledge than the Catholics without the encumbering disciplines of the apostolic tradition, expressly identified the Church as Paradise:

. . . flee to the Church, and be brought up in her bosom, and be nourished with the Lord's Scriptures. For the Church has been planted as a *paradisus* in this world; therefore says the Spirit of God (Genesis 2:16), "Thou mayest freely eat from every tree of the garden," that is, Eat ye from every Scripture of the Lord; but ye shall not eat with an uplifted mind, nor touch any heretical discord. For these men [the Gnostics] do profess that they have themselves the knowledge of good and evil; and they set their own impious minds above the God who made them. They therefore form opinions on what is beyond the limits of human understanding.[7]

Irenaeus goes on to quote Romans 12:3 on the importance of not being wise beyond what is fitting to be wise, "that we be not cast forth, by eating of *gnosis*, . . . from the paradise of life."

Irenaeus elsewhere also suggests the precariousness of the Church as the provisional paradise when he appeals to Paul's image of the wild olive grafted onto the orchard olive (Romans 11:17 ff.) and tries to make the apostle's analogy horticulturally more plausible by picking up the prophetic wilderness-garden motif, stressing not Paul's original thought of the wild Gentile being grafted onto the good stock of Israel but rather Paul's warning that Christians through Gnostic temptation and the concurrent evasion of the Church's corporate disciplines might become wild again. In a mood more eschatological than the passage above, Irenaeus says that

---

[6] Lucien de Bruyne, "La décoration des baptistères paléochrétiens," *Miscellanea liturgica in honorem L. Cuniberti Mohlberg* (Rome, 1948), I, 189–220; Franz-Joseph Dölger, "Die Achtzahl in der altchristlichen Symbolik," *Antike und Christentum*, IV (1933–1934), 154–187.

[7] *Against Heresies*, V, xx, 2; Harvey, ed., II, 379; translation from *ANF*, I, 548.

men, if they do truly progress by faith towards better things, and receive the Spirit of God, and bring forth the fruit thereof, shall be spiritual (*spirituales*), as being planted in the [provisional] paradise of God. . . . [and will eventually] arrive at the pristine nature of man—that which was created after the image and likeness of God.

But if they do not, here is his warning:

. . . the good olive, if neglected for a certain time, if left to grow wild and to run to wood [lusts], does itself become a wild olive.[8]

A famous letter to an otherwise unknown Diognetus in the second century reflects this same conviction as to the restoration of the paradisic state in respect of knowledge and behavior:

If you chance upon these [Christian] truths and listen earnestly to them, you will know what things God provides for those who love Him rightly, who are become "a Paradise of delight," raising up in themselves a tree all-fruitful and flourishing, and are adorned with divers fruits. For in this garden has been planted "the tree of knowledge and the tree of life." . . . But the tree of knowledge does not kill; disobedience kills. For that which stands written is not without significance, how that God from the beginning planted "the tree [of knowledge and the tree] of life in the midst of Paradise," showing that life is through knowledge. Because our first parents did not make pure use of this knowledge they were left naked by the deceit of the serpent. . . . If you [in the Spirit, however,] bear the tree of this and pluck its fruit, you will ever gather in the things desired with God, which the serpent does not touch and deceit does not taint.[9]

The roughly contemporary Christianizing *Testament of Levi* (18:10–13) also "foresees" that the Messiah "shall open the gates of paradise . . . and shall give to the saints to eat from the tree of life and the Spirit of holiness shall be on them."[10]

Aphrahat the Sage of Persia (c. 280–345), after discussing the vision of the grape and vine in Isaiah 65:8 and the tree of knowledge, refers to the healing of the olive trees and suggests that sacramental unction reopens the door of Paradise to the newly baptized:

But to those seeking peace the door is opened and confusion flees from the

---

[8] *Against Heresies,* V, x, 1; Harvey, ed., II, 345; *ANF,* I, 536. There is an illuminating article on theological dendrology by Gerhart Ladner in *De Artibus* in honor of Erwin Panofsky ed. by Millard Meiss (New York, 1961).

[9] *The Epistle to Diognetus,* xii, 1; tr. Henry G. Meecham (Manchester, 1949), p. 91; H. I. Marrou, ed., *Sources chrétiennes,* XXXIII (1951), 80 f., 235, derives the Paradise of delight from Psalms of Solomon 14:2. Here the saints themselves are likened to the aromatic trees of Paradise.

[10] On the date, c. 190 = c. 225, see Marinus de Jonge, *The Testaments of the Twelve Patriarchs: A Study of their Text, Composition and Origin* (Assen, 1953), p. 125.

mind of many; the light of the mind has begun to shine; the splendid olive trees have produced their fruits in which is the sign of the sacrament of life whereby Christians are made *priests, kings,* and *prophets.*[11]

The disciplined Christian in the ancient Church had an indelible "ordination" as priest, prophet, and king, no longer in bondage to the world but freed through Christ to join in the corporate thanksgiving of the redeemed, to exercise sovereignty over the inner temple, and to know the truth in the illumination of the Spirit. The Church as the provisional paradise in which truth is restored through the disciplines of grace was set in the wilderness of the world.

It was the schismatic bishop of Rome, Hippolytus (c. 170–c. 236), who was perhaps the first to make use of the wilderness motif in the special context in which it appears in the Song of Songs (3:16; 8:5). He answered the query of "who is that coming up out of the wilderness" or wasteland by pointing to the pagans who had hitherto been "left waste" but had now been included in the divine dispensation, leaning as a bride and companion upon the heavenly Bridegroom, Christ.[12]

In endeavoring to ascertain how all the prophecies of the Old Covenant had been completely fulfilled in the New, the Old Catholic Fathers, for example, Bishop Cyprian of Carthage (d. 258), commonly interpreted baptism as the fulfillment of Isaiah's prophecy (43:18–21), Christ having made "a way in the wilderness of heathen cults and rivers of baptismal purification in the desert of pagan abominations"; and they interpreted the wine of the eucharist as the quenching water foretold by Isaiah in 48:21, the Church being the *paradisus cum fructu pomorum* of Canticles wherein the spouse once again partakes of holy food.[13] For the Gentiles who had long thirsted in the desert God made water to flow from the cleft of that rock which is Christ the Redeemer of men.

As the age of persecution and martyrdom drew to a close, the North African Lactantius (d. c. 320) rhetorically brought Judaeo-Christian millennialism and the Isaianic vision of a second Eden in the wilderness

---

[11] *Demonstratio,* xxiii, *De Acino,* 3; *Patrologia Syriaca, pars prima,* Vol. II, col. 10.

[12] *Eis to asma,* slavisches Fragment xvi (iii, 6), ed. Bonwetsch, Berlin Corpus, *Hippolytus,* I, pp. 355 f. Origen, who about 240 wrote a commentary on Canticles and two surviving homilies, did not have occasion to develop the wilderness theme in connection with the nuptial imagery of his ecclesiology because the Septuagint renders the wilderness passage (3:8) differently from the Hebrew, which Hippolytus, in contrast, was aware of. The extant text of Origen, surviving only in Latin, does not, in any event, expressly deal with our three key passages.

[13] For example, Cyprian, *Ep.* LXIII (LXII), viii, 1; *Ep.* LXIX, ii, 1; LXXIV, xi, 2; LXXV, xv, 1; *To Quirinus,* i, 12.

together with the cyclical return of the golden age of Saturn. In the *Divine Institutes* (304–311) Lactantius systematized the Christian hope for Christ's descent after a period of war and destruction, his preliminary judgment, and his rule with the saints for a thousand years, in a grand vision that conflates the Isaianic vision of the peace of nature (Paradise restored), the millennium as the provisional Kingdom (of Christ), and the golden age renewed:

Then that darkness will be taken away from the world with which the heaven will be overspread and darkened, and the moon will receive the brightness of the sun, nor will it be further diminished; but the sun will become seven times brighter than it now is; and the earth will open its fruitfulness, and bring forth most abundant fruits of its own accord; the rocky mountains shall drop with honey; streams of wine shall run down, and rivers flow with milk: in short, the world itself shall rejoice, and all nature exult, being rescued and set free from the dominion of evil and impiety, and guilt and error. Throughout this time beasts shall not be nourished by blood, nor birds by prey; but all things shall be peaceful and tranquil. Lions and calves shall stand together at the manger, the wolf shall not carry off the sheep, the hound shall not hunt for prey; hawks and eagles shall not injure; the infant shall play with serpents. In short, those things shall then come to pass which the poets spoke of as being done in the reign of Saturnus.[14]

Bishop Eusebius of Caesarea (c. 260–c. 340), a later contemporary of Lactantius and the biographer and eulogist of Constantine, as well as the father of Church history, was tempted to believe that the millennium was indeed being ushered in by the first Christian emperor. Eusebius laid the scriptural and theological foundations in the widespread conviction in Eastern Orthodoxy that the Christian *Basileia* reflects on earth the Kingdom or Paradise above.

Eusebius, like Cyprian and the Old Catholic Fathers, frequently resorted to the Exodus motifs in interpreting redemption through "the water bath broken out in the wilderness." He likened the imperial persecutions to the sufferings of old Israel in "the desert and wilderness." In the converted Constantine he saw the Christian Moses, who, having defeated Maxentius and his hosts in the crossing of the Tiber at Saxa Rubra, was repeating the providential destruction of Pharaoh in the Red Sea,[15] to prepare the way for the Christianization of the world.

It is significant, in view of the imminent limitation of the paradisic

---

[14] *Divine Institutes*, VII, xxiv; *ANF*, VII, 218 f.

[15] *Discourse at Tyre*, c. 315, in Eusebius, *Ecclesiastical History*, X, iv, 32–36; in Philip Schaff and Henry Wace, eds., *Nicene and Post-Nicene Fathers* (henceforth *NPF*) (New York, 1890), I, 374 f.; *Life of Constantine*, i, 38; in *NPF*, I, 492 f.

motif to the monks in flight from the Christianized empire, that in the interpretation of Christ's post-baptismal temptation in the wilderness of Jordan Eusebius chose to extinguish entirely the motif of paradisic harmony in the Marcan version and, confirming the major tradition in applying Psalm 91:13 thereto, pictured Christ as crushing by his divine virtue the asp and the adder, the lion and the dragon in the wilderness.[16] With this concept of Christ as *Victor* rather than as *Via in deserto,* Eusebius readily imagined Constantine completing the resolute action of the Saviour in crushing by force of arms the demons of divisiveness, disorder, and the depraved cults. Commingling the imperial and his own episcopal ideal of the Christian commonwealth, Eusebius described a lofty painted tablet erected by Constantine in front of the portico of his palace.[17] This icon displayed Constantine and his sons under a representation of the salutary sign (of the cross) trampling on the head of a dragon stricken through with a dart and cast headlong into the depths of the sea. Eusebius interpreted the icon, "divinely inspired," as the emperor's discerning representation of his own fulfillment in the realm of war and politics of what Paul (Ephesians 1:22) had said of Christ after his crucifixion and also as an imperial fulfillment of what Isaiah (27:1) had foreseen of the Messiah, doing battle amid "thorns and briers," making peace and a "pleasant vineyard" after overcoming Satan: "God with his great and terrible sword will punish the twisting dragon, the fleeing serpent, and we will slay the dragon that is in the sea."[18] In the history of the cross-dragon-deserttemptation motif in liturgy and iconography it may well have been precisely Eusebius' paralleling of Constantine's victory *in hoc signo* with Christ's victory on the cross which finally brought about the eclipse of the Old Catholic interpretation of Jesus among the animals in the wilderness in Mark 1:13 as the New Covenantal Adam in Paradise, which is the Church.

More and more, in Byzantine art it is the figure of Orpheus that replaces Adam among the animals, while a growing interest in the

---

[16] *Praeparatio Evangelii,* vii, 16.

[17] *Life of Constantine,* iii, 3; in *NPF,* I, 520.

[18] Only this much of Isaiah is actually quoted (in a version closer to the Hebrew than to the Septuagint). The briers and peaceful vineyard belong to vv. 2 f. The most detailed and yet comprehensive study of the wilderness and paradise motif in connection with the cross and with due attention to Eusebius is that of Meyer Schapiro in a fascinating iconographic and textual analysis, "The Religious Meaning of the Ruthwell Cross [end of the seventh century]," *The Art Bulletin,* XXVI (1944), 235 f. Cf. F. Saxl, "The Ruthwell Cross," *Journal of the Warburg and Courtauld Institutes,* VI (1943), 1–19, where the stress is upon the Mediterranean origin of the iconographic items rather than the wilderness theme. More recently Ernst Kantorowicz has identified the one remaining obscure figure in the cross as Ishmael in the wilderness of Paran, "The Archer in the Ruthwell Cross," *The Art Bulletin,* XLII (1960), 57–59.

classical motifs of the chase and of the creature in the clutches of a bird or beast of prey becomes unpleasantly prominent in Byzantine mosaics and frescoes often as a symbol of the conquest of vice by virtue and of Christian conversion under the Christianized Empire.

But if Eusebius in his own period contributed to the general retreat of the feeling for the Church as a provisional paradise[19] in preference to the idea of the Christianized empire as the terrestrial image of the celestial Kingdom, he also saw fit to include in his *Ecclesiastical History* (I, iv, 5–15) a primitivist element which was destined to sway the imaginations of monks and sectaries alike throughout the succeeding centuries in reinforcement of the wilderness-paradise motif. For Eusebius took over from the apologists (like Theophilus of Antioch, Justin Martyr, Tertullian, and Lactantius) the idea that Abraham was in effect a Christian before he was a Jew, "a friend of God" by faith alone (cf. James 2:23) before he submitted to covenantal circumcision, and that accordingly all the venerable company before him "as friends of God" and "as in verity Christians by their action if not by name" were likewise in no need of the mediation of the cultus of tabernacle and temple, or of the codification of a law already written primordially upon their hearts. In fact, "these friends of God" not only were visited on occasion by the pre-existent Christ but were themselves called "christs," as in Psalm 105:15. Thus, though Eusebius did not himself call the habitat of the pre-Covenantal Christians or the friends of God either a desert or a garden, generations of Christian primitivists and secessionists on scrutinizing his *History* would inevitably construe his influential testimony as to the identity of "the religion of Abraham" and "the religion transmitted and taught by Christ" as a sanction for their wandering quest in the wilderness of a formalized Christianity and as a warrant for their retreat from the complexities of an elaborate Christian cultus and canon to the simplicity of the desert or into the exaltation of a spiritualized creed.[20] But this is to anticipate. We have yet to mention the connection of Eusebius with another aspect of desert theology very much cultivated in his own day.

Eusebius, as bishop of Caesarea in Palestine, was the principal ad-

[19] The conception of the whole Church as paradise survives in the post-Constantinian age in several writers, among them Methodius of Olympus (*Symposium*, ix, 3), Zeno of Verona (*Sermo*, ii, 63), Optatus of Mileve (*Contra Donatum*, ii, 11), and Ephraem Syrus (on whom more presently); but it is no longer a dominant idea.
The contrasting conception of the Christian life in terms of the chase has been traced in Byzantine art by André Grabar, *L'Empereur dans l'art byzantin* (Paris, 1936).

[20] For the history of the mystical-spiritualist conception of the friends of God (James 2:23 and John 15:14), see E. Peterson, "Der Gottesfreund: Beiträge zur Geschichte eines religiösen Terminus," *Zeitschrift für Kirchengeschichte*, XLII (1923), 161–202. Cf. Irenaeus, *Against Heresies*, IV, 13, 4.

viser of Constantine and Constantine's mother Helen in the erection of
the three great Constantinian basilicas in the Holy Land. As all three
of them are connected with sacred caves or grottoes, we may conveniently at this point introduce another strand in the Christian elaboration of the wilderness-paradise motif as it centers in the sacred cave.[21]

The three churches built by Constantine and Helen to celebrate the
Christian victory over the "cave cultus" of the pagan world were the
basilica over the Grotto of the Nativity in Bethlehem,[22] that over the
Holy Sepulchre,[23] and that over "the very cave [on the Mount of
Olives] where the Saviour imparted his secret revelations to his disciples," according to the Little Apocalypse of Matthew 24. This site
was traditionally identified as the locus of his ascension.[24]

That Jesus was born in a cave rather than in the stable of an inn, that
he was buried in a cave rather than in a stone tomb, that he ascended
from a cavern on the top of the Mount of Olives—all this mystery of
the cave belongs to the Eastern tradition and rests not upon the canonical Gospels but, contrary to this testimony, upon an ancient tradition
that goes back to the Septuagintal text of Isaiah 33:16 f.: "He shall
dwell in the lofty cave of a strong rock. Bread shall be given him, and
his water [shall be] sure. You shall see the king with glory."[25] Very
early this prophecy was regarded as messianic and applied presently to
the birth of Christ in a cave in Bethlehem. This Isaianic prophecy is referred to in Pseudo-Barnabas (11:9), in Justin Martyr's *Dialogue with
Trypho* (lxx), and in the Proto-evangelium (21:3) ascribed to James,
the brother of the Lord. In the patristic tradition already mentioned of
finding the sacraments foreshadowed in the wilderness, Barnabas
stressed the water in the Isaianic prophecy as a reference to the redemptive baptism brought by Christ, while Justin stressed the reference
to bread as a prophecy of the eucharist and connected the vision with
that of Isaiah 35:1–7, placing the lofty cave of sacramental salvation in
the wilderness, which through that redemptive water blossoms like a
rose.[26] It is quite possible that the claim of the devotes of the rock-

---

[21] Ernst Benz is the first to have brought together the theology of the sacred cave
into the larger setting; "Die heilige Höhle in der alten Christenheit und in den
östlich-orthodoxen Kirche," *Eranos-Jahrbuch*, XXII (1953), 365–432.

[22] *Life of Constantine*, iii, 41 and 43; in *NPF*, I, 530 f.

[23] *Ibid.*, iii, 25 ff.; in *NPF*, I, 526 ff.

[24] *Ibid.*, iii, 41 and 43; in *NPF*, I, 530 f. Neither Matthew 24 nor the account of
the ascension from the Mount of Olives in Mark 16:19, Luke 24:50 f., and Acts 1:1
f. mentions any cave on the Mount.

[25] The reading "in a lofty cave" is found in neither the Hebrew Bible nor the Vulgate.

[26] *Dialogue*, lxix, where Justin vigorously refutes the apparent claim of the Mithraists
to the Isaianic prophecy.

born Mithras that Isaiah's prophecy was fulfilled in the nativity and underground cultus of this deity prompted the Eastern churches to claim the prophecy for Christ and to elaborate a speluncar nativity of Christ in their liturgy and iconography.

In the course of time, as the scriptural passages were collected and collated concerning the cave of the nativity, the cave of the burial and resurrection, and the cavern of the ascension, a veritable speluncar theology developed which, in the Eastern tradition, became a distinctive element in the monastic conception of the desert with its caves.

When the Isaianic prophecy was brought into relation with that of Daniel (2:45) concerning the stone taken from the mountain, it was possible to think of Mary as the spiritual Rock and her womb as the lofty cave foretold.

Along with the double sense of the cave of the nativity, a double sense could also be given to the Sepulchre. In the elaboration of speluncar theology, hell itself, harrowed by Christ for three days after the crucifixion, was thought of as the collective sepulchre of unredeemed mankind, into which Christ had descended to extend the scope of his redemption before rising on Easter morn.

In view of the long association of death, the demonic, the deep, and the desert in the tradition of the Old Testament, it is of special interest that for some time after the destruction of Jerusalem by Titus the very cave reconsecrated by Constantine's basilica of the nativity was occupied by a shrine of the dying and rising god Tammuz-Adonis.[27]

By the time of Eusebius and Constantine, caves sacred to the tradition of the biblical people were identified and hallowed with shrines all over the Holy Land—for example, the cave where Mary herself was born, the cave of the annunciation in Nazareth, the cave of the resurrection of Lazarus in Bethany, the cave of Abraham in the valley of Mamre, and the cave of Elijah on Mount Carmel.

Whatever the religio-historical connections and details may have been, the potency and fascination of these speluncar sites must have been considerable to have captured the learned attention of Eusebius, to have fostered the architectural zeal of Constantine, and, especially in the case of the Grotto of the Nativity, to have completely displaced in popular imagination, in the Eastern liturgies, and in iconography the canonical account of Christ's birth not in a cave but in a stable.

It is not certain at what period the Grotto of the Nativity was referred to in the Eastern liturgies as also paradise; but in all the sur-

---

[27] Jerome, *Ep.* LVIII, 3, *Ad Paulinum;* for a synopsis of the learned discussion, see Benz, *op. cit.,* pp. 392 ff.

viving liturgies in the Septuagintal tradition, the cave of Isaiah 33:16 f. has become also a provisional paradise:

> Today the Virgin gives birth to the Creator of all;
> The Grotto brings forth Paradise
> And the Star refers to Christ,
> The Sun to those who sit in darkness.[28]

In another Christmas service the same hymnal exclaims: "Bethlehem has opened Eden: . . . Come, let us receive in the Cave that which is of Paradise."[29]

It was natural that the monks, retreating to the deserts, should find in the cave not only their minimal shelter but also their divinely sanctioned site for the exercise of their sacred asceticism, for here in the cave the hermits died with Christ to the world; here they fought demons, as Christ in Hades vanquished the devil; here they fought demons in the sands like the martyrs surrounded by the beasts of the arena; here they were reborn; here they tasted the fruits of paradise.

Ignatius, bishop of Antioch, a prototype of the martyr, had longed for the Roman Colosseum, there to be "in the claws of the lion" as "in the hands of God." Anthony, the prototype of all hermits, went into the desert to fight the demons of the caves, and in the sands, the dragon and *lilith.* In the spiritualization of geography and in the evolution of Christian anthropological types, the desert of the ascetic with its wild beasts was at once the sublimation of the arena of the pre-Constantinian martyr and the intimation of the paradise of Adam before the Fall.

2. *The Flight to the Desert: The Monastery as a Provisional Paradise*[30]

Eusebius, if not Lactantius, lived long enough to realize that there were to be as many temptations, vexations, and murmurings under the Christian Moses as under the old. And many Christians, some of them the most conscientious, began to flee the so-called Christian empire. It was among the hermits and monks that the biblical sense lived on of the ambiguity[31] of the wilderness of Sinai and the wilderness of Jordan, the wilderness of temptation and the wilderness which is a pro-

---

[28] Hymn of Germanos for the Vespers of the Feast of Christmas; *Menologion* (Athens), XII (December, 1904), 307. Benz has collected many of the cave-paradise passages, *op. cit.,* pp. 412–416. That the cave with its cradle was thought of theologically as in the wilderness, though it was located in Bethlehem, is borne out by a sticheron in the liturgy for December 26; *Men.,* XII, 319.

[29] *Men.,* XII, 312.

[30] Georges Florovsky has suggested this theme in "Empire and Desert: Antinomies of Christian History," *Greek Orthodox Theological Review,* III (1957), 133–159.

[31] In commenting on the tympanum of the Portal of the Goldsmiths in Santiago, in which Christ's temptation is fashioned as a re-enactment of that of Adam in Paradise, Schapiro, *op. cit.,* p. 234, remarks: "The desert becomes an ambiguous concept. . . , for it is both the fearful wilderness, uninhabited by man, and the earthly paradise

visional paradise with saints and beasts in harmony, obedient unto Christ.

The flight of the hermits into the desert was, for them, a fifth exodus from bondage. Basil the Great (c. 330–379), the organizer of Eastern monasticism, spoke for the whole company of those who fled into the desert when, before his elevation to the episcopal throne in Caesarea in Cappadocia, he wrote:

I am living . . . in the wilderness wherein the Lord dwelt. Here is the oak of Mamre; here is the ladder which leads to heaven, and the encampments of the angels which Jacob saw; here is the wilderness where the people, purified, received the law, and then going into the land of promise beheld God. Here is Mount Carmel where Elijah abode and pleased God. Here is the plain whither Ezra [IV:14:37–38] withdrew [for forty days], and at God's bidding poured forth from his mouth all his divinely inspired books. Here is the wilderness where the blessed John ate locusts and preached repentance to men. Here is the Mount of Olives, which Christ ascended and there prayed, teaching us how to pray. Here is Christ, the lover of the wilderness; for He says (Matthew 18:20), "Where there are two or three gathered in My name, *there* am I in the midst of them [!]." Here is the narrow and strait way that leadeth to life. Here are teachers and prophets, "wandering in deserts, in mountains, and in dens, and in caves of the earth" (Heb. 11:38). Here are apostles and evangelists and the life of monks, citizens of the desert.[82]

Basil's younger brother, Gregory of Nyssa (d. c. 395) was quite specific about the importance of the rejection of marriage, admittedly the holiest of human ties, as a prerequisite for achieving in the solitude of the wilderness the return to the original beatitude of Adam in Paradise.[83]

Gregory, like other Greek Fathers, tended to use interchangeably as essentially one the state of Paradise before the Fall, the realm of Paul's rapture (II Corinthians 12:2 ff.), and the celestial realm whither the soul of the good thief departed from his cross at the side of Christ. He was among the first to see in the paradisic rapture of Paul a model of the mystical experience accessible to all devout Christians,[84] first through baptism, and then through further illumination:

Jordan alone of rivers, receiving in itself the first-fruits of sanctification and

where the first man lived in harmony with the beasts." This generalization holds for the whole Christian development of the biblical motif.

[82] *Ep.* XLIII, ed. and tr. Roy J. Deferrari, Loeb Library, *Letters,* I, 261.

[83] *De Virginitate,* 12, ed. John Cavarnos, in Werner Jaeger, ed., *Opera* of Gregory of Nyssa, VIII:1 (Brill, 1952), pp. 302 ff.; cited by Ladner, *op. cit.,* pp. 76 f .

[84] Cf. Ladner, *op. cit.,* p. 78. Gregory's mystical interpretation of paradise as the individual soul was, to this extent, preceded by Origen, who held that the individual believer can become a paradise of God (*ibid.,* p. 74), and before him by Philo (Daniélou, *op. cit.,* pp. 468 ff.).

benediction, conveyed in its channel to the whole world, as it were from some fount in the type afforded by itself, the grace of Baptism. . . . And where shall we place that oracle of Isaiah, which cries to the wilderness: "Be glad, O thirsty wilderness: let the desert rejoice and blossom as a lily: and the desolate places of the Jordan shall blossom and rejoice" (Isaiah 35:1)?[35] For it is clear that it is not to places without soul or sense that he proclaims the good tidings of joy: but he speaks, by the figure of the desert, of the soul that is parched and unadorned, even as David (Psalm 144:6) also, when he says, "My soul is unto thee as a thirsty land." . . . For as great Lebanon presents a sufficient cause of wonder in the very trees which it brings forth and nourishes, so is the Jordan glorified by regenerating men and planting them in the Paradise of God.[36]

Gregory was at the same time quite specific about the desert or wilderness as signifying sin, personalizing the conquest of the Canaanites by Joshua in his allegory:

Carry the Gospel like Joshua the Ark. Leave the desert, that is sin. Cross the Jordan. Hasten toward the life according to Christ, toward the Land which bears the fruit of joy, which according to the promise flows with milk and honey.[37]

Thinking of the devout individual, Gregory, in his Homily XV on Canticles and in allusion to Paul's simile in I Corinthians 3:6-9, compares the sinner to a wasted field converted again into a garden cultivated by Christ:

The [true husbandman] is he who at the beginning in Paradise cultivated human nature, which the heavenly Father planted. But the wild boar [Psalm 80:13; from the forest] has ravaged our garden and spoiled the planting of God. That is why he [the husbandman] has descended a second time to transform the desert into a garden, ornamenting it by planting virtues and making it to flourish with the pure and divine stream of solicitous instruction by means of the Word.[38]

For Gregory of Nyssa the single converted soul in its elevated state was also in a sense a Paradise. It is therefore of special interest to anticipate at this point the fact that it is precisely the opposite word, *wilderness* (*desert*), which will discharge in Western medieval mysticism a function comparable to Gregory's *paradise* in the elaboration of spiritual terminology.

[35] The reference to the Jordan is Septuagintal.

[36] *On the Baptism of Christ*, Migne, *Patrologia Graeca* (henceforth *PG*), XLVI, cols. 92 f.; *PNF*, 2nd ser., V, 522 f.

[37] *On Baptism, PG*, XLVI, cols. 420 f.

[38] *In Canticum canticorum*, ed. Hermann Langerbeck in Werner Jaeger, ed., *Opera*, VI (Brill, 1960), pp. 436 f.; *PG*, XLIV, col. 1092 D.

After the accommodation of the Church to the empire, some of the most devout of the Church Fathers and the new Christian race of hermits and monks, dissatisfied by the paradisic pretension of the Church as a whole, claimed rather that Paradise was being realized instead either ecstatically within the devotee as an individual or, by extension, within the precincts of the hermit's cell or the monk's monastery. In any event it was only in mystical flight from the suddenly enlarged Church of the people or from the but partially Christianized empire into the wilderness and into the solitude of the desert that these devout believers could hope to experience that inner and external harmony consonant with their conviction about the restoration of Paradise.

The desert was, in effect, for the ascetics as for the biblical Israelites at once the haunt of demons and the realm of bliss and of harmony with the creaturely world. The monks withdrew to the desert both to carry their warfare into the enemy's territory and to contemplate the Author of their victory. As John Cassian (d. 435) later wrote, preserving the colloquies of the desert Fathers:

> They were anchorites, i.e., withdrawers, because, being by no means satisfied with that victory whereby they had trodden under foot the hidden snares of the devil (while still living among men), they were eager to fight with the devils in open conflict, and a straightforward battle, and so feared not to penetrate the vast recesses of the desert.

At the same time in "the freedom of the vast wilderness" they sought to enjoy "that life which can only be compared to the bliss of angels."[39]

Anthony the Hermit seriously instructed his followers in the techniques of diabolic warfare. *The Lausaic History or Book of Paradise* of Palladius (d. 425) and the closely related *Historia Monachorum* of Rufinus of Aquileia (d. 411) are full of demons, of Satan with his animal and human disguises, of devils and monsters whose crafts and assaults the untrained multitudes could not endure; for these evil spirits resisted the efforts of holy men who, intruding themselves in the caves and ruins of the desert still becharmed with hieroglyphs and the visages of ancient animal deities, sought to dislodge these evil spirits of an earlier age. Because of the success in holding back the demons, the holy men could think of their habitations as the fulfillment of the prophecy of Isaiah 35:1 that "the dry desert shall rejoice."[40]

---

[39] *Colloquia* (III), xviii, 6, and xix, 5.
[40] Abbâ Apollo in Palladius' *Paradise* (Syriac version), ed. and tr. E. A. Wallis Budge (London, 1904), I, 525.

That the haunt of the monks, charged with the effluvium of their sanctity, was a kind of provisional paradise is suggested by the very title of Palladius' *History,* as also by frequent references in it to the paradisic vision and to paradisic nurture and to the paradisic power of the holy men over and peace with the creatures of the wild, including lions and crocodiles which made friends with the recluses (in fulfillment of the Isaianic prophecy of 35:1). One Postumianus[41] recalls how a holy man, on encountering a lion amid the palms, bade it withdraw until his terrified visitors were appeased, and then plucked dates for the beast; how a lioness in the wilderness beyond Memphis sought out a hermit to help recover the sight of her five cubs blind from birth; and how a she-wolf accustomed to receiving bits of food from another hermit, after one day stealing a loaf, "repented" and was forgiven by the monk's stroking her head. Whatever the actual episodes may have been, it is significant that both the saints and the hagiographer felt that only through the recovery of pristine holiness could man help undo the ferocity brought into the world by man's primordial disobedience in the first Paradise. Postumianus muses:

. . . Behold, I beg of you, . . . the power of Christ, to whom all is wise that is irrational, and to whom all is mild that is by nature savage. A wolf discharges duty; a wolf acknowledges the crime of theft; a wolf is confounded with a sense of shame: when called for, it presents itself, it offers its head to be stroked; and it has a perception of the pardon granted to it, just as if it had a feeling of shame on account of its misconduct,—this is thy power, O Christ—these, O Christ, are thy marvelous works. For in truth, whatever things thy servants do in thy name are thy doings; and in this only we find cause for deepest grief that, while wild beasts acknowledge thy majesty, intelligent beings fail to do thee reverence.[42]

In the *Pratum spirituale* is preserved the famous story of the Palestinian abbot Gerasimus (in an account resembling that concerning Androcles), who relieved the pain of a lion by removing a thorn from its paw, in return for which the lion served him in the capacity of guardian and draught animal and at length, mourning the death of his benefactor, died over his grave. The narrator concludes his story:

All this was done, not because it is necessary to attribute to the lion a rational soul, but rather because God wished . . . to show how the animals

[41] Preserved in Sulpitius Severus, *Dialogi,* xiii–xv.
[42] *Ibid., cap.* xiv; translation in *NPF,* XI, 31. For other references to the saints and tamed beasts in the wilderness, see the long note in Herbert Workman, *The Evolution of the Monastic Ideal* (London, 1913), p. 36.

were subject to Adam before his disobedience and his expulsion from the Paradise of delights.[43]

In due course this lion of abbot Gerasimus became attached, as a tell-tale attribute, to the scholar monk Jerome in his paradisic study.

Jerome (c. 342–420), translator of the Vulgate from the Hebrew and Greek, may be taken as a representative Latin theorist of the monastic flight into the wilderness. Jerome reworked a number of the desert themes. Writing about the efficacy of baptism,[44] he spoke of Eden, of the Red Sea as a figure of baptism, of the dragons of the deep, of the adders and scorpions that haunt dry places and "behave as if rabid or insane" when brought near water (forever sanctified by Christ in the Jordan). In his famous Epistle CXXV he, like Basil, traced the lineage of Christian monasticism into biblical times and went on to intertwine the wilderness and paradisic themes we have been following:

He [John the Baptist] lived in the desert, and seeking Christ with his eyes, refused to look at anything else. His rough garb, his girdle made of skins, his diet of locusts and wild honey were all alike designed to encourage virtue and continence. The sons of the prophets, who were the monks of the Old Testament, built for themselves huts by the waters of Jordan and forsaking the crowded cities lived in these on pottage and wild herbs (II Kings 4:38 f.; 6:1 f.). As long as you are at home, make your cell your paradise, gather there the varied fruits of Scripture, let this be your favourite companion, and take its precepts to your heart. . . . The sons of Jonadab, we are told, drank neither wine nor strong drink and dwelt in tents pitched wherever night overtook them (Jeremiah 35:6 f.). Others may think what they like and follow each his own bent. But to me a town is a prison and a solitude, paradise. Why do we long for the bustle of cities, we whose very name (*monachus*) speaks of loneliness? To fit him for the leadership of the Jewish people Moses was trained for forty years in the wilderness (Acts 7:29 f.), and it was not till after these that the shepherd of sheep became the shepherd of men.[45]

Jerome was not merely using a figure of speech when he spoke of the monastic cell as the provisional paradise, a garden in the wilderness. He connected the eating of the apple in Paradise quite literally with both hunger and sexual desire and regarded the forty days of Moses in meditative solitude and of Jesus in the wilderness of temptation as primarily concerned with the struggle against the demon of hunger.

---

[43] The *Pratum spirituale*, by John Moschus Eucrates (d. 619); PL, LXXIV, col. 174.
[44] *Ep.* LXIX, 6.
[45] *Ibid.*, 7 and 8; translation from *NPF*, VI, 246 f. See also *Ep.* XX and John Cassian, *Colloquia*, xviii, 6.

By following Moses and Jesus into the wilderness, he says, and "by fasting we can return to paradise."[46] "Care must be taken," he writes, "that abstinence may bring back to paradise those whom satiety once drove out." Jerome sees in the original wilderness experience of the children of Israel as applied by Paul to Christians (I Corinthians 10:1 ff.) the willing endurance of chastisement with respect to food and sex, and in "the dashing of little ones" (Psalm 137:9) the breaking of sexual impulses and evil thoughts against the Rock which is Christ in the desert of desirelessness.[47]

Bishop Ambrose of Milan (c. 339–397), strongly committed to the extension of continence and celibacy among Christians, whenever practicable, wrote a whole book on paradise and another on Naboth's vineyard as the Church of Christ. He likewise developed the idea of the disciplined return to Paradise,[48] notably in connection with Christ at his baptism in the Jordanian wilderness, and again in connection with the beginning of his passion in the garden of Gethsemane.

In commenting on the meaning of the temptation of Christ in the wilderness after his baptism in the Jordan, Ambrose says that just as the first Adam was driven from Paradise into the desert, so also the second Adam, in order to reassemble mankind in the Paradise originally intended for men before the fateful act of disobedience, had to begin his ministry in that very desert, overcoming the temptation of that same serpentine Satan and all his wiles. Thereafter, the believer in Christ, putting off all the garments of this world, might, through baptismal regeneration instituted by him who was bare of all guilt (*nuda a culpa*), become once again an inhabitant of Paradise. To be sure, to complete his redemptive work Christ had to face Satan once also in a garden. For wandering mankind might still have been lost if the second Adam had not, in addition to overcoming Satan in the immemorial wasteland of temptation, also, through an act of utter self-sacrificial obedience to the will of the heavenly Father, allowed himself unresistingly to be taken prisoner "in a new paradise" (Matthew 26, Mark 14, Luke 22), that is, the Mount of Olives. In order that fallen man might be effectually taken up into Christ, and the Adamic "exile" thereby re-formed in his original Garden state of grace, Christ died that he might conduct him into Paradise and thence into the Kingdom of God.[49] Ambrose, unlike some of the Fathers, clearly distinguished

[46] *Contra Jovinanum*, ii, 15.
[47] *Ep.* XXII, 6 and 10.
[48] The most recent study here is that of C. Morino, *Il ritorno al Paradiso di Adamo in S. Ambrogio* (Vatican City, 1952).
[49] *Ep.* LXXI, *Ad Horontianum*, 3 f.; Migne, *Patrologia Latina* (henceforth *PL*), XVI, 1295, p. 13 f.

between Paradise (as the first stage of the Kingdom) and the Kingdom proper.[50]

Ambrose describes the itinerary or pilgrimage of the believer's return to Paradise from the wilderness of this world in three stages.

First, the convert must recognize that he is in the desert of worldliness and must arm himself against its temptation through catechetical instruction, episcopal exorcism, immersion, and that unction which symbolizes both the anointment of burial and the anointment of royalty. Then his followers pass through the sown fields, symbolized by the grain plucked by Christ's disciples on the Sabbath day (Matthew 12:1 ff.), and by the garden beyond the brook Kedron (John 18:1) into which he took them, a garden enclosed, symbolic of the inwardness of the Church in the Songs of Songs (4:12 ff.). And finally Christ conducts his true followers into Paradise itself, as when on the cross he said to the believing thief: "This day wilt thou be with me in Paradise" (Luke 23:43).[51]

Ambrose of Milan, though he came late in the fourth century, and shared with other post-Constantinian Fathers the disillusionment of the age of extended Arian controversy and the apostasy of the Emperor Julian, nevertheless perpetuated the earlier ideal of the Church as a provisional paradise. And this view persisted in attenuation after him;[52] but for the most part it was the hermit in his cave and the monk in his desert monastery who could most naturally draw upon the wilderness-paradise tradition.

Eucharius (d. c. 449), for example, a once-married ascetic of Lyons and saintly bishop of Lyons, admirably restated our basic theme in the Latin monastic mode when, in *De laude eremi,* he observed that the desert in its limitlessness has, since the Fall, been the abode and "the temple of God"; for, since Paradise had proved fatefully beautiful for man, attaching him to the earth, God in his mercy henceforth beckoned him into the desert in order there to direct the gaze of man beyond himself to heaven.

It will be useful here to summarize certain differences and phases in the use of the desert motif in Eastern and Western monasticism.

In the East it was the theology of the cave that was dominant with the quest for the inner illumination amidst the external darkness. Absent

---

[50] Pointed out and clarified by Ladner, *op. cit.,* p. 144.

[51] *Expositio Evangelii secundum Lucam,* IV, 7–15 on Luke 4:1–13.

[52] Ephraem (d. 373) in his Paradise hymns is a good example of the survival of the paradisic claim of the Church in the Syrian tradition. He went so far as to speak of the Spirit entering the primitive Church at Pentecost as the perfume from Paradise. Hymn XI, 13 f. All his hymns have been edited by Edmund Beck, *Ephraems Hymnen über das Paradies,* Studia Anselmiana, XXVI (Rome, 1953).

from Eastern desert mysticism was the nuptial imagery, partly because, as we noted earlier, the Hebrew word for desert is absent in the Septuagintal version of Canticles 8:5. The attitude toward the animals of the desert was ambiguous in the East. They were interchangeably the minions of Satan and the denizens of Paradise precariously restored in the environs of the hermit or monk. At the same time Eastern spirituality, both Greek and non-Greek, drawing upon such universalists as Origen, Gregory of Nyssa, Theodore of Mopsuestia, and Maximus Confessor, held open the possibility of the eventual salvation (*apokatastasis pantōn*), not only of all human beings including Adam and Eve and perhaps even Judas, but also of the demons (the fallen spirits) and possibly even the animals. Ever since Elijah the desert had been the preordained place for the restoration of all things (Malachi 4:5; Acts 3:21).

In contrast to the East, the West, reinforced by the strong predestinarianism of Augustine, was much more disposed to stress the biblical texts in which the saints and sinners are sharply distinguished, and accordingly emphasized the selective character of salvation and in many forms found itself drawn to the idea of the remnant. As for the wilderness or desert tradition within the West, it tended to bring out the ideal of spiritual warfare more than the idea of contemplation, both of which elements belong to the original desert ideal. In Celtic monasticism the desert motif had the effect of reinforcing the idea of penitential wandering in imitation of the children of Israel on the march. Instead of the contemplative cave, for the Celtic monks it was the peniential mission that was most characteristic. The monastic quest for ever new and unpeopled deserts undoubtedly explains the penitential mobility of the Celtic missionaries and the penetration of unsubdued forests and swamps by successive waves of monastic reformers and planters, constantly seeking a more isolated *disert* or *disart*.[53] In Celtic and Anglo-Saxon monasticism the paradisic harmony of the hermit with the creaturely world was nevertheless prominent. Undoubtedly, pre-Christian totemism and a natural fondness for animals intensified this feature in the lives of the Celtic saints. But the observation of the Venerable Bede (d. 735) in connection with the life of Cuthbert, "We lose our empire over the creature because we neglect to serve God," strikes the Western note.[54]

[53] See John Ryan on the Celtic monks as *milites Christi* in *Irish Monasticism* (London, New York, 1931), pp. 195 ff., and the Carthusian *Liber de quadripertito exercitio cellae*, which deals with desert and paradise; *PL*, CLIII, cols. 799–884.

[54] For the numerous instances of saintly peace with the animal world, see Charles

3. *Certain Marginal Developments of the Garden Theme in the Middle Ages*

From time to time in the course of the Middle Ages, the ideal of the hermit as the lone warrior in the desert, as distinguished from the encamped monastic militia, was revived.[55] The idea of the monastery as a provisional paradise persisted. But the most distinctive medieval developments of our paradise and wilderness themes were (a) the architectural use of the term "paradise" for the atrium of basilicas and monasteries, (b) the elaboration of the paradisic and marital motifs in the emergence of a Christian theory of the school and university within the basic Christian presupposition that reason had been impaired by the Fall but could be sustained by grace, (c) the elaboration in medieval romance, iconography, and devotional literature of a distinction between the good garden of *sapientia* and the evil garden of *scientia* with special reference to the ways of love and Christian behavior, (d) the differentiation between the heavenly and the terrestrial paradise and speculation concerning the latter leading to the great age of exploration and discovery, (e) the mystical interiorization of the wilderness as state of mind through which the mystic passes to the consummation of the divine nuptials, and (f) the sectarian appropriation of the scriptural texts which would justify the flight of a Church of the remnant into the literal wilderness of mountains and forests to escape the clutches of the red dragon of papal ecclesiasticism.

As for the architectural use of the term, it must suffice to observe that the great forecourts of the Constantinian basilicas of the Holy Sepulchre and St. Peter's in Rome, along with an increasing number of such constructions in subsequent Romanesque cathedrals and monastic cloisters, were called paradises (*paradis*).[56] It was in this area, at the center of which flowed a fountain (*phialē, vasca*) in four streams, sometimes surrounded by potted trees and other plantings suggestive of a

---

Plummer, *Vitae Sanctorum Hiberniae* (Oxford, 1910), I, pp. cxliii–cxlvii. Especially interesting is Jonas' *Vita Columbani,* xxv, xxvii, xxviii, xxx, lix, lv. Schapiro, *op. cit.,* has gathered all this material together in explaining the Ruthwell Cross with the beasts adoring Christ in the desert rather than being trampled on.

[55] E.g., the Cluniacs, Carthusians, and Camaldolesi. See, for example, Peter Damian, *Ep.* XII; *PL,* CXLIV, cols. 392 ff.; also Kurt Hassinger, *Die Anfänge Clunys,* Forschungen zur Geschichte des Mittelalters, 1940.

[56] The development and the literature may be found conveniently in Ernst Schlee, *Die Ikonographie der Paradiesesflüsse,* Studien über christliche Denkmäler, N.F., XXIV (Leipzig, 1937), esp. pp. 133 ff.

garden, that the worshiper renewed the blessing of holy water on entering the sanctuary proper, a precinct to which the poor repaired to be
served at agapes, and to which the panting outlaw fled to attain the
right of sacred asylum. The clerical encyclopedist Honorius of "Autun"
(actually Bavaria) summed up the traditions and the observations from
such disparate sources as Eusebius of Caesarea, the *Liber Pontificalis,*
and Bishop Paulinus of Nola (d. 431), when early in the twelfth century he made it quite clear that the cloister was a paradise because it
was constructed like the portico of Solomon as an adjunct of the temple
(or church), and that it had been in the portico or cloister that the first
apostles preached about the faith and lived their lives in a loving
community of goods.[57]

As for the paradisic motif in the elaboration of the monastic theory
of education, we shall be dealing with it elsewhere in this book in
the rise of the medieval university (Part Two).

With regard to the medieval speculations concerning the terrestrial
paradise and its influence in the era of global navigation, we shall mention them briefly as we pursue our themes into the New World
(Chapter IV). Suffice it to observe that even here much of the Old
Testament polarity and interrelatedness of garden and desert persisted
in the medieval belief that the terrestrial paradise was to be found in a
warm clime at the antipodes of the wilderness of Zion. It was Dante
who near the end clearly distinguished between the terrestrial and celestial paradise and the two kinds of regeneration necessary for entry into
one and the other. At the threshold of the Renaissance he suggested that
through the poet's vision one might become incorporated with the first
Adam, *umanità,* and thereby participate in the rights and pleasures of a
human paradise before entry into that above.[58]

As for the literary and iconographic development, we shall have to
limit our observation to the fact that for the first time in our survey
the biblical concept of the garden when applied to the realm of courtly
love, chivalric conduct, and the Christian life in general also proves
ambivalent and divides (like the meaning of the wilderness in the

[57] *Gemma Animae,* I, cxlviii; *PL,* col. 590.

[58] Ernst Kantorowicz, *The King's Two Bodies: A Study in Medieval Political Theology* (Princeton, 1957), pp. 451–484. Dante opened his *Divine Comedy* as one lost
in a dark, dense, savage wood faced by three hostile beasts (Jeremiah 5:6), notably the
she-wolf "per la piaggia diserta." It was, moreover, precisely "nel gran diserto" that
Dante espied his advancing guide, Virgil, who would conduct him on his subterranean
pilgrimage to the pole opposite the wilderness of Zion, namely: *Paradiso.* On Dante's
medieval and ancient sources for locating the earthly Paradise in the Southern Hemisphere, opposite Jerusalem, see Charles S. Singleton, "Stars over Eden," *Seventy-fifth
Annual Report* of the Dante Society (Cambridge, 1957), pp. 1–18.

Bible itself) into a good and bad sense with considerable variation and sophistication both ethically and culturally.[59] In brief, the pleasance (*locus amoenus*) with its background in pagan literature supplemented by the image of the nuptial garden enclosed of Canticles played itself out over against and intermingled with the more strictly religious garden (*hortus caelestium deliciarum*). The fact that the Garden of Eden had been a place both of virtue and of the Fall, of the divinely sanctioned *sapientia* and the humanly craved *scientia*, made it possible for the paradisic representations, and all the trees and other flora and fauna therein, to symbolize either *caritas* or *cupiditas*. The central tree could be either the fateful tree of the knowledge of good and evil, the leaves of which wither and in the shade of which no one can therefore eternally rest,[60] or the tree of life, symbolic of the cross which restores man to prelapsarian bliss. The love portrayed in the garden can be either that which leads to mystical or that which leads to sexual ecstasy. Although divines and mystics contributed to the elaboration of the concept of the two gardens in art and literature, the most extensive development came at the hands of the great medieval romancers; and we shall later take note of the persistence of their metaphors, saturated with chivalric emotions, in the religious permutations of both wilderness and paradise themes, especially in the English seventeenth century (Chapter III, sec. 2).

There is, however, one modern survival and innocent deformation of the cult of the tree of Paradise, so often falsely thought of as a revival of a postulated pagan Germanic cult of the winter solstice, that can be mentioned here in passing. The modern Christmas tree has, to be sure, certain Roman, Celtic, Germanic, and medieval legendary roots and branches; but it is essentially the grafting one into the other of the tree of Paradise that caused death and the tree of eternal life which is the cross. In the morality play enacted in front of the medieval cathedral at Christmas the only tree that could serve as a tree of Paradise was an evergreen cut in the forest. The earliest records of the modern Christmas tree come from Alsace at the beginning of the sixteenth century and undoubtedly represent a domestication during the period of Protestant ascendancy in Strassburg and elsewhere when what had hitherto been a community celebration in front of the

---

[59] The major probing into this extensive and complicated material extending from Beowulf to Chaucer is that of D. R. Robertson, Jr., "The Doctrine of Charity in Medieval Literary Gardens: A Topical Approach through Symbolism and Allegory," *Speculum*, XXVI (1951), 24–49.

[60] See the meditation of Hugh of St. Victor, *Homilia IX in Ecclesiasten; PL,* CLXXV, cols. 171 f.

cathedral was transferred to private homes.[61] In the tympanum of the central portal of that cathedral Christ, the second Adam, is portrayed upon the cross planted on the mount of Calvary which is shown in cross section to expose the skeleton of the first Adam. One may conjecture that in the local morality play an evergreen was featured in an annual representation of the fall and the redemption of man through the incarnation and the crucifixion of the Son of God. But it is not until the sixteenth century that we actually glimpse this tree in the records, already by now reproduced in the homes of Protestant Strassburg and Sélestat (Schlettstadt). These first Christmas trees had no candles, only two kinds of "decorations," the symbolism of which was theologically clear: the apples of the tree of perdition and the (unconsecrated) eucharistic wafers (*Hostien*) of the new tree of life.

With this brief reference to a few marginal developments of our theme, we shall henceforth be limited in this chapter to a sampling of the mystical and then the sectarian appropriations and modifications of the wilderness motif in the Middle Ages.

4. The Wilderness in Mystical Theology and in the Formation of Heretical Conventicles in the Late Middle Ages

i. The Inner Desert of Western Mysticism

We have already anticipated the fact that where Eastern mysticism used *paradeisos* for the mystical state, in the West the comparable term was *desertum*. In the East one strove contemplatively to recover primordial manhood before the Fall. In the West one sought the promised land through mystical elevation in the covenanted company of pilgrims in the wilderness.

Richard of St. Victor (d. 1173) may be taken to illustrate the transition from the desert theology of antiquity, when the interiorized *desertum* became a technical term in mystical theology for a stage in the itinerary of the inner life. Its mystical sense was drawn from an allegorization and harmonization of most of the desert texts we have thus far noticed. The mystic Richard in his monastery of St. Victor, going beyond the use of *solitudo* and *desertum* of Revelation and using particularly the imagery of Exodus and Canticles, completely interior-

---

[61] The first mention of apples and eucharistic wafers is dated for Sélestat in 1600, in Strassburg in 1605; but the cutting of Christmas trees for the home is recorded from 1525 on. See J. Lefftz and A. Pfleger, *Elsässische Weihnacht: Ein Heimatbuch* (Colmar, 1941), pp. 51–57; René Herdt, "L'arbre de Noël," *Foi et Vie*, XXX (1927), 1193–1202.

ized the meaning of desert and thus moved in a somewhat different realm of piety from that of Jerome, Basil, and Postumianus, who had firsthand acquaintance with sand, serpents, and scorpions; and from that also of Cassian, Columbanus, and Cuthbert, who had sought out bleak isles. Richard's allegorization of the stages of the passage from bondage in Egypt to the Promised Land had, to be sure, antecedents going back to Origen and earlier:

. . . the human mind [reports Richard] may fall into ecstasy and transcend itself through intensity of joy and exultation. This kind of going forth seems to be sufficiently well expressed in the Song of Songs (8:5). . . : "Who is she," saith the Scripture, "that cometh up from the desert? . . ." If we rightly interpret the desert as being the human heart, what is this rising up from the desert, but the passing of the human mind into ecstasy?

. . . the soul is led by God into the wilderness where it is fed with milk so that it may be inebriated with inward sweetness. Hearken what is said of this state when the Lord speaks by the prophet (Hosea 2:16): "Therefore," he saith, "I will feed her with milk and will lead her into the wilderness and will speak to her heart." But first we must leave Egypt behind, first we must cross the Red Sea. First the Egyptians must perish in the waves, first we must suffer famine in the land of Egypt before we can receive this spiritual nourishment and heavenly food. He who desires that food of heavenly solitude let him abandon Egypt both in body and heart, and altogether set aside the love of the world.[62]

The contemporary recluse and sometime Benedictine Abbess Hildegard of Bingen (d. 1179) in her *Liber Scivias,* a first fruit of German mysticism, could still use Canticles (8:5) as an allegory of the barbarians and other Gentiles coming up out of the wilderness of history to be joined in covenant with Christ. With the Cistercian Mechthild of Magdeburg (d. c. 1280) we have the fully woven mystical theology of the inner wilderness. In her revelation, "The desert (*woestin*) has twelve things," she enjoins:

> Thou shalt love the naughting
> And flee the self.
> Thou shalt stand alone
> Seeking help from none,
> That thy being may be quiet,
> Free from the bondage of all things.
> Thou shalt loose those who are bound,

[62] *Selected Writings on Contemplation,* tr. Clare Kirchberger (London, [1957]), pp. 203, 224. In the text of Hosea, the usual reading is *vineyard,* not *milk.*

And exhort the free.
Thou shalt care for the sick
And yet have nothing for thyself.
Thou shalt drink the waters of sorrow,
And kindle the fire of love with the faggot of virtue.
Thus shalt thou dwell in the true wilderness (*Wüstenunge*).[63]

By the thirteenth century, Western mystical nomenclature seems to have further refined the meaning or meanings of wilderness. We can distinguish, in fact, at least two somewhat divergent traditions in respect to the use of the concept. These traditions reflect, as we have come to expect, the ambiguity of the word in Scripture and in effect represent two somewhat different reports on the sequence of experiences at the interior of the mystical mind. By the close of the Middle Ages the terms appear distinct in the representatives of Rhenish and Iberian (Carmelite) mysticism. In the latter the desert was thought of as a phase of darkness, frustration, and temptation in line with one of the strands of interpretation of the experience in the Bible itself. In the Rhenish tradition of Meister Eckhart and his school, the meaning of desert was the empty vastness, the passive yieldedness (*Gelassenheit*) of the soul of man unencumbered by the world.

In Rhenish mysticism the stress and arrangement of the biblical texts was thus such as to yield a quite new and distinctive feeling for the term "wilderness" or *Wüste*. Besides bewilderment and the desert of the unencumbered self, there was the corresponding or answering void or desert of the ultimate ground or abyss within the divine being itself. Unlike the early desert Fathers, Eckhart (d. 1327) and the other Rhenish mystics, including the anonymous Friends of God (*Theologia Germanica*), attached little or no importance to a literal wilderness or desert as the locale of the mystical itinerary. More influenced than the early Carmelites by Plotinian nomenclature, Eckhart seems to have reinforced the metaphysical meaning of the *Wüste* of the soul by making the German word carry both the imagery of the scriptural *desertum* and Neoplationist *vastitas* (*adyton*), which could be used both of the divine abyss or ground of being and of the superior part of the soul adapted for contemplation.[64] The Pseudo-Dionysian *vastitas* in the sense of emptiness could be, moreover, readily linked by the

[63] Adapted from the translation of Lucy Menzies, *Revelations* (London, 1953), pp. 17 f.; from the German text edited by Gall Morel (Regensburg, 1869), p. 7.

[64] Curt Kirmaze, in connection with his *Die Terminologie des Mystikers Johannes Tauler* (Leipzig, 1930), p. 92, believes that the confluence of scriptural and Neoplatonist usage in *Wüste* was brought about under the intensification of native Pseudo-Dionysian Neoplatonism by the spread of Arabic versions; and he refers specifically to

mystical exegetes with several scriptural passages where *vastitas* as desolation and *desertum* are used as synonyms.

The philosophical reinforcement of the mystical sense of wilderness made it possible for Eckhart boldly to extend the meaning of *Wüste* as a technical term of apophatic theology. He spoke of "the *barren* Godhead, of which the Trinity is a revelation:"

> In this barren Godhead, activity has ceased and therefore the soul will be most perfect when it is thrown into the Desert of the Godhead where both activity and forms are no more, so that it is sunk and lost in this Desert where its identity is destroyed and it has no more to do with things than it had before it existed. Then it is dead to self and alive to God. What is dead in this sense has ceased to be so that that soul will be dead to self which is buried in the Godhead-desert.[65]

Man, whose deepest self is the divinely created image of the divine *Wüste,* must prepare the way for " 'the voice of One crying in the wilderness.' Let this voice cry in you at will. Be like a desert as far as self and the things of this world are concerned."[66] The mystic is alone in "that darkness of unself-consciousness," Eckhart preaches another time, "tracking and tracing [every clue] and never retracing his steps," "and the more he makes himself like a desert, unconscious of everything," the nearer he comes to that estate. In the traditional language of scriptural mysticism, he relates desert and revelation, citing Hosea 2:12: "The genuine word of eternity is spoken only in the spirit of that man who is himself a wilderness alienated from [denuded of] self and all multiplicity."[67]

Eckhart recognizes the divine initiative in the visitation that follows upon the mystic's elementary preparations:

---

the following from Algazel's *Liber philosophiae,* iv, 5, as edited by Petrus Lichtensteyn (Venice, 1506):

"Anima vero humana habet duas facies; unam ad partem superiorem, quae est *vastitas* superior, eo quod ab illa acquirit scientias, nec habet anima virtutem speculativam, nisi respectu illius partis, cuius debitum erat, ut semper reciperit, et aliam faciem ad partem inferiorem, scilicet ad regendum corpus. Artur Schneider, *Die Psychologie Albert des Grossen, Beiträge zur Geschichte der Philosophie des Mittelalters,* IV, Heft 6, p. 447, n. 1."

[65] Sermon, *Expedit vobis,* ed. by Raymond B. Blakney, *Meister Eckhart: A Modern Translation* (New York, 1941), pp. 200 f. He goes on to cite Colossians 3:3: "You are dead and your life is hidden with Christ in God," and Dionysius: "To be buried in God is nothing but to be transported into uncreated life."

For other references to *Gotes wüestunge, die wüeste der gotheit,* see *Werke,* ed. F. Pfeiffer, pp. 26, 153, 215, 242, 249, 266, 402, 412, 439, 511.

[66] *Expedit vobis,* p. 202; cf. *Qui audit,* Blakney, *op. cit.,* pp. 203 ff.

[67] *Et cum factus esset Jesus,* Blakney, *op. cit.,* p. 120; cf. *Beati pauperes,* Blakney, *op. cit.,* pp. 227 ff.

Above all, claim nothing for yourself. Relax and let God operate you and do what he will with you. The deed is his; the word is his; and all you are in his, for you have surrendered self to him with all your soul's agents and other functions and even your personal nature. Then at once, God comes into your being and faculties, for you are like a desert despoiled of what was peculiarly your own.[68]

Having insisted that the "hearing of God's word requires complete self-surrender," alluding to Luke 14:26, he makes bold to seize upon the baptismal scene in the wilderness of Jordan and declare that every mystic is in a sense the unique Son of God: "To deny one's self is to be the only begotten Son of God and one who does so has for himself all the properties of that Son. All God's acts are performed and his teachings conveyed through the Son, to the point that we should be his only begotten Son."[69]

For perhaps the first time in the evolution of the wilderness motif the epiphany of the Father's relationship to the Son, regenerated in the baptismal scene in the wilderness of Jordan, is made to carry the same mystical meaning as elsewhere the nuptial imagery of the divine Bridegroom and his spouse in the desert (Hosea 2:14, Jeremiah 2:2, Canticles 8:5).[70]

It will not be necessary to examine the later representatives of Rhenish mysticism in the school of Eckhart. Suffice it to say that John Tauler (d. 1361),[71] Henry Suso (d. 1366),[72] and Ruysbroeck the Admirable (d. 1381)[73] amply document the importance of the wilder-

---

[68] *In hic, quae patris mei sunt*, Blakney, *op. cit.*, p. 115.

[69] *The Defense*, viii, 1b, and ix, 15a, Blakney, *op. cit.*, pp. 280, 287.

[70] A development still in the future is the conflation of the nuptial language of the Red Sea wilderness and the generative image of the Jordan wilderness in the baptismal theology of Reformation sectarianism (Chapter III, sec. 1).

[71] See *Die Predigten*, ed. Ferdinand Vetter (Berlin, 1910), pp. 54 f. and 277 f., where he speaks of *wueste wilde, wuester grunt*, the wild animals of one's own senses and impulses, the *stille wueste, wueste Gotz*, and *goetliche wuesternunge*.

[72] Anna Nicklas summarizes the use of *wueste* and related terms in *Die Terminologie des Mystikers Heinrich Seuse* (Königsberg, 1914), *s.v.*

[73] Joseph Kuckhoff identified the Pseudo-Dionysian *adyton* behind the *woestine, grondelose abys* or *zee*. Earlier Melline d'Asbeck had devoted a whole book to this substratum, *La Mystique de Ruysbroeck l'Admirable: un echo du néoplatonisme au xive siècle* (Paris, 1930), esp. pp. 84, 92, 147, 256, on *woestine*. A typical passage is this from *The Sparkling Stone*:
"There is a great difference between the brightness of the saints and the highest brightness or enlightenment to which we may attain in this life. For it is only the shadow of God which enlightened our inward wilderness (*vlakte*), but on the high mountains of the Promised Land there is no shadow; and yet it is one and the same Sun, and one radiance, which enlightens both our *wilderness* and the high mountains. But the state of the saints is transparent and shining, and therefore they receive the brightness without intermediary; but our state is still mortal and gross, and this sets up an obstacle which causes the shadow, which so darkens our understanding that we cannot know God and heavenly things so clearly as the saints can and do. . . . But

ness concept as a technical term of mystical theology. One may simply remark that the Dutch mystic unexpectedly appears to make much more of the brightnes of the desert experience than, say, the Carmelite author of the *Dark Night of the Soul.*

In the second development of mystical vocabulary, that of the Spanish Carmelites, the dazzling and dry desert preserved its historic and literal significance beneath the allegorization. The Carmelite tradition traced its spiritual lineage back through St. Berthold (d. 1154) and the earlier hermits who had settled on Mount Carmel to Elijah and Elisha, and the revered cave of the sons of the prophet on its slopes.[74] The wilderness tradition of Old Testament piety was consequently very strong, and when the order was replanted in western Europe the practice of isolated cells was reproduced.

In Spain the Carmelites constructed desert retreats called "deserts" to which they went periodically for solitude before returning to the life of the convent and of *caritas* toward humankind.[75] Carmelite mysticism recognized the necessity of recurrent passages from a physical wilderness and back to Christian society for the health of the Christian soul. When the Spanish mystics used the term "desert" or "wilderness," they meant both the dryness of the soul and the need of being physically in these desert retreats for mortification and contemplation.

St. John of the Cross (1542–1591) is generally taken as the most advanced exponent of Carmelite mysticism; and, although he brings us out of our chronological frame, for the purpose of the present sketch he is the best resource. In his *Ascent of Mount Carmel, The Spiritual Canticle,* and *The Dark Night of the Soul,* St. John draws upon the desert-betrothal imagery of Hosea (2:14), Jeremiah (2:2), and Canticles (8:5) and shows how when the soul follows God into the desert,

---

if we would become one with the brightness of the Sun, we must follow love and go out of ourselves into the Wayless (*omvijze*), and then the Sun will draw us with our blinded eyes into its own brightness, in which we shall possess unity with God. So soon as we feel and understand ourselves thus, we are in that contemplative life which is within reach of our mortal state. And this it was that the bride in the Book of Love (1:7) desired when she said unto Christ: 'Tell me, O Thou whom my soul loveth, where thou feedest, where thou makest Thy flock to rest at noon,' that is in the light of Glory, as Saint Bernard says."

This passage was translated by C. A. Wynschenk Dorn in *John of Ruysbroeck,* ed. Evelyn Underhill (London, 1916), pp. 213 f.

[74] II Kings 2:25. For the medieval literature, see Robert A. Koch, "Elijah the Prophet, Founder of the Carmelite Order," *Speculum,* XXXIV (1959), 547 ff. According to the Carmelite legend the pre-Christian hermits were baptized by the apostles in the course of their mission. Clemens Kopp, *Elias und Christentum auf dem Karmel* (Paderborn, 1929).

[75] See Benoit Marie de la Sainte Croix, *Les saints déserts des Carmes Déschaussés* (Paris, 1927), and also the article "Déserts" in *Dictionnaire de la Spiritualité.* The fascicule with the projected article on *érémitisme* and the theology of the desert has not yet appeared.

the divine Spouse speaks to her heart and how she is then "well prepared to go up, leaning upon her Beloved, through the wilderness of
death, abounding in delights, to the glorious seats and resting-places of
her Spouse."[76]

In *The Dark Night of the Soul* St. John combines the physical and
spiritual senses of wilderness and shows how the wilderness experience
may be initially resisted and finally rejoiced in as preparatory to the
highest bliss. He knows there are many who get started on the mystical
exodus—

> Whom God begins to lead through the solitude of the wilderness and
> like the children of Israel, who, though God began to feed them, as soon
> as they were in the wilderness, with the manna of heaven, which was so
> sweet that, as it is written, it turned to what every man liked (Exodus
> 16:15, Wisdom 16:2), were more sensible to the loss of the onions and
> flesh of Egypt than to the delicious sweetness of the angelical food.[77]

As in the Old Testament, death, desert, and darkness are interrelated, but in the spiritual sense of mortification; and the attendant
darkness or night of the soul is a preparation for the divine betrothal
and luminous ecstasy:

> In order to show . . . [St. John of the Cross says] how effectual is the
> night of sense, in its aridity and desolation, to enlighten the soul more and
> more, I produce here the words of the Psalmist (63:6 f.; 52:3), which so
> clearly explain how greatly efficacious is this night in bringing forth the
> knowledge of God: "In a desert land, and inaccessible, and without water;
> so in the holy have I appeared to Thee, that I might see Thy strength and
> Thy glory."[78]

He presently describes the darkling soul which is absorbed in the
wilderness:

> . . . the soul sees itself distinctly as far away from, and abandoned by,
> all created things; it looks upon itself as one that is placed in a wild and
> vast solitude whither no human being can come, as in an immense wilder-
> ness without limits; a wilderness, the more delicious, sweet, and lovely, the
> more it is wide, vast, and lonely, where the soul is the more hidden, the
> more it is raised up above all created things.[79]

From the mystical interiorization of the desert we may now turn
back to the medieval sectarian appropriation of the wilderness motif

[76] *Complete Works*, ed. Allison Peers (London, 1934), I, 163, 235, 171, 403.
[77] As translated by Benedict Zimmerman (London, 1924), p. 40. He repeats the same
thought on p. 109.
[78] *Ibid.*, p. 58.
[79] *Ibid.*, p. 160.

in a fully recovered ethical and eschatological seriousness.

ii. The Wilderness Church

Schematically one can say that a renewed eschatological intensity, coupled with dissatisfaction or even despair with the apostolic see—finally transformed into a papal monarchy under Innocent III (1198–1216)—tended to convert the monastic impulse into fully separatist sectarianism and to encourage the replacement of the cloistered paradise with the conventicle of the wilderness. Benedictine abbot Rupert of Deutz (d. 1135?), the visionary Cistercian abbot Joachim of Flora (d. 1202), and the sectarian Peter Waldo (d. 1217), successively illustrate this shift.

Rupert of Deutz in his commentary on Revelation[80] was apparently the first to break away from the theology of history and periodization which Augustine embodied in his *City of God*. Rupert found concentrated in Revelation what Augustine had seen in the whole of the Old Testament, namely, the chronicle of the conflict between the two cities. Dividing Revelation into twelve parts, Rupert discerned in it allusions to events from Moses to Constantine. Rupert was unprepared, however, to press for a revelatory or apocalyptic interpretation of events into his own time. He made no attempts to construe the 1260 days of the woman in the wilderness (Revelation 12:6) in anything but a literal sense. He understood the passage as a reference to the primitive Church in Jerusalem which, according to Acts, held all things in common for approximately this time, namely, three and a half years, which was again about the length of time that Jesus' first followers lived with him joyfully with a common purse. The place prepared by God is in a sense none other than Christ himself. The primitive Christians (and following them the hermits, the monks, and the canons) fled, according to Rupert, from the world with its *sollicitudo* in respect of earthly possessions to enjoy that *solitudo* in the practice of the community of goods which enabled them to live a life of contemplation. For "to posseses or desire nothing in this world is the trusting and peaceful solitude of the mind," which may, indeed, be called a *desertum* because of the removal of cares "for the pursuit of the truth of God."[81]

Cistercian Abbot Joachim of Flora likewise loved the solitude, like-

[80] Wilhelm Kamlah, *Apocalypse und Geschichtstheologie: Die mittelalterliche Auslegung der Apocalypse vor Joachim von Fiore*, Historische Studien, Heft 285 (Berlin, 1935), p. 87.
[81] *Commentarius in Apocalypsim*, PL, CLXIX, cols. 1049 f. and 1131; *De victoria verbi Dei, ibid.*, col. 1489.

step toward the monastic-sectarian appropriation of the idea of the wise commented on the Apocalypse, and then took the epoch-making Church of the wilderness in Revelation 12:6 in an eschatological context. A characterization of Joachim's contribution to the elaboration of the wilderness motif is indispensable for our later account, because he was the first to apply the day-year principle to the 1260 days of prophetic preaching in Revelation 11:3.

As a restless noble youth, Joachim left the Norman court of Sicily and visited Constantinople. Disgusted by the glittering court of the Eastern emperor, he made a pilgrimage to the blazing Syrian desert and Mount Tabor, where after forty days of fasting and prayer he received, on Easter Eve, a vision of the Eternal Gospel (Revelation 14:6). Returning from the opulence of East Rome and the deadly desert of Syria, which had cost his traveling-companion his life, he became a Cistercian and worked on his commentary on Revelation.

In accordance with his desert vision he postulated three typologically interconnected ages of man under the triune God, successively under the prevailing influence, first of the Father, namely, the age of the married patriarchs; then of the Son, namely, the age of the clerics; and at length of the Holy Spirit, namely, the age of the monks or the age of the *Ecclesia Spiritualis*.[82] For Joachim, the world was not growing older, but younger: the age of the patriarchs led to the age of maturity, and that will lead to the age of childhood, when the Child will be born again. The lost morning of Paradise, the infancy of the world, is at the same time the future Kingdom of God. Joachim thought of these ages not only as typologically interconnected but also as in part overlapping, a conception of dispensational history that enabled him to anticipate the future on the basis of analogy to related events in an earlier age. Himself a reformed Benedictine, the Cistercian abbot saw in Benedict of not-so-distant Monte Cassino the beginning of the spiritual community already forming within the aeon destined to pass away. Joachim thus opened a new epoch in the theological interpretation of history, for he construed the whole papal Church

Therefore this woman clothed with the sun in general designates the universal Catholic Church . . . the Church of the teachers (*doctorum*) and according to the prerogative of grace that glorious queen of heaven who, since she is the pure virgin, will give birth to the king of glory. . . .

And she . . . will remain hidden in the solitude threatened by the serpent. . . .[83]

---

[82] A major study here is that of Ernst Benz, *Ecclesia Spiritualis* (Stuttgart, 1934).
[83] The quotation combines *Liber concordiae Novi ac Veteris Testamenti*, folio 12 v.;

(*universa catholicorum ecclesia*), the church of the clerics, as the woman living in the wilderness of world history:

The Church as a whole could now be thought of as moving under the papal vicar of the Son of God through the wilderness of the world for some 1260 years toward a third age to become, under a *novus dux* (later, retrospectively, identified by the Spiritual Franciscans as St. Francis), a *novus populus,* ushering in the age of the Holy Spirit, the age of the monks and friars. Although the Cistercian abbot's eschatology was not directly anti-papal, he had supplied critics of the papal monarchy with a fresh interest in descrying the signs of its imminent dissolution and its giving way to a third dispensation in the providence of the triune God.

Joachim, though of aristocratic birth, calling himself a *homo agricola a juventute mea,*[84] probably in allusion to the rustic prophet in Zechariah 13:5,[85] sought the wilderness for himself and a stricter Cistercian rule. He escaped into the mountainous wastes of Pietralata in Calabria and presently organized his followers and founded the abbey of St. John the Baptist of Flora (Fiore) in the wilderness of La Sila which was finally approved by the Pope as the Order of Flora two years after Joachim's death.

Joachim predicted the Third Kingdom of the Spirit, but it was Francis of Assisi (1181[2]–1226) who showed what it was for his contemporaries. After Christ, he considered himself the freest of men, ending his life with the prayer "I thank thee, Lord, that thou lettest me die free of all things."[86] He thought of his order, committed to a life of fraternal poverty (going far beyond the community of goods of the earlier orders), as a cedar in the Garden of God,[87] or as a new and fruitful winestock in the desert.[88]

It was through possessionlessness that he and his followers could participate in that wilderness intuition of the creaturely world, animate

Expositio in Apocalypsim, folio 154v.; and the report of the conversation in 1190 between Richard the Lion-Hearted and Philip Augustus with Abbot Joachim in Messina in Roger of Hoveden's *Chronica,* ed. Stubbs, III, 75. The significance of Joachim's contribution is admirably analyzed in the context of the history of eschatological exegesis by LeRoy Edwin Froom, *The Prophetic Faith of Our Fathers: The Historic Development of Prophetic Interpretation* (Washington, 1950), I, esp. 685–716.

[84] He calls himself this in the *Expositio.* Without heeding the scriptural allusion, Ernesto Buonaiuti makes this a basic datum for inferring that Joachim was not from a noble family as in the traditional biographies, but a peasant, *Gioacchimo da Fiore* (Rome, 1931).

[85] "Non sum propheta, homo agricola ego sum: quoniam Adam exemplum meum ab adolescentia mea."

[86] *Thomas of Celano, Leben und Wunder des Heiligen Franziskus von Assisi,* Franziskanische Quellenschriften, V (Werl, Westphalia, 1955), Second Life, 216 (p. 437).

[87] *Ibid.,* § 100.

[88] *Ibid.,* § 89.

and inanimate, as made up of brothers and sisters, alike dependent upon the heavenly Father. This joyful perception of the fullness of unencumbered being in a nonutilitarian relationship to other creatures found memorable expression in the *Canticle to the Sun*. The flowers of the meadows were for Francis the designs in the tapestry of the Garden of Eden. Legend tells how he preached to the birds, saved lambs from the slaughter, persuaded a wolf to cease molesting the townspeople of Greccio, and the townspeople to feed the wolf. It was in this same town that Francis instituted the first observance of Christmas with a crèche, an ox, and an ass, in dependence upon the account of the manger in the apocryphal gospels and in allusion to Isaiah 1:3. The straw from this Franciscan manger, when eaten by sick animals round about Greccio, was said to have made them well.[89] The peace of the animal kingdom betokened a provisional restoration of paradise. The most striking example of Francis' conviction occurred when he was undergoing cauterization with a red-hot lancet for an affliction of the eye. The attending brethren, unable to bear the sight of the operation, had withdrawn, but the saint spoke to the fire in which the doctor was preparing his instrument, "Brother Fire, more beautiful and useful than other things, . . . be kind to me, I pray thee in this hour, for long have I loved thee in the Lord."[90] After the operation, he attested that he had felt no pain, to the astonishment of the physician; for, as his biographer says: "He had returned to the innocence of Paradise, and if he chose, even the wild elements were tame before him."[91]

Francis' ideal of holy poverty or paradisic possessionlessness did not survive his death intact. In spite of his pleas that his Rule be followed *senza glossa*, as identical with the gospel, his erstwhile friend Hugolino, on becoming Pope as Gregory IX (1227-1241), declared that as Francis' intimate he best knew how to interpret it; and in his bull *Quo elongati* he made the first legal breach in the ideal of corporate as well as individual poverty by permitting the order to hold property corporately under the guise of a legal fiction. This ruling was too transparent to find acceptance among the saint's loyalest followers, and the

---

[89] *Ibid.*, § 35; Celano, First Life, §§ 84 f.; cf. also Joseph Bernhart, "Heilige und Tiere," *Ars Sacra*, 1937.
[90] Celano, Second Life, §166.
[91] *Ibid.*, § 166. The paintings of Francis by Giotto (d. 1337) and the Dominican Giovanni da Fiesole, called Fra Angelico (d. 1455), carry out the paradisic theme. See also Henry Thode, *Franz von Assisi und die Anfänge der Kunst in Italien* (2nd ed., Berlin, 1904). F. D. Klingender in "St. Francis and the Birds of the Apocalypse," *Journal of Warburg and Courtauld Institutes*, XVI (1953), 13–23, has shown how in English iconography the paradise motif in respect to the birds was in some instances converted into an apocalyptic view. The daws and sparrows were painted as birds of prey and carrion and interpreted in the garish light of Revelation 19:17-20.

hundred years after the founder's death in 1226 are characterized by a series of struggles between the zealots and the comfortable moderates in the order, with frequent drastic intervention by successive popes.

The paradisic ideal of Francis and the eschatological idea of Joachim of Flora were combined by the Spiritual Franciscans and Fraticelli, who considered themselves as constituting Joachim's new order of spiritual men (*novus populus spiritualis*). The attempt of the Franciscan minister general John of Parma (1247–1257) to resuscitate the pristine ideal of Francis failed as a result of the conflict which arose over the publication by certain Franciscans in Paris in 1254 of the so-called *Eternal Gospel*. This was a reworking of Joachim's ideas, condemning the Papacy for its reluctance to make room for the coming Spiritual Church of the Third Age, foreshadowed in the Franciscan order. The general indignation which this book caused provided the incentive or the excuse for the suppression of the radical party.

The great Franciscan scholastic Bonaventure, minister-general (1257–1274), wrote his *Apologia Pauperum* to refute the arguments of the strict Spirituals, distinguishing between control (i.e. ownership), which was forbidden by the Rule of Francis, and simple use (*usus pauper*), which was licit. The accession of the aged hermit Peter Morrone to the Papacy as Celestine V in 1294 renewed the hopes of the Spirituals for a real change in the attitude of the Papacy toward their ideal of poverty, but his prompt abdication the same year ended their hopes. Pope Clement V in his bull *Exivi de paradiso* (1312) confirmed the subterfuge which permitted conventual ownership of property, and Pope John XXII in two bulls, *Sancta Romana* (1317) and *Gloriosam ecclesiam* (1318), enjoined the radicals to submit under pain of excommunication, actually executing four recalcitrants.

In 1321 the controversy broke out anew, when Franciscan teachers reasserted their conviction that Christ and the disciples (despite the common purse in the custody of Judas) had owned no property, either individually or collectively. John XXII replied with *Cum inter nonnullos* (1323), condemning this view as heretical. Despite further sallies by Richard FitzRalph, archbishop of Armagh, in *De pauperie Salvatoris*, and by John Wyclif in *De domino divino*, the attempt to associate paradisic-apostolic poverty with true obedience to the gospel was a failure, except as radical publicists insisted that the secular as well as the regular clergy should live as would become the denizens of Paradise before the Fall and in imitation of the saints of the primitive Church in Jerusalem, while in contrast the princes and kings of Christendom might properly continue to use property and power in order to perform their God-assigned duties in a fallen world.

The quasi-sectarian and vigorously excommunicated Spiritual Franciscans came close to identifying their fraternity with the Church of the wilderness. The appropriation of the monastic-apocalyptic wilderness theology proceeded further with the completely sectarian Waldensians; with the Taborites, Horebites, and Adamites among the radicals in Bohemia; and with the devotees of Girolamo Savonarola in Florence.

In the wilderness to the north of the same peninsula where Joachim had commented on the Apocalypse, namely, in the Piedmontese Alps, and at about the same time, the followers of Peter Waldo had fled for the protection from papal ban (1179), inquisition, and crusade (1209). In the beginning the Waldenses had confidently sought episcopal and then papal recognition for their apostolic form of Christianity with lay evangelism, but under persecution they withdrew as a sect and soon came to interpret the whole papal system as Antichrist. The early Waldensian *Qual cosa sia Antichrist* enjoined true Christians, in appealing to Jeremiah 50, Leviticus 20, Exodus 34, and Revelation 18, thus: "Withdraw, withdraw yourselves, go forth thence," "flee out of Babylon, and come out of the land of the Chaldeans."[92]

Once the Waldensians were completely separated from the Catholic Church, they came to think of their daily repasts as love feasts; and before their pastors (barbs) sat down to table, they blessed the food in phrasings reminiscent of Christ's feeding the multitude in the wilderness: "God, who blessed the five barley loaves and two fishes for His disciples in the wilderness, bless this table, whatever is upon it, and whatever may be brought to it."[93]

At what moment in their history the Waldensians in their mountain retreats began to apply to their persecuted conventicles the passage which Joachim had applied to the papal Church approaching its term is not documented, but it was inevitable that the aptness of the description of the Church in the wilderness of Revelation 12:6 would come to be recognized as the scriptural sanction of their flight and their meaningful suffering as a remnant. At that moment the desert-betrothal imagery passed from the convent and the church to the conventicle.

A later interpreter of the ancient Waldensian documents may not

---

[92] Translated by Samuel Moreland, *History of the Evangelical Churches of the Valleys of Piemont* (London, 1658), p. 151.

[93] On the rare Waldensian custom of taking fish along with the bread and wine at their eucharist, see the newer literature brought in incidentally but profusely by Kurt Goldammer, "Der Naumburger Meister und die Häretiker," *Zeitschrift für Kirchengeschichte*, LXIV (1952–1953), esp. 97–102.

have gone much beyond the self-interpretation of the later medieval Waldensians themselves when he wrote out in his introduction to the collected documents the conviction:

. . . this is the Desart whither the woman fled when she was persecuted by the Dragon with seven heads and ten horns. And where she had a place prepared of God, that they should feed her one thousand two hundred and sixty daies; That here it was that the Church fled, and where she made her Flocks to rest at noon, in those hot and scorching seasons of the ninth and tenth Centuries: Then it may be thou wilt begin to believe with me, that it was in the clefts of these Rocks, and in the secret places of the stairs of these Valleys of Piemont, that the Dove of Christ then remained, where also the Italian Foxes then began to spoil the Vines with their tender Grapes although they were never able utterly to destroy or pluck them up by the roots.[94]

Sectarian, Joachimite, and Renaissance expectations of a new age of Gold and of the Spirit received an abortive political expression on the eve of the Reformation Era in the Florence of the Dominican prophet Girolamo Savonarola (1452–1498).

Savonarola's inner religious experience and his fatal involvement in the intricate system of civil and religious intrigue in Renaissance Italy led him to think of God as having led his chosen people into the new wilderness of the world (Ezekiel 20:10) in order to isolate them from their idolatry.[95] Varying the image slightly, he also observed that for the good man, the world is like a solitude and a desert.[96] In this desert he will come to long like the hart for the water brooks (Psalm 42:1).[97] He thought of the French king as Cyrus restoring Zion in the wilderness. In a series of sermons on Ezekiel preached in Florence, which he compared first to Rome and then to Jerusalem,[98] Savonarola delineated the steps by which men are to be led out of the waste places and into the city of Zion, the company of the elect.[99] To some of his contemporaries he seemed indeed to have succeeded in transforming Florence: "This city seemed an earnest of Paradise; all were one, and great peace

[94] Samuel Moreland, the authorized Cromwellian collector, *op. cit.*, Introduction, pp. vi and vii. In postulating a more or less continuous apostolic community surviving in the Alps from the ninth and tenth centuries, Moreland was probably adding a link in the chain of which the medieval Waldensians themselves were unconscious. On the role of the Waldensians in the evolution of Puritan wilderness theology, see below Chapter III, Sec. 2, i.
[95] *Prediche sopra Ezechiele*, ed. Roberto Ridolfi (Rome, n.d.), II, 264 ff.
[96] *Ibid.*, p. 277.
[97] *Ibid.*, pp. 284 ff.
[98] *Prediche e Scritti*, ed. Mario Ferrara (Milan, 1930), pp. 380 f.
[99] *Prediche sopra Ezechiele*, II, 254 ff.

was everywhere."[100] Savonarola promised the wicked man in this life "an earnest of hell," but the righteous "an earnest of Paradise."[101] When the unwavering enmity of Pope Alexander VI, the intrigues of other enemies, and the fickleness of his friends had brought him to the prison from which his only escape would be the stake, Savonarola could still attest his loyalty to this vision:

> What is Jerusalem, which is interpreted Vision of Peace, except the Holy City of the Blessed, which is our Mother? . . . Therefore, O Lord, do favourably unto Zion, and quickly make up the number of the elect; and the walls of Jerusalem shall be built and perfected out of new stones, which shall give Thee praise, and endure for ever.[102]

The prophetic Dominican conception of the Florentine Zion amidst the desert of papal Italy, the radical Franciscan conception of the brotherhood living in the perfection of paradisic poverty, the Waldensian conception of the Church of the wilderness, the experience of the inner wilderness and the divine desert of the mystics—all these medieval permutations of our theme were to live on into the age of the Reformation, but primarily among the Radical Reformers. Not until the seventeenth century would these same impulses break forth within the context of the established Reformed churches.

[100] Roberto Ridolfi, *Vita di Girolamo Savonarola* (Rome, n.d.), I, 195, citing Marietta Rucellai.
[101] *Prediche sopra Ezechiele*, II, 255.
[102] *Exposition of the Psalm Miserere Mei Deus,* tr. F. C. Cowper (Milwaukee, 1889), p. 74.

Chapter III.   Fleeing to and Planting in the Wilderness in the Reformation Period and Modern Times

The Magisterial Reformation of the classical Protestants was concerned to purify the Church where it stood. The Protestant Reformers were in no mood to flee into the wilderness, and were sober-minded about Paradise. They were concerned only with the Fall therefrom and man's inveterate sin. They pilloried monasticism and for the most part had little sympathy with mysticism. To be sure, John Calvin (1509–1564), for example, in his scriptural commentaries recognized that the word *wilderness* might occasionally be used metaphorically for desolation or the frightful ruin of the Jewish nation, such as existed in the time of the Babylonian Captivity, and thus that at the time of John the Baptist "Jerusalem was in this sense a wilderness: for all had been reduced to wild and frightful confusion";[1] but he was at pains to clear Christ's forty days in the desert of any ascetic significance. The arena of Protestant combat with evil forces was the burgher's walled town, not the monk's enclosed garden in the wilderness.

It was thus in the sixteenth century primarily among the proponents of the Radical Reformation that the wilderness motif of the medieval monks and mystics survived, and, of course, in Catholicism, where it remained unbroken, as in the Spain of the great Carmelite mystic, St. John of the Cross, already dealt with. In the Radical Reformation of the sixteenth century we shall have occasion to mention Anabaptists like Menno Simons, Spiritualists like Caspar Schwenckfeld, and Evangelical Rationalists like Michael Servetus.

1. The Church of the Wilderness in the Radical Reformation[2]

In the writings and the apostolic zeal of the Mennonites, the Hutterites, and one at least of the early Unitarians we can see the confluence of several impulses from medieval piety in respect to the wilderness motif, and the reanimation of the restitutionist aspirations of antiquity. In seeing how plausibly they combined primitivist, mystical, and sectarian conceptions of the wilderness experience and connected it either

[1] *Commentary on a Harmony of the Gospels* (Matthew 3:3); *Opera omnia* (Amsterdam, 1667), VI, 44.

[2] The larger context of our theme has been dealt with in *The Radical Reformation 1520–1580* (Philadelphia, 1962).

with a spiritualized inward Christianity or specifically with the sub-
mission to the rite of adult baptism on the pattern of Jesus in the
wilderness of Jordan, we sharpen our understanding of the extraordinary mobility, missionary zeal, and readiness to accept martyrdom
on the part of hundreds of thousands of earnest people, harried
from town to town and fleeing for protection to the fastness of the
mountains and forests. With the re-emergence of the wilderness concept
as literally a divinely secured place of refuge as distinguished from the
contemplative desert-state of the soul, it is understandable that, beginning in the Reformation era, the persecuted sectarians readily assimilated the occasional references to the forest in Scriptures and
thereby enriched the image of *desertum*. In any event the wilderness in
northern Europe and eventually in the New World could no longer be
thought of as a vast expanse of brightness and dryness; it became rather
the darkling and toilsome but also protective wooded wilds.

In representative figures of the Radical Reformation we can identify
the full range of pre-Constantinian, medieval mystical, and sectarian
meanings for the biblically synonymous terms *wilderness* and *desert*,
now on their way toward a differentiation of meaning, especially in
the English language. It was, for example, the Spiritualists Caspar
Schwenckfeld (1490–1561) and Sebastian Franck (1499–1542) who
picked up from the medieval mystical Friends of God (*Theologia
Germanica*) and without doubt directly from Eusebius' *Ecclesiastical
History* the primitivist-restitutionist idea that Abraham was a Christian before he was a Jew and that the true friends of God are they who
constitute everywhere in the world away from divisive creeds and
cults the Church of the Spirit, nourished inwardly by the celestial flesh
of the eternal Christ, as the children of Israel were nourished by the
bread of heaven in the wilderness.

Also a primitivist for a period in his career was the Spiritualist and
egalitarian Dr. Andreas Bodenstein von Carlstadt (d. 1541), sometime
colleague of Luther at the University of Wittenberg, who, after he had
introduced the first "Protestant" communion in Luther's absence, removed to rural Orlamünde and there donned the garb of a simple
peasant, to preach to his parishioners as Amos, the gatherer of syca-
more fruit. Significantly the radical Spiritualist professor left his university course at that point in his comment on Zechariah, namely, 13:5,
which had earlier made Abbot Joachim of Flora style himself a
propheta, homo agricola.[8]

[8] Hermann Barge, *Andreas Bodenstein von Karlstadt* (Leipzig, 1905). See above,
Chapter II, at n. 84.

Though the Spiritualists Carlstadt and Schwenckfeld evoke our theme, it is primarily among the Anabaptists that the medieval mystical-sectarian interest in the wilderness lived on. The furrier turned prophet, the sometime Lutheran evangelist and then charismatic Anabaptist visionary, Melchior Hofmann (c. 1495–1543), best illustrates the survival and fresh combination of medieval impulses. Hofmann took over from Rhenish mysticism the concepts of the wilderness (*Wüste, desertum*) as the utter emptiness of the soul at leisure from itself and of the soul as the bride of the heavenly Bridegroom. His innovation was to locate the regenerative experience of the divine nuptials of the wilderness in the public act of repentance and believers' baptism.

Eckhart, it will be recalled, had held to the doctrine of a mystical regeneration whereby each believer might become truly the son of God. Hofmann, in exteriorizing the experience, connected it with adult baptism, which he construed as a covenanting and betrothal, in fact as an espousal of Christ and man; for Christ is the head of man, as a man is head of his spouse (I Corinthians 11:1).[4] In the baptismal marriage "all children of God and brothers of the Lord Jesus Christ imitate him and also covenant and betroth themselves to the Lord Jesus Christ . . . as a freewill offering."[5] The language with which Hofmann describes the self-surrender of the bride in the baptismal espousal to Christ recalls the bold imagery employed by the medieval mystics. Before believers give themselves individually or corporately to the Bridegroom, they have already been sought out by him in the wilderness in the double sense of being in flight from the established Church and of being utterly opened to Christ in mystical *Gelassenheit* ("yieldedness"). The Anabaptist in publicly espousing his faith was a martyr in the triple sense of one who testifies, who is prepared to die for his testimony, and who is impelled to proclaim his faith in itinerant evangelism on his martyr pilgrimage from some Germanic Jordan to the Jerusalem that is above.

The wilderness motif was a strong strand in the missionary impulse of the Radical Reformation. Just as Abraham sent forth a servant to procure a bride for his son in the land of kinsmen, so now the heavenly Bridegroom sends out his apostolic servants to gather together a Bride, his Church, in the wilderness of the world, "out of the bonds of darkness, out of the realm and all the power of the devil and Satan, out of all that belongs to this world."[6] Like Yahweh in Jeremiah 2:2 and

---

[4] *Ordinance of God*, translated in *Spiritual and Anabaptist Writers*, Library of Christian Classics (henceforth *LCC*) (Philadelphia, 1957), XXV, 193.
[5] *Ibid.*, p. 190.
[6] *Ibid.*, p. 185.

Hosea 2:14 f., "in this final age the true apostolic emissaries of the Lord Jesus Christ will gather the elect flock and call it through the gospel and lead the Bride of the Lord into the spiritual wilderness, betroth, and covenant her through baptism to the Lord." So Paul "betrothed the church of Corinth to the Lord as a virgin to her husband" (II Corinthians 11:2).[7]

For Hofmann, of course, appealing to the biblical accounts of the children of Israel brought safely through the Red Sea and of Jesus lifted up from the waters of the Jordan to face temptation in the wilderness for forty days, there was also an inner wilderness through which the baptized elect has to pass even after having been saved from the wilderness of the world. More than any other spokesman of the Radical Reformation, Hofmann stressed the post-baptismal temptations that beset the Anabaptists. Many mystics had written about the wilderness or desert experience that followed upon the ecstasy of contemplation. Now that Hofmann had connected this mystical ecstasy with the act of adult baptism, he could also externalize the experience of the mystics with spiritual drought in terms of the post-baptismal desert temptations of Jesus himself. The newly converted Anabaptists, "being led and driven through the Spirit and the will of God and the anointed Saviour," he said, must be prepared to "spend forty days and forty nights in the wilderness, all of them according to the will and pleasure of the Lord with spiritual fasts," reminiscent of "the forty years long" in Sinai. They can be assured, however, that they will be found "loyal and unblameable in all God's testings," none of which will be unbearable to the truly elect (I Corinthians 10).[8] But the Bride, as the woman with child of Revelation 12:6, must be prepared to sojourn in the wilderness until her now imminent vindication.

In Münster certain Anabaptists, having appropriated Hofmann's ideas of Jerusalem descending as a Bride, distorted them in the form of a revolutionary restitutionism of Maccabean violence. One of the factors in the restoration of the communism of the primitive Church and eventually also of the establishment of polygamy with the sanction of the Old Testament patriarchs was the hope that in siring *without fleshly lust* a progeny for the new baptismal covenant, the Münsterites might the more swiftly fill up the number of 144,000 saints (Revelation 4:4; 14:1 ff.) and thereby advance the Kingdom!

One of the peace-loving followers of Hofmann in the Netherlands, Dietrich Philips (1504–1568), an associate of Menno Simons, wrote

[7] *Ibid.*, p. 188.
[8] *Ibid.*, p. 190.

against the vagaries of the Münsterites in his *Spiritual Restitution*. Herein he likened Jesus to Moses, and the Satan tempting Christ in the wilderness to Pharaoh. He drew lessons from the sufferings of God's people in the wilderness of Sinai and pointed out that, while Moses and Aaron had died in the wilderness, Jesus brought his own through to the Promised Land. For true Christians the blood of Christ is their Red Sea, and the pillar of cloud the comforting presence of the Holy Spirit. These believers, nourished by the celestial flesh of Christ, the manna of the New Covenant people, must find "their right way" (without the use of any external force but their readiness for martyrdom and without any in-group force but the lovingly exercised ban) "through the wilderness of this world"; for the Congregation of God is none other than the woman great with child, upon her head the sun symbolizing the brilliance of Christ in Revelation and the twelve stars representing the true uncorrupted teachings.[9]

The whole Mennonite church, of which Dietrich Philips was a major spokesman, had fled for protection from the red dragon of persecution into the partially protective wilderness of anonymity.[10] Menno Simons (1496-1561) himself wrote of the Satanic Antichrist and crooked serpent of persecution perpetrated by Catholic and Protestant alike:

He casts out of his mouth the terrible streams of his tyranny, by means of the rulers and mighty ones of the earth, at the glorious woman pregnant with the Word of the Lord, in hope of exterminating and destroying her seed. But God be eternally praised, who has protected her against the red dragon and has prepared a place in the wilderness for her.[11]

The communistic Anabaptists, called after their leader, Jacob Hutter, the Hutterites, who had taken refuge in the war- and plague-devastated districts of Moravia and who organized themselves on the model of the primitive community as recorded in Acts, also thought of themselves collectively as the woman of the wilderness. They held that none who, outside Christ and his community of goods, failed to acknowledge her as fostering mother could claim God for Father in heaven:

In this time a place has been given to the bride of the Lamb in which to dwell amid the wilderness of this world, there to put on the beautiful linen garment and thus to await the Lord until he leads her after him here in tribulation and afterward receives her with eternal joy.[12]

[9] The twelve marks of the true Church are detailed in Philips' tract, *The Church of God*, translated in *LCC*, XXV, esp. 255 ff.

[10] *Bibliotheca Reformatoria Neerlandica*, X, 344, 354-356, 359 f.

[11] From "The True Christian Faith" (1541), in *The Complete Writings of Menno Simons*, tr. Leonard Verduin (Scottdale, Pa., 1956), pp. 324 f.

[12] Ulrich Stadler in *LCC*, XXV, 281.

By the middle of the century when Hutterite emissaries were recruiting among the stranded or divided Anabaptist communities in Germany and Switzerland, they contended that the Hutterite Church was not only a matter of faith and order. It was also a matter of place. The Moravian wilderness, then being turned by pious colonists from everywhere into fruitful farmland, was manifestly the providentially determined place of refuge foreseen by the Seer of Revelation 12:6. Just as the Anabaptist brethren in Germany should be separated in conventicles from the wicked, so also should they, to prosper, be separated from the whole wicked society of the territorial churches, in which a sham Christianity corrupts even the most devout and sturdy soul. One Hutterite missionary stresses the woman of the wilderness not only as pregnant with the true Word but as bearing many children:

Since God through his Spirit has in all times led the pious according to his word and will to the place which has pleased him or which he had provided for them to dwell in and thus leads and separates them, that he may be to them their ruler and governor and has a special delight in dwelling in the midst of the pious and accordingly since God especially with the primitive Church had joy and pleasure in seeing his own drawn together from all tongues under heaven (Acts 2:7 f.), wherein his heavenly work and rule was established on earth, [so likewise that he] might see his bride in the place determined for her in the wilderness (Revelation 12:6) wherever it should please him on earth and wherever he should ordain that she might rest awhile from the dragon and might bear her children,—for this reason God's spirit has [implanted] in the hearts of the pious a yearning to dwell in that very place.[13]

To satisfy this holy yearning, God sent forth Hutterite apostles or missionaries to gather together the scattered sheep under the protection and discipline of his pastors in Moravia.

The foregoing selection from the Hutterite *Chronicle* is eloquent testimony to the missionary zeal and cosmic sense of exclusive mission that inspired the Hutterites well into the second half of the century and goes far to explain the tremendous attraction exercised by the patriarchal Hutterites over the other radical but less seasoned churches like the proto-Unitarians in Poland.

These Polish Brethren combined radical trends deriving from the Italian Evangelical Rationalists, from the Dutch, German, and Hutterite Anabaptists, and from the Anabaptist anti-Nicene Spaniard Michael Servetus.

[13] A. J. F. Zieglschmid, *Die Älteste Chronik der Hütterischen Brüder* (Ithaca, N.Y., 1943). This and other Hutterite passages on the wilderness theme are documented in *The Radical Reformation.*

Michael Servetus (1511–1553) in his *Restitutio Christianismi* (1553) used Revelation 12 (and Daniel 12:1 f.) to argue that Christ was with the true Church driven into the wilderness to remain harassed for 1260 years from the Council of Nicaea (325), when his true relationship with the Father was creedally misconceived; and Servetus therefore looked for the restitution of the apostolic Church about 1585 (or 1560 if one reckoned from the emergence of Constantine to prominence about 300).[14] Servetus in some obscure way thought of himself as trumpeting the advent of the new age of restitution as a deputy of the archangel whose name he bore.

Although Servetus is more commonly associated with his attempt to restate the doctrine of the Trinity, he might with equal propriety be called the apostle of Anabaptist immersion. In the baptismal scene at Jordan's bank, he saw not only the epiphany of the three persons of the Trinity but also the model baptism by immersion for every true believer at Jesus' age of thirty. His baptismal theology was much more closely linked with a doctrine of the fall of man from Paradise than was that of the Swiss Brethren and the South German Anabaptists. In fact, it was the very physical sense of original sin and the pervasiveness of demonical temptation that for him made baptismal reparation such a relief and remedy for the assaults of wickedness from within and without. "Continuously," he wrote, "we have in us two princes (*principes*) in combat, God in the spirit and the serpent in the flesh."[15] Servetus thought even of the highest science as "serpentine" when not baptized in Christ.

He visualized the two trees in Paradise, the tree of life and the tree of the knowledge of good and evil, and considered them both as representing Christ. The latter, no less than the former, "was good . . . because in the Paradise of God no evil tree could grow up." Adam's fall was occasioned by his eating *prematurely* of "the unripe fruit" of the second tree, and thereby he was deprived of the fruit of both trees and became subject to death and liable to even greater delinquency: "It [the fruit of the second tree] was at the time forbidden to Adam and reserved for Christ alone, in order that we, when we should have acquired *through him* knowledge without deceit, would become like gods." For even if Adam had not sinned, "Christ who was as Word with God would have ultimately shared that knowledge with the world," making the state of the reborn in Christ superior to that of Adam before the Fall. (The concept of *felix culpa* was seldom so

---

[14] *Restitutio*, iii, 1.
[15] The remainder of this section on Servetus is taken with permission from *The Radical Reformation*.

strongly stressed in the Reformation era.) Thus God, who had intended that man should have life and some day also the knowledge of good and evil, established in his program of redemption first the Law. From fallen Adam to the establishment of the Law under Moses unmitigated death reigned (Romans 5:14), but with the Law the elect people were enabled to distinguish between good and evil and prepare themselves for an eternal salvation. Provisionally they were encouraged in a temporal way by the promise of entry into a land flowing with milk and honey. Canaan in Servetus' speculations was, in fact, a small portion of what had once been Paradise, now blasted by man's sin and only partly and precariously restored with but two of the original four rivers still flowing, and even these at too great a distance to produce verdure in Canaan.

The identification of Eden and Canaan was very important in Servetus' baptismal theology. It was grounded textually in Isaiah 51:3; 58:11; Ezekiel 36:35; and Joel 2:3, where Zion like a desert is variously described as becoming like Paradise, with the spiritual verdure made possible by the flowing of waters interpreted by Servetus as anticipatory of the life-giving waters of baptism. Servetus made the whole of his paradise-wilderness theology baptismally specific in appealing to Christ's word in John 7:38: "He who believes in me, as the Scripture [Isaiah 44:3; 55:1; 58:11] has said, 'Out of his heart shall flow [the four] rivers of living water.'" Servetus, seizing upon this text, in which the evangelist specifically refers to the gift of the Holy Spirit and says it cannot be imparted until Christ himself is glorified, developed the great conviction about the restoration of Paradise made possible by Christ's death, resurrection, and glorification, and by his institution of believers' baptism ("believes in me"). Redemptive rebirth is from above in water and the spirit (citing Colossians 1:13 and Ephesians 2:6), whereby the believer is delivered from the dominion of death and serpentine darkness and transferred to the kingdom of the Son.

Salvation for Servetus was very rich in meaning, involving the body, mind, and heart, namely, salvation from physical death (ultimately at the resurrection), salvation from distorted (serpentine) science, and salvation from all manifestation of hate. Harking back to the original cause of the Fall, Servetus stressed the ubiquity of "serpentine knowledge from the coils of which the believer can be released only in dying with Christ in baptism."

The *early* anti-Nicene Anabaptists in Poland under the influence of the wilderness theology of Michael Servetus, the Hutterites, and possibly also the Mennonites, at length fleeing "from Babylonian faith" (both Catholic and Calvinist), converged on a sandy wilderness given them by a protecting castellan and there founded the colony of Raków (1569), destined to be the center of Socinianism and the Racovian Catechism (1605). One of the earliest Racovians, the Anabaptist anti-trinitarian Martin Czechowic, in his Polish Bible of 1577 expressly adapted his translation to the northern European experience, driving Jesus after his baptism (Luke 4:1) not into the desert but into the forest (*puszcza*).

2. The Wilderness Theme in the Puritan Reformation of the Seventeenth Century

As with the Calvinist and the Lutheran territorial churches on the Continent, so in the Reformation establishment in England in the sixteenth century there was no mood to flee into the wilderness. But by the seventeenth century the wilderness impulse appeared everywhere in the piety and the ecclesiology of Puritan England. Indeed all Christians in the Britain of the King James Bible, of Civil War, Commonwealth, Restoration, and Glorious Revolution—whether they were Irish Catholics or Presbyterians, Caroline divines or Quakers—knew that they were wandering in the wilderness of an age of religious and constitutional turmoil toward that better state which God had most certainly promised his English Israel.

The tutelage of the Book of Common Prayer may well have contributed to the prominence of the wilderness strands in the violent sectarian unraveling of the tapestry of English Christianity in the seventeenth century. Thomas Cranmer had taken over from the medieval monastic office Psalm 95, *Venite*, as an integral part of Morning Prayer; and the wilderness theme, in both the personal-mystical and the national-prophetic senses, was consequently indelibly imprinted on the national consciousness:

Harden not your hearts: as in the provocation, as in the day of temptation in the wilderness . . . forty years long was I grieved with this generation, and said: It is a people that do err in their hearts, for they have not known my ways. Unto whom I sware in my wrath: That they should not enter into my rest.

The word *wilderness* became indeed, in the seventeenth century, an almost incantational term. It had absorbed the Wyclifite *wastity* (in rendering the Vulgate *vastitas* as "desolation"), also such older words as *wastine* and *wastern,* to carry the full charge of all the biblical-nuptial connotations traced thus far. It was admirably suited also to describe the state of the sects as a righteous remnant in a stricken land.[16]

The inherently duplex meaning of *wilderness* and its close relationship to the conception of reformed England as God's ongoing Israel were suggested by Richard Baxter (1615–1691) when he wrote in *The Saints' Everlasting Rest:*

> If they [the Israelites] had not felt their Wilderness-necessities, God should not have exercised his Wilderness-Providences and Mercies. If Man had kept his first Rest in Paradise, God had not had opportunity to manifest that far greater Love to the World in the giving of his Son. If Man had not fallen into the depth of misery, Christ had not come down from the height of Glory, nor died, nor risen, nor been believed on in the World.[17]

An indication of the gradual reconception of the Puritan church as itself the righteous remnant within a wayward Anglican Israel is the gradual idealization of the Waldensian church of the wilderness on the part of the more radical Puritans and their self-identification with "the Israel of the Alps." This development represents an unexpected diversification of our theme which deserves a special heading.

i. The Role of the Waldensians in the Puritan Vision of the Wilderness

One of the extraordinary features of the mystical and sectarian Puritans was their adoption of the medieval Waldensians as the connecting link between the re-Reforming church of England and the pure Christianity of the apostolic age. There had always been a certain reserve among the English Reformers about adopting the native Lollards as forerunners. And, as for the Waldensians, good English Protestants all knew that Luther for his part had heartily disliked them and that the Swiss Reformers had been willing to acknowledge them as truly Reformed only when they at their synod in Cianforan in 1532 submitted to the exacting canons of the Reformed churches. But gradually the English and Scottish Reformed churches in the seventeenth century, like the Mennonites and the Hutterites before them, began to look for connecting links with the apostolic age and found in medieval Waldensianism the idealization of this alleged continuity. It is perhaps pertinent to add that whereas the sixteenth-century radicals began to annex the Waldensian story to their chronicles at the close of their heroic age,

---

[16] Of incidental interest as a comment on the *wilderness* as a word of the age is the fact that in formal "gardens of delight" in the seventeenth century a certain section was set aside as the "wilderness" which was a labyrinth of box and other hedges and plantings, elaborately designed to bewilder the stroller pleasantly.

[17] *The Practical Works of . . . Richard Baxter* (London, 1707), p. 109.

the English sectarian Calvinists appropriated the same Waldensian story in programmatic fervor near the beginning of what was to be their heroic age in conflict with what they regarded as Anglican "Popery." We have already noted how Oliver Cromwell's representative visited Waldensian Piedmont "where those poor wretches had their abode, which was in the Clefts of ragged Rocks, and in the Caves of snowy mountains."

Within the English Calvinist context, Samuel Moreland's identification of the Waldensian church as the woman of the wilderness goes back to John Bale who in his *The Image of Bothe Churches after the most Wonderfull and Heavenlie Revelacion of Saincte John* (1550) suggested a connection between Protestantism and the persecuted churches of the wilderness like the Paulicians, the Albigensians, and the Waldensians. Bale, former Carmelite, author of *A Brefe Comedy or Enterlude of Johan Baptystes Preachinge in the Wylderness* (1538), sometime bishop of Ossory in Ireland, had during his exile in the Netherlands become acquainted with the work of the Anabaptist Melchior Hofmann (above, section 1), as he acknowledged in his preface.

Especially influential in the Puritan idealization of the Waldensian church was a book published by Jean Perrin at the international headquarters of Calvinism, *Histoire des Vaudois* (Geneva, 1619). This was translated into English a decade later and was widely read under the title *Luther's Forerunners or a Cloud of Witnesses Deposing for the Protestant Faith*. In this book Perrin projected the fully *Protestant* character of the Reformed Waldensians into their medieval phase and declared "that the Reformation of the Church . . . began in France, by means of Waldo," "as it were from a new Sion, causing rivers of his holy Law and pure doctrine to distill and drop downe upon the rest of the world" (Ezekiel 47:12; Isaiah 35:1 ff.). At the conclusion of this influential book, Perrin wrote thus of the persecutions of the Waldensians for four hundred years:

Which enforced them to disperse themselves here and there, where they could have any abiding, wandring through desert places; and yet nevertheless the Lord hath in such part preserved the remainder of them, that notwithstanding the rage of Satan, they have continued invincible against Antichrist, to whom they have offered a spiritual combat, destroying him by the blast of the Spirit of God.[18]

The suffering of the Waldensians persecuted anew kindled the

[18] *Op. cit.*, English version, pp. 143 f. Giorgio Spini has worked out this theme with special reference to New England, "Riforma Italiana e mediazioni Genevrine nella Nuova Inghilterra Puritana," *Genevra e l'Italia* (Florence, [1959]).

apocalyptic imaginations of the radical Puritans (the Independents) and also stirred their compassion. Under Cromwell's sponsorship Samuel Moreland tramped through the Waldensian valleys again to distribute the benefits of England's generosity. Moreland's *A Distinct and Faithful Accompt of all the Receipts, Disbursments and Remainder of the Moneys collected in England, Wales, and Ireland, for the Relief of the Poor Distressed Protestants in the Valleys of Piedmont* (London, 1658) must be put down as a major document in the history of international philanthropy; and the eschatological motivation of this huge national subscription should be stressed. It was to the true Church of the Wilderness that the money was given, as Moreland declared in his subscription appeal in language almost identical with that quoted above (Chapter III, at n. 94) from his later book about them.

From Cromwell's commissioner for Waldensian affairs, we pass to Cromwell's Latin secretary; for John Milton, too, occupies a special place in the elaboration of our theme.

ii. Wilderness and Paradise in John Milton

John Milton (1608-1674) in his opposition to a hireling ministry with "flaminical vestures" may speak for many a Puritan of the seventeenth century when in *The Reason of Church-government urg'd against Prelatry* (1641) he took it for granted that the true Church, despite its earlier Reformation, had in fact taken "flight into the wilderness" because of "the perverse iniquity of sixteen hundred years."[19] In the same year in *Animadversions upon the Remonstrants against Smectymnuus* Milton spoke bitterly against the Anglican arguments from "succession," "custom," and "visibility" and deplored the way England had vexed God and his Spirit "in this our wilderness since Reformation began" with "these rotten Principles." He was confident in the present age, in which the Church as Bride was descending from heaven as foreseen by the Seer of Revelation and wrote against the defenders of traditional episcopacy:

[To] twit us [Puritans] with the present age, which is to us an age of ages wherein God is manifestly come downe among us, to do some remarkable good to our Church or state, is as if a man should taxe the renovating and re-ingendring Spirit of God with innovation, and that new creature for an upstart noveltie; yea the new Jerusalem, which without your

[19] *The Works of John Milton*, ed. Frank Allen Patterson (New York, 1931–1940) III:1, p. 246.

admired linke of succession descends from Heaven, could not scape some such centure.[20]

In the *Areopagitica,* written a dozen years after the two preceding works, Milton in national pride referred to Wyclif when he said that out of England "as out of Sion . . . sounded forth the first tidings and trumpet of Reformation to all Europe," which had it been heeded "the glory of reforming all our neighbours had bin compleatly ours." He went on to prophesy:

Now once again by all concurrence of signs, and by the generall instinct of holy and devout men, . . . God is decreeing to begin some new and great period in his Church, ev'n to the reforming of the Reformation it self: What does he then but reveal Himself to his servants, and as his manner is, first to his English-men. . . .[21]

It is against the background of this great national confidence and sense of the impending reformation of the Reformation that Milton's two great poems on Paradise (1667 and 1671) are to be seen. To enter very deeply into the garden and wilderness themes in these two major works of world literature would disturb the balance of the present essay. It must suffice to note that almost all the variations of our themes come out prominently in *Paradise Lost* and *Paradise Regain'd,* and in Milton's other writings as well.

It is of special interest, for example, to observe that Milton distinguishes in the Jordanian wilderness at the beginning of Jesus' ministry between the "Desert wild" into which Christ went to engage in preliminary "holy meditation" and the same wilderness into which he was driven to engage in spiritual combat with Satanic temptation. Milton ascribed to God the plan to "exercise" Jesus in the wilderness that he might there, against the assaults of Satan, fashion the disciplines or instruments of spiritual warfare and thereby convert the wilderness into paradise. Milton has Jesus saying:

> ["]And now by some strange motion I am led
> Into this Wilderness, to what intent
> I learn not yet, perhaps I need not know;
> For what concerns my knowledge God reveals.["]

Then the poet comments:

> So spake our Morning Star then in his rise,
> And looking round on every side beheld
> A pathless Desert, dusk with horrid shades;

[20] *Ibid.,* p. 144.
[21] *Ibid.,* IV, p. 340.

> The way he came not having mark'd, return
> Was difficult, by humane steps untrod. . . .
> Full forty days he pass'd, whether on hill
> Sometimes, anon in shady vale, each night
> Under the covert of some ancient Oak,
> Or Cedar, to defend him from the dew,
> Or harbour'd in one Cave, is not reveal'd;
> Nor tasted humane food, nor hunger felt
> Till those days ended, hunger'd then at last
> Among wild Beasts: they at his sight grew mild,
> Nor sleeping him nor waking harm'd, his walk
> The fiery Serpent fled, and noxious Worm,
> The Lion and fierce Tiger glar'd aloof.[22]

Paradise was in fact regained when Christ "the glorious Hermit" went into the wilderness and from his cave of meditation raised it by his redemptive presence to become an Eden, as Milton sang at the beginning of his poem:

> I who e're while the happy Garden sung,
> By one mans disobedience lost, now sing
> Recover'd Paradise to all mankind,
> By one mans firm obedience fully tri'd
> Through all temptation, and the Tempter foil'd
> In all his wiles, defeated and repuls'd,
> And Eden rais'd in the wast Wilderness.[23]

Thus within a few lines of the opening book of *Paradise Regain'd*, Milton described the desert as a place of meditative refuge, as a realm of temptation, as a provisional paradise in which the animals were rendered mild by the Hermit redeemer of mankind.

The most extraordinary and controversial feature of Milton's poetic portrayal of Christ's temptations in the wilderness was, of course, his including knowledge, both theological and philosophical, among the temptations spurned. In *Paradise Regain'd*, Milton the opponent of a hireling ministry, a ministry recruited in his day partly by the allures of a university education and the languid leisure of the pursuit of "trifles," made possible by ancient endowments and tithes, imagined that Satan tempted Jesus by reminding him of his boyhood attraction to Temple learning and suggesting that he might well substitute the empire of the mind for the kingdoms of this world. He puts these words on Satan's lips:

---

[22] *Paradise Regain'd*, I, lines 290–313; *Works*, II:2, pp. 415 f.
[23] *Paradise Regain'd*, I, lines 1–7; *Works*, II:2, p. 405.

Therefore let pass, as they are transitory,
The Kingdoms of this world; I shall no more
Advise thee, gain them as thou canst, or not.
And thou thy self seem'st otherwise inclin'd
Then to a worldly Crown, addicted more
To contemplation and profound dispute,
As by that early action may be judg'd,
When slipping from thy Mothers eye thou went'st
Alone into the Temple; there was found
Among the gravest Rabbies disputant
On points and questions fitting *Moses* Chair,
Teaching not taught; the childhood shews the man,
As morning shews the day. Be famous then
By wisdom; as thy Empire must extend,
So let extend thy mind o're all the world,
In knowledge, all things in it comprehend,
All knowledge is not couch't in *Moses* Law,
The *Pentateuch* or what the Prophets wrote,
The *Gentiles* also know, and write, and teach
To admiration, led by Natures light;
And with the *Gentiles* much thou must converse,
Ruling them by persuasion as thou mean'st,
Without thir learning how wilt thou with them,
Or they with thee hold conversation meet?
How wilt thou reason with them, how refute
Thir Idolisms, Traditions, Paradoxes?
Error by his own arms is best evinc't.
Look once more e're we leave this specular Mount
Westward, much nearer by Southwest, behold
Where on the *AEgean* shore a City stands
Built nobly, pure the air, and light the soil,
Athens the eye of *Greece*, Mother of Arts
And Eloquence, native to famous wits
Or hospitable, in her sweet recess,
City or Suburban, studious walks and shades;
See there the Olive Grove of *Academie*. . . .[24]

Jesus in answer to Satan refused to confuse "light from above" with "conjectures, fancies, built on nothing firm," to become in Satan's eyes "a king compleat" by joining to himself the empire of *scientia*. Milton, in making natural knowledge one of the temptations of Christ and by implication of the devout minister, thus ranged himself, to the despair of Christian humanists, with those who have relegated *scientia* to the

[24] *Paradise Regain'd*, IV, lines 208–244.

cunning of the wilderness rather than finding it restored to the provisional paradise of the Church and school.[25]

There are other Miltonian meanings of *wilderness*. When, for example, Milton in *Eikonoklastes* (1649) made his answer to the royalist *Eikōn Basilikē*, he rebuked Charles I for his encroaching upon the rights of Parliament and told how his tyrannical exercise of the royal prerogative would have returned Englishmen to bondage as under Pharaoh or forced upon them "a second wandring over that horrid Wilderness of distraction and civil slaughter."[26] After the king had been executed, Milton in his *Defensio* of 1651 continued to use the term *wilderness* or *desertum* for the disorder and vices which stemmed from life under the English Pharaohs and which could not be at once and completely eliminated though England be now "under God's immediate government."[27]

It is, of course, in the left wing of Puritanism that we find the wilderness motif especially prominent, among the Baptists, Diggers, Seekers, Quakers, and Ranters.

iii. The Wilderness of the Sects

The Digger Gerrard Winstanley in *The Mystery of God* (1648) combined the garden and the wilderness motifs with both psychological and social implications reminiscent of the claim of Origen and Gregory of Nyssa that each individual soul may be a paradise:

> God declares, That Adam himselfe, or that living flesh, mankinde, is a Garden which God hath made for his own delight, to dwell, and walk in, wherein he has planted variety of Hearbs, and pleasant Plants, as love, joy, peace, humility, knowledge, obedience, delight and purity of life.[28]

Here Winstanley alludes to Canticles 4:12 and Isaiah 58:11, and goes on to show how the original serpent of the Garden was the pride of the creaturely trying to act the Creator. Adam was driven from the Garden into the wilderness; and amidst the competing claims of all the mutually exclusive sects on the eve of the Commonwealth period, Winstanley declares:

> Think it not strange to see many of the saints of God at a stand in the

---

[25] The Miltonian problem of knowledge and grace has been admirably analyzed and placed in its broad seventeenth-century setting by Howard Schultz, *Milton and Forbidden Knowledge* (New York, 1955).

[26] *Works*, V, p. 288.

[27] *The First Defence; Works*, VII, pp. 178 and 179.

[28] *Op. cit.*, p. 2.

wilderness, and at a loss and so waiting upon God to discover Himself to them.[29]

John Jackson, the prinicpal English Seeker,[30] in his *The Pedigree and Peregrination of Israel* (1649) exclaimed:

. . . sprinkle the posts and lintles of my heart with the hysope of thy grace, and the precious bloud of thy salvation; that I may be knowne to be thine, and be received into thy mercy when thou shalt come to visit me, and to bring me through the Red Sea of that dangerous passage to the heavenly Canaan of eternitie.[31]

Jackson interprets the testing of the wilderness as an expression of God's love:

. . . in this desart he kept thee the longer to acquaint thee with the disposition of thine owne heart, that thou mightest see, what was in thee, and that he might cause the carkases of the rebells (murmurings and unbeliefs) to fall and perish in this wildernesse.[32]

It is possible that the term *wilderness* acquired a quite peculiar meaning among the Ranters, an outcropping in seventeenth-century England of what were called on the Continent in the sixteenth century the Spiritual Libertines and in the fifteenth century the Adamites. There can be no doubt about the antinomian meaning of the wilderness experience for such a Ranter as Lawrence Claxton (1615–1667), who in *The Lost Sheep Found* (1660) told how he moved from Baptism to Ranterism, taking his "progress into the Wilderness."[33] The basic thrust of Ranterism as of all Libertinage was to make programmatic Paul's persuasion (Romans 14:14)[34] that "nothing is unclean in itself." The English Ranters, drawing upon the medieval Adamite tradition, apparently considered the society of law and order a wilderness until step by step they could be completely delivered from the bondage of the Law and all laws and customs and live "in the perfect liberty of the sons of God" without any sense of guilt, like Adam before the Fall.

The Ranters' conversion of the biblical desert or wilderness into the

[29] *Ibid.*, p. 39.
[30] See James Vendettuoli, Jr., "The Seeker Path Through the Wilderness," Chap. VIII in his Harvard doctoral thesis, "The English Seekers," Cambridge, 1958.
[31] *Op. cit.*, p. 119.
[32] *Hosannah to the Son of David* (1657), III, 43.
[33] An extensive collection of Ranter excerpts is printed and interpreted by Norman Cohn, *The Pursuit of the Millennium* (Fairlawn, N.J., 1957). The excerpt from Claxton is on p. 345.
[34] Likewise important was Titus 1:15: To the pure all things are pure. The author in *The Radical Reformation*, chap. XII:2 and chap. XXIII:3, has sought to draw some distinction between licentious Libertinage and spiritual Libertinism.

nothingness of the moral law was an extraordinary perversion of the metaphor in view of the fact that it was precisely in the wilderness that the Law had first been given. The Ranters appropriated the wilderness passage of Isaiah 42:11–16 and permitted themselves to interpret God's successively drying up and refreshing with grace the dry places as his sanction of making moral "darkness light before them." The Adamite-Libertine-Ranter antinomian exploitation of the aboriginal ambivalence of the wilderness motif therefore belongs to our survey. Fortunately for the historic resonance of this great word from Scripture there is no subsequent echo of this moral aberration in the usage of the word outside the small Ranter circle.

Much more consonant with the long history of the word is the Quaker usage in the seventeenth century.

George Fox (d. 1691) likened the world to "a briary, thorny wilderness" and James Nayler (d. 1660) purposed "to plant in the wilderness." Another Quaker, Charles Marshall (d. 1698), took quite literally the injunction to fly for a season of solace and reflective solitude into the forests and glades. He recalled how before becoming a Quaker he had grown dissatisfied with the Independents and the Baptists, although moved by the "tender" earnestness of their quest; and, feeling burdened with his own sin and the overpowering sense of the fallen state of mankind as a whole over against the humility of other creatures, he

became like the solitary desert, and mourned like a dove without a mate. And seeing I could not find the living among the dead professions, I spent much time in retirements alone, in the fields and woods, and by springs of water, which I delighted to lie by, and drink of. And in those days of retirement, strong, great, and many were my cries unto the Lord. . . . Oh, that my soul might be eased from these heavy burdens and loads of death and darkness! That out of the state of gross Egyptian darkness I might be saved, and from the land of drought, a land of anguish, a land of horrible darkness! Oh, undeclarable fall! said my soul. . . . And in those days, as I walked and beheld the creation of God Almighty, everything testified against me, heaven and earth, the day and the night . . . , the watercourses and the springs of the great deep, keeping in their respective places: the grass and flowers of the field; the fish of the sea and fowls of the air, keeping their order; but man alone, the chief of the work of God's hand, [I saw was] degenerated.[35]

[35] *The Journal . . . of Charles Marshall*, printed by Richard Barrett (London, 1844), p. 26. Much later still another Quaker, Stephen Crisp, in *A Short History of a Long Travel from Babylon to Bethel* (1792) tells how the concept of the world as a wilderness made of him a true pilgrim in search of the eternal Jerusalem:
"I had no Comfort Night nor Day, but still kept going on, whether right or wrong

This markedly English, religiously motivated interest in the animals and the birds and the other denizens of the wilderness, which found expression in the seventeenth century, was later reinforced in the eighteenth century by romanticism and in the nineteenth century by humanitarianism, to become in the end an English cultural trait, the sources of which have never been satisfactorily explained. In the seventeenth century, at least, and especially on the dissenting side, the positive attitude toward nature and hence toward the wilderness in the literal sense seems to have been compounded of two somewhat contradictory biblical or theological ingredients.

One of these ingredients was the paradisic motif among those radicals who went so far in their belief that Christ's atoning work had indeed taken away sin from the whole world, nature included, that nature in contrast to largely unregenerate people reflected the pristine or primeval glory of Paradise. Such indeed appears to have been the thought of the Quaker cited above, who assumed that nature was either from the beginning or since the atonement exempted from the disorderly effects of man's fall from Paradise.

Another ingredient in the English theology of nature was the radical, sectarian eschatology which tended to withdraw the church, man in the church (the conventicle), and all of nature from the direct government of Christ, pending his imminent advent in glory.[36] This interpretation of nature liberated it as a realm free for scientific inquiry and for decisive human action. In some cases this eschatological view had also the effect of endowing man with a special responsibility for this realm in the interim.

For example, as early indeed as the sixteenth century in the meditations, sermons, and examinations of John Bradford, royal chaplain under Edward and martyr at the fiery stake under Mary in 1555, we observe an extraordinary concern for the redemption of the realm of the creatures. Openly declaring that the Established Church had some things to learn from the despised Anabaptists, Bradford in his meditation on "Thy kingdom come" in the Lord's Prayer distinguished between God's present kingship over all creatures in general like the

---

I knew not, nor durst I ask any Body, for fear of being beguiled as before. Thus I got into a vast howling Wilderness, where there seemed to be no Way in it, only now and then I found some Men and Women's footsteps, which was some Comfort to me in my Sorrow; but whether they got out, without being devoured of wild Beasts, or whither I should go I knew not. But in this woful State I travelled from Day to Day, casting within myself what Condition, or whether I had best to seek some other Town or City, to see if I could get some other Guide."

[36] See the suggestive essay by George L. Mosse, "Puritan Radicalism and the Enlightenment," *Church History*, XXIX (1960), 424–439.

demons, the angels, mankind everywhere, the animals, the birds, the fishes, and all other creatures, and his imminent personal rule over the elect. Then just before his execution Bradford clearly propounded a doctrine of a truly universal salvation or restitution of all things (Acts 3:21), interpreting the term *creature* in its fullest sense. Appealing to Paul's outcry for the whole of creation groaning in pain together with man because of the Fall (Romans 8:22), and alluding to the angels (and the peaceable animals) serving Christ in the wilderness of temptation, Bradford proclaimed that "without any doubt" all creatures, that is, the plants, the animals, and all living things, would be freed along with men and restored to the perfection and harmony of Paradise.[37]

The wilderness motif was especially developed in the Baptist thinker John Bunyan (1638–1688), who combined Quaker, Seeker, and mystical elements and reinforced the theme by assimilating hitherto unused scriptural passages in his interpretations of life as a confident pilgrimage from bewilderment to certainty. It was in Bunyan that for the first time the biblical term *wilderness* absorbed the coloration of the forest texts in Scripture and acquired its peculiarly haunting resonance for English ears. Bunyan developed the wilderness theme notably in *Differences in Judgement about Water Baptism* (1673), *Pilgrim's Progress* (1678), and *The House of the Forest of Lebanon* (published posthumously, 1692).

The first of these is of interest for the fact that, though Bunyan was himself rebaptized in 1653, he did not withhold three of his children from the infant rite; and in *Differences* he argued that, since the ancient "church of the wilderness" had no circumcision and yet the uncircumcised were admitted to the partaking of the manna, so the contemporary Church in the wilderness of sectarian turmoil should not make of believers' baptism "the rule, the door, the bolt, . . . the bar, the wall of division between the righteous and the unrighteous."[38]

It was, of course, in *Pilgrim's Progress* that Bunyan gathered up so much of the wilderness concept from the religious literature which preceded him and in turn powerfully tinctured the connotation of the word in popular Anglo-American piety for more than two centuries. He opened the Pilgrimage with these words:

As I walk'd through the wilderness of this world, I lighted on a certain

[37] *Writings,* ed. Aubrey Townsend (London, 1853), pp. 127, 350 f., 359.
[38] Bunyan will be quoted from the standard three-volume edition of his works, in this case *The Whole Works,* ed. George Offor (London, 1862), II, 616–674, esp. 625 ff. Bunyan's New Testament basis for arguing from the Old Covenantal was of course I Corinthians 10:5–10.

place, where was a den; and I laid me down in that place to sleep: and as I slept I dreamed a dream.[39]

The den or cave was the prison in which he spent most of the years between 1660 and 1672 because of his recalcitrance in not conforming to the Restoration Settlement under Charles II. The dream, of course, was the *Progress* of Christian and later his spouse Christiana as pilgrims through the wilderness of the religious and political turmoil of the English seventeenth century.

From his biblical allusions it is clear that the wilderness for Bunyan was darkness, disorder, death, and the demoniacal (Job 3:5; 10:22; Jeremiah 2:6) and that the Apollyon whom Christian overcame was a combination of Abaddon, the angel of the bottomless pit (Revelation) and of Leviathan (Revelation and Job). After the defeat of Apollyon, Christian had still to wander through a trackless waste:

Now at the end of this Valley, was another, called the Valley of the Shadow of Death, and Christian must needs go through it, because the way to the Coelestial City lay through the midst of it: Now this Valley is a very solitary place. The Prophet Jeremiah [2:6] describes it, A Wilderness, a Land of Desarts, and of Pits, a Land of Drought and of the shadow of death, a Land that no Man (but a Christian) passeth through, and where no man dwelt.[40]

In *The House of the Forest of Lebanon,* based on I Kings 7:2, written about 1688, Bunyan wove a new scriptural strand into the wilderness motif, the darkling forest. He interpreted four buildings described in Scripture typologically as representing phases of the ongoing Church, namely, the tabernacle of the wilderness, the temple of Solomon, the porch of Solomon, and his "house of the forest of Lebanon." Bunyan surmised that Solomon, besides his palace with its portico (made of Lebanese timbers) in Jerusalem, had also a country seat or hunting lodge located in the Lebanese forest. This house of the forest typified the scattered and persecuted Church "in her sackcloth state." With the by now quite traditional combination of the idyllic ecclesiology of the wilderness of Exodus and the prophets, the mystically perceived bridal ecclesiology of Canticles, and the eschatalogical ecclesiology of Revelation 12, Bunyan brought in the concept of the Church "scattered in the wilderness of the nations" of Ezekiel 20:35 ff. He contrasted Ezekiel's remnant "scattered among the nations, as a

[39] *Works,* III, 89.
[40] *Ibid.,* p. 65. On chivalric romances among the literary sources of Bunyan's religious melancholia and his wilderness imagery, see Harold Golder, "Bunyan's Valley of the Shadow," *Modern Philology,* XXVII (1929–1930), 55–72.

flock of sheep are scattered in a wood or wilderness" with the Church at worship in the temple and in peace. He compared the symbolism of Solomon's temple and his house in the forest:

> We read, before this house was built, that there was a church in the wilderness; and also, after this house was demolished, that there would be a church in the wilderness (Acts 7:38; Revelation 12:14). But we now respect that wilderness state that the church of the New Testament is in, and conclude that this house of the forest of Lebanon was a type and figure of that; that is, her wilderness state. And, methinks, the very place where this house was built does intimate such a thing; for this house was not built in a town, a city, etc., as was that called the temple of the Lord, but was built in the forest of Lebanon, unto which that saying seems directly to answer. "And to the woman," the church, "were given two wings of a great eagle, that she might fly into her place."[41]

Bunyan proceeds to speak of "the terror, or majesty and fortitude, which God has put upon the church in the wilderness, that makes the Gentiles so bestir them to have her under foot."[42] He insists that the Anglicans "misapprehend concerning her, as if she was for destroying kings, for subverting kingdoms, and for bringing all to desolation." To be sure, in their eyes she is "terrible as an army with banners" (Canticles 6:10); and, as the house was made up of great timbers, so this Church of the wilderness is "made up of giants of grace" with "the faces of lions." Yet "she moveth no sedition, she abideth in her place; let her temple-worshippers but alone, and she will be as if she were not in the world; but if you afflict her, 'Fire proceedeth out of their mouth and devoureth their enemies; and if any man will hurt them, he must in this manner be killed'" (Revelation 11:5) "by the sword of the Spirit."

In his fresh reworking of the scriptural texts, Bunyan conveys powerfully his deep sense of the latent strength and imminent massiveness of the now persecuted and suffering Church of the wilderness state; for "when the combustion for religion is in the church in the wilderness it is said to be in heaven" (Revelation 12:7) between the angels and the dragon.

3. The Pietist Protestant Missions to and Plantations in the Wilderness

In the Magisterial Reformation of the sixteenth century Luther and Zwingli, Cranmer and Calvin had been concerned to reform the

[41] *Works*, III, p. 513.
[42] *Ibid.*, p. 516.

Church. They had no thought of engaging in a world mission like the Counter-Reformation or of evangelizing Christendom itself like the Anabaptists and others in the Radical Reformation. Even in the "second Reformation" of England in the seventeenth century, the parties of the left were almost as nationalistic as the Anglicans and in some cases even more so, and were so preoccupied with personal and conventicular perfection that little thought could be given to evangelization outside English Christendom.

In the eighteenth century it was otherwise. First German, then English Pietism took to heart the evangelical mission initiated by the Radical Reformers of the sixteenth century and appropriated directly from the Bible and perhaps indirectly from these Radicals themselves the eschatological theology of the wilderness destined to blossom as the rose and of that true Church which is to be as a garden in the wilderness of the world beyond the seas and of the merely nominal or rationalistic and political Christianity at home.

John Arndt (d. 1621), a mystical Lutheran pastor in Brunswick, who wrote a popular devotional *Paradiesgärtlein,* published in 1606 *Of True Christianity,* later to be much admired by the German Pietists of the eighteenth century. True Christianity was identified with "the eternal Gospel" of Revelation 14:6, which was to be proclaimed "to those who dwell on earth, to every nation and tribe and tongue and people."

It is of great interest to observe how in respect to our own wilderness theme the phrasings of John Bunyan join with those of the German Pietists in the letter of Anthony William Boehm (1673-1722), German chaplain at St. James's under Queen Anne and the first Hanoverians, wherein he dedicated to Anne his translation of Arndt's *Of True Christianity* in 1707. Boehm, educated in the Pietist community of Halle, commended Arndt's distillation of the essence of Christianity as a healing balm for the earnest Christian, as a prescription for the world mission of the Church, and notably as a cure for sectarian divisiveness. The German, with his eyes opened to the vast dominion of Britain beyond the seas, for perhaps the first time identified the wilderness with nationalistic churchmanship, which had for so long kept Protestantism from performing its proper evangelical function. Going beyond the Independent Milton and the Seeker Jackson, who respectively identified the wilderness with civil strife and with sectarian claims, Boehm echoed the language of Canticles in his appeal to the Queen to sponsor that ecumenical Church soon to "come up from the wilderness" of a vain ecclesiasticism and ethnic pride:

Many that are ashamed of the Meanness of the Gospel, and of True Christianity raised thereon, would be powerfully convinced of its eminent *Dignity,* if ever they should see Kings and Queens of the Earth bring their Honour and Glory into the Kingdom of Christ. There will be a Time, when the Church of Christ will *come up from the Wilderness* of various Sects, Parties, Nations, Languages, Forms, and Ways of Worship, nay of Crosses and Afflictions, *leaning upon her Beloved,* and in his Power bidding Defiance to all her Enemies. Then shall that Church, which now doth but look forth as the Morning in its Dawn, after a continual Growth in Strength and Beauty, appear *Terrible as an Army with Banners;* but terrible to those only that despised her whilst she was in her Minority, and would not have her Beloved to reign over them.[43]

Boehm was himself very active in promoting the evangelization of the natives of the New World from the Barbados to Boston and was tireless in translating the voluminous correspondence between the German Pietists in Halle and notably the divines in Boston. We shall have occasion further to observe his influence (chapter IV).

Representative of indigenous nonconformist piety in the eighteenth century in England was the Baptist John Fawcett (1740–1817). Best known for the hymn "Lord, dismiss us with thy blessing ... Trav'ling thro' this wilderness" (1773), Fawcett in his widely used two-volume devotional commentary on the Bible (London, 1811) preserved in attenuated strength something of the wilderness mood of the more violent English seventeenth century and then went on to stress the great commission to evangelize the world. In commenting on Canticles 3:6 and 8:5 he observed:

... a wilderness is the common emblem of this present evil world. The believer comes out of it, when he renounces its friendship, and is delivered from the love of it, when he leaves its sinful pleasures and pursuits. . . . A sinful state is a wilderness, barren and dry, and remote from communion with God. Out of this state sinners are brought by repentance, through the power and grace of Christ. A soul convinced of sin, and truly humbled for it, finds itself in a wilderness, and at a loss what way to take, till brought acquainted with Jesus Christ, and enabled to lean upon him. There is then a coming up from the wilderness of this world, . . . living as strangers and pilgrims, and aiming at a better country. But every step of the way it is necessary to lean upon the beloved.[44]

---

[43] *Of True Christianity* (London, 1707), pp. xiv, 169.
[44] *Op. cit., in loc.* The missionary theme was stressed by a somewhat later Baptist, Andrew Fuller (1754–1815), of Ketteringham, where the English Baptist Missionary Society was organized in 1782. In his *Expository Discourses on the Apocalypse* preached here, he pointed to North America as the wilderness afforded by God, "for the second

From this typically inward though not mystical sense of the wilderness, Fawcett turned in his commentary on Isaiah 35:1 and elsewhere, like so many of his fellow eighteenth-century divines, to identify in the world missionary movement the fulfillment of the prophecy that the wilderness and the solitary place will rejoice and blossom as a rose, when

> the glory and excellency of the most favoured and fruitful spots of ground shall be conferred on those dark, desolate and barren regions of the earth, where sin and Satan had reigned from age to age.[45]

Notably influential in the evolution of the wilderness concept was John Wesley (1703–1791), who drew not only on the English seventeenth-century elaboration of our theme, as summed up by Bunyan, but also upon fresh drafts of the medieval mystical and perfectionist traditions as represented specifically by the desert Fathers, by Madame Guyon in France, and by Gregory Lopez of Mexico.[46] The "wilderness state" came to be a fairly important term in his moral theology and in his hymnody, intermingled with certain romantic notions about nature that were later to find fullest expression in such poets as William Wordsworth.[47]

The earliest significant reference to the wilderness is in Wesley's *Journal* under date of March 28, 1740: "From these words, 'Then was Jesus led by the Spirit into the wilderness to be tempted of the devil,' I took occasion to describe that *wilderness state,* that state of doubts, and fears, and strong temptation, which so many go through, though in different degrees, after they have received remission of sins."[48] Thus, from the outset the term in Wesley presupposed a state of grace. Just as the Israelites were provisionally saved once they had been delivered from bondage to Egypt and were wandering in the wilderness, so every Christian is provisionally saved by baptism, but he must continue

---

flight," "to be nourished during the remainder of the 1260 years." On Fuller, see LeRoy Edwin Froom, *The Prophetic Faith of Our Fathers* (Washington, 1950), III, 350–354.

[45] Besides Fawcett there is another good summary of the meaning of the wilderness at the end of the eighteenth century in Benjamin Keach, *A Key to Open Scripture Metaphors* (London, 1779), p. 935.

[46] The Spanish solitary Lopez (1542–1596), whose life Wesley read, is several times referred to by him. On Madame Guyon, see below at n. 54.

[47] The parallel and contagion are noted by Margaret M. Fitzgerald, *First Follow Nature: Primitivism in English Poetry 1725–1750* (New York, 1947), pp. 8, 152, 168 f., 174, 180 f., 186. To illustrate her thesis she quotes the following hymn, p. 49:

> "For in some lonely, *desert* place
> Forever I would sit,
> Languish to see the Saviour's face,
> And perish, weeping at His feet."

[48] Standard Edition, II, 339; italics mine.

to submit to the discipline of the Spirit until he reaches the promised realm or state of perfection. For Wesley the wilderness was clearly a theological term referring to the life of the redeemed, not to the life of the reprobate.

The influence of the Moravian Brethren may well have been working in the back of Wesley's mind at this point, and behind this the testimony of the Anabaptists. It will be recalled that the Anabaptist Melchior Hofmann was particularly conscious of the temptations that beset the Christian after his regeneration in the public act of adult rebaptism. Wesley and the Moravians connected regeneration, of course, not primarily with (infant) baptism but rather with the sanctifying descent of the Holy Spirit in the redemptive change of heart; but all Pietists knew the temptations that had to be faced after such regeneration; and hence Wesley looked also for "the second blessing" when "people that do err in their hearts . . . enter into my [God's] rest" (Psalm 95, *Venite,* in the Anglican Prayer Book). For example, Wesley wrote in a letter of spiritual counsel to one Miss Marsh (October 13, 1764): "From what not only you, but many others likewise have experienced, we find there is very frequently a kind of wilderness state, not only after justification, but even after deliverance from sin, . . . the most frequent cause of this second darkness and distress, I believe, is evil reasoning. . . ."[49]

Presently, Wesley was to distinguish the "wilderness state" from "heaviness," ascribing only the former to sin, *unacknowledged,* which must be probed into until confessed and forgiven.[50] Heaviness, in contrast, must be put down to physical disability, which the sufferer should seek to cure medically, or failing this, put up with, as a divinely imposed trial of patience. In 1774, for example, he wrote a letter of spiritual comfort to one Mary Bishop:

The differences between heaviness and darkness of soul (the wilderness state) should never be forgotten. Darkness (unless in the case of bodily disorder) seldom comes upon us but by our own fault. It is not so with respect to heaviness, which may be occasioned by a 1000 circumstances, such as frequently neither our wisdom can forsee nor our power prevent.[51]

In his Sermon XLVI, "The Wilderness State,"[52] Wesley was aware

[49] *Letters,* Standard Edition, IV, 270.
[50] This seems inconsistent with the fact that Wesley's first identification of the wilderness state was in connection with the Jordan baptismal scene where no sinfulness in Christ could be theologically acknowledged.
[51] *Letters,* VI, 111. The matter in parenthesis is Wesley's own. Cf. the letter to Rebecca Yeoman, February 5, 1772, *ibid.,* V, 303.
[52] *Works,* ed. John Emory (New York, 1856), III, 408.

of the monastic experience of accidie (sloth), also of the mystical meaning of the desert as the emptiness preparatory to receiving God, of the darkness before the light; but he here expressly rejected the positive connotation of the term *wilderness* in the mystics. Opposing their traditional interpretation of Hosea 2:14 on the allurement of the Bride into the wilderness, Wesley says the text "manifestly refers to the Jewish nation; and, perhaps, to that only" and goes on soberly: "But if it is applicable to particular persons, the plain meaning of it is this: I will draw him by love; I will convince him of sin; and then comfort him by pardoning mercy." Wesley thus rejected the mystics' conception of the wilderness state as desirable; but he took over, with only a moderate challenge, their individualistic application of the wilderness texts. For the first time in our survey the wilderness has acquired in Wesley an exclusively negative sense (except as it was, to be sure, descriptive of errant Christians, and not benighted pagans). Henceforth the Methodist meaning for "coming out of the wilderness" would be the personal revivalistic exodus of the individual from the wilderness of nominal Christianity. But the sentiment and even sentimentality of later expressions of Methodist conversion language (coming up out of the wilderness, leaning on the Lord) unwittingly perpetuated in respect to public revival the betrothal imagery which the rejected mystics had used discretely or only esoterically in respect to private contemplation.

In his Sermon XLVII, "Heaviness through Manifold Temptations,"[53] Wesley was aware of the special meaning of heaviness among "mystic authors" whose "notion, has crept in, I know not how, even among plain people, who have no [direct] acquaintance with them." However, precisely at this point, he himself quotes approvingly from the Quietist authoress Madame Guyon (1648–1717):

I continued [says Madame Guyon] so happy in my Beloved, that, although I should have been forced to live a vagabond in a desert, I should have found no difficulty in it. This state had not lasted long when, in effect, I found myself led into a desert. I found myself in a forlorn condition, altogether poor, wretched, and miserable. The proper source of this grief is the knowledge of ourselves, by which we find, that there is an extreme unlikeness between God and us. . . .[54]

[53] *Ibid.*, p. 417.
[54] *Apud* Wesley, *ibid.* Madame Guyon's twenty-volume commentary on the Bible "avec des explications et réflexions qui regardent la vie intérieure" is replete with references to the wilderness. Wesley was at first quite annoyed with the pervasive influence of quietism, which, for all its merit, was frequently unscriptural, he averred, and tended "to make us rest contented without either faith or works." Finally in 1776 he was prompted to edit an expurgated edition of Madame Guyon's autobiography with a preface. The latter is printed in *Works*, VII, pp. 561–563.

In France in the century following Madame Guyon's death, the desert of which she had written mystically was a very real wilderness for her Protestant compatriots. With the revocation of the Edict of Nantes (1685), the Huguenots took flight to the caves, forests, and desolate places. They called their forbidden conventicles *"les églises du désert."* Even their synods and their forbidden baptismal and marriage certificates were dated "from the wilderness."

The wilderness sermons of Claude Brousson were published in Amsterdam in 1695 with the title *La Manne Mystique du Désert.* In one of these the text is Canticles 2:14 on the fugitive Church of Christ likened to a dove hidden in the clefts of the rocks. Identification is made with the Waldensians who had been similarly forced to flee into the wilderness of the Alps. Much under the continuing influence of Pierre Jurieu, who had predicted the universal triumph of Protestantism in 1689 in his *L'accomplissements des prophéties, ou la délivrance de l'Église,* the Church of the Desert kept revising its eschatology, never losing confidence in itself as the true Church temporarily hiding in the wilderness (Revelation 12:6).

The more fanatical Camisards, who rose in revolt in 1702, let go the more mystical and quietistic desert texts and, considering themselves a colony of Israel, spoke of God as Jehovah, of their place of meeting as Zion, of their camp as the encampment of the Eternal, and of their inspirers as prophets. Corporately, under military discipline they styled themselves the children of God and they gave to their leaders biblical sobriquets. Their foes were the priests of Baal, Pharaoh, and Babylon.[55]

In Scotland among the Covenanters and especially the Cameronians the pattern of ancient Israel wandering and covenanting in the wilderness was likewise powerful. One thinks of Samuel Rutherford, *Joshua Redivivus* (1664), of Alexander Peden, *The Lord's Trumpet Sounding*

We have left out of our account the development of the Catholic use of the paradise-wilderness theme in the age of the baroque. It is of incidental interest, however, that Paradise pictures became very prominent around 1600. One thinks here of Jan Brueghel (1581–1625) and Roelant Savery (1576–1639). Interestingly, it was the rather late baroque painter of monastic landscapes and kindred scenes, Alessandro Magnasco (1677–1749), who alone, apparently, in our period revived St. Mark's symbolism of Christ at peace with the animals in the wilderness in painting "Christ Ministered to by the Angels" with at least one wild creature pictured at his feet.

[55] There is a considerable literature on and documentation of the eighteenth-century Huguenots, but the wilderness motif is easier to generalize on than to trace. See N. Peyrat, *Histoire des pasteurs du Désert . . . 1685–1789* (Paris, 1842), II, 521. The term "Les Églises du Désert" was the phrasing in the eighteenth century. See D. Ligou, *Documents sur le Protestantisme montalbanais au xviii⁰ siècle* ([Montauban], n.d.), p. v. On the consciousness of "les vaudois nos ancêtres," see *Les Sermons de Paul Rabaut: Pasteur du Désert (1738–1795),* ed. Albert Monod (Paris, n.d.), p. 94; also for the desert motif in general, esp. pp. 93, 136, 146.

Alarm Against Scotland (1682), and of all the harassed preacher-martyrs of the moors who fought the demons of the heath and cave no less than Satan ensconced as Antichrist in the compromised Kirk and the imperious Anglican Church of the burghs (Walter Scott, *Heart of Mid-Lothian,* Chap. XV).

In Sweden, in an entirely different atmosphere, a scholarly prophet quite unlike the fierce Camisard of the Cévennes and the Cameronian of Caledonia, unlike also the rationalist Pietist of Oxford and Bristol, pondered the biblical meaning of the desert. He was Emanuel Swedenborg (1688–1772). Son of a Lutheran bishop, a natural scientist of considerable attainment, he came to devote himself almost exclusively to the study of Scripture and the recruitment of the New Church as a spiritual fraternity of the few who felt called together amid the wilderness of the sects and a (state) church that was itself dried out like a desert. Commenting in *The Apocalypse Explained* (1795)[56] on Revelation 12:6, Swedenborg wrote:

. . . a new church that is called the Holy Jerusalem, and is signified by "the woman," can as yet be instituted only with a few, by reason that the former church is become a desert. . . .

Swedenborg found the natural man guided through a rational phase to a spiritual state by having to face and overcome temptations. Only thus can the true Church of God be formed:

Every man is born natural, and so lives until he becomes rational, and when he has become rational, he can be led by the Lord and become spiritual; and this is effected by the implanting of knowledge of truth from the Word, and at the same time by the opening of the spiritual mind which receives the things of heaven. . . . This opening and conjunction [with a spiritual affection for truth] is possible only through temptations, because in temptations man fights interiorly against the falsities and evils that are in the natural man. In a word, man is brought into the church and becomes a church through temptations. All this was represented by the wandering and leading about of the sons of Israel in the desert.

Swedenborg's spiritualism could be achieved only through the punitive discipline of ecclesiasticism! Never before had the historical sacramental Church been called so unequivocally the Desert in the specific sense of a stage of religion prerequisite to membership in the true New Church. In his commentary on certain wilderness and paradise pas-

---

[56] Published posthumously. Quotations are from the American edition (New York, 1894), pp. 2024, 2034, 2036. Besides this work, Swedenborg wrote on the desert theme in the *Arcana Coelestia* (eight quarto volumes on Genesis and Exodus), *Apocalypse Revealed,* etc.

sages in Isaiah (43:19 f. and 51:3), Swedenborg, the visionary and sometime royal commissioner for mines, went perhaps farther than any other in drawing out the double meaning of the desert in the Old Testament texts.

In Germany, Pietism of the kind that found expression in Pastor Anthony Boehm made extensive use of the wilderness motif. Many Pietists, especially those who took a sectarian and millennialist turn, sought in the wilderness of the West, as we shall see in the next chapter, an opportunity to build up their conventicles. Especially interesting was the relocation of the redemptive wilderness in the East in the lands of Orthodoxy and beyond, a new eschatological orientation connected in part with the romantic aspirations of the Germanies in the Napoleonic age and the period of the Holy Alliance.

It was the German physician and visionary, novelist and friend of Goethe, Johann Heinrich Jung-Stilling (1740–1817), who turned the eyes of many Pietists from the New World to the East and engendered widespread expectations that Russia might be the protecting eagle of the Church of the wilderness in the steppes and desert.[57] In his novel *Das Heimweh* (1795) Jung-Stilling reflected on what he had observed was an inborn homesickness for the land of the rising sun. He described the seven redemptive steps to be taken by the inner man in his return to the original light and hinted guardedly at the need of an external pilgrimage. He saw in the French Revolution a near-final phase in the cosmic struggle before the true Church would be gathered in the East. In *Der Graue Mann* (1814) he quoted Isaiah 64:4 and looked for the Bride of the Lamb, the Woman of the Sun, to assemble her followers in the desert of Samarkand under the protection of Tsar Alexander I after the defeat of Napoleon.[58] Like the Zurich pastor Johann Casper Lavater and the Alsatian philanthropist Johann Friedrich Oberlin, Stilling believed in the eventual salvation of all creatures.

Between 1817 and 1819 a number of Württembergers removed to Asiatic Georgia, founding seven Pietiest communities in the region of the Kur River (perhaps in conscious imitation of the seven churches of Asia), there to await as in a holy land the return of Christ.[59]

---

[57] I am drawing here on the typescript of the Berlin doctoral dissertation by Tatjana Lanko, "Untersuchung des Verhältnisses Jung-Stillings zu Russland und zum 'Osten' während der Regierungszeit Alexanders I" (Marburg, 1954), of which there is a copy in the Bethel College Library, North Newton, Kansas.

[58] "Sie sehen also, dass auch dem Sonnenweib in der Wüste ihr Ort zubereitet wird; der russische Adler wird ihr also die Flügel leihen, mit denen sie dorthin fliegt."

[59] Aaron Williams, *The Harmony Society* (Pittsburgh, 1866), pp. 18–19, 121–123. For the growing belief, especially among the Württembergers, of an eventual salvation of all creatures, including the demons and perhaps also the animals, see the rectoral

Under the influence of Jung-Stilling, many Dutch-Prussian Mennonites also migrated to Russia. One of their settlements was called Alexanderwohl, allegedly from the fact that on their trek in 1821 they encountered the Tsar, who greeted the immigrants and gave them his special blessing for their plans of colonization.[60]

In 1877, after the government canceled some of the special privileges of the Mennonites (and many sought to migrate to America) Claasz Epp, Jr., still under the influence of Jung-Stilling, published *Die entsiegelte Weissagung des Propheten David und die Deutung der Offenbarung Johannis,* urging his followers to move still farther East in an exodus to the unknown, barren wilderness of Turkestan in the heart of Mohammedan territory recently annexed by the Cossacks, there to meet the Lord and inaugurate the millennium.[61]

Turning from the migration eastward and westward in certain German circles especially influenced by the vision of the woman of the wilderness of Revelation 12:6, we come to an extraordinary migration, this time in South Africa, the trek north of the Dutch Boers from British jurisdiction in Cape Town.

It has not yet been determined to what extent the Huguenot settlers (who had been especially prompted to emigrate from France because of their stern religious convictions) contributed to Afrikaaner national self-consciousness as a biblical people. French names are, in any event, very prominent in the formulations. The belligerent spirit[62] of the Camisards and the Cameronians, as well as of the Dutch Sea Beggars, is reproduced in South Africa, all four groups having been sustained by their strongly biblical Calvinism. The full sense of being God's on-going Israel became explicit only after the Huguenots were completely assimilated to the Dutch, and when, as one people, they resisted definitive British control at the end of the Napoleonic period.

In his *Algemene Oproeping* of April 8, 1848, from beyond the British frontier, Andries Pretorius ended with a prayer to him "Who has so long protected us here in the wilderness."[63]

At first the Reformed pastors declined to participate in the trek,

---

address of Ernst Staehelin, *Die Wiederbringung aller Dinge,* Basler Universitatätsreden, No. 45 (Basel, 1960), pp. 28 ff.

[60] Years later when descendants left Russia for the prairies of Kansas, they called their chief settlement New-Alexanderwohl.

[61] See the article by Franz Bartsch on Epp in *The Mennonite Encyclopedia,* II (Scottdale, Pa., 1956), with the literature.

[62] The only comprehensive treatment I have found of the biblical elements in South African nationalism is that of F. A. van Jaarsveld, *Die ontwaking van die Afrikaanse Nasionale Bewussyn 1868-1881* (Johannesburg, 1957), esp. p. 26 with notes.

[63] H. S. Pretorius and D. W. Kruger, eds., *Voortrekker-Argiefstukke 1829-1849* (Pretoria, 1937), p. 314.

which was led by the more violent. One of their grievances was the British abolition of slavery.[64] But because of this biblical ideology, trekkers greatly desired "pastors and teachers for the extension of Christ's Kingdom" to labor "in the almost utterly devastated vineyard."[65] Though the government of Britain was stronger than they, they felt the power and divine sanction of the Israelites, who, though they had to wander about in the desert for forty years, in the end came to power in Canaan.[66]

The letters of Andrew Murray, the Scottish Free Church Presbyterian who for the most part sympathized with the more moderate of the trekkers, preserve glimpses into the mood of the Afrikaaners. They considered themselves carried away into the wilderness, where they were enabled to see, on the basis of a marginal note in their *Statenvertaling* of the Bible, that the ten horns of Revelation 17:3 and 12 referred to kings of ten nations in Europe (exclusive of Holland), collectively representing the Beast. In their trek northward they considered themselves "Jerusalem pilgrims."

Next day [wrote Murray, November 27, 1850] I took my seat upon the waggonbox, while some forty Boers stood round to put me on trial. [A book by William] à Brakel [d. 1711], a Reformed theologian of irreproachable orthodoxy, . . . was brought forward, and all sorts of nonsensical demonstrations about the duty of coming out of Antichrist were urged, in order to prove that I could not be a true minister till I came out from under the English Government to this side of the Vaal River. . . . On Monday there was again a public dispute with the part of those who wish to go to Jerusalem. . . . The three heroes came forward, and immediately began to prove that England is a horn of the beast (Rev. 17:3), and that I could not be a true servant of Christ.[67]

Just before and during the Boer War (1899–1902) the biblical self-consciousness of the Afrikaaners was intensified. A sermon by C. Spoelstra in Pretoria on June 13, 1897, based on Isaiah 5 is a rich tapestry of biblio-political ideology.[68] The preacher reminded his congregation of the many parallels between the Afrikaaners and the Israelites, so often noted by friend and foe alike. Insisting that the Boers divided by the British frontier must become again one people, Judah

---

[64] See Anna Stienkamp (sister of Piet Retrief) in "Journal of our Migration," printed by J. Bird, *Annals of Natal, 1495 to 1845* (Pietermaritzburg, 1888), I, 459.
[65] *Vortrekker-Argiefstukke*, pp. 363 ff.
[66] *Ibid.*, p. 365.
[67] J. Du Plessis, *The Life of Andrew Murray* (London, 1919), p. 121. See also his letter of November 22, 1849, *ibid.*, p. 103.
[68] Printed in full in his *Het Kerkelijk en Godsdinstig leven der Boeren na den Grooten Trek* (Kampen, 1915), pp. 383 ff.

and Israel reunited, the Boer preacher went on to liken his people to the wasted vineyard of his Isaianic text and contended that the noble vines had grown wild despite the loving care of the heavenly Gardener, and that their failure to obey his commandments would account for the temporary blasting of Afrikaaner national destiny; he exhorted them to repent and return to the disciplined way of their fathers lest utter disaster befall.

Writing in 1915, after the Boer War and interpreting defeat as a divine chastisement, the same pastor Spoelstra could still look forward, *soli Deo gloria,* to the time when the Dutch-Afrikaaner race, predestined to extend into the wilderness and desert "from the Cape to Cairo," would expand to North Africa and "the sons of Calvin reach out their hands to the children of Augustine."[69]

Other Christian nations have appropriated the image of ancient Israel, especially in strengthening the ideal of liturgical kinship, as idealized in the reigns of David and Solomon. But the Dutch South Africans are the only nation to have taken Israel on the march in the wilderness of Exodus and the Church fleeing into the wilderness of Revelation as major ingredients in the shaping of national self-consciousness—except for the Americans.

Apart from an occasional allusion, the development of the wilderness motif in American history has been segregated from the account thus far, in order that it might be presented as a unit in the last section of the survey.

[69] *Ibid.,* p. 15.

Chapter V. The Enclosed Garden in the Wilderness of the New World

In the retrospect of the nineteenth century the epic gathering of a mighty Christian nation beginning in the scattered settlements of the eastern seaboard, a nation made up of peoples fleeing in successive generations from the bondage of the Old World across the Atlantic Ocean to a land of promise and of liberty, has been seen as a providential repetition, in majestic, continental proportions, of the exodus of God's ancient elect from bondage to Egypt. To be an American has been for successive immigrant generations to know a new birth of freedom. In fact, first citizenship papers have been for countless yearning thousands the outward sign of an invisible change of allegiance, a sense of belonging within the covenant of a new people of destiny. This sense of being a new people who had sloughed off the accents and the attributes of the Old World was perpetuated within these families unto the second and even the third generation. But if America has been for them the community of rebirth, the Old World churches brought over with them have represented the community, so to speak, of birth, their native land. In them they found weekly solace from their being buffeted about in a new world whose ways and words, though fascinating, were not immediately understood; and during the Sunday sermon or mass their homesick hearts were drawn not only upwards to the Jerusalem above but also backwards and across to the villages and hills of their homeland whence came also their inner strength. The immigrant church, to speak collectively, was the conservative, ethnico-cultural community of birth. No broad interpretation of American culture and American denominationalism can be complete without a full documentation of this epic reversal of, or at least continuous strain upon, the respective roles of church and commonwealth in the unfolding of American society.

But the interpretation in terms of the biblical exodus of the Pilgrim crossing of the Atlantic and later the trek of the pioneers from the eastern seaboard settlements into the opening West has in point of fact been largely an interpretation by the Revolutionary generation and their descendants. In the colonial period, it was not the wilderness of Sinai that the New England forefathers had mostly in mind, but rather much more commonly the eschatologically oriented conception of the wilderness in Revelation 12:6 and the mystically saturated imagery of the wilderness in Canticles and the allied texts of the pre-exilic prophets. Thus the fourth chapter of our survey is entitled "The Enclosed Garden in the Wilderness."

In the previous chapter we reached modern times in the development of the wilderness theme and followed several sectarian groups in their attempts to realize their ideal not only in Europe, Asia, and Africa, but also in the New World. In the present chapter we shall be exclusively concerned with the New World, especially with the American mind as it has been shaped by the tradition and religious presuppositions of New England. The most distinctive of these presuppositions was the conception of the Puritans (shared and clearly enunciated, as we have already noted, by John Milton) that they were inaugurating a new age of the Church, a new Reformation.[1] The Pilgrim Father John Robinson, in his farewell speech at Delft on July 21, 1620, articulated this conviction in the oft-quoted promise "of more light yet to breake forth":

For my part, I cannot sufficiently bewail the condition of the reformed Churches, who . . . will go at present no further than the instruments of their first Reformation. The Lutherans cannot be drawn to go beyond what Luther saw: whatever part of his will our good God has imparted and revealed unto Calvin, they will rather die than embrace it. And the Calvinists, you see, stick fast where they were left by that great man of God, who yet saw not all things.

This is a misery much to be lamented; for though they were burning and shining lights in their times; yet they penetrated not into the whole counsel of God, but were they now living, they would be as willing to embrace further light, as that which they first received.[2]

Pilgrims and Puritans thought of this re-reformed Church as taking shape like a garden in the protective wilderness of the New World.

It was, for example, in commentary on Canticles 6:2 about the beloved as a garden that the Boston Puritan divine John Cotton (d. 1652) took occasion to make clear over against the churches of the Old World in what sense the self-disciplined churches of the New were the gardens of the Lord:

[1] See notably Ernst Benz' article "Ecumenical Relations between Boston Puritanism and German Pietism: Cotton Mather and August Hermann Francke," *Harvard Theological Review;* also his preliminary article in *Church History* (August, 1961), XX, 28–55.

[2] As quoted by Cotton Mather in *Magnalia Christi Americana* (Hartford edition of 1855), I, 64. Mather put in the first person the account of Robinson's speech recalled by Edward Winslow twenty-six years after the event and printed in his *Hypocrisie Unmasked* (London, 1646).

Wittenberge was a meaner place then Rome, or Constantinople, or Alexandria, or Hierusalem, or Antioch, where Christ had formerly his pleasant gardens. Yea, in this [respect] the garden or Church at Wittenberge was inferiour to the primitive Churches before Constantine, for they were gardens enclosed (Canticles 4:12), not so Wittenberge.[3]

The larger cultural implications of the Puritan quest in the wilderness of the New World for the garden enclosed can be seen at a glance if, in the terms of the present essay, we contrast it with the search on the part of the Spaniards and the Portuguese for the terrestrial paradise to the south. The sectarian Calvinist cultivators of the garden in the primeval wilderness and the Iberian Catholic conquistadors in search of El Dorado in his terrestrial paradise, having set out from the Old World with different objectives, laid down such contrasting patterns of life in the two new continents that to the present day these two impulses, even in their completely secularized versions, namely, the paradisic motif in the exploration and colonization of South America and the wilderness motif in the colonization of (sectarian) English North America, provide us with a refined set of keys for the unlocking of certain parts of Latin and English New World civilizations which would be inaccessible to the blunter or more standardized keys, such as the contrasting pair: Catholic and Protestant.

While the Calvinist John Cotton of Boston, expounding Canticles, thought of the new plantation of Puritan churches coming up out of the wilderness of the New World as collectively a garden enclosed, "a Paradise, as if this were the garden of Eden," the priests, monks, and friars in the exploring parties to the south were sustained by the vision of an earthly paradise merely waiting to be gained.[4] Thus Catholic Christopher Columbus was prompted to report to his sovereigns that he had almost certainly discovered the terrestrial paradise.

We shall not go into the development in Latin America, except to note that Columbus knew from Genesis 2:8 that the Lord God had planted a garden eastward in Eden; and, basing his further calculations on Pierre d'Ailly's *Imago Mundi,* he was prepared to find the terrestrial paradise at the first point of the Far East where the sun rose on the day of creation near the stem-prominence of the supposedly pear-shaped earth. To his royal patrons he wrote:

[3] *A Brief Exposition with Practical Observations Upon the whole Book of Canticles* (London, 1655), p. 164.
[4] The "Edenic" motif in the discovery and colonization of Latin America has been most recently presented by Sergio Buarque de Hollanda, *Visão do Paraíso: Os Motivos Edênicos no Descobrimento e Colonização do Brasil* (Rio de Janeiro, 1959).

I have already described my ideas concerning this hemisphere and its form, and I have no doubt, that if I could pass below the equinoctial line . . . I should find the earthly paradise, whither no one can go but by God's permission; but this land which your Highnesses have now sent me to explore, is very extensive, and I think there are many other countries in the south, of which the world has never had any knowledge. I do not suppose that the earthly paradise is in the form of a rugged mountain, as the descriptions of it have made it appear, but that it is on the summit of the spot, which I have described. . . . I think also, that the water I have described may proceed from it, though it be far off, and that stopping at the place which I have just left, it forms this lake. There are great indications of this being the terrestrial paradise, for its site coincides with the opinion of the holy and wise theologians whom I have mentioned. . . .[5]

With this glimpse into the mood of the great explorer of milder climes we return to the sterner mood of the Bay Colony, where the "desert" theme in its theological (as well as literal) sense appears in almost every imprint from the colonial period.[6]

1. Choice Grain in the Wilderness of New England

John Eliot (d. 1690) of Roxbury, apostle to the Indians, will at once make us more familiar with the northern mood. In his refutation of the charge in England that the Puritans were new fangled, he puns: The "Novangles are not New Fangles but No Fangles (in respect to worship)"; and he goes on to say that they have come purposely into the barren wilderness in just their present location on the Bay, neither further north where furs are plentiful, nor to the south where the warm sun makes both for gold and tobacco:

Assuredly [he goes on] the better part of our plantations did undertake the

---

[5] *Select Letters of Christopher Columbus,* tr. and ed. R. H. Major (2nd ed., London, 1870), pp. 140–143. George Boas has edited the paradisic material in his anthology with interpretation, *Essays on Primitivism and Related Ideas in the Middle Ages* (Baltimore, 1948).

For the medieval and Byzantine antecedents, see Milton Anastos, "Pletho, Strabo, and Columbus," *Mélanges Henri Grégoire* (Brussels, 1952), IV, 1–18, and Leonardo Olschki, *Storia Letteria delle Scoperte Geografiche: Studi e Richerche* (Florence, 1937).

[6] Though often noticed, the first systematic study of it is that of Alan Heimert, "Puritanism, the Wilderness, and the Frontier," *New England Quarterly,* XXVI (1953), 361. He points out that at first the Pilgrims and Puritans thought of America as a promised land, then as a wilderness through which to pass into Zion. Heimert was not in a position to sort out the diverse scriptural meanings of the wilderness and the solid tapestry woven of them on the ancient loom of mystical and sectarian piety.

Perry Miller has recognized the importance of the theme by using it poetically in his collection of essays, *Errand into the Wilderness* (Cambridge, 1956), and Kenneth Murdock likewise recognized its prominence in entitling his article "Clio in the Wilderness: History and Biography in Puritan New England," *Church History,* XXIV (1955).

enterprise with a suffering minde . . . to go into a wilderness where nothing appeareth but hard labour, wants, and wilderness-temptations (stumble not countrymen, at the repetition of that word, wilderness-temptations), of which it is written that they are trying times and places, Deuteronomy 8. There must be more then golden hopes to bear up the godly wise in such an undertaking, but when the injoyment of Christ in his pure Ordinances is better to the soul than all worldly comforts, then these things are but light afflictions. . . .[7]

Yankee frugality is not only a consequence of the climate but a biblical interpretation of the proper dress and deportment of the elect in the wilderness state.

The work from which we have quoted appears in a larger publication on the Indians as Judah scattered westward. The title-page quotes Canticles 8:8 on the little sister without breasts in application to the admittedly still immature spiritual state of the bewildered descendants of Judah. But Eliot was confident that their speech, which he had mastered the better to proclaim the gospel among them, was akin to Hebrew, which he knew well and thought of not only as the divine and the primordial language but also as the universal tongue of the future of mankind.

Thomas Shepard in nearby Cambridge was likewise concerned for the evangelization of the Indians, and the sympathizing editor in England introduced Shepard's *Clear Sunshine of the Gospell, Breaking forth upon the Indians in New England* (1648) with these words:

. . . there can be no reason given why God should fence us, and suffer other places to lye wast, that we [white Englishmen] should bee his Garden, and other places a Wilderness, that he should feed us with the bread of Heaven, and suffer others to starve.

He then used Paul's argument (Romans 11:14) about the conversion of the Gentiles with a new twist:

Let these poor Indians stand up incentives to us, as the Apostle set up the Gentiles a provocation to the Iews: who knows but God gave life to New England to quicken [the] Old . . . ?[8]

Another, more radical Puritan, Roger Williams (d. 1682 or 1683), likewise conspicuously concerned for the Indians, was the American counterpart of the English Seeker John Jackson, already quoted. In

[7] John Eliot, "The Learned Conjectures touching the Americas," in Thomas Thorowgood, *Iews in America, or, Probabilities That the Americans are of that Race* (London, 1650), Part II, p. 23.
[8] In Edmund Calamy's editorial letter to the reader.

his *Key into the Language of America* (1643) Williams offered not only a dictionary of Indian words and phrases but also valuable observations on life in the wilderness and reflections on its theological meaning.[9] The orderly "Mould or forme of Government" among the aborigines and their relatively high sexual and family morality despite their nakedness prompted him to place a poem on their lips:

> We weare no Cloaths, have many Gods,
>   And yet our sinnes are lesse:
> You are Barbarians, Pagans wild,
>   *Your* Land's the Wilderness.[10]

Observing the fruitfulness of the American wilderness, Williams turned to rebuke his fellow European:

> The Wildernesse remembers this [God's command],
>   The wild and howling land
> Answers the toyling labour of,
>   The wildest Indians hand.
> But man [in Christian Europe] forgets his Maker, who,
>   Framed him in Righteousnesse.
> A paradise in Paradise, now worse
>   Then Indian wildernesse.

No pantheist but a mystical Calvinist with a deep sense of God's sovereignty as Creator of the universe, Williams read the book of the wilderness with its emblems much as he read Scripture typologically, as though it were a vast palimpsest unrolled before him. On one level of legibility he observed: "As the same Sun shines on the Wildernesse that doth on a Garden so the same faithfull and all sufficient God, can comfort, feede and safely guide even through a desolate howling Wilderness." Or again: "How sweetly doe all the severall sorts of Heavens Birds, in all Coasts of the World, preach unto Men the prayse of their Makers Wisedome, Power, and Goodness, who feedes them and their young ones Summer and Winter . . . ?" But on the more obscure level he discerned the lineaments of the fallen world: "The Wildernesse is a cleere resemblance of the world, where greedie and furious men persecute and devoure the harmlesse and innocent as the wilde

[9] Perry Miller calls him "Prophet in the Wilderness" and remarks concerning him: "No other New England writer makes quite so much of an incantation out of the very word 'wilderness.' . . ." *Roger Williams: His Contribution to the American Tradition* (Indianapolis, New York, 1953), p. 52.

[10] From the edition in *Publications* of the Narragansett Club, 1st ser. (Providence, 1866), I, 167. The same theme appears on p. 146: "The best clad English-man, Not cloth'd with Christ, more naked is: Than naked Indian." The quotations which follow from *A Key* are from pp. 126, 103, 118, and 130.

beasts pursue and devour the Hinds and Roes." Thus the ambiguity of the desert in the Old Testament reasserted itself in Williams' understanding of the wilderness of the New World.

Driven from Congregational Salem into a Providentially prepared wilderness, Williams turned quickly from a three-months experiment with believers' baptism in Providence to a mature Seekerism, despairing of the rival pretensions of mutually exclusive sects. He interpreted Revelation 6:19, from which the "white horsemen" of the earlier chapters (understood to be the apostles of Christ) are absent, as indicative of the "routing of the Church and Ministry of Christ Jesus, put to flight, and returned into the Wildernesse of desolation."[11] He was convinced that

there were no churches since those founded by the apostles and evangelists, nor could there be any, nor any pastors ordained, nor seals administered but by such, and that the Church was to want these all the time she continued in the Wilderness.

Unlike the Quakers, Williams recognized both a "nurturing" and a "generating" ministry. The latter he knew was possible only when the ministers were truly sent, in other words, apostles. He beheld no apostles at work in his world; but he still looked for the coming of truly apostolic men. In the meantime against George Fox he contended that

. . . there is a time of the coming out of the Babylonian Apostacy & Wilderness: there is a time of many Flocks pretending to be Christs and saying [Matt. 24:26]: Loe here he is &c. and a Command of Christ Jesus, goe not into the Wilderness, goe not into the private Chambers: There is a time when Christ Jesus his doves and loves cry out to him, O thou whome my Soule loveth, tell me where thou feedest, where thou makest thy Flock to rest at noon. . . .[12]

Against the godly commonwealth of the Bay Colony, Williams averred that the Puritans there "make the [enclosed] garden and the wilderness (as often I have intimated)—I say, the garden and the wilderness, the church and the world all one." He continued:

The unknowing zeale of Constantine and other Emperours, did more hurt to Christ Jesus his Crowne and Kingdome, then the raging fury of the most bloody Neroes. In the persecutions of the latter, Christians were sweet and fragrant, like spice pounded and beaten in morters: But those good

[11] *The Hireling Ministry* (London, 1652), p. 2.
[12] *George Fox Digg'd Out of His Burrowes* (1676), ed. Lewis Diman (Providence, 1872), pp. 103 f.

Emperours, persecuting some erroneous persons, Arrius, &c. and advancing the professours of some Truths of Christ (for there was no small number of Truths lost in those times) and maintaining their Religion by the materiall Sword, I say by this meanes Christianity was ecclipsed, and the Professours of it fell asleep, Cant. 5. Babel or confusion was usher'd in, and by degrees the Gardens of the Churches of Saints were turned into the wildernesse of whole Nations, untill the whole World became Christian or Christendome, Revel. 12 & 13.[18]

Sir Henry Vane, governor of Massachusetts Bay and leader of the Long Parliament, sympathetic with Antinomians and Seekers in old and New England, completely interiorized the Kingdom of God as a state of conscience; but like Williams he understood the wilderness as a real place outside the mind where the eschatological combat was to be fought out "between the seed of the woman and the seed of the serpent":

The Kingdom of God is within you and is the dominion of God in the conscience and spirit of the mind. . . . This Kingdom of Christ is capable of subsisting and being managed inwardly in the minds of His people, in hidden state concealed from the world. . . . Those that are in this Kingdom, and in whom the power of it is, are fitted to fly with the Church into the wilderness, and to continue in such a solitary, dispersed, desolate condition till God call them out of it. They have wells and springs opened to them in the wilderness, whence they draw the waters of salvation, without being in bondage to the life of sense.[14]

The principal opponent of Williams was one with whom Antinomians and Seekers knew they had much in common, John Cotton. We now return to him and to other, more typical New England Puritans who, unlike Eliot, Shepard, and Williams, were not much interested in the evangelization of the Indians in the wilderness.

But in the conception of the garden in the wilderness Williams and Cotton were, as in the following quotation from Cotton, virtually interchangeable:

. . . under the Christian Emperors, Constantine and the rest opened the doors of the Church so wide, that all the garden of God was become a wilderness by an inundation of carnall people, Christian in name, but Pagans in heart, that were let in; and then that which was once a garden enclosed, was now made a wildernesse. . . .[15]

---

[18] *The Bloudy Tenent of Persecution* . . . (London, 1644); section headed "A Reply to the aforesaid *Answer* of Mr. Cotton," Chap. LXIV, p. 95.

[14] From *An Epistle to the Mystical Body of Christ on Earth: The Church Universal in Babylon* (London, 1662).

[15] *The Powring Out of the Seven Vials or an Exposition of the 16. Chapter of the Revelation, with an Application of it to our Times* (London, 1642), IV, 11.

In his *Exposition of Canticles,* as already indicated, Cotton dealt extensively with the Church as the garden amid the wilderness (3:6, 8:5 ff.). Though without express reference to the American situation, he returned to the claim made by the early Church of being the provisional paradise:

. . . All the world is a wildernesse, or at least a wilde field; onely, the Church is Gods garden or orchard, in these three respects,

First, as the garden of Paradise was the habitation of Adam in the estate of innocence, so is the Church of all those who are renewed into innocency.

Secondly, as in the garden were all manner of pleasant and wholesome hearbs and trees growing, so in the Church are all manner of usefull and savoury spirits.

Thirdly, as a man walketh in his garden to refresh himselfe; so doth Christ walke in his Church, yea calleth his friends thither to walke with him.[16]

At home in the medieval monastic-sectarian tradition, Cotton rejoiced in the wilderness state as conducive to greater spiritual perspicuity. In introducing the work of a fellow New Englander on their Congregational Way to those of the Reformed Churches in Britain and on the Continent, Cotton wrote confidently:

Let no one despise this as the inelegant production of exiled and abandoned brethren, as long as it can be said of them, as Jehoshaphat (II Kings 3:12) once said of Elisha, who was living temporarily in the wilderness of Edom: "The word of the Lord is with him." John, the beloved disciple of Christ, writes that he himself was carried away into the wilderness that he might see more clearly not only the judgment of the great whore but also the coming down from heaven of the chaste bride, the New Jerusalem (Revelation 17:11, 21:2).[17]

The book which Cotton thus introduced was *The Answer to* [the Dutch divine] *Apollonius* by the Ipswich pastor John Norton, designated for the task. In this work another feature of the New England wilderness theme was programmatically expressed, over against the Anglican right and the Baptist left. At issue with the Baptists, though otherwise Calvinistic, was believers' baptism. Norton used the practice

---

On the garden-wilderness theme see further, Elizabeth Hirsch, "John Cotton and Roger Williams," *Church History,* X (1941), 382.

[16] *Op. cit.,* London edition of 1642, p. 130.

[17] Foreword to John Norton's *The Answer to . . . Apollonius* (Latin: London, 1648), tr. and ed. Douglas Horton (Cambridge, 1958), p. 14.

of the wilderness church of old Israel as a precedent for that of the new, and contended that the offspring of covenanted parents were already by virtue of their birth members of Christ's Church. The uncircumcised Israelites were called "the congregation (*ekklesia*) in the wilderness" (Acts 7:38). Hence, "the church may [even] be deprived of baptism for a time and yet remain a [true] church."[18]

Against the *de jure divino* Episcopalians Norton was, of course, adamant, but he deplored the bitter disagreements on polity among those who could broadly regard themselves as Reformed, and went so far as to hold that the

discord of brothers about the polity of the Gospel holds Christ away from his dominion, keeps the woman [the true Church] in the wilderness, and the [Anglican-Papal] harlot on the throne.[19]

The provisional though protective character of the wilderness state based upon Revelation was clearly reflected in a speech on the wharf, in England, preserved by Edward Johnson, which may well have been his own on departing: "I am now prest for the service of our Lord Christ, to re-build the most glorious Edifice of Mount Sion in a Wildernesse [cf. Isaiah 61:4], and as John Baptist, I must cry, prepare yee the way of the Lord, make his paths strait, for behold hee is comming againe, he is comming to destroy Antichrist, and give the whore double to drinke the very dregs of his wrath [Revelation 18:6]."[20]

And William Stoughton (1631–1701) in an election sermon in Boston in 1668 or 1669 stamped a phrase which has remained indelible in the memory of his descendants to this day: "God sifted a whole nation that he might send choice grain over into the wilderness."[21]

By the end of the colonial and the beginning of the provincial history of Massachusetts Cotton Mather (d. 1727 or 1728), still filled with hope for the holy experiment and yet depressed by the vagaries which even the Puritans were not spared, reflected in his extensive writings the full ambiguity of the meaning of the desert and wilderness in the Old Testament and the New. In one mood he held that the North American wilderness was ordained by Providence as a refuge and pro-

[18] We have met this argument already (though actually for a later day) in the irenic Baptist John Bunyan. Horton, *op. cit.*, p. 49, n. 3, traces this argument in Norton back to William Perkins, *Cases of Conscience* (London, 1606), Bk. 2, Chap. 9, qu. 1, sec. 1.

[19] *Op. cit.*, p. 6.

[20] *A History of New England: From the English Planting in the Yeare 1628 untill the Yeare 1652* . . . (London, 1653); reprinted and ed. by J. F. Jameson as *The Wonder-Working Providence* (New York, 1910), p. 52.

[21] *New England's True Interest, Not to Lie* (Boston, 1668–1669), p. 19.

tection of the Reformed Church. In the other he thought of the wilderness as the empire of Antichrist, filled with frightful hazards and the demonic minions of Satan.

In the latter frame of mind, in *The Wonders of the Invisible World* (1693), a discourse based on Revelation 12:12, he wrote:

The first Planters of these Colonies were a Chosen Generation of men, who were first so Pure, as to disrelish many things which they thought wanted Reformation elsewhere; and yet withal so peaceable, that they Embraced a Voluntary Exile in a Squalid, horrid, American Desart, rather than to Live in Contentions with their Brethren. . . . The New-Englanders are a People of God settled in those, which were once the Devil's Territories; and it may easily be supposed that the Devil was Exceddingly disturbed, when he perceived such a people here accomplishing the Promise of old made unto our Blessed Jesus, That He should have the Utmost parts of the Earth for His possession. . . . The Devil thus Irritated, immediately try'd all sorts of Methods to overturn this poor Plantation and so much of the Church, as was Fled into this Wilderness [Revelation 12], immediately found, The Serpent cast out of his Mouth a Flood for the carrying of it away.[22]

Witchcraft in Salem was clearly the work of Satan. Here we find very much alive the Old Testament feeling for the desert as the haunt of death and the demonic. Being interested in the sciences of his day, Mather charged Satan and his devils with holding up the invention of such wholesome scientific aids and comforts as spectacles, the printing press, and the telescope.[23] In the American wilderness he felt surrounded by devils and also the red savages who were in the service of the French-Catholic Antichrist:

The Wilderness thro' which we are passing to the Promised Land [he continues] is all over fill'd with Fiery flying serpents. . . . All our way to Heaven, lies by the Dens of Lions, and the Mounts of Leopards [Canticles 4:8]; there are incredible Droves of Devils in our way.

In *The Devil Discovered* (1693), he noted that it was precisely "when he was alone in the Wilderness" that Satan "fell upon our Lord." And more fully in *Magnalia Christi Americana or The Ecclesiastical History of New England* (1702), he said:

It is written concerning our Lord Jesus Christ that he was led into the wilderness to be tempted of the devil; and the people of the Lord Jesus

22 *Op. cit.*, folio 5b.
23 *Ibid.*, pp. 16 f.

Christ, led into the wilderness of New England, have not only met with continual temptation of the devil there; the wilderness having always had serpents in it; but also they have had in almost every new lustre of years, a new assault of extraordinary temptation upon them; a more than common hour and power of darkness.[24]

But besides the demon-infested howling desert, Cotton Mather shared and significantly propagated the idea that in the wilderness of North America James I had as the unwitting instrument of Providence given in letters patent "all that part of America, lying . . . from forty degrees . . . to the forty-eighth degree . . . throughout all the firm lands *from sea to sea*" as "the spot of earth, which the God of heaven spied out for the seat of such evangelical, and ecclesiastical, and very remarkable transactions, as require to be made an history; here 'twas that our blessed Jesus intended a resting place, must I say? or only a hiding place for those reformed Churches, which have given him a little accomplishment of his eternal Father's promise upon him; to be, we hope, yet further accomplished, *of having the utmost parts of the earth for his possession?*" Mather had at this point already declared his intention of writing the history to date "of a New-English Israel" and now went on to be eschatologically specific, however modestly, namely, "an history of some feeble attempts made in the American hemisphere to anticipate the state of the New-Jerusalem, as far as the unavoidable vanity of human affairs and influence of Satan upon them would allow. . . ."[25] Cotton Mather, like the English Independents, drew inspiration from the Waldensians.

Revising the traditional formula and reposing his hope in "Light from the West," Cotton Mather was neither a proto-nationalist nor a narrow sectarian. Inspired by the Pietist vision mediated by his German-English correspondent Anthony Boehm, Mather had an ecumenical view of the spiritually re-Reformed churches. In his sermon *American Tears upon the Ruines of the Greek Church* (1701), he manifested his concern for the regeneration of Eastern Orthodoxy; and in his sermon *A Joyful Sound Reaching to both the Indias* before the (still extant) Society for the Propagating of the Gospel in New England, he summarized Johann Arndt's *Evangelium aeternum* in three points for the Indians and went on to interpret his own age, in which Protestantism was being awakened to its missionary duties, as an age of the Spirit pouring out gifts upon young men and old.

Perhaps the most sober and authentically scriptural balance in inter-

[24] Edition of Hartford, 1855, in two volumes, II, 426.
[25] *Ibid.*, I, 44, 46.

preting the negative and positive senses of the desert for New Englanders was struck by John Higginson (1616–1708) in his "Attestation" printed as a foreword to the *Magnalia,* wherein he presented the ten reasons why his colleague Cotton Mather had undertaken the *Magnalia.* Four of the reasons advanced for the writing of the book admirably summarize the theological meaning which the wilderness held for New Englanders as they looked back on their heroic period:

That the present generation may remember the way wherein the Lord hath led his people in this wilderness, for so many years past unto this day; [according to Deuteronomy 8:2 . . .]. All considering persons cannot but observe, that our wilderness-condition hath been full of humbling, trying, distressing providences. . . .

[That] whereas it may be truly said, (as Jeremiah 2:3, 21) that when this people began to follow the Lord unto this wilderness, they were holiness to the Lord, and he planted them as a noble vine; yet if in process of time, when they are greatly increased and multiplied, they should so far degenerate, as to forget the religious design of their fathers, and forsake the holy ways of God . . . then this Book may be a witness against them. . . .

That the little daughter [without breasts, Canticles] of New-England in America, may bow down herself to her mother [the Spouse] England, in Europe, presenting this memorial unto her; assuring her, that though by some of her angry brethren, she was forced to make a local secession; yet not a separation, but hath always retained a dutiful respect to the Church of God in England; and giving some account to her, how graciously the Lord has dealt with herself in "a remote wilderness.". . .

That this present history may stand as a monument, in relation to future times, of a fuller and better reformation of the Church of God, than it hath yet appeared in the world. For by this Essay it may be seen, that a farther practical reformation than that which began at the first coming out of the darkness of Popery, was aimed at, and endeavoured by a great number of voluntary exiles, that came into a wilderness for that very end, that hence they might be free from human additions and inventions in the worship of God, and might produce the positive part of divine institutions, according to the word of God. . . .[26]

Higginson and Mather like Robinson and Cotton before them, still awaited a second reformation preparatory to the final building up of Zion.

Jonathan Edwards (1703–1758) was likewise bent upon reformation, but like his contemporary John Wesley he largely interiorized and individualized the meaning of wilderness; and for him the promised

[26] *Ibid.,* I, 13 and 16. Higginson had also written his own history, *The Cause of God and the People in New-England* (1663).

land was heaven and not a realizable godly commonwealth. The revival which he preached was the ordained means of coming out of the wilderness of the world. In his sermon "The True Christian's Life, A Journey Towards Heaven,"[27] Edwards appropriately used Hebrews (11:13 f.), which anciently represented the stages of the exodus as the rungs of a ladder:

The land that we have to travel through is a wilderness; there are many mountains, rockes, and rough places that we must go over in the way; and there is a necessity that we should lay out our strength. . . .

What better end can you propose to your journey than to obtain heaven? Here you are placed in this world, in this wilderness, and have your choice given you, that you may travel which way you please. And there is one way which leads to heaven. . . .

If we spend our lives so as to [be] only a journeying towards heaven, this will be the way to have death, that is the end of the journey, an entrance into heaven, not terrible but comfortable. . . . Is it terrible for him [the traveler] to think that he is almost got to his journey's end? . . . Were the children of Israel sorry, after forty years travel in the Wilderness, when they had almost got to Canaan?

The demythologizing of the biblical term *wilderness* merely to denote the disciplines of life and the world to which the believers should never become too much attached was not the whole of Edwards' theology of nature; for in fact he saw everywhere about him signs and emblems of the Creator, and his observations and intuitions prepared the ground in New England for a more positive view of nature at the end of his century.

But the more spectacular change in the meaning of the wilderness was the belated appropriation of the exodus motif in interpreting the achievement and aspiration of the restive colonies over against the mother country.

With the Treaty of Quebec in 1763 and the subsequent generous concessions made to the Catholics by the British in the north, the fear of Catholicism was suddenly intensified, especially in New England. An Ipswich New Light pastor, John Cleaveland, who opposed both the theology of Jonathan Mayhew and the political policy of the royal governor Thomas Hutchinson, signed his articles in the Essex *Gazette* as "Johannes in Eremo."[28]

As the break with Britain approached, some of the language formerly

---

[27] Sermon XXXVI, *Works*, IV, see esp. 515, 582.
[28] Noted by Alice Baldwin, *The New England Clergy and the American Revolution* (Durham, N.C., 1928), pp. 144 f.

used of Rome was transferred to the Anglican Tories. Escape from bondage to Pharaoh became a stock allusion in the sermons preached annually before the uniformed militia on Lexington green in commemoration of the decisive action of April 19, 1775.

In 1776 the patriot preacher Samuel Sherwood (1730–1783) of Lexington delivered a sermon, "The Church's Flight into the Wilderness: An Address on the Times," in which he enlarged on the persecuted Waldensians and their Protestant successors and expressed the belief that the American wilderness was the refuge reserved by Providence.[29]

When Samuel Cooke (1739–1783) of nearby Arlington came to commemorate in a sermon the opening action which he had himself witnessed, he was filled with righteous indignation at the barbarity of the British; and, choosing as his text Isaiah 10:1–13, he gave expression to the deep biblical conviction that Britain must have been the rod of God's anger against the colonists for their moral failings. But in another sermon based on John 21:15–19 after the Revolution seemed assured, he voiced the more popular conviction that God in his providence had great hopes for his Reformed people gathering as a new nation in what had been a howling wilderness. Cooke was so fascinated by the wilderness theme that on one occasion he even spoke of "Satan, whom the Indians worshipped," as having driven Christ into the wilderness, where Satan raised "armies of fierce and devouring beasts to tear Him in pieces or at least with the Indians roaring."[30] Cooke virtually identified the apostolic and early Christian martyrs, the dissenters of the seventeenth century, and the patriots who had recently given their lives to separate Reformed America from episcopal and oppressive England as alike members of the true Church Militant and as the Bride of Christ. Turning to Revelation 6:9–11 in reference to the souls of those slain for the Word of God who cry out in vengeance, Cooke predicted that the "martyrs" of the Revolution "should rest yet for a little season, until their fellow servants also and their brethren that

---

[29] As late as 1844 George Junkin, Presbyterian divine and president of three colleges in Virginia, Pennsylvania, and Ohio, in his *The Little Stone and the Great Image* averred that the wilderness of Revelation 12:6 was America, providing sanctuary for Huguenots from France, the Scots, the English Independents, and other godly Reformed refugees from the scarlet woman and the red dragon. And in the same year the music press of Oliver Ditson sang in *The Puritan's Mistake* (1844) the anti-Anglican Republican lines:

"Oh, we are weary pilgrims; to this wilderness we bring
A Church without a bishop, a State without a king."

Sherwood, Junkin, and many other eschatologically sustained nationalistic divines, on the eve of the Revolution and in the early national period, are admirably treated by LeRoy Edwin Froom, *The Prophetic Faith of Our Fathers* (Washington, 1950), III, IV.

[30] The whole sermon has been transcribed by Elizabeth Abbot Smith as "Sermon on the Wilderness," and is deposited at the public library in Arlington, Massachusetts.

should be killed [in the Revolution] . . . should be fulfilled."

Cooke then goes on to identify the martyr church, the church in the wilderness assailed by the dragon, as the new *nation:*

But the Gates of Hell have not, nor shall they ever be able to overthrow ye Church of Christ, it being founded on him who is ye rock of ages. The blood of the martyrs has been ye seed of ye Church. Our pious forefathers were driven into this wilderness [Revelation 12:6] by the persecuting rage of the High Church party in Britain. But Christ over-ruled the wicked and cruel designs of his adversaries [Satan and his minions], to advance his own kingdom, by erecting and establishing his Churches in these benighted parts of his world. May the King of Glory still defend us and add to his churches such as shall be saved!

We trust in this day of distress that God will remember for us the kindness of our Youth: as for Jeremiah [2:2], when our fathers followed him into the Wilderness, then a land not sown. Christ is now calling us as he did the Apostles and many of our forefathers, to resist even to blood, striving against sin, against oppression and violence.[31]

2. Sectarian Developments Outside of New England

Having reached the beginning of the national period in one culturally homogeneous region, New England, we may now turn back to glance at the development of our theme in the middle colonies and elsewhere, especially among the German sectaries.

i. The Vision of Paradise Among German Sectarians, Quakers, and Swedenborgians

We have in an earlier section noted the emergence of the wilderness theology of Pietism within and without the state churches of central Europe and have anticipated the arrival of Germanic seekers of the wilderness Church in the New World.[32]

For example, Johann Kelpius (1673-c. 1708), moved by the prophecy of Böhmist Johann Jakob Zimmermann of the advent of the millennium in 1694, set out on an expedition to the primeval solitudes of

---

[31] MS sermon, September 20, 1778, in the custody of the Arlington Historical Society; partly printed in Benjamin and William Cutter, *History of the Town of Arlington* (Boston, 1880), p. 87.

[32] Julius Friedrich Sachse, *The German Pietists of Provincial Pennsylvania* (Philadelphia, 1895), esp. p. 8. He entitles the whole first half of the book "The Woman in the Wilderness." See further *The German Sectarians of Pennsylvania*, 2 vols. (Philadelphia, 1899-1900); Friedrich Nieper, *Die ersten deutschen Auswanderen von Krefeld nach Pennsylvanien: Ein Bild aus der religiösen Ideengeschichte des 17. und 18. Jahrhunderts* (Neukirchen, 1940); and Walter C. Klein, *Johan Conrad Beissel: Mystic and Martinet* (Philadelphia, 1942).

Pennsylvania and set up a hermitage in what is now Fairmount Park in Philadelphia. The community called itself "The Contented of the God-loving Soul" and identified itself as "Das Weib der Wüste." On the death of Zimmermann in 1693, Kelpius assumed the leadership of the band. His followers believed that their community, having fled to the wilderness (Revelation) and now coming up from the wilderness (Canticles), should lay aside all other engagements and, trimming their lamps and adorning themselves with holiness, prepare themselves to meet the Bridegroom with joy. They believed that there was a three-fold wilderness state of progression in spiritual holiness, namely, the barren, the fruitful, and the wilderness state proper of the elect of God. It was for the third mystical phase, entry into which betokened their divine election, that they were waiting. To qualify for it, they believed it essential to dwell literally in the wilds. In so far as in their period of waiting they were living at the level of the "fruitful wilderness" they occupied themselves with the conversion of the Indians. Conrad Beissel, a later leader (d. 1768), modified the organization of the wilderness quest in his fully monastic colony of the Solitary Brethren and Sisters of Ephrata (1721).

A Catholic, monastic ingredient had clearly entered the German conventicles that were breaking away from the state churches committed to salvation by faith alone. For example, back in Germany Gerhard Tersteegen (1697-1769), converted to Pietism under the influence of English Puritan Independents like William Perkins and William Ames, retired to his pilgrims' hut at Otterbeck in 1727 and there published the lives of several Catholic mystics, translated Madame Guyon, and, in his hymnody thus inspired, made extensive use of the wilderness theme. Several of his hymns were translated by John Wesley. All five of the selections in a standard American hymnal deal with "the darksome wild," "wild stranger land," and wandering. This mystical, monasticizing trend appeared also in the founder of the Rappists.

Johann George Rapp (1757-1847) of Württemberg, removed to the New World to establish a communitarian venture at "Harmony" in Pennsylvania. Harmony was organized as a disciplined means for returning to paradisic androgyny, symbolized by communal work, by social equality, and, as the ideal, by continence or celibacy. The terrain at Harmony soon proved to be unsuitable for cultivating the vine (the traditional crop of these Württembergers); and in 1806, when Rapp was in the national capital appealing for a fresh grant of land to the west more suitable for vintners, he wrote home, enclosing some strangely beautiful verses which, he said, had been composed in "the desert of wisdom." It is not certain whether this "desert" referred to Washington or the Rappite colony!

> Children, all rejoice anew
> For love's inner amadou [tinder]
> Jesus' friends re-pair thuswise:
> Sunlight flashes, rays agleaming,
> Sending spirit-sparks forth streaming
> On seed-fields of the Paradise. . . .[33]

In 1815, removing his colony to New Harmony in Indiana, Rapp, in allusion to the paradise of pleasure in Genesis 2:8, 2:15, and 3:23-24, reported to a friend that the Indiana site afforded far better opportunity than Pennsylvania "to make of a wild country, fertile fields and *gardens of pleasure.*"[34] It should be added that there is only a trace of our theme in the colonization of the theologically conservative Lutheran immigrants "raising a Lutheran Zion" on the Mississippi.[35]

To return to the eastern seaboard. Here along with the other sectarian seekers of paradise in the middle colonies and states mention should be made of the Quakers, whose wilderness theology in England we have already noted (Chapter III, sec. 2). The interest centers on Edward Hicks (1780-1849), kinsman of the liberal Hicksite leader Elias. He painted over a hundred scenes of "The Peaceable Kingdom," today widely reproduced as Christmas cards. Hicks' primitives illustrated the fulfillment of the prophecy of Isaiah 11:6-9 with special reference to the Quaker policy of peaceful coexistence with the Indians. Hicks commonly painted Penn and other Quakers in his paradise scenes with the animals and the noble savages. Hicks was quite clear about his intention in these pictures, setting down his reflections on the text in a "miscellaneous discourse" based upon an earlier sermon.[36]

In brief, his religious pictures illustrate not only the specific achievement of Penn's peaceful policy of coexistence but also, and more universally, various natural human types symbolized by wild animals living alongside converted or regenerate Christians, symbolized by congruent types of domestic animals. Working with the traditional

---

[33] John S. Duss, *The Harmonists* (Harrisburg, Pa., 1943), p. 26.

[34] Italics mine; John A. Bole, *The Harmony Society* (Philadelphia, 1904), p. 77. In thus making use of the Vulgate rendering of Garden, where the German and English Protestant translations of Genesis leave it Eden, Rapp reveals his dependence on the medieval mystical tradition.

[35] Cf. Carl S. Meyer, "Lutheran Immigrant Churches Face the Problems of the Frontier," *Church History*, XXIX (1960), 440-462.

[36] "A Little Present for Friends and Friendly People," published as an appendix in his *Memoirs of the Life and Religious Labors* (Philadelphia, 1851), pp. 263-331.

four elements of creation and the four humors of the body, Hicks observed that regeneration could not completely alter the melancholy, the sanguine, the phlegmatic, and the choleric, whom he found both within and without the Church of the regenerate, even within the Quaker fellowship and in varying assortments. With a little artifice, he found in Isaiah's vision of four pairs of wild and domestic animals led by the Child a prophecy of the way in which the grace of Christ might turn the fiercest lion type roaring in the wilderness of the world into a still, strong, but mild ox, a helpful denizen of the provisional paradise which is the community of the regenerate. As a lion may by grace become an ox, so the wolf type, a lamb; the leopard, a kid; the bear, a cow. His scheme is amply supported by discerning observation and analysis, and his presentation is enlivened by his strong conviction about the rights of women and the iniquity of slavery, war, and usury. He vividly recounts, for example, how the nominal Christian, even a birthright Quaker and weighty Friend, is sometimes more like a usurious bear in business, preoccupied with his affairs, fierce and carnivorous when pursued to his den, than a uberous cow who generously shares her substance in ruminating patience and charity. He cites St. Paul as the fierce and strong lion type who through regeneration in Christ becomes the equally powerful but mild and reliable ox. Hicks also recalls:

The most valuable father in the church of Christ I ever knew, was a man of coleric complexion, and in his first nature like a lion; but when I knew him [after his saving experience], he was as patient, submissive and powerful as an ox. He was truly to me a precious father, taking me by the hand in my youth, and leading by precept and example. . . .

Hicks gives evidence in his *Memoirs* and sermons of a love of real animals of the forest and barnyard and he had a deep feeling for the individuality of all the creatures of nature, but in his sermon on Isaiah and in his numerous paradisic paintings he is portraying the peaceable kingdom of regenerate men and women who, though formerly wolves, leopards, bears, and lions, have been drawn from the world into the Church:

Oh that you, my dear friends, . . . may so follow the Captain of our salvation as to know the Seed or Word of God, to bruise the head of that serpent that is the author of all hatred against fathers and mothers, husbands and wives, brethren and sisters; and so overcome as to be permitted to eat of the tree of life, that stands in the paradise of God.[37]

[37] *Ibid.*, p. 325.

An even better-known character in the American frontier development of our theme was the extraordinary Swedenborgian missionary
and planter of apple nurseries on the expanding frontier of the old
Northwest Territory, John Chapman (d. 1845). Johnny Appleseed
had grasped Swedenborg's theory of correspondences even when he
could not very often make his spiritual theology coherent to rough
frontiersmen. In the War of 1812 he moved about as a watchman in
the wilderness, warning the settlers in Ohio of raids by the Indians.
But among the Indians, too, he moved freely as one who would hurt
neither man nor beast. Like Hicks and Rapp and the friars and monks
before them, Chapman was at peace with the animal kingdom. In his
religiously inspired mercies to wild creatures, he was one with Francis
of Assisi and the desert Fathers. He was even opposed to cutting and
grafting apple scions; hence his stress on seeds and seedling apple trees
in his paradise in the wilderness. Although his apple nurseries were the
serious frontier business of a shrewd merchant, his vocation as barefoot
orchardist cannot be separated from his Swedenborgian vision of a
peaceful Zion burgeoning in the desert. Nor was he merely a col-
porteur of Swedenborgian books. A missionary as well as a seedsman,
he even considered giving some of his lands for the founding of a New
Church school on the frontier, another kind of seedbed in the wilderness.[38]

We turn now from these immigrant visions of a paradise in the
wilderness to an indigenous and distinctively American religious
movement which found motivation and sanction in the idea of the
true Church of the Wilderness of both Sinai and the seer and Revelation.

*ii. Isaiah and Canticles in the Desert of Joseph Smith Before the Mormon
Exodus to Utah*

In making this transition to Mormonism we shall remember that,
despite great geographical and theological distance between it and
German Pietism in the middle states and Puritanism in New England,
Joseph Smith (d. 1844) had his roots in the same cultural and religious
soil from which John Cotton and Samuel Sherwood drew their
strength.

The trek of the Mormons from Ohio, Missouri, and Illinois under
severe persecution to Utah at once suggests the epic of Exodus and is
obviously the closest American parallel to the flight of the Boers to

---

[38] See, on the plan for a school, for instance, Robert Price, *Johnny Appleseed: Man
and Myth* (Bloomington, Ind., 1954), p. 129. A more popular account is that of Robert
Price *et al.*, *Johnny Appleseed: A Voice in the Wilderness: The Story of the Pioneer
John Chapman* (Paterson, N.J., 1954).

escape British control. Surprisingly, however, the language of Exodus is not at all prominent in the extant documents. This can be only partly explained by the fact that Joseph Smith's own *Book of Mormon* and his *Commandments* had been interposed between the Bible and the daily experience of the Mormons on the frontier.[39] In any event it is in the works of Smith himself that the wilderness motif in Mormonism can be best examined at its source.

Mormon restorationism stressed the recovery of not only the apostolic Church but also the Aaronic (lower) and the Melchizedek (higher) priesthoods.[40] This took place in two stages in 1829, a year before the printing of *The Book of Mormon*. Smith declared that he had gone into the woods along the Susquehanna River near the New York-Pennsylvania boundary to pray and inquire of the Lord respecting baptism for the remission of sins. John the Baptist descended in a cloud from heaven ordaining him and his associate Oliver Cowdery to the Aaronic priesthood with the power to baptize. Accordingly, on May 15 Joseph and Oliver immersed each other in turn "by being buried in the liquid grave." The power of ordination, however, was still understood to be wanting. The restoration of the Melchizedek priesthood was authorized by a second oracle:

A voice of the Lord in the wilderness of Fayette, Seneca county, declaring the three witnesses to bear record of the book. The voice of Michael on the banks of the Susquehanna, detecting the devil when he appeared as an angel of light. The voice of Peter, James, and John in the wilderness between [George Rapp's] Harmony, Susquehanna county, and Colesville, Broome county, on the Susquehanna river, declaring themselves as possessing the keys of the kingdom, and of the dispensation of the fullness of times.[41]

With the baptismal and apostolic powers of the two priesthoods restored, Smith and his collaborator proceeded to organize their strictly immersionist Church of Jesus Christ of Latter Day Saints, April 6, 1830. A new Israel had begun to gather in the wilderness, moving westward under the compulsion of both persecution and a phantom promise.

[39] The only study of our particular theme that I have located is the Harvard honors thesis by Richard L. Bushman, "New Jerusalem, U.S.A.: The Early Development of the Latter-day Saint Zion Concept on the American Frontier," Cambridge, 1955.
[40] B. H. Roberts, *A Comprehensive History of the Church of Jesus Christ of Latter Day Saints* (Salt Lake City, 1930), I, 177–198; John D. Giles, "Restoration of the Melchizedek Priesthood," *Era*, XLVIII (1945), 338 ff.
[41] *Op. cit.*, Section 128:20.

In his *Commandment*[42] at the dedication of the Temple in Kirtland, Ohio, March 27, 1836, Smith declared:

[Remember all thy Church] that thy Church may [rise up and][43] come forth out of the wilderness [Canticles 6:10] of darkness, and shine forth fair as the moon, clear as the sun, and terrible as an army with banners [Canticles 6:43.]

That [She] be adorned as a bride [Revelation 21:2] for that day when thou shalt unvail the heavens, and cause the mountains to flow down at thy presence, and the valleys to be exalted, the rough places made smooth [Isaiah 40:3]; and the glory may fill the earth.

The allusion to the army terrible with banners in combination with other scriptural passages suggests John Bunyan's *House in the Forest of Lebanon.*

In *The Book of Mormon*[44] it is written:

For the Lord shall comfort Zion: he will make her wilderness like Eden, and her desert like the Garden of the Lord.

The wilderness tabernacle suggested the Mormon term for the local meetings, namely, "stakes," in dependence on Isaiah 33:20 and 54:2: "Enlarge the place of your tent, and let the curtains of your habitations be stretched out, hold not back, lengthen your cords and strengthen your stakes." Zion was thus an overarching concept, an invisible canopy above a people gathering from all sides. Yet Zion could be thought of as quite localized in Jackson County, Missouri, for example, which had been spied out and identified by Joseph Smith and his men as its eventual location.[45]

Driven to Utah, interpreters of the trek looked back upon their experience as providential. Commenting on Zion in the wilderness in Section 97 of Smith's *Doctrines and Covenants,* the commentators appealed to Revelation 12:6 in accounting for the way in which the Mormon Church had escaped, among other disasters, the scourge of the Civil War by going into the Rocky Mountain wilderness prepared by God.

[42] *Commandment*, Sec. 109:73 and 74.
[43] Inserted from the fuller phrasing in Sec. 5:4.
[44] II Nephi 5:72 f. Smith's *Commandment*, Sec. 1:30, on "the Church brought forth out of obscurity and out of darkness" and the establishment of the Church of Latter Day Saints have been regarded by some Mormons as the fulfillment of Revelation 12:6. See F. H. Edwards, *A Commentary on the Doctrine and Covenants* (Independence, Mo., 1946), p. 30.
[45] Hyrum H. Smith and Janne M. Sjodahl, *Commentary* (Salt Lake City, 1954), p. 614.
[46] The only systematic treatment is that of Miles Fisher, *Negro Slave Songs in the*

Turning from the Mormons to the Negroes, we take up another peculiarly American permutation of the wilderness theme.

iii. *Yo' Wan'na Fin' Jesus, Go in de Wilderness*[46]

As in the Bible and most of the traditions (with the almost unique exception of Wesley), so in the Negro spirituals the wilderness has both a positive and a negative sense. On the negative side are those spirituals of Methodist lineage like "Ain't I glad I got out of the wilderness," "Done foun' my lost sheep . . . Go to de wilderness, seek an' fin',"[47] and "In his name we come out 'd' wilderness," wherein the experience of spiritual and moral struggle is portrayed. But by far the more distinctive meaning (even when the associated tune is derived from a Methodist hymn with the negative sense of the term) is that which has as its background the slave assemblies in the forest. The aboriginal secret meetings brought over from Africa and stealthily perpetuated were gradually given an increasingly Christian reinforcement and coloration by what the slaves overheard in sermon and hymn about the Bride (Canticles) or the Woman in the Wilderness (Revelation). Their early morning "valley" or "wilderness" assemblies were sometimes magnanimously countenanced by the white masters during a revival but were more often furtively attended while the masters were sleeping. There was usually a tub of water allegedly to drown the sound, actually carrying over a forgotten African jungle appurtenance, possibly also interpreted as the pool of water in the wilderness in so many of the desert passages in the Bible. In the following spiritual the imagery of the Bride, the Woman, and the Devil of the Jordanian temptation scene seem to be intertwined. In other words the positive and negative senses of the wilderness experience are combined:

Ef ye want to see Jesus, Go in de wilderness, . . . Leanin' on de Lord. Oh, brother, how d'ye feel, when ye come out de wilderness, Leanin' on de Lord? . . . I heard de deb'l howlin', when I come out de wilderness I gib de deb'l a battle, when I come out de wilderness.[48]

The quest for Jesus in the wilderness for secret solace and revival

---

United States (Ithaca, N.Y., 1953). He summarizes his idea about the wilderness motif on p. 186. Paul F. Laubenstein, unaware of the millennial history we have traced, connected the word solely with the Exodus in his "An Apocalyptic Reincarnation," *Journal of Biblical Literature*, LI (1932), p. 238.

[47] James Weldon Johnson *et al., The Book of Negro Spirituals* (New York, 1925).

[48] M. F. Armstrong *et al., Hampton and its Students* (New York, 1874) pp. 184 f.

and fellowship appears frequently: "Jesus a waitin' to meet you in de wilderness,"[49] "I seek my Lord in de wilderness, for I am goin' home," etc.[50]

Because the wilderness meeting was at once the Bride, the Woman, and, by extension, Mary the Mother of Jesus, the slaves of St. Helena Island had a tradition that the much-sought Jesus was actually born in the secret meetings in the woods, and they tiptoed in the early morning in order not to disturb the Babe of Bethlehem.[51]

In some spirituals Mary, Mary Magdalene, and the Woman of the Wilderness are combined as "Weeping Mary," symbol of the Negro Christians, their church of the wilderness outside the white man's church. In one spiritual she rocks her child all night in "a weary lan.' "[52] Another spiritual addresses the more or less secret Negro Christian fellowship:

Run, Mary, Run, Mary, run, Oh, run, Mary, run, I know de oder worl' 'm not like dis. Fire in de east, an' fire in de west, I know de oder worl' 'm not like dis, Bound to burn de wilderness, I know de oder worl' 'm not like dis. Jordan's riber is a riber to cross, I know de oder worl' 'm not like dis, Stretch your rod an' come across, I know de oder worl' 'm not like dis.

The allusion here to the burning of the wilderness is not entirely clear from purely scriptural sources. It reappears in "What Yo' Gwine to do When Yo' Lamp Burn Down?" and fire "burn down de wilderness."[53] There may well be here a confused allusion to John the Baptist's proclamation in the wilderness that a mightier one would soon come with the Spirit and then with fire, another fiery Elijah.

From wilderness assembly and its big-city equivalent "the praise house" several modern Negro denominational movements have sprung.

From the haunting spirituals of the slaves and the suras and commandments of the seer of Palmyra, New York, we turn back to that major cultural expression of our theme, the building of the seminary in the wilderness with which our long survey began.

[49] William Francis Allen *et al., Slave Songs of the United States* (New York, 1867), p. 14. See emendation by Fisher, *op. cit.,* p. 69.

[50] Allen, *op. cit.,* p. 84; Fisher, *op. cit.,* p. 74.

[51] Fisher, *op. cit.,* pp. 63, 136, 178.

[52] Nicholas Gallanta (Taylor), *Saint Helena Island Spirituals* (New York, 1925), p. 5. On John's preaching and Joel's vision of fire see above, I, at n. 6 and at n. 20.

[53] Armstrong, *op. cit.,* p. 188; Johnson, *op. cit.,* p. 170. For a literary impulse from the Negro wilderness, see Faulkner's *The Bear* and W. V. O'Connor, "The Wilderness Theme in Faulkner's *The Bear," Accent,* XIII (1953), 12.

3. The Seminary in the Wilderness[54]

We have shown elsewhere how the conception of the Church as the provisional paradise was at length largely limited to the monastic community (Chapter II, sec. 2) and how the quasi-monastic medieval university (Chapter II, sec. 3) laid claim to the paradisic motif in sanctioning its pursuit of knowledge within the corporate disciplines of sacramental grace. In a supplementary essay (Part II) we shall expand the second point to show how the medieval idea of the university as a garden of knowledge survived into seventeenth-century England and was in turn translated to America by way of Harvard College.

At this point therefore we shall be limited to that transformation of the wilderness-garden motif as it found expression in the emergence in America of the theological seminary as a seedbed for the missionary propagation of the true Church of the wilderness. But, inasmuch as many of these seminary or missionary colleges were to evolve into standard American colleges or universities, we are dealing here not only with early American theological education but also with a hitherto unnoticed biblical or religious motivation in the rise of general American higher education. Dartmouth College, for example, was originally designed as a mission school for Indians and a seminary for ministers and especially for missionaries on the frontier.

The domestic and foreign missionary impulse in the founding of Dartmouth, stemming from the Great Awakening in New England, and the role of Dr. Eleazar Wheelock (d. 1779) and his school for the Indians are well brought out in the following passage (by two early nineteenth-century collaborators in editing Wheelock's *Memoirs*),[55] which points up once again the persistently ambiguous meaning of the wilderness motif. After observing that the winds of revivalism in the aftermath of the Great Awakening did good in ruthlessly uprooting barren trees, but that they also strewed the seeds of sectarianism in the garden of the Lord, the co-editors continue:

At the close of this glorious day, when spiritual slumbers began to steal upon the church, the enemy sowed tares. A race of Separatists, of Anabaptists, and other sectaries, darkened the heavens with the smoke of their

---

[54] I have dealt with this theme monographically in connection with the rise of a short-lived seminary in Gilmanton, New Hampshire, in "The Seminary in the Wilderness: A Representative Episode in the Cultural History of Northern New England," *Harvard Library Bulletin*, XIII (1959), 369–400; XIV (1960), 27–58. Several of the following paragraphs are adapted from this article, with most of the documentation removed.

[55] David M'Clure and Elijah Parish, *Memoirs of the Rev. Eleazar Wheelock, Founder and President of Dartmouth College and Moor's Charity School: with a Summary History of the College and School* (Newburyport, Mass., 1811), pp. 17 and 57.

unhallowed fires. The foundations of religious society were shaken. A spiritual tornado tore up the barren trees in the garden of the Lord; the most precious fruit was bruised, and the enclosures [the Congregational parishes] in many places were thrown down; the laborers [the ministers of the Standing Order] trembled for their own safety. They were called "hirelings, wolves in sheep's clothing, formal legalists, destitute of the power of godliness, dumb dogs that could not bark." In this dismal tempest Dr. Wheelock stood secure, like Moses on Sinai's fiery summit.[56]

In the mood of this wilderness eschatology, Dr. Wheelock, when he came to found his mission school, had in fact appealed to the wilderness motif in choosing for the college seal, *Vox Clamantis in Deserto.* The eschatological conviction that a seminary, as the seedbed of proclaimers of the gospel, was the God-ordained means of building up the wastes places of Zion (the collective term for the churches of the Congregational Way) was everywhere stressed.

Dr. Wheelock, like the earlier John Eliot of Roxbury, was convinced that God had manifested his displeasure against New Englanders for their failure to bring the gospel to the Indians. Hence his great interest in founding a missionary school for them. In moving north from his first work in Lebanon to Hanover on the Connecticut River, Wheelock "derived support from the example of the prophet Elisha (II Kings 6:1–7) who founded a college, or school of the prophets in the wilderness of Jordan."

A poem written in his lifetime by a pupil of Wheelock alluded with echoes from Milton to the college as the garden of the Lord, a provisional paradise in the desert:

> Thus we behold, in pathless forests sprung,
> A fruitful tree, with golden apples hung,
> Inclos'd around with shades and gloomy wastes,
> Expos'd to beating rains, and stormy blasts,
> So Dartmouth seated on her desert plain,
> Try'd, disappointed, and oppress'd with pain,
> Look'd back, and long'd for her old seat again.[57]

In the founding and interpreting of Dartmouth the missionary motif and the recovery of the apple of paradise through the study of the golden apples of the classical tradition are here all brought together in the seminary in the wilderness.

[56] *Ibid.,* pp. 127–128.
[57] Other instances of the wilderness motif in connection with education are found in *ibid.,* pp. 94, 99.

In 1811 Wheelock's biographers could write of him and his missionary school, now a leading college:

How would the good Doctor, like aged Simeon, with the infant Redeemer in his arms, have rejoiced to see our day, when the tongue of the dumb sings for joy, and the wilderness blossoms as the rose. Perhaps God designed him as the morning star, to be the harbinger of this resplendent light.
. . . The rock smitten by the hand of faith watered the camp, and sustained the church of God in her travels through the wilderness.[58]

The wilderness motif, as interpreted by all New Englanders, included, as we have seen, the experience of punitive testing (Exodus) and the concept of a providentially prepared environment in which the true but hidden church (Revelation 12) could gather strength for a world mission to the pagans near and far. Thus the establishment of a seminary, a seed-plot of preachers and missionaries, in the wilderness or desert after a "long drought," sustained by copious "showers of grace," the revivals, was a mark of "the grand era of missions" at home and abroad, setting off the present from "all former ages."[59]

President Timothy Dwight of Yale, for example, preaching in 1812, spoke of all the colleges in the New World as seminaries, for the training of evangelical preachers, defining their evangel as the whole design of both the Old and the New Testaments, and he pictured the revival as a shower upon the desert:

The Gospel is the rain and sun-shine of heaven upon the moral world. Wherever its beams are shed, and its showers fall, the wilderness blossoms as the rose, and the desert as the garden of God: while the world beside is an Arabian waste, where no fountains flow, and no verdure springs, and where life itself fades, languishes and expires.[60]

Into "the wilderness of Zion," he declared, preachers were coming like angels from heaven, preaching another gospel—Unitarians, Universalists, Methodists, Freewill Baptists all thinly veiled behind his characterizations, while all about were multitudes who did not even pretend to any other conviction than French infidelity. It was the clear implication of his sermon that every man preparing to "enter the desk" would have to be adequately fitted intellectually and morally to challenge the angels of both heresy and infidelity. Approaching the close of his sermon Dwight reminded his largely clerical congregation:

[58] *Ibid.*, pp. 122, 126.
[59] Froom, *op. cit.*, IV, 106.
[60] *Sermons* (New Haven, 1828), II, 433–452.

Every Minister is here constituted by Christ the shepherd of his flock, "to watch as one that must give an account"; to feed them with the bread of life; and to conduct them through this wilderness to regions of everlasting rest!

The specific occasion of President Dwight's sermon was a convention in Windsor, Vermont, of New England Congregationalists, who were considering a plan for the establishment of a northern New England seminary that would be so constituted that its graduates might directly enter the ministry or the mission field without attending college.

At a critical juncture in the development of New England theological education, Dwight headed off this first major move to establish in America a pattern of professional education "with a partial and limited course of studies." He realized in so doing that the supply of preachers would be delayed temporarily. As a result of Dwight's efforts, the original plan for a New Hampshire and Vermont theological seminary was altered and instead of a terminal theological seminary, an academy was established with special financial and curricular provisions to give a biblical education to indigent and pious young men who intended to enter the gospel ministry but who would go on to college and a post-collegiate theological education.

In appealing for the support of this new seminary on a revised basis the Windsor convention reflected Dwight's eschatological convictions when it urged that without a seminary in the north "our new settlements, where they have not faithful ministers, will be left a prey to sectarian preachers, who diseminate errors, as ruinous to the soul, as poison is to the body; who create divisions, which weaken society," "That the millennial state of the church is not far distant, and is swiftly approaching," "that we are living in the last days of blasphemous infidelity, when the prince of darkness is making great efforts to maintain his dominion over the earth," and that therefore the churches must give "bountifully" lest the talents of "the pious but indigent" youthful recruits for the (precollegiate) seminary be "buried in obscurity and the good they might do in building up Zion" be lost. Strongly appealing to the world mission of the New England churches, the Windsor Convention declared: "We have reason to conclude, that as soon as the nations of the earth are supplied with Bibles in their own language, accompanied with faithful preachers . . . God will pour out his Spirit."

The desire to have a terminal (noncollegiate) theological seminary was not easily suppressed, however, in the midst of the sense of eschatological urgency. The embers of the doused Windsor plan were easily blown into flame by the spirit of successive revivals and the intensity of concern for quickly and inexpensively trained ministers and missionaries.

Thus a society for promoting theological education in the District of Maine, which had not been represented at the New England ecclesiastical convention at Windsor, proceeded to incorporate in the very year of that convention (1812); and, instead of locating their school in the western and more thickly settled parts, they determined "to march to the front, and plant it in the midst of those spiritual wastes which it was intended to build up." Their seminary opened at Hampden in conjunction with an academy there in 1816. It was proposed to give the pious young men two years of classical training in the latter and two years of theology in the seminary, on the model of the four-year program of the English dissenting institutions. Jehudi Ashmun (later a colonial agent in Liberia), in a masterly essay designed to show the importance of the seminary on the Maine frontier rising under his care, wrote in the middle of the first winter:

The Holy Ghost, in less than six months after the establishment of it, converted the desert spot upon which it had been seated, into a spiritual Eden; and in less than a year, from the stones of the wilderness, reared up a living Church [gathered in Hampden where before there had been no ministrations] of more than thirty members, into which the members of the School were immediately incorporated.[61]

In 1819 the seminary moved up the Penobscot River a few miles to Bangor. The Missouri Compromise and Maine's admission as a state in 1820 made Bangor Seminary especially conscious of the importance of its mission, to send Puritan free-soilers into the imperiled West and pastors into the northern wilderness:

. . . the tide of population is fast rolling back upon the forests at the north. . . . Very many churches are destitute of the stated means of grace, because ministers cannot be obtained. Towns and plantations are growing up in almost every section of the State, whose moral condition is deplorable almost beyond description—and if suffered to remain destitute as they now are, another generation will find them sunk in the most hopeless kind of heathenism. . . . The call is loud and thrilling, and is wafted to our ears by every wind that blows. We are told of multitudes of children and youth who are growing up in ignorance of their highest interests, while vice and

---

[61] The MS essay so characterized is quoted by Ralph R. Gurley, *Life of Jehudi Ashmun* (New York, 1839), p. 32.

error of every name are fastening upon them the bands and cords of a most degrading servitude. What shall be done? . . . We cannot obtain them [preachers] from Auburn, or Princeton, or New Haven. Andover, heretofore, has not sent us on an average more than two annually. . . . The trumpet is sounding an alarm in the valley of the Mississippi, and every young man who can be pressed into the service must go thither. And while we rejoice in these efforts to save the western country, we can readily perceive that their tendency is to prevent young men in our Theological Seminaries from turning their attention to the East. We must therefore have a Seminary of our own. . . .[62]

The recurrent theme of the seminary as the fulfillment of Isaiah's prophecy of the garden in the wilderness (3:18–21) is alluded to in a despairing cry for more funds at the conclusion of the Bangor *Survey:*

We, who sit under the droppings of the sanctuary, and whose hearts are daily cheered with the hopes and promises and consolations of the Gospel —shall we tell them [the faithful] that the Fountain, from whence they have expected streams to gladden the desolate places around them, is dried up? That no more sons of consolation will ever go forth from this Seminary? . . . This Institution must be sustained. . . . Many Christians, scattered abroad in the wilderness, have been cheered and strengthened— many poor, guilty wanderers from God, have been turned from the error of their ways—and many desolate regions have been made to rejoice and blossom as the rose, by the instrumentality of this Institution.[63]

The eschatological tone of this message was clear to all who read the appeal, combining phrases as it does in allusion to the Fountain of the heavenly Jerusalem (Revelation 21:6) that issues from under the sanctuary of the new Zion (Ezekiel 47:12) to make glad the desert in the wilderness round about Zion (Isaiah 35:1 ff.).

Lyman Beecher, later president of Lane Theological Seminary in Ohio, expressed similar sentiments in his more famous *A Plea for the West* (1835).

The American Home Missionary Society was in fact founded in the conviction that with the showers of revival preaching the whole American wilderness would become like the garden of the Lord. One of the founders read a paper before fellow students at Andover Theological Seminary on the connection between domestic missions and the political prospects of the country, in which he called for the unification of all the resources "of philanthropy, patriotism and Christian sympathy throughout our country, into one vast reservoir, from which a stream

---

[62] *A Survey of the Theological Seminary at Bangor, Maine* (Bangor, 1830), p. 11.
[63] *Ibid.*, p. 14.

will flow to Georgia, to Louisiana, to Missouri, and to Maine, fertilizing every barren spot and causing our whole country to flourish like the garden of the Lord."[64]

It is of interest further that in the work of the American Board of Commissioners for Foreign Missions the young seminarians of New England felt especially drawn to the (Moslem) desert of Lebanon, which Isaiah 35:1 ff. had promised would one day be given (to Christ) and blossom as a rose.

It is also of interest to add that a leading spokesman of Unitarianism, Henry Whitney Bellows, alarmed by the ruthless utilitarianism of American economic expansion but with special reference to its erosion of traditional features which he regarded as essential even for a liberal or progressive Church, prophetically intoned the hallowed language of New England in his famous address before the Harvard Divinity School, *Suspense of Faith,* and its *Sequel* (1859):

I believe wholly and devoutly in the permanency of Christianity, and in the coexistence of the Church with the civilization which is its child, and is now half ready to be its parricide; and I expect confidently, absolutely, that memory and hope, history and progress, gratitude and longing, institutions and a free spirit—imagination, conscience, reason, affection—will all unite again, as they have formerly united, in building up *the waste places of Zion,* in clothing in beautiful garments the faith and worship of Christendom, now shivering with nakedness, and in bringing back the intellect, aspiration, and artistic genius of the world, now divorced and languishing with home sickness, to the fountain and shelter whence they drew their ancient inspiration, and even the strength that has supported them in exile.[65]

4. "Landscape Righteousness and the Devil"

At this point our account blends into many standard and more specialized treatments of the Christian factors in the rise of American culture and nationality, like the secularization of the doctrine of election as "manifest destiny," and the conversion of the colonist (sloughing off his Old World inheritance) into the American Adam. In the romantic vision of the nineteenth century the North American wilderness, without losing any of the storied resonance that echoes in the multiple

[64] John Maltby, quoted in "The Seminary in the Wilderness," *Harvard Library Bulletin,* XIII (1959), 388. See also Collin B. Goodykoontz, *Home Missions on the American Frontier with Particular Reference to the American Home Missionary Society* (Caldwell, Ida., 1939), p. 176.
[65] *Op. cit.*

biblical and traditional Christian meanings of desert, was now often by preference fondly called Nature.

R. W. B. Lewis in *The American Adam: Innocence, Tragedy, and Tradition in the Nineteenth Century* (1955) has documented the conflict in American literature, from 1820 to 1860, between the romantic feeling for the new nation of Nature in paradisic innocence and "separation from Europe" and the emergence of a new sense of the fall of man and nature even in the New World, notably in the works of Nathaniel Hawthorne and Herman Melville.

In the same year Perry Miller, in "The Romantic Dielmma in American Nationalism and the Concept of Nature,"[66] showed how in the romantic mood the American wilderness had been converted into a bountiful and beneficent Nature with some of the attributes of Paradise. He quoted from a popular essay of the age:

God has promised us a renowned existence, if we will but deserve it. He speaks this promise in the sublimity of Nature. . . . The august Temple in which we dwell was built for lofty purposes.[67]

Then, with special reference to the five gigantic canvases by Thomas Cole (d. 1848) entitled "The Course of Empire," Miller showed that at least some entrepreneurial romantics were not entirely confident that Nature could be at once worshiped and ravished with impunity. Miller pointed out that the logic of Cole's prophetic paintings was that a nation committed to Nature could in the end never escape the ineluctable cycle of the rise from its innocent barbarism to a fall of which Rome's final ruin was for Cole the prototype. In his paintings and in allied writings of the period, all from the hands of avowed Christians, the inherent contradiction between the Christian conception of man and his fall and the romantic sense of the benignity of the American wilderness personified as Nature was thus vaguely apprehended.

Henry Nash Smith in his *Virgin Land: The American West as Symbol and Myth* (1950) has dealt quite specifically with our theme and notably in two chapters on "The Garden and the Desert" and "The Myth of the Garden and Turner's Frontier Hypothesis." In tracing, however, the conflicting sentiments concerning the pioneer who was at once the scout of civilization and the escapee from culture and in analyzing the contradictory images of the desert beyond Kansas and Nebraska as at once the haunt of lawless half-breeds and the realm

---

[66] *Harvard Theological Review*, XLVIII (1955), 239-253.
[67] Quoted by Miller from a popular and widely republished essay by James Brooks, written in 1835 in *The Knickerbocker; loc. cit.*, p. 245.

which "in the fulness of time will blossom into the fulfilment of its early promise" ("Rain Follows the Plough"), Smith seems to have been unaware of the millennial elaboration of the biblical garden-desert theme, which will have been as much in the minds of the nineteenth-century denizens and interpreters of the wild West as, according to his thesis, the French Physiocratic agrarian theory! Richard Hofstadter, with his grasp of the agrarian myth and the folklore of Populism in *The Age of Reform* (1955), might likewise have gone farther in assessing the biblical factor in the ideology of American agrarianism.

It cannot be here our purpose to explore the American conception of the primeval wilderness as Nature. But we cannot take leave of the romantic and Christian conceptions of the American forests and prairies without noting how pioneer conservationists and naturalists, sensing in their turn that the wilderness was inextricably bound up with national character and destiny, sought, often with the invective of the ancient prophets, to save reserved parts of the American heritage.

After the period of Ralph Waldo Emerson and David Thoreau the most influential nature essayist was John Burroughs (1837–1921) and the most important conservationist was John Muir (1838–1914). Like John the Baptist theirs were voices crying in the wilderness, but for the wilderness—for the saving of nature in order to save society.

Scotch-born John Muir, his mind resounding with passages from the Bible three-fourths of which he had committed to memory as a boy under the tutelage of his sometime vegetarian father, set forth from his new pioneer home in Wisconsin for the university and then "for the University of the Wilderness." This involved a thousand-mile walk to the Gulf. In his journal he confided his reflections on man's attitude toward nature and the animal world. After settling near Martinez and devoting himself to horticulture, he emerged as a towering national publicist who defended the American wilderness against exploitation and desecration. In memorable phrases he appealed for a national program of conservation, declaring that "God began the reservation system in Eden," that "the forests of America . . . must have been a great delight to God; for they were the best he ever planted," the whole continent being "a garden; and [that] from the beginning it seemed to be favored above all the other wild parks and gardens of the globe . . . and happy birds and beasts gave delightful animation." He declared that the battle was joined between the defenders and the exploiters of this American heritage, "between landscape righteousness and the Devil."[68]

---

[68] *The Story of My Boyhood and Youth* (Boston, New York, 1913); *A Thousand-*

Through the efforts of John Muir and Robert Underwood Johnson, then an editor of *The Century Magazine,* a national campaign was launched to preserve Yosemite Valley from the ravages of the timber-men and the grazers. It is significant that it was precisely in 1890, the year in which the American Census Bureau formally reported the closing of the frontier, that this monumental wilderness area was definitively and inalienably set aside as a national park. In a booming America in which any attempt to bring any aspect of life under any national control was at once pilloried as a repudiation of the American principle of freedom and free enterprise, the conservationists were in the end able to persuade the American people that the preservation of primeval forests and monumental landscapes was the proper concern of the federal government in the interest of Americanism. In the terms of our essay the significant aspect of the American conservation movement and the associated nature societies is that the wilderness should now be enclosed as a park and that the preservation of that wilderness should be widely felt to be the duty of the national government. In this development the wilderness, from being a desert of death and devils, has, with its variegated flora and fauna living in peace, been converted into a kind of paradise. The devil now prowls outside the wilderness—the combination of selfish economic powers that would despoil the "continental garden" for private greed.

mile Walk to the Gulf (Boston, New York, 1916); "Forest Reservations and National Parks," *Harper's Weekly,* XLIII (June 5, 1897), 563–567; "The American Forests," *Atlantic Monthly,* LXXXII (August, 1897), 145–157; Linnie Marsh Wolfe, *Son of the Wilderness: The Life of John Muir* (New York, 1945).

Chapter V. Conclusion: Wasteland and Wilderness

In the Palestinian world the Hebrew equivalents of *desert* and *wilderness* denoted roughly the same terrain. In Europe, outside the relatively dry Iberian Peninsula, the terms have become over the centuries differentiated. On the geophysical level *desert* denotes dry, sandy terrain; *wilderness* and its equivalents in other European languages suggests the wildness of the dark forest, the dismal swamp, and the mountain fastness.

In the long evolution of the biblical terms and their translation and transformation in the course of European history, the term *desert* has by now largely lost all but its geophysical sense, and the term *garden* has come to be used only in its horticultural sense. In contrast, the biblical term *paradise,* which originally could have the horticultural sense of a *royal park,* as well as its primordial meaning in Genesis, has now become exclusively religio-mythical or poetic in its application.

In between, it is the word *wilderness* which has retained both its purely geophysical and its potently religious meanings. Indeed, the one word in its theological sense has drawn into itself the power of the associated designations and still suggests all the mystery and ambiguity of its Hebraic antecedents. It is a word that can be intoned or invoked. Its incantational potency is felt.

To be sure, like every metaphor, that of the wilderness can become merely a rhetorical gesture. But even in a muted or mutilated version one can detect something of the sweep of a great tradition into modern times. One may instance examples from the extremes of Christendom.

When in Washington the possibility of bringing about atomic and conventional disarmament was under discussion and the prospect of world peace seemed momentarily brighter, with a vast federal network of super highways in mind Atlanta banker Edward D. Smith declared:

If we could get rid of the unproductive use of that forty billion [defense expenditure] and put it into highways or anything else, it would make this country bloom like a rose.[1]

Metropolitan Evlogius, at the consecration of the Russian Orthodox theological seminary of St. Sergius in Paris, declared:

Five hundred years ago St. Sergius built his monastery in the heart of an impenetrable forest. We are setting up this cloister in the midst of a noisy city, the heart of a world civilization. . . . But does not this culture, which

[1] *Life,* August 24, 1959, p. 26.

long since grew away from its Christian foundations, represent a desert more savage and fruitless than was that of St. Sergius?[2]

When in 1960 Brazil moved its capital to Brasilia, it was implementing Title i, Article 3 of the Constitution of 1891 and also fulfilling the prophetic dream of St. Giovanni Bosco (1815–1888), the founder of the Salesian order devoted to work among neglected boys, to education, and to evangelization, and who sent his Salesians into Brazil to bring this vast land of squalor and wealth, of Indians and Negroes hitherto scarcely touched by Christ into the fold of the Church. Don Bosco shortly before his death beheld in a prophetic dream a new energization and commingling of the races in Brazil, recentered in a vast wilderness, where the jaguar screamed at night and naked savages devoured a prisoner after battle. A voice came to the saint: "The Salesians will tame them."

I saw [continued Bosco] a great civilization rising on a plateau on the shores of a lake between the 15th and 20th parallels, a promised land of rich milk and honey blest.[3]

In precisely this area the new capital has now in fact been built with prodigal haste and national pride; and the city planners, to sanction their selection of the site, have appealed to Bosco's dream and have even made an artificial lake to conform to the prophecy.

Don Giovanni Bosco might not be entirely happy at the ruthless prodigality of the city of which he has become the patron saint, and surely Isaiah would not have understood the Atlanta banker's peaceful super highways, but there is obviously history-shaping power in the ancient imagery of Scripture.

A glance at the permutations of the wilderness motif in contemporary American philosophy, literature, and art likewise reveals the persistence and the power of the ancient ambiguities within our metaphor.[4] *The Inward Morning* of Henry G. Bugbee, Jr. (1958), for example, brings the reader at once into contact with current reflections on the meaning of the wilderness.

---

[2] Quoted by Donald A. Lowrie, *Saint Sergius in Paris: the Orthodox Theological Institute* (London, 1954), p. 11.

[3] The *sogno missionario* of 30 August 1883 is set down in *Memorie Biografiche*, ed. Eugenio Cerchi, XVI (Turin, 1883), 380–390. For his place in the founding of Brasilia, see Osvaldo Ovico, *Brasília* (New York, Brazilian Government Trade Bureau, n.d.), p. 26 f. and *Bolletino Salesiano*, LXXXIV (1960), 506 f.

[4] Among contemporary writers who have most clearly discerned the ambiguous character of the wilderness motif are T. S. Eliot, *The Wasteland*, directly influenced by Jessie Weston, *From Ritual to Romance* (1920); W. H. Auden, *The Enchafèd Flood* (the desert and the sea as literary symbols); Nathan Scott, *The Tragic Vision and the Christian Faith*; and Sidney Keyes, "The Wilderness."

Bugbee acknowledges his indebtedness to and kinship with John M. Anderson, whose *The Individual and the New World* (1955) summarizes well one aspect of the American commitment, when he writes:

Americans often thought of their conquering of the wilderness in the terms of the development of a garden for mankind; and they have continuously seen the frontier experiment in the terms of an ideal human community. . . . In such institutions, Americans have seen themselves as marching across the wilderness and with more or less clarity have conceived of themselves as representatives of mankind's ultimate place in the unknown universe.[5]

But while Bugbee has the literal wilderness of America in mind and more specifically the swamps and woods explored as a boy and notably the ocean during his three years of service at sea in World War II, he has gone much farther than Anderson in transmuting the term *wilderness*. And although he never appeals directly to scriptural or Christian tradition, except for frequent citation of Eckhart, it is his redefinition of the ambiguity of our metaphor that best fits into our survey as a representative and concluding modern document.

His philosophical exploration in the form of a journal is sympathetically introduced by Gabriel Marcel, who recognizes from his vantage point at the Institut de France what a young American philosopher, greatly indebted to him, means when he writes: "Here is what I miss most in the thought of Marcel—the wilderness theme."[6] And an American Catholic interpreter of the philosophical journal, sympathetically reviewing Bugbee's effort to "flush" philosophical meaning out of his concept of the wilderness, points out that the theme, however philosophically and artistically elaborated, remains indeed as authentically American as the greeting, "Howdy, stranger," which likewise emerged out of the American frontier experience.[7]

The wilderness for Bugbee is at once the world without and within perceived no longer as wasteland but as reality beheld contemplatively as "our true home";[8] as "the world of every day," experienced in faith. Here for the first time in our long survey of the permutations of the metaphor of the desert, the ambiguity is terminologically eliminated by making *wasteland* the equivalent of *desert* in the primitive, negative sense while *wilderness* has come to bear the combined meaning of

[5] *Op. cit.,* Preface.
[6] *Ibid.,* p. 164.
[7] Walter S. Ong, S.J., "Personalism and the Wilderness," *Kenyon Review,* XXI (1959), 297–304.
[8] *Op. cit.,* p. 76.

wilderness in the protective sense and also paradise. Yet even here the
two terms are related as two phases in the redemptive vision of the
world; for to experience it first as wasteland is a prerequisite for enjoy-
ing it as "wilderness." Speaking of Jean Paul Sartre, Bugbee writes:

> He has laid bare the wasteland in which we find ourselves in so far as
> we lack good faith—faith, that is. And this can also be a step upon the
> threshold that opens out into the wilderness that is the reality of faith.
> It is to this theme of reality as a wilderness that I want to move.
>
> This, so far as I can tell, is the theme which unifies my own life. It en-
> folds and simplifies, comprehends and completes. Whenever I awaken, I
> awaken to it. It carries with it the gift of life. And it lives in the authen-
> ticity of every authentic gift, every true blessing confirms it deeper; it is
> always with me when I come to myself. Through it I find my vocation,
> for the wilderness is reality experienced as call and explained in responding
> to it absolutely.[9]

Bugbee's frequent citation of Eckhart and specifically of his "still
desert" (*wueste*)[10] and the frequent allusion to early American exponents of the idea of the wilderness, like Henry Thoreau and Herman
Melville, make especially significant, within the context of the present
survey, Bugbee's extraordinary definition of philosophy itself as "learning to leave things be: restoration in the wilderness here and now." By
this he means not inaction but "being still in the presence of things,
letting them speak."[11] Thus he can speak of his boyhood experience of
"the gladness of being in the swamp" as "the immanence of the wilderness there,"[12] of a wartime "Christmas in the wilderness of the sea,"[13]
of the world as "a holy place, a universe of things ['existing in their
own right'], a wilderness."[14] Here for the first time in our survey it is
through the aesthetic discipline of solitude in the wilderness rather
than through the ethical discipline of the wilderness that paradisic
understanding is restored:

> Things exist in their own right; it is a lesson that escapes us except as
> they hold us in awe. Except we stand on the threshold of the wilderness,
> knowingly, how can our position be true, how can essential truth be
> enacted in our hearts?[15]

[9] *Ibid.*, p. 128.
[10] *Ibid.*, p. 75, where Bugbee refers to Ernst Cassirer, *Language and Myth* (New
York, 1946).
[11] *Ibid.*, p. 155, where besides referring to Oriental literature, he again cites Eckhart.
[12] *Ibid.*, p. 43.
[13] *Ibid.*, pp. 71 f.
[14] *Ibid.*, p. 165.
[15] *Ibid.*, p. 164.

Bugbee's description of the wilderness is both a testimony and a helpful analysis. Indeed it serves to clarify much of the insight which we have been studying through the centuries: the wilderness must be first experienced as wasteland to be known as paradise. But this definition is too exclusively aesthetic and epistemological. It must be enlarged and diversified to include also the ethical, the ecclesiological, and the eschatological connotations of the term. Moreover, in the fullness of human history, precisely the literal designation of the word is acquiring an unexpected religious significance.

Man, according to the biblical myth, was primordially set in a garden at harmony with the multitudes of God's other creatures. Even after the Fall, man in the cataclysm of the divine wrath was charged with the care not only of the domestic beasts of immediate utility to him but also of all creatures, "of clean animals, and of animals that are not clean, and of birds, and of everything that creeps on the ground" in order "to keep their kind alive upon the face of all the earth." Truly the stewardship of Adam for all creatures in the Park of the Great King and the redemptive assignment laid upon Noah before the Deluge is literally in man's keeping today.

Ours is the age of the bulldozer as much as it is the age of the atomic bomb. For good or ill, we need no longer conform to the contours of the earth. The only wilderness that will be left is what we determine shall remain untouched and that other wilderness in the heart of man that only God can touch.

For the first time in the long history of the redemptive meaning of the wilderness, it is in our age that the forest, the jungle, the plain, the unencumbered shore, the desert, the mountain fastness, each with its myriad denizens fashioned by the hand of the Creator in their natural haunts, are becoming, surely more than he now knows, necessary for the completeness of man himself, the only creature fashioned in the image and likeness of God. Man would be less than man without his fellow creatures in all their variety and divine immediacy. Man needs now some companion in the garden bigger and freer than himself.[16]

Without prejudice to the ecclesiastical meanings of the wilderness traced in the foregoing essay, we know with St. Paul that the whole creation has been in travail together with us until now. Only amidst the circumambient wilderness of tundra with its musk oxen, of the sea with its whales, the mountain fastness with its condor and its puma,

---

[16] This, with special reference to the threatened elephants of Africa, is the theme of Romain Gary, *Les Racines du Ciel* (Paris, 1958).

the jungle with its tiger, the woods with its warblers and crows, the veldt or prairie with its gnu and its bison, can man tend the garden in which through the discipline and the grace of the arts and the sciences and his faith he maintains his hold upon that life which God created and called good.

Unless some believers in every generation can, through that poverty by which we divest ourselves of all lordliness, join St. Francis in his canticle addressed to the sun and to the bears as brethren, to the snow and to the swallows as sisters, then in the present stage of mankind's awesome capacity for enforcing lordship over nature—whether in ruthless urbanization of the countryside, or in exploitation of natural resources heedless of generations to come, or in any careless experimentation in the realm of life, disease, and death—we shall presently find that we can no longer address even one another as brother and sister and that a utilitarian view of nature will have blasted our human nature. We shall find that the garden of culture, like the garden which is the Church, will wither or bewilder when it is by artifice fenced off from the ground of our creatureliness.

Wherever we live and work, we must have in our being or refresh within us the awareness of a real wilderness, which now we are called upon not only to contemplate periodically as did the desert Fathers but also to conserve for ourselves and our posterity as well as in the interest the myriad creaturely forms themselves.

Ultimately of course this outer wilderness, both as savage and as benign, as the mystics knew, is also within. It is our true creaturely estate. The long history we have traced gives substance to the hope that the image within us mirroring That which can alone assure us from beyond is indeed glimpsed and recognized only in the serenity of the primeval and the primordial solitude, which are one.

Part Two

THE THEOLOGICAL IDEA
OF THE UNIVERSITY

*The Paradise Theme and Related Motifs
in the History of Higher Education*

ADAM IN THE TERRESTRIAL PARADISE

Let us fly with succoring wings to every creature and bring to it what is wanting to complete that universal confession it essays, suffering and groaning in travail. . . . Yes, I understand . . . that gospel which we have been commanded to bring to every creature. . . .

It is the whole work of Adam in the terrestrial paradise which we now take upon ourselves in a magisterial and systematic way. And what will this terrestrial paradise become from which not a single particle of creation will be excluded? Yes, it is necessary that we come to the rescue of this creation which groans and has need of us. It is necessary to go first of all to the rescue of mankind, but after that, to the rescue of the forest, of the bramble that would be a rose, of the river that implores our aid to prevent its overflowing its banks; it is necessary to come to the aid of the birds and of the savage beasts and of all animals, according to their kinds. It behooves us, placed as we are between God and the earth, to come to the aid of one and all. For all, we should open the passages and the ways by which compassion may be joined with righteousness. We should aid creation to unite not only in faith and in the recollection of our common fall, but also in the paschal and the pentecostal plenitude. We must carry order, moderation, fruitfulness, and the law everywhere. It is needful that nature at the very core of her being heed the order which we bring to her in the name of the Creator. Everything that the creative Word has brought forth must in the end hear also the redemptive Word, that nothing in his creation be stranger to his revelation in glory. Before that solemn mass begin, all the aisles of creation must be cleared that the Priest may pass freely from one end of the church to the other in order to baptize all, while the children of God intone the Vidi aquam *and the* Asperges [*from the cosmic liturgy of the Resurrection*].

PAUL CLAUDEL
Conversations dans le Loir-et-Cher
(Paris: Librairie Gallimard), p. 257.

Introduction

As the oldest university in the United States, Harvard more than any other has preserved the theological memory and the constitutional substance from which derives our feeling in America for the autonomy of the academic community. Concentration in the following sketch on the tradition of one college is intended to clarify its experience and to identify certain theological or quasi-theological motifs that already belong to or may be appropriated by other academic institutions in America, wherever the problem of religion and higher education is under discussion.[1] By reason of its tremendous influence in the rise of American colleges and universities, the history of Harvard is an essential link in the long chronicle of the "transfer of learning" from antiquity to the present day.

Many aspects of the proper relationship among Church, Commonwealth, and College; many laws, privileges, and customs of the university; and, in particular, the nature and function of a university had been fixed by the medieval *studium generale* and by the Reformation academy long before they were translated to the New World shores to constitute, as Cotton Mather once proudly boasted, a truly "American University, presenting herself, with her sons, before her European mothers for their blessing."[2] In dealing with the theological conception of one university, we are ultimately concerned with the Christian meaning of every college or university. We shall trace here, not the history of Harvard University or even the history of theology in Harvard[3] to the founding of the Divinity School in 1811-1816, but rather the theological conception is illustrated by Harvard of what constitutes and motivates a university and the divine sanctions to which it has appealed in defending the interior life of the Republic of Letters.[4] After distinguishing and establishing five university themes

[1] Out of the current situation at Harvard, concerned with defining the proper role of its enlarged Divinity School in the University, have come two other essays on a related theme approached from the point of view of a scholar standing in the Faculty of Arts and Sciences, Morton White, "Religion, Politics, and the Higher Learning," *Confluence*, III (1954); "Religious Commitment and Higher Education," *ibid.*, VI (1957), 137-146.

[2] *Magnalia Christi Americana* (Boston, 1702), iv.

[3] In addition to the earlier histories of Harvard, there are the three basic works of Samuel Eliot Morison: *Three Centuries of Harvard 1636-1936* (Cambridge, 1936); *The Founding of Harvard College* (Cambridge, 1935); *Harvard in the Seventeenth Century*, 2 vols. (Cambridge, 1936); "The History of Universities," *Rice Institute Pamphlet*, XXIII (1936), No. 4, pp. 211-281. A whole chapter is devoted to Harvard in Dunster Metzger, *The Development of Academic Freedom in the United States* (New York, 1955), pp. 78-113; 177-185. See also Charles Lyttle, "A Sketch of the Theological Development of Harvard University, 1636-1805," in *Church History*, V (1936), 301.

[4] This is the designation of Harvard University in the Constitution of the Commonwealth of Massachusetts of 1780, Chap. V.

surviving from antiquity and the Middle Ages in the Harvard of the seventeenth and eighteenth centuries, we shall go back to trace their Old World origins and then return to the nineteenth and twentieth centuries to assess their significance today in respect both to the problem of religion in the university and to the freedom of the university.

Chapter I. The Conception of a University in the Theology of the Founders and Fathers of Harvard

Increase Mather, president of Harvard from 1685 to 1701—the only American president to assume also the title of "rector" and the originator of the university's often-controversial seal *Christo et Ecclesiae*— in one of his now-lost Latin orations paid the following tribute to his presidential predecessor Charles Chauncy (1654–1672):

> That illustrious Charles Chauncy, whom we may properly style *Charlemagne* (*Carolus Magnus*) was a venerable old man, most accomplished in the resources (*presidiis*) of the [sacred] languages [Hebrew and Greek], an uncommonly learned *gymnasiarch*, who devoted himself with exemplary and unfailing diligence to the instruction of the *Sons of the Prophets*. The departure and death of such a man have left the College crippled and debilitated.[1]

The words here italicized all have great significance for the theological conception of a university. The significance of this allusion to the organizer of the palace school in Frankish Gaul will be clear when related material is adduced.

Cotton Mather—almost as much involved in ecclesiastical, academic, and political affairs as his presidential father—could not bring himself to consider antipaedobaptist Henry Dunster (1640–54) as Harvard's first president; he was therefore at pains to find ways of interpreting Dunster's successor, the fully orthodox Chauncy, as the effective founder of learning in the New World. Having followed his father in likening the role of Chauncy to that of Charlemagne, Cotton Mather at another point in his *Magnalia* carried out the military imagery in evoking the memory of the venerable martyr Polycarp, who refused to yield to the earthly emperor out of loyalty to the heavenly Christ, and also in recalling Chauncy's own allusion to the imperial valor of Vespasian:

This eminent *soldier* [Chauncy] of our Lord Jesus Christ, after he was

---

[1] This brief paragraph in Latin survives only in Cotton Mather, *Magnalia*, iv, pt. 1, p. 2. In the Boston edition of 1702, the paragraph appears on p. 14 of Volume II. Hereafter the more available Hartford edition will be cited. The translations from the Latin depend upon those in the Hartford edition; but where the latter are faulty or obscure they have been altered.

come to be fourscore years of age, continued still to "endure hardness as
a good *soldier* of [the Lord] Jesus Christ" [II Tim. 2:3]; and still professed with the aged Polycarp, that he "was not willing to leave the service
of the Lord, that had more than fourscore years been a good master to
him."[2] When his friends pressed him to remit and abate his vast labours,
he would reply, *Oportet Imperatorem stantem mori;*[3] according[ly] he
stood beyond expectation, directing in the learned *camp,* where he had been
a *commander.*[4]

In this conflated image, Cotton Mather is alluding to the university as
the *militia* of Christ, with its commander a stalwart lieutenant of the
King of kings. Just as the 86-year-old bishop-martyr Polycarp declined
to be secured to the stake, insisting that he could stand for execution
unmoved in the power of Christ, and just as the ailing Emperor Vespasian insisted on dying in the posture of command, so the presidential
commander of the *milites Christi* in New England prepared to die in
the posture of duty, be it in the pulpit or at the podium.

Thus far we have identified only one complex of ideas about the
university in the New World—namely, that it was a learned encampment of the militia of Christ. But the allusion to Emperor Charlemagne
had an additional significance.

When Rector Increase Mather referred to Chauncy as the "gymnasiarch . . . of the Sons of the Prophets" in Cambridge, he was giving
expression to a second university theme. This was the deep conviction of the New England Puritans that they had participated epochally
in the transfer of learning to the New World. The two Mathers were
evidently well acquainted with the storied *translatio studii,* from the
schools of the prophets, through the Academy of Athens and the
palace school of Charlemagne, to the medieval universities and Reformation academies. They felt deeply the New World mission of their
university as corporate heir of all the ages in the communication of
Veritas.

In his extravagant nomenclature, Cotton Mather even called Charles
Chauncy the American Cadmus, in reference to the legendary bearer
of letters from Phoenicia to Greece. The story behind this appellation
throws further light upon his conception of the university.

The Mathers and their contemporaries fondly referred to Cambridge
as Kirjath-Sepher (Joshua 15:15), the City of Books.[5] Kirjath-Sepher,

---

[2] Eusebius, *Ecclesiastical History,* iv, xv; cf. *Martyrdom of Polycarp,* ix, 3.
[3] Suetonius, *XII Caesares, Vespasian,* xxiv.
[4] *Magnalia,* iii, § 11 (I, 474).
[5] *Magnalia,* iv, pt. 1, § 2 (II, 9). Kenneth B. Murdock has demonstrated the seriousness of the Matherian appeal to tradition in "Clio in the Wilderness: History and

Debir (Joshua 11:21; 21:15), interpreted as Oracle of Wisdom, and Kirjath-Sannah (Joshua 15:49), interpreted as the City of Acumen, were understood as identical or related cities and together with Hebron as among "the universities of Palestine" at the time of Joshua. On the basis of his readings in classical and biblical lore, Cotton Mather was pleased to perpetuate two etymological surmises in the interest of tracing the continuity of learning. The first was that Cadmus, who in classical mythology vanquished the dragon Pytho, was none other than the Hivite mentioned in Joshua 9:7–17: "for an Hivite signifies as serpent in the language of Syria." The second surmise was that Cadmus had been educated in Hebron or Debir (Kirjath-Sepher) at the time of the "great commander" Joshua and later carried his divine knowledge to Greece. The Lacedemonians in this view were really Cadmonians. Moreover, Cotton Mather continued, "among the old Grecians" a college or university was first called a "Cadmia or Cadmea," subsequently altered to Academy, "in commemoration of Cadmus the Phoenician."[6]

Having thus recalled the significance of the ancient Cadmus, Cotton Mather continued with his application in the lofty style of the epic chronicler:

. . . when some ecclesiastical oppressions [of Cushan-Rishathaim (=Cushan of double wickedness)][7] drove a colony of the truest Israelites into the remoter parts of the world, there was an academy quickly founded in that colony: and our Chauncy was the Cadmus of that academy [he had been once appointed as professor of Hebrew and Greek in old Cambridge]; by whose vast labour and learning the knowledge of the Lord Jesus Christ, served by all human sciences, hath been conveyed unto posterity.[8]

One need not be convinced by this forced, rhetorical effort to estab-

Biography in Puritan New England," *Church History,* XXIV (1955), esp. 232. Ernst Benz has, on the basis of the correspondence involving some four thousand letters between the Mathers and the German Pietists at Halle, indicated a Continental source of many of the Matherian ideas about the university. See "The Wilderness Theme" above, Chapter IV, at n. 1.

[6] *Magnalia,* iii, pt. 2, ch. 23, § 1 (I, 463–464). Some of this construction is made plausible by Cotton's reference to Maccabees, where the Lacedemonians are spoken of as "near of kin" and the Spartans are addressed as "brethren" (II, 6:9; I, 12:6–7); and to Strabo, who confuses Israelites and Arabians; but much of it seems to be Cotton's own imaginative conjecture. The kinship alleged in Maccabees between the Hebrews and Hellenes rested on the supposd connection between Peleg (eponymous ancestor of the Hebrews, Genesis 10:25; 11:16) and the Pelasgians, a prehistoric Aegean maritime race.

[7] The allusion (*ibid.,* I, p. 463) is to double wickedness in Church and State under Laud and Charles. Othniel, upon whom the Spirit of the Lord came, rose up to save Israel against Cushan (Judges 3:7–11).

[8] *Magnalia,* I, 464. Cf. Edmond Dickenson, *Delphi Phoenicezantes* (Oxford, 1655), pp. 22 f.

lish the continuity of the community of letters to be nevertheless impressed by the way Cotton Mather and his contemporaries felt indebted equally to Hebrews and Hellenes for their conception of *Veritas,* and by the sense of stewardship they felt for the communication of divine and human truth to be handed down as a torch from generation to pious generation.

Jonathan Mitchell, writing about 1663,[9] reproduced the traditional *translatio studii* in somewhat attenuated form in ascribing to "the Light of nature" the encouragement of schools among "the Egyptians, Babylonians, Persians, Grecians and Romans," alongside "of sundry Schools or colledges in Israel wherein scholars (or sons of ye prophets) were trained up, some of which Elijah (as their visitor [=Overseer]) did visit."[10]

The sense of responsibility that "the knowledge of the Lord" and "the Light of nature" be "conveyed unto posterity" in "a succession of a learned ministry"[11] is the basic theme of the *translatio studii,* to the long history of which we shall presently turn.

In addition to the conception of the providential transfer of learning from land to land and from people to people, and the other conception of the university as a local encampment of the universal militia of Christ, we find a third educational theory—namely, that the continuity of instruction is thought to be maintained in part by inspiration; and consequently that the *doctor* of a university is in succession to the *prophets* and the *apostles.*

In the *Funeral Discourse upon the Death of the Very Reverend and Aged Dr. Increase Mather,*[12] Benjamin Colman gave expression to the view then common that "Elijah and Elisha, after Samuel, seem to have been the Heads and Presidents of Israel's Colleges";[13] and Increase Mather was therefore mourned and lauded as "Patriarch and Prophet," "Minister and Doctor." In a funeral sermon for President John Leverett (1708–1724) the following year, Colman could be even more specific in his elaboration of the theme, since, unlike Increase Mather, Leverett had died while in presidential office. "Prophets," he said, "were their masters and Presidents, and the Spirit of prophecy rested

[9] *A Modell for the Maintaining of Students and Fellows of Choise Abilities at the Colledge in Cambridge,* in *Harvard College Records,* III (Publications of the Colonial Society of Massachusetts, XXXI), 309.

[10] Mitchell has another reference to sons of the prophets and Nazirites on p. 312. *A Modell* also quotes at length Luther's *Letter in Behalf of Christian Education* (1524), pp. 310–311.

[11] *Magnalia,* iv, pt. 1, § 1 (II, 8).

[12] Boston, 1723.

[13] II Kings 4:38 ff. The biblical word is band, not school.

upon many of them."[14] Everywhere the notion was quite familiar that "The Sons of the Prophets were the Scholars that dwelt and studied and worship'd in the Colleges of Israel."[15] Colman felt it useful, however, to quote Symeon Patrick (1627-1707), successively bishop of Chichester and Ely, on an additional point. By "the Sons of the Prophets" are meant the Scholars of the Prophets," on some of whom God bestowed the spirit of prophecy; and these schools of the prophets flourished by God's grace in precisely those areas which need most the heavenly teaching and rebuke.[16]

Elisha is the only prophet recorded as having received an unction comparable to that of the king and priest in ancient Israel. In I Kings 19:16, Elijah is enjoined: ". . . and Elisha the son of Shaphat of Abelmeholah shalt thou anoint to be prophet in thy room." Thus the annointed Elisha, as a type of Christ, was understood to exercise an authority over the school of the prophets with a specifically *christological* sanction; and, in the schools of the prophets in succession to his, the authority of the masters was consequently felt to be in part grounded upon the doctoral authority of Christ himself in his threefold office of *prophet* (in the sense of teacher), priest, and king. Benjamin Colman, for example, in preaching on President Leverett as the "Master taken up from the sons of the prophets," referred to Christ as a great prophet[17] and to God as the Father of spirits,[18] observing that prophets belong to "a Supreme Order"[19] and "though called Gods on earth yet must die like men."[20] President Chauncy in an earlier sermon on the sons of the prophets distinguished even in the school of Elisha between "sons of the prophets" who were taught and disciplined and other prophets who "had their calling *immediately* from God."[21] But the distinction between the two in the old and the new Israel was never absolute, and Chauncy was emphatic that "the calling of a Prophet is such an honour as the title was given to the Lord Jesus himself."[22]

---

[14] *The Master Taken up from the Sons of the Prophets:/ A Sermon Preached at Cambridge/ Upon the Sudden Death/ of the Reverend and Learned John Leverett,/ President of Harvard College* (Boston, 1724), p. 2.

[15] *Ibid.*, p. 3.

[16] *A Commentary upon the Historical Books of the Old Testament.* I could consult only the fourth edition (London, 1732), II, 451.

[17] Colman, *The Master Taken up*, p. 10; cf. his *Funeral Discourse*, p. 31.

[18] *The Master Taken up*, p. 12.

[19] *Funeral Discourse*, p. 14.

[20] *Funeral Discourse*, pp. 13-14.

[21] *God's Mercy Shewed to His People* (Cambridge, 1658), p. 3.

[22] *God's Mercy*, p. 12. Jonathan Mitchell, confident that the prophetical and priestly office of Christ was completely vindicated in the "First Times of the Reformation," felt "that it only remained in New England to Clear the Rights of Christ's Kingly Office."

The conviction that the knowledge and wisdom, the *Veritas,* of which the university was custodian by virtue of the succession in which it stood in the millennial transfer of studies from the school of the anointed Elisha through Athens and Paris to the inspired instruction of the new Cambridge, the new Kirjath-Sepher, is related to a fourth theme: the paradisic motif.

Basic here, as we have already observed in Part I, is the guarded theological surmise that, in some sense, what had been lost in Paradise by Adam's overweening grasp for the knowledge of good and evil had been partially restored in the disciplined fellowship of the school of the prophets. The New England Puritans were unaware of the extent to which the whole Church, in the period before Constantine especially, had considered itself a provisional paradise precisely in respect to redemptive truth. Instead (in a nascent clericalism imperceptibly at variance with their professed congregationalism) they thought of paradisic truth as being limited to duly ordained teachers. According to this view, the truth of Paradise as possessed by Adam before the Fall, a universal truth, had been safeguarded in the corporate custody of disciplined teachers devoted to Christ and his Church and dutifully communicated to posterity. Only in some such manner could a Christian institution of learning justify its existence in the face of the anti-intellectual implications of the biblical account of Adam's fall. Adam had not sufficiently feared God to obey him on a seemingly arbitrary order. Therefore a wholesome reverence for God might be, for fallen reason, the beginning of wisdom.

Harvard's early leaders were fully conscious of the long history of the conflict between faith and reason, inspiration and education. Cotton Mather recalled, for example, the threat to the Christian cause embodied in the legislation of the Emperor Julian the Apostate, who demanded the closing of schools in which instruction in the classics was in the hands of Christians.[23] Because of the long controversy in old England and new on the legitimacy of clerical training over against direct inspiration, Harvard had to contend against the recurrent popular threat to the College from the withdrawal or reduction of tax support.

Charles Chauncy, writing in 1658,[24] distinguishes two kinds of opponents of education—namely, those who opposed the university

---

The Great End and Interest of New-England, 1662; reprinted by Increase Mather in *Elijah's Mantle* (Boston, 1722), p. 2.

[23] *Magnalia,* iv, pt. 1, § 1 (II, 8).

[24] *God's Mercy,* esp. pp. 31 ff. Cf. Samuel Eliot Morison, *Harvard in the Seventeenth Century* (Cambridge, 1936), I, 331, n. 2.

altogether and those who merely opposed it as a center of ministerial training, on the ground that inspiration was alone sufficient for a truly godly clergy. Although Chauncy's named foes and allies were English antagonists outside the colony,[25] the occasion of his writing was the aversion of "The Separation" to a learned ministry; and he urged them to consider "the college" in Jerusalem to which Hilkiah the priest repaired to consult the prophetess Huldah (II Kings 22:14), and to be mindful of the fact that Jesus taught disciples and Gamaliel taught Paul.

Cotton Mather, in his defense of ministerial education, enthusiastically cited Dr. John Arrowsmith (1602–1659), vice-chancellor (1647) and Regius professor of divinity (1651) at Cambridge, and his reasoned refutation of the Weigelians.[26] The Lutheran Spiritualist Valentin Weigel (1533–1588) had come to the conclusion that learning clogged the conduits of divine inspiration. Mather summarized Weigel's thought about clerical education with a Latin characterization found in Arrowsmith to the effect that "there is no Academy in the world, where Christ is to be found: in such institutions not a particle of the knowledge of Christ can be obtained; that Christ did not wish to have the Gospel preached by devils and therefore not by academicians."[27]

Thus the defenders of Harvard had in various ways to counter the allegedly Christian or biblical arguments against a learned clergy and the consequent repudiation of a Christian academy as a contradiction in terms. In Harvard's defense they elaborated a series of interrelated propositions according to which the universal light of reason and the

25 William Dell, Sydrach Simpson, John Crandon, Richard Baxter. Chauncy does not mention John Milton (see above, Part One, Chapter III, sec. 2), or Roger Williams (Part One, Chapter IV, sec. 1). The latter, however, well represents the view in *The Hireling Ministry* (1652) that, though universities are excellent in their general purpose, they are not for the training of "the begetting ministry of the apostles or messengers to the nations" as distinguished from "the merely prudential" feeding ministry of pastors and teachers"; and he points with satisfaction to the fact that just as Thomas Cromwell destroyed the monasteries so Oliver Cromwell was destroying the monastic universities as "seed-plots" for "mystical merchants." A representative defense of the walled garden against the "wild boars coming out of Rome's wood and wilderness" (Psalm 80:13) is that of Robert Borman, *Paidea Thriambos* (London, 1653). Borman makes much of the two ministries of pastor and *doctor*, both essential to the well-being of Church, School, and Kingdom.

On the whole problem, see Richard Schlatter, "The Higher Learning in Puritan England," *Historical Magazine of the Protestant Episcopal Church*, XXIII (1954), 167–187, and more recently, Howard Schultz, *Milton and Forbidden Knowledge* (New York, 1955), esp. pp. 184 ff.

26 *Tactica sacra; sive, de milite spirituali pugnante, vincente, et triumphante Dissertatio: Accesserunt Orationes aliquot anti-Weigelianae* (1657).

27 *Magnalia*, iv (II, 7). One of Weigel's numerous learned works against clerical learning is *Anweisung zur rechten Schule Gottes; Erweisung, dass heut zu Tage fast allenthalben in Europa in allen Kirchen und Schulen kein einziger Stuhl sey, darauf nicht ein Pseudo-Propheta und Pseudo-Christus sitze* (Halle, 1609).

incarnate Word had in separate dispensations ordained schools of learning, while the direct inspiration of the Spirit experienced in the schools of the prophets survived unabated in the carefully guarded traditions of the academic community—traditions that went back indeed to Paradise before the Fall, when faith and reason were as one.

The *libido sciendi* and the *libido sentiendi* had together compassed the fall of man; and thus, in the monastic tradition of learned celibacy out of which the ideal of the medieval university in part developed, faith and continence were held to be the two ordained means of restoring reason to something of its paradisic perfection. In the Calvinist mutation of this ascetic tradition which brought with it the abandonment of clerical celibacy, the paradisic ideal persisted in the rigorous discipline of the academy and in the programmatic situating of the academy in the community of love under Christ the new Adam. Hence the dedication of the University under Increase Mather to Christ and the Church (*Christo et Ecclesiae*).

Even human as distinguished from divine knowledge (revelation) was thought to be most certainly secured from distortion and fragmentation through the dedication of the fellowship of learning to Christ the Truth as perceived from the vantage point of the community of faith. Cotton Mather, in insisting on the reliability of reason in tutelage to faith and on the universality of truth, thought it worth noting that what his contemporaries called *academiae* their forefathers had more commonly called *universitates,* "quod universarum divinarumque rerum cognitio, in iis, ut thesauro conservato aperiatur."[28] The revelation of universal stores of human and divine knowledge like a hidden treasure suggests a striking cabalistic passage in two of the histories of universities to which Increase Mather refers[29]—namely, that of the Christian Hebraist Jacob Alting,[30] and that of the German jurist Johann Wilhelm Itter.[31] According to these writers, Adam, on leaving Paradise, tried to carry out with him the book of wisdom (Genesis 5:1—the book of the generations of Adam), whereupon the book was wafted up into heaven; only in response to his supplication was it restored to him by God, on condition that he not permit knowledge to be lost among the children of men and that he devise means for its orderly succession in each generation.[32]

---

[28] *Magnalia*, iv, pt. 1, § 1 (II, 8).

[29] *Magnalia*, iv, pt. 1, § 6 (II, 19–20).

[30] *Hebraeorum respublica scholastica: sive historia academiarum* (Amsterdam, 1652), pp. 62–63.

[31] *De honoribus sive gradibus academicis* (Frankfurt, 1698), pp. 74–75.

[32] Alting himself gives as his source for what "the most ancient rabbis" said about

Benjamin Colman, without referring expressly to the truth of Paradise, was quite explicit about the proper relationship between theology and "all human literature, Arts and Sciences," which are "as humble hand maids to wait and minister to the other as their mistress and queen."[33]

Both Increase and Cotton Mather were widely read in the history of universities. Rector Mather apparently improved his time between audiences with three British sovereigns—from whom he besought a new charter for the colony in 1691 and a confirmation, if possible, of the old charter of the college—by reading the history of university law and custom. Before, during, and after his English sojourn, he became acquainted not only with Jacob Alting (d. 1676) and Johann Itter (d. 1725) but also with the Swiss anti-Lutheran polemicist Rudolph Hospinian (d. 1626), the Wittenberg jurisconsult Caspar Ziegler (d. 1690),[34] Jacob Middendorp (d. 1611),[35] the Catholic classicist Valentin Rotmar (d. 1581),[36] the Leyden theologian Francis Junius (d. 1602),[37] Edward Leigh (d. 1671),[38] and Hermann Conring (d. 1681). Increase Mather is known to have had in his library at least three of their works.[39] Part of his erudition in the history of education found institutional expression in Increase Mather's assumption of the dignity of "rector" (1686–1692)[40] and especially in his acceptance of the doctoral dignity,

---

this book the late thirteenth-century Menahem ben Benjamin Recanati, in whose *Commentary on the Pentateuch* is quoted the Cabalistic *Zohar*, folio 55b. Professor Harry Wolfson finds the reference in the Venetian edition of Recanati (1523), folio 25, cols. 2–3; he notes that Alting's reference to the restoration of the book *"ea conditione*, ne oblivione periret a filiis hominum ejus sapientia, sed ut eam posteris communicaret" reads not "on condition that" but simply "in order that." For the English rendering of the passage, see *The Zohar*, translated by Harry Sperling and Maurice Simon (London, 1931), I, 176–177. Another place in which Jewish educational theory was influential at Harvard was in the claim that the school was superior to the synagogue (meetinghouse) in President John Leverett's *Discourse on John Harvard* (1670). The doctrine that "the sanctity of a school is greater than the sanctity of a synagogue" goes back by way of Thomas Godwyn's *Moses and Aaron* (1641), *lib*. ii, *cap*. ii, p. 72, to Maimonides. See Samuel Eliot Morison, *The Founding of Harvard College* (Cambridge, 1935), p. 221, n. 1.

[33] *The Master* [Leverett] *Taken up*, p. 9.

[34] *De juribus majestatis*. Only the emperor can authorize a university.

[35] *Academiarum celebrium universi terrarum orbis libri viii* (Cologne, 1602).

[36] *Annales Academiae Ingolstadiensis*.

[37] *De Academiis*.

[38] *Treatise of Religion and Learning and Religion and Learned Men (1652)*. Conring's work is *De antiquitatibus Academicis* (1739).

[39] In the *Catalogue* of Dr. Cotton Mather's library purchased by Isaiah Thomas, Itter's work of 1685 has the following inscription: "I. Mather. London, November 19, 1691 . . ." See Julius Herbert Tuttle, "The Libraries of the Mathers," in *Proceedings*, American Antiquarian Society, II (1909–1910), 333. Cf. Henry Joel Cadbury, "Harvard College Library and the Libraries of the Mathers," *ibid.*, L (1939–1940), 8, 22. On Itter, see also note 52 below. Increase seems to have had some personal knowledge of Itter: "juvenis doctissimus Christianus."

[40] After 1692, when a new college charter was in force, he was styled president. Both

proffered him by the university corporation of which he was himself the president and his son a fellow.

President Mather's S.T.D., construed at the time as earned rather than merely honorific, was the first doctorate to be awarded in America. The bestowal has been variously interpreted by modern scholars[41] as an act of mutual admiration, as an act of gratitude for Mather's securing a college charter pointedly omitting overseers or any visitorial power, and as a "gesture of sovereignty." In any event, the bestowal of a doctorate and two baccalaureate degrees in theology on September 5, 1692, was a self-conscious departure in the history of the college.[42]

It is the sense of the sovereignty or autonomy of the university which should be especially emphasized in the light of all the references to the history of the doctorate which survive from the pens of the Mathers, father and son. In bringing together his father's papers in the *Parentator*,[43] Cotton recalled that Increase "had nothing more at Heart than the Interest of the College," and that his status as rector enhanced his mission with the nominally Calvinist King William, to whom he appealed with success for protection lest "the College built by Non-Conformists should be taken from them, and put into the Hands of Conformists."

Fear of the visitorial encroachments of the visible Anglican Church prompted the rector to make explicit the dedication of Harvard's quest of *Veritas* both to the Universal but wholly invisible Church of Calvinist Congregationalism and to the King of kings above all earthly magistrates and their academic visitors. Hence the mention in the college charter of 1692 of a "Common Seale" (*Christo et Ecclesiae*)[44]— intended as a shield against interference from Massachusetts magistrates unsympathetic with the strict Calvinism of the founding fathers of the commonwealth and college.

The college charter of 1692 contains other Matherian gestures of academic sovereignty. The exemption of the president, fellows,

---

Kenneth B. Murdock and Samuel E. Morison give as the reason for a temporary deviation in usage the fact that the president of the New England Council had pre-empted the presidential title; but Mather's own interest in drawing upon the usage of the Continental university tradition may have been a more important consideration. See Murdock's *Increase Mather* (Cambridge, 1926) and Morison's *Seventeenth Century*, Vol. II.

[41] Kenneth B. Murdock, Samuel E. Morison, Perry Miller.

[42] *Harvard College Records,* I (Massachusetts Historical Records, XV), 340.

[43] *Memoirs of Remarkables in the Life and Death of the Ever-Memorable Dr. Increase Mather* (Boston, 1724), esp. pp. 112–113, 154, 171–172.

[44] *Harvard College Records,* I, 335–338. Ordered and thereupon cut by John Coney in 1693. Samuel E. Morison, "Harvard Seals and Arms," *Harvard Graduates Magazine,* XLII (September, 1933), 5.

scholars, and a specified number of their servants "from all Personal Civil Offices, Military Exercises, watchings and wardings, And the Estates [of these same officers] . . . free from all Rates and Taxes" are provisions and immunities that ultimately hark back to the privileges accorded the University of Bologna and the *doctores* of civil and canon law by Emperor Frederick I.[45]

Especially important in the Matherian charter of 1692 is the assertion of the "power from time to time, to grant and admit to Academical Degrees, as in the Universities in England." The sense of institutional maturation and independence is very close to the surface of the formal, imitative Latin formularies of Mather's doctoral citation.[46] Extensive reading in the history of universities and academic degrees had informed the Mathers, father and son, that the first doctorates were granted by Emperor Lothair II (1125-1138) to professors of civil law about 1135:

Lotharius the emperor, having found in Italy a copy of the "Roman civil law,"[47] which he was greatly taken withal, he ordained that it should be "publickly expounded in the schools"; and that he might give encouragement unto this employment, it was ordained that the public professors of this law should be dignified with the style of doctors, whereof Bulgarus Hugolinus, with others, was the first.[48] Not long after, this rite of creating doctors was borrowed of the lawyers by divines, who in their schools publickly taught divinity; and the imitation took place first in Bononia, Paris and Oxford.[49] But I see not why such marks of honour may not be properly given by an American University. . . .[50]

Here follows a transcription of Increase's diploma, interesting as "the

[45] For the history of the liberties beyond Frederick I back to Vespasian, see Pearl Kibre, "Scholarly Privileges," *American Historical Review*, LIX (1954), 543. With the transfer of empire went the transfer of scholarly liberties assimilated to those clerics.

I have shown elsewhere that certain American academies likewise secured comparable immunities in their charters, probably under the influence of Harvard's charter. At the end of the colonial period and the beginning of the national period the college, the university, the academy, and the seminary were not clearly differentiated. See my "The Seminary in the Wilderness," *Harvard Library Bulletin*, XIII (1959), esp. 384 ff.

[46] Cotton Mather, *Parentator*, pp. 171-172; *Magnalia*, iv, pt. 1, § 9 (II, 26).

[47] This oversimplification was first corrected by Savigny. It is to be found, among other places, in a university history known to Mather, namely, Itter's *De gradibus*, pp. 73, 86.

[48] Cotton considers the two as one. Itter gives Bulgarus, Hugolinus, Martinus, Pileus. *De gradibus*, p. 86. The four doctors, glossators on the text of Irnerius, were Hugolinus, Rogerius, Placentinus, Azo. So Hastings Rashdall, *History of Medieval Universities* (2nd ed., Oxford, 1936), p. 255.

[49] Itter (p. 86) mentioned Peter Lombard at Paris as possibly the first to receive the theological doctorate. His position as chancellor and first doctor of theology in the Old World would thus correspond to Rector Mather's in the New; but Cotton Mather does not make this express comparison.

[50] *Magnalia*, iv, pt. 1, § 9 (II, 26).

sole instance of such a thing done in the whole English America."

The Mathers, conscious of the Catholic "Seminaries of Canada and Mexico," were zealous for the assumption of full university status by the only American university of "this protestant and puritan country."[51] At the same time, both of the Mathers were keenly conscious of the problem at Harvard of maintaining both academic liberty and the full status of a degree-granting university. Academic liberty meant to the Mathers, of course, only two things: (1) over against distant Anglicans and local Congregationalists of latitudinarian sympathies, the right to perpetuate the pristine Puritanism of the founders of the Bay Colony; and (2) over against the Spiritual successors of Anne Hutchinson, the right to raise up a clergy learned both in the classical and the biblical traditions. The according of full university status to Harvard, connected with the right to grant degrees, the Mathers acknowledged to be a prerogative of the Crown. As Protestants, reluctant to acknowledge the prerogative of the Pope in chartering medieval universities, they stressed the imperial and royal lineage of the university tradition. They were familiar with Catholic Valentin Rotmar's distinction between *collegia* as ecclesiastical bodies endowed with privileges by the Pope and *academiae,* which derive their authority from the prince.[52] But Increase Mather expressly rejected this distinction. In a Latin address, delivered at the first commencement after his return, Mather dealt with the question, if this degree-granting prerogative be one of sovereignty, ". . . what has New-England to do with an academy?"—or "What has the New-England Cambridge to do with an academic degree?" His was the proud asseveration of the returned diplomat: "I would have such objectors understand that our academy is now established and confirmed by royal authority." But confirmation of the rights of Harvard was not the same as the bestowal of these rights. It is quite possible that there played in the back of the rector-president's mind, as a result of his extensive reading in the history of universities, the mounting conviction that the Reformed Church—and specifically the New England *Ecclesia* under Christ (like the medieval Church under the Pope)—might charter, sanction, or confirm a true

---

[51] *Ibid.,* § 1 (II, 9). Cotton boasts with Voetius "that whereas there are no less than ten provinces in the Popish Belgium, and there are no more than two Universities in them, there are but seven provinces in the reformed Belgium, and there are five Universities therein, besides other academical societies."

[52] *Magnalia,* iv, pt. 1, § 6 (II, 19): "Mitto Rotmarum, qui collegia corpora ecclesiastica esse vult ac igitur *pro academiis non habendae, quae privilegiis pontificorum non sunt donatae.*" This may be derived directly from Rotmar or may be adapted from Itter, *De gradibus,* pp. 118–119: ". . . Rotmar *pro Academiis non habendas* ait, *quae non munitae sunt privilegiis Pontificum.*"

university. Indeed, under the college charter of 1650, Baptist President Dunster had proceeded to the granting of degrees without express permission.[53] And in the measure that Increase Mather met political opposition, he found himself increasingly articulate as to the political autonomy of Harvard, even if it meant the sacrifice of the external privilege of granting degrees; for Harvard was in prophetic—i.e., doctoral—succession by way of the Genevan Academy with the school of the prophets under Elijah, from whom the mantle of teaching authority passed from "president" to "president." To this point he had come in his theory of what constitutes a university when he wrote down among five despairing queries in June or July of 1700:

If they [the General Court] consent to have a clause in the Colledge Charter expressly declaring that the Corporation may if they will Chuse such to be Presidents and Fellows as are known to espouse these principles which our Fathers came into this Land for no other reason but that so they and their posterity might not be Corrupted therewith, will there not be sin in it?

It is clear that he was almost ready to argue that it would be better to have the college "turned into a school for Academical Learning without privilege of Conferring degrees, as in Geneva . . . than to consent to such fatal alterations in the government of the Colledge."[54]

In the end, after a decade of charter-mongering, the old charter of 1650 (under which Harvard still operates) was declared in force by Governor Dudley in return for the General Court's confirmation of tolerant John Leverett in the succession to the presidency by their voting a proper salary. It is generally emphasized by the historians of Harvard University that Increase Mather, by reason of his stubborn nonresidency, his attempt in 1699 to secure a college charter directed against liberals like Leverett and Brattle, his effort to impose strict Congregationalism as a future condition of election to the presidency and to fellowship, and his despairing suggestion that the university might dispense with degrees on the Genevan model, can be set down as at best only a qualified success in his administration of the university, despite his incomparable learning. Nevertheless, a fresh reading of the sources upon which he drew in articulating his theory of the university leads to the conclusion that, within the limitations of his own culture, he was groping for the defense of what one could consider

[53] See Samuel Eliot Morison, *Three Centuries of Harvard 1636–1936* (Cambridge, 1936), p. 35: "The granting of degrees was the boldest thing President Dunster and the first Board of Overseers did; for the conferring of academic titles was a jealously guarded prerogative of sovereignty."
[54] These are Queries 3 and 5. All five queries and the reason for dating the manuscript are to be found in Morison, *Seventeenth Century*, II, 526–527.

academic freedom—the freedom of the interior life of the university from interference at the hands of the magistracy and electorate, even though dependent upon them for financial support. He was abreast of and open to the secular scholarship of his time. Though equivocal in his utterances and successive policies, he must be accorded a place in the history of the efforts to maintain the spiritual autonomy of the academic community. As his son said of him, he endeavored to secure for the Province both its English and its Christian liberties.[55] Among beneficiaries of the latter he would have included the college itself, dedicated to the invisible Church under Christ.

Cotton, his son, was quite clear about the illegitimacy of inter-mingling magisterial and ecclesiastical functions. He was careful in the appropriate section in the *Magnalia*[56] to point out that Moses and David in the Old Dispensation were exceptional and inimitable in their combination of the offices of prince and prophet. He cited even within the Old Covenant the divine chastisement of King Uzziah for presuming to offer incense (II Chronicles 26:16-17), i.e., to combine religious and civil functions. Both of the Mathers, in keeping with their Calvinist heritage, understood the doctoral and pastoral functions to be subsumed under the office of prophet. Church officers and magis-trates should not interfere in the affairs proper to the other. The Teacher of the Second Church of Boston, who was at the same time the Rector of the School of the Prophets in Kirjath-Sepher, held that the definition of doctrine lay within the competence of the Church and the University—not of the Magistrate.

Benjamin Colman, in the already cited sermon on the death of Presi-dent Leverett, referred to the three co-ordinate societies as School, Sanctuary, and State.[57] Nevertheless, in his and other writings of the period, though the Church and the State and the University are vaguely co-ordinate, the College is much closer to the Church than to the State upon which it may depend for its exterior form and privi-leges. The interior life of the Academy was more like that of the gathered Church than of the elected General Court.

We may now conclude this survey of the theological conception of Harvard in the formative years with a summary enumeration of all the venerable themes and theories about the university that had been successfully transplanted to American shores.

We can refer to the last principle—that of the co-ordinate authority

---

[55] *Magnalia*, iv, pt. 1, § 6 (II, 18).
[56] *Magnalia*, v, pt. 2, 17, § 5 (II, 235).
[57] *The Master Taken up*, esp. pp. 8–9.

and the relative autonomy of the University in respect both to the Church and to the State—as the *critical* theme. As we have seen, it was only imperfectly represented in the period under discussion.

Second, though the corporate right to grant degrees is confirmed by the State, the doctoral or professorial authority is akin to and in succession to prophetic authority and finds its ultimate sanction in Christ, whose threefold office was that of priest, prophet (*doctor*), and king. We can refer to this and related motifs as the *christological* theme, whereby divine sanction is appealed to for the co-ordinate authority and relative autonomy of the university and the professor.

Third, though Theodore Beza was known to have called some universities "fans of Satan"[58] and Luther to have castigated the "Popish" universities,[59] nevertheless the founders and builders of Harvard in the seventeenth century were conscious that their college stood in the epic succession whereby, under God's providence, learning had been transferred from antiquity through the medieval universities to the New World. With this providential translation came the divine compulsion to provide for the orderly succession of knowledge from generation to generation. We can refer to the *translatio studii* as the *transferential* theme.

Fourth, though reason had been impaired by the Fall, the dedicated community of scholars might still hope, through self-discipline and the integration of faith and reason, to rectify the error of primal man and safeguard knowledge, human and divine, from distortion and fragmentation. We shall continue to refer to this motif as the *paradisic* theme in the community of learning.

Fifth, the discipline of the academic community is a special kind of spiritual warfare, and hence the university may be thought of as an encampment of the militia of Christ. We can refer to this recurrent strand as learned warfare, the academic adaptation of Christian spiritual warfare, which is itself a continuation of the polemical parallelism by which the primitive Church first drew the contrast between the Kingdom of Christ and the kingdoms of this world—notably, the Roman Empire. This is the *martial* theme.

Having shown how these five themes or motifs were variously present in the minds of the makers of seventeenth-century Harvard, we shall now fill out their Old World lineage, of which we have only here and there indicated the development. Then we shall return to the America of Increase Mather's successors, prepared to trace the interweaving of these same themes into the modern period.

[58] Cited in *Magnalia*, iv (II, 7).
[59] *Ibid.*; also Chauncy, *God's Mercy*, p. 31.

Chapter II. The Five Themes in the History of the University in the Old World to the Reformation

The history of the theological idea of the university begins, not with the catechetical schools of Christian antiquity, but rather with asceticism conceived as the true philosophy and with the ancient church and later the monastery in the desert considered as a provisional restoration of Paradise.

The relatively independent order (*taxis*) or choir (*choros*) of teachers as a ministry in the ancient Church distinct from that of the liturgical clergy did not, to be sure, long survive the Gnostic crisis of the second century. Nor could the catechetical schools under such free and winsome laical *doctores* or *didaskaloi* as Justin Martyr in Rome and Clement and Origen in Alexandria long resist the steadily mounting pressure to bring catechetical instruction and doctrinal formulation under the magisterial authority of the bishop and the bishops collectively in synod.[1] We have dealt elsewhere with the claim of the whole Church to be a paradise. Group discipline, catechetical instruction, sacramental rebirth were, as we have seen,[2] the ordained means of recovering that clarity of mind and purity of will lost in the Fall from Paradise. We are, in the present essay, limited to the claim of the ancient monastery to be a provisional paradise and especially to the rootage of Christian scholarship in that tradition and to the allied monastic theme of spiritual warfare.

We therefore begin our survey of the theological history of the university in terms of the five motifs we have distinguished in the conception of the nature and function of Harvard College in the colonial period by recalling Jerome's conception of the monastery as a provisional paradise in his *Letter to Rusticus* (411):

[1] I have briefly traced the extinction of the teaching order in *The Ministry in Historical Perspectives*, ed. H. Richard Niebuhr and Daniel D. Williams (New York, 1956), esp. pp. 45 ff., with the recent literature. For quite recent contributions to the history of Christian education in the post-Constantinian period and the problem of the place of the classics therein, see Glanville Downey, "Education in the Christian Roman Empire: Christian and Pagan Theories under Constantine and his Successors," *Speculum*, XXXII (1957), 48; "The Emperor Julian and the Schools," *The Classical Journal*, LIII (1957), 97; "Justinian's View of the Classics in Christian Education," *The Anglican Theological Review*, January, 1958. In the latter, Downey shows that the University of Athens was "closed" because the pagan teachers could not conscientiously turn Christian, which was the condition laid down by Justinian for any further instruction in classical subjects. The oft-noted coincidence of this action and the founding of Monte Cassino as the center of a new kind of discipline and philosophy retains its significance.

[2] "The Wilderness Theme" above, Part One, Chapter II, sec. 1.

The sons of the prophets, whom we consider the monks of the Old Testament, built for themselves huts by the waters of Jordan and, forsaking crowded cities, lived in these on pottage and wild herbs [II Kings 4:38–39; 6:1–2]. As long as you are in your native land, make your cell your *Paradise,* gather there the varied fruits (*poma*) of Scripture: make the use of these your sole delight, the embrace of these your only pleasure. To spare your soul spare nothing else.[3]

The allusion to the Fall is clear. Learned celibacy in the garden of faith is the prescribed means of restoring in one hermt's hut, at least, the wisdom of Paradise. Thus had the Christian Hebraist Jerome found a vital and purportedly Christian sanction for the pursuit of Christian studies, albeit in isolation.

Leaving out of account the history of formal Christian education as such and concentrating on our selected themes, we can note that some four centuries after Jerome, amidst the Carolingian Renaissance, Alcuin among others picked up the paradisic theme of the pre-Constantinian Christians and the post-Constantinian monks. In a letter (796–797) from St. Martin's to Charlemagne, he likened the Garden of Eden, which was York, and its extension to Tours, to sprigs taken from (the tree of) Paradise with its fruits—which, in the language of King Solomon's canticles, were to be eaten in paradisic abandon.[4] And in another letter to Charlemagne (799) he compared the Carolingian school and the Athenian academy, noting that the latter had shone with the *science* of the seven arts, while the Christian school exceeded all in *wisdom* because the seven arts had been enriched by the fullness of the seven gifts of the Holy Spirit.[5] Smaragdus, abbot of St. Mihiel-sur-Meuse, elaborated the paradisic motif. In the prefatory poem of his widely circulated commentary on the Rule of St. Benedict around 817, he compared the ablution of baptism with the laver of contrite tears, whereby simple Christians advanced to the status of denizens of the monastic paradise.[6]

This confidence in the superiority of ascetic Christian learning over the pagan—of the sciences integrated by faith—is vividly expressed in a St. Gall codex describing a now-vanished fresco of the monastery under Abbot Grimold (841–872); here St. Sophia is apostrophized as

[3] This is *Ep.* CXXV (formerly numbered as IV and also as XCV); Migne, *PL,* XXII, p. 1076; *NPF,* VI, p. 246. A similar conception is to be found in *Ep.* LVIII, 7, *Ad Paulinum,* quoted above in Part One, Chapter II, at n. 45.

[4] *Monumenta Germaniae Historica* (henceforth *MGH*), *Ep.* IV, No. 121, p. 177, 4 ff.: "emissiones paradisi cum pomorum fructibus."

[5] *Ibid.,* No. 170, p. 279, 16 ff.

[6] *PL,* CII, 691. A variant text is printed by C. B. du Boulay, *Historia Universitatis Parisiensis* (Paris, 1665–1673), I, 643.

the mother of the seven arts, and the suggestion is very close that theology, pictured as a woman (suggested in part by the figure of philosophy in Boethius' *De consolatione*), is the source of all sciences.[7] This view becomes explicit in a related manuscript.[8]

It was in St. Gall in 884 (just a few years after the poem describing the monastery fresco) that Notker the Stammerer, among the first, announced another of our five university themes—the transferential. In his *Gesta Karoli,* later much quoted, Notker wrote that Charlemagne gave the Abbey of St. Martin's to Alcuin, "whose teaching had proved to be of such fruitfulness that the modern Gauls or Franks might be said to equal the ancient Romans and Athenians."[9] In this same spirit, Heiric of Auxerre, writing about 875 to Charles the Bald, praised him even above Charlemagne for his love of knowledge and showed how, in imitation of wisest Solomon, by his alertness to and patronage of scholarship wherever it could be found, Charles the Bald had succeeded in transferring the privileges of Greece "to our climes."[10]

Before tracing the development of this strand, we must reach back to pick up one other Carolingian contribution to the woven tapestry of the academic tradition. Charlemagne himself in an undated letter (780–800) urged bishops and abbots to bestir themselves in the cause of education "as befits the soldiers of the Church."[11]

The martial imagery in describing the children of Israel is, of course, well grounded in the Old Testament; and Paul gave prominence to the ideal of the individual soldier of Christ.

Before Christianity had been established as the religion of the Roman Empire, Origen argued, against the pagan detractors of Christianity as unpatriotic, that in point of fact the whole Christian community through its prayers in the Holy Spirit was more effective than the imperial legions. The concept of the Christian as a soldier of Christ and martyr-combatant was elaborated in polemical parallelism over against

---

[7] This iconographic and literary evidence of the conflation of theology and philosophy as the mother of seven daughters, the arts and sciences, is discussed by Julius von Schlosser, "Beiträge zur Kunstgeschichte aus den Schriftquellen des frühen Mittelalters," in *Sitzungsberichte der Wiener Akademie der Wissenschaft,* philosophisch-historische Klasse, CXXIII (1890), esp. 138.

[8] "Philosophia docet inquirere quid sit honestum: In septem pares sapienter dividit artes. Has quondam peperit Theologia parens." P. Gabriel Meier, "Die 7 freien Künste des MAs," in *Jahresberichte der Lehr- und Erziehungsanstalt des Benedictinerstiftes zu Maria-Einsiedeln* (1886–1887), p. 7.

[9] *MGH,* Scriptores, II, 739, 35 ff.: "Cuius in tantum doctrina fructificavit, ut moderni Galli sive Franci *antiquis* Romanis et Atheniensibus aequarentur."

[10] *MGH,* Poetae, III, 429, 23. Ernst Robert Curtius considers this passage as the oldest form of the *translatio studii* and notes that the literary model was Horace, *Ep.* ii, I, 156; *Europäische Literatur und lateinisches Mittelalter* (Bern, 1948), p. 36, n. 4.

[11] "Karoli epistola de litteris colendis," in *MGH,* Leges, II, i, 79, 38 ff.

the empire. But with the imperial establishment of the Church, the military imagery of pre-Constantinian Christianity moved from the center to the margin of Christian life and was appropriated by the monks in their spiritual warfare.[12] Spiritual warfare meant not only self-discipline but the practice of the "true philosophy."

In the Carolingian age, the specifically "military" function of the Church was the prosecution of learning and, to a lesser extent, the defense of the faith against heresy. Twice in the capitularies of Louis the Pious (829) the bishops, recovering for the clergy of the world what had been cloistered with the regular clergy, referred to themselves and their charges as *milites Christi* precisely in emphasizing their educational responsibilities.[13]

Abbo of Fleury (d. 1004), a representative monastic theorist,[14] adumbrates the critical theme in his tripartite scheme of society with the monastic or celibate university as a third force in Christendom when he describes the three orders as (1) the laymen, including *agricolae, agonistae,* and *principes;* (2) the clerics, consisting of deacons, presbyters, and bishops; and (3) the various monks, whose *vita monastica* is proudly described as a *laboriosum spiritualis philosophiæ otium.*

St. Anselm, a first flower of the scholarship of the monastery, the father of the emerging scholasticism destined to be transferred from the monastic school to the *studium generale* (the university), responded to the last echoes of Tertullian's scornful query "What has Jerusalem to do with Athens?" with the renowned asseveration: "I believe in order that I may know." A distant pupil of Anselm, the encyclopedist Honorius of "Autun," had completely and unconsciously assimilated the arts and sciences of Athens to the grace and wisdom of Jerusalem when, in a brief and popular tract devoted to the problem of the exile of man, he situated natural man in Babylonian Exile, yearning to return to the Jerusalem which is above. For "the exile of men is ignorance; their homeland wisdom, and their way thither passes through the several cities of the arts, sciences, and the philosophies."[15]

[12] On the monk as soldier see H. Edmonds, "Geistlicher Kriegsdienst," *Beiträge zur Geschichte des alten Mönchtums,* Supplement I; E. von Hippel, *Die Krieger Gottes: Die Regel Benedikts als Ausdruck frühchristlicher Gemeinschaftsbildung* (2nd ed., Paderborn, 1953).

[13] *MGH, Leges,* II, vol. ii, p. 35, 19–20 and 40. The goal common to both paradisic contemplation and spiritual warfare is peace; and the idea is not remote that the anointed ruler as the *rex pacificus,* the Christian Solomon, is at once the patron of wisdom and the protector of the peace, of the Church. On the *rex pacificus* and his role in the peace of the Church, see Roger B. Delamare, *L'Idée de la paix à l'époque carolingienne* (Paris, 1939).

[14] *Apologeticus; PL,* CXXXIX.

[15] *PL,* CLXXII, 1243. Honorius flourished in the first quarter of the twelfth century.

Especially interesting is the role of Abelard in weaving the transferential, the paradisic, and the christological themes into the enlarging concept of what constituted the Christian community of learning. In his *Historia calamitatum* (1132), Abelard endeavored to provide the rationale for the life of learned celibacy.[16] He regarded Jesus Christ as the founder of the order of monks and nuns. He was at pains, in fact, in his communications to Héloïse to point out that women were prominent among the disciples of Jesus. Moreover, of the three anointments received by Jesus, two were from the hand of a woman, who, in pouring ointment upon his feet and presumably upon his head, "as by corporal sacraments consecrated Jesus King and Priest."[17] But even before his incarnation the eternal Christ had called forth women (like Anna) as well as men to the disciplined life. Abelard sought indeed to find a common divine source of inspiration for both biblical and classical examples of learned celibacy:

This view is maintained, for example, in the love of God by those among us who are truly called monastics, and the love of wisdom by those who have stood out among men as sincere philosophers. . . . Among the Jews of old there were the Nazirites . . . and the *sons of the prophets,* followers of both Elijah and Elisha, whom, on the authority of St. Jerome,[18] we consider the monks in the Old Testament.[19]

Abelard, clearly indebted to Jerome, was unprepared to draw a radical

His is an interesting adaptation of Augustine's idea that both *scientia* and *sapientia* are gifts of the Spirit (cf. *Confessions*) and his individualizing of the collective experience of the race as portrayed in *De civitate Dei.*

[16] Abelard's role in the history of learning has been admirably worked out in the essay of Ernst Kantorowicz, *Die Wiederkehr gelehrter Anachorese im Mittelalter* (Stuttgart, 1937). To Kantorowicz the present writer is much indebted for the whole conception of this essay. Successively professor in Frankfurt, Oxford, Berkeley, and Princeton, he has valorously defended the Republic of Letters in the course of his own personal *translatio studii* to the New World. He was one of the heroic minority who refused to take the special oath at the University of California, defining the corporate rights of the universal community of scholarship in his tract for the times, *The Fundamental Issue* (Berkeley, 1950). He led his former colleagues in vindicating before the California courts the basic principle that professors are *officers* of the university and not its employees.

[17] The third anointment, preparing Jesus for the sepulchre, was alone the work of men (Joseph of Arimathea and Nicodemus). The threefold anointment of Christ corresponds to the threefold anointment of David, and to the threefold anointment of every Christian at baptism, confirmation, and extreme unction; here Abelard cites Jerome, on Psalm XXVI. *Opera,* ed. by Victor Cousin (Paris, 1849), I, 122–123.

[18] *Epp.* LVIII and CXXV; see note 1 above.

[19] *Opera,* I, 14; cf. I, 26, where he incorrectly cites Jerome's *Ad Eustochium* and where he in addition cites Jerome's *Contra Jovianum* (II, 9) on the importance of getting away from the lures of both the city and the charming countryside—as Pythagoras and Plato had done.

distinction between philosophers and prophets, between the love of wisdom and the love of God.

Long before Abelard found his way to the royal Abbey of St. Denis, the tradition had become firmly established that Dionysius (Denis) the Areopagite, Paul's Athenian convert, had brought the apostolic faith to Gaul. To him had been ascribed in due course the rich, mystical, Neoplatonist corpus made available in Latin translation from the pseudonymous fifth-century Monophysite by John Scotus Erigena, scholar in the court of Charles the Bald. By Abelard's day, the monks of St. Denis considered their patron as having been indeed bishop of Athens. When Abelard, driven from Paris, drew to the attention of his hosts a passage by the Venerable Bede upon which he had chanced and which asserted that the Areopagite had become bishop of Corinth, not Athens, they became incensed. After being threatened with violence by the abbot and the brethren, Abelard fled under cover of darkness and eventually took refuge in a spot where his renown as a scholar would presently draw students from far away. He rededicated the oratory in the heath to the Holy Spirit, not only as Comforter, but as patron of Christian learning. Critics assailed him for this unprecedented consecration, on the ground that only to the Three Persons as one or to Christ the Son was it permissible to dedicate a church. But Abelard argued that, just as the Son was especially recognized in the Feast of the Incarnation, so was the Holy Spirit in the Feast of Pentecost; and that a Church could therefore with as much propriety be dedicated to the Third as to the Second Person. "Nay," he said, "it seems more fitting to dedicate a temple to It than to either of the other Persons of the Trinity, if we but carefully study the apostolic authority, . . . for to none of the three Persons did the Apostle dedicate a special temple save to the Holy Spirit alone (I Corinthians 6:17 ff.)."[20] Thus in the Holy Spirit as well as in the eternal Christ, founder of the monastic *ordo*, Abelard located the divine sanction for the tremendous intellectual effort he was making to reconcile the classical and biblical traditions of reason and faith over against Bernard of Clairvaux.

A contemporary of Abelard in Germany, Imperial Bishop Otto of Freising (d. 1158), uncle of Frederick I Barbarossa and former student in France, when he came to write his *Historia de duabus civitatibus*, found also a place for a third city embodied in the semi-autonomous community of learning, whose history, like that of the empire and the Church, he could trace back to the East:

[20] *Ibid.*

That wisdom was found first in the East (that is, in Babylonia) and was carried thence into Egypt, because Abraham went down to Egypt in a time of famine, Josephus makes clear in the first book of his *Antiquities*. . . . That wisdom passed from Egypt to the Greeks in the time of the philosophers the same author indicates. . . . From the Greeks it appears to have been carried to the Romans . . . and afterwards to the extreme West—that is, to the Gauls and the Spains—very recently, in the days of those illustrous scholars Berengar [of Tours, d. 1088], Manegold [of Lautenbach, d. after 1103], and Anselm [of Laon, d. 1117].[21]

Otto of Freising did not feel that there was an insuperable conflict between faith, learning, and government.

In the third quarter of the twelfth century, a less well-known antagonist of Bernard of Clairvaux, Philip de Harvengt (d. 1182), carried on the effort of Abelard to justify the attempt to reconcile faith and reason.[22] Abbot of the Premonstratensian Abbey of Bona Spes, he wrote two letters concerning the Paris in which the university was beginning to take form among the cathedral and monastic schools.[23] He wrote of Paris as the new Jerusalem in which David's psalms, Isaiah's prophecies, and Solomon's wisdom were studied:

Just as the Queen of Sheba is said to have come with a large retinue, that by the sight of her own eyes she might have surer knowledge of those things whose fame she had eagerly absorbed from afar, so you too [he writes to Hergald, as student] came to Paris and found, sought out by many, compressed as in a replica—Jerusalem. . . . Here the wisdom of Solomon is open for the instruction of all who have converged upon the city. Here his treasure house is thrown open to eager students. . . . Happy city! in which the sacred tomes are pored over with much zeal and their involved mysteries resolved by the gift of the outpoured Spirit, in which there is so much diligence upon the part of the lecturers, so much, in short, science of Scriptures that it truly deserves to be called Kirjath-Sepher, that

---

[21] *Op. cit.*, V, Prologue; translated by Charles Christopher Mierow, *The Two Cities . . . by Otto* (New York, 1928), pp. 332 f. Josephus writes in *Antiquities*, i, 8, 2: "He communicated to them [the Egyptians] arithmetic, and delivered to them the science of astronomy; for before Abram came into Egypt they were unacquainted with those parts of learning, for that science came from the Chaldeans into Egypt, and from thence to the Greeks also." In i, 2, 3, Josephus says that Seth's children "were the inventors of that peculiar sort of wisdom, which is concerned with the heavenly bodies, and their order," and made special provision (inscribed *stelae*) for its transmission to posterity in anticipation of great disasters prophesied by Adam. Josephus also mentions the role of Cadmus in the transmission of letters from Phoenicia to the Greeks. *Contra Apionem*, i, 2.

[22] The only study of the life and thought of this neglected writer is in the *Revue Bénédictine*, IX (1892), 24, 69, 130, 193, 244. He is, however, written up at some length in *Histoire littéraire*, XIV, esp. 274, 282.

[23] *PL*, CCIII, *Epp.* iii and xx; reprinted in H. Denifle and E. Chatelain, *Chartularium Universitatis Parisiensis* (Paris, 1889), I, No. 50, p. 50; No. 52, p. 51.

is the City of Letters. Therein would I have you instructed like Othniel, not so much literally as spiritually, and so to possess the Scriptures[24] that you may take delight in searching out their inner sweetness.[25]

Elsewhere also he refers to Paris as Kirjath-Sepher.[26] Like Abelard he quotes Jerome's two epistles on the sons of the prophets as the Old Testament monks.[27] The learned abbot, drawing in part upon Isidore's *Etymologiae*,[28] dwelt also upon the achievement of Cadmus as the carrier of the alphabet and wisdom from Phoenicia to Greece in the time of the Judges in succession to Othniel (Gothoniel).[29] The warrior Othniel is the symbol of learned warfare *as redemptive*.

The Hieronymic interpretation of the sons of the prophets as the Old Covenantal scholars and monks was in turn made use of by Pope Honorius III in his constitutionally important regulation of 1219, whereby the clerics of the University of Paris were not permitted to study civil law out of deference to the king's preference for customary law. The biblical argument given was the necessarily "straitened circumstances" of Elisha's prophetic school (II Kings 6:1).[30]

Gregory IX (1227–1241) picked up the biblical and classical themes. He wrote of Paris as Kirjath-Sepher, where "as in a special factory of wisdom" ornaments were fashioned and arms were forged—especially "the sword of the spirit" whereby the "Christian militia," whose "stony hearts were enkindled by the fervor of the Holy Spirit," were enabled to fight against "the brazen powers."[31]

So concerned was the Pope for the independence of the university from the local authorities, both royal and episcopal, that he granted it a special privilege with the penalty of excommunication if violated, that

[24] The younger brother of Caleb and the capturer of Kirjath-Sepher (Debir), Joshua 15:17. The text reads "Gothoniel," but this is in the Hebrew identical with "Othniel." It may be, however, that something of the Gothoniel of Judith 6:15 has been, by contagion, assimilated to the cycle of stories in Joshua. Othniel received the Spirit of God as savior of his people (Judges 9:10).
Othniel gave up his daughter in marriage that he might capture the City of Letters (Joshua 15:16–17).
[25] *PL*, CCIII, *Ep.* iii, col. 14; *Chartularium*, I, No. 50, p. 50; translation based upon but varying from that by Arthur O. Norton, *Readings in the History of Education: Medieval Universities* (Cambridge, 1909), p. 146.
[26] *Ep.* xx; *Chartularium*, I, p. 51.
[27] Jerome, *Epp.* LVIII and CXXV are quoted by Philip, in *PL*, CCIII, col. 793.
[28] I, iii, 6; V, xxxix, 10.
[29] *De institutione clericorum*, vi, *cap.* xlv, cols. 1019 ff. But he does not, like Cotton Mather, connect Cadmus with Academia.
[30] *Chartularium*, I, No. 32, p. 92.
[31] *Chartularium*, I, No. 79 (1231), p. 136. This same section of the letter to the scholars of Paris is reproduced verbatim in the letter to the king, No. 81. The same imagery reappears in less literate form in a letter from the cathedral chapter of Rheims to Pope Alexander IV, dated 1256; *Chartularium*, I, No. 295, p. 341.

"neither the bishop nor his official nor the chancellor shall require a fine" from the masters or scholars for *any crime;* and all alumni of Paris were expected to heed their university oath of solidarity even when in later years they might be recruited for service with the king or the archbishop of Paris.[32]

In another letter[33] Gregory spoke of the University of Paris as the veritable paradise of the Church universal; and then, in allusion to the irrigation of paradise by the grace of the Holy Spirit, he warned (St.) Louis IX and his mother Blanche, regent at the time, of the hazard to France of allowing the university to flow from its accustomed banks of the Seine and to become diffused as in a network of lesser channels. He warned the rulers that they should make just restitution and compensation to the students and teachers who, having suffered at the hands of the local magistrates, fled the city. They should be secured in their persons and property and scholastic rights for the good also of the kingdom and the good of the Church, lest the constitutional "traces of the Trinity be deleted from the realm."

Gregory speculates that just as the Triune God has the three attributes of *potentia, sapientia,* and *benignitas,* so the three orders of society, though they be one in Christ, should enjoy a measure of autonomy. The knights (*milites*) in their might (*strenuitas*) correspond by implication to the Father (*potentia*); the clerics of the university in their science and letters correspond to the Son (*sapientia*); and the king and peers (*principes*), by reason of their clement goodness (*clemens bonitas*), to the Holy Spirit (*benignitas*). In this triadic arrangement, the teaching clergy and the parochial clergy are grouped together in the Pope's preoccupation with the freedom of the university. Very important are the Pope's recognition of the co-ordinate authority of the university and the magistracy and especially his discerning declaration that

[32] In 1329 the archbishop, Hugh of Besançon, was formally expelled from association with the university for violation of the Gregorian privilege of 1231 in pursuit of his episcopal duties of maintaining order and decorum. He was vehemently rebuked and likened to Judas:

"This then is he who among us 'dippeth his hand . . . in the dish,' now, however, about to betray us [Matthew 26:23]. He who a short time ago was educated as an alumnus among us, was richly endowed with our liberties, and now strives damnably to weaken them. In truth, there is no more injurious person than the enemy who is an intimate."

This passage from *Chartularium,* II, No. 899, pp. 335 f., is quoted by Pearl Kibre in an important study of "Academic Oaths at the University of Paris in the Middle Ages," in *Essays in Medieval Life and Thought,* presented in honor of Austin Patterson Evans (New York, 1955), pp. 123–137. She shows how the solidarity of the university, achieved through the academic oath to the rector, was undercut in the reign of Louis XI through the royal insistence upon an oath of fidelity to the monarch.

[33] *Chartularium,* I, No. 71 (1229), pp. 128–129.

"if of the middle [the university] the other two are deprived, they fall into extreme corruption, because power, unless it is tempered by wisdom, luxuriates in presumption and gives itself over to arrogance, while benignity, too, if it is unsupported by knowledge, becomes amorphously degenerate and rendered akin to fatuousness."[34]

Pope Gregory's trinitarian sanction of his triadic scheme of co-ordinated orders does not provide exactly the same triad of intersecting societies within the later *corpus Christianum* which we shall take note of—namely, State, University, Church. But the triadic motif which we saw forming in Abbo of Fleury's tripartite society and in Abelard's conception of the threefold unction of Christ appears here in a theologically significant form. And it is noteworthy that in the nearly contemporary Joachimite *Liber figurarum* (c. 1190) the threefold office of Christ is recognized in a negative but instructive form—namely, that the Antichrist will appear as at once prince and pontiff and prophet.[35]

The paradisic theme woven into Gregory's letter was picked up by the university itself in a communication to the prelates of the Church and scholars throughout the world, dated 1254,[36] which opened thus:

The hand of the Almighty planted aforetime a Paradise of pleasures in Paris, a venerable *gignasium*[37] of letters, whence arises the font of wisdom, which, channeled in the four faculties—namely, theology, jurisprudence, medicine, and philosophy (rational, natural, and moral)—like unto the four rivers of Paradise is distributed throughout the four climes, drains and irrigates the whole world, and from which, further, how much and diverse spiritual and temporal progress Christianity has experienced![38]

[34] "In tribus, que appropriatione nominis tribus in sancta Trinitate personis attributa noscuntur, potentia, sapientia et benignitate videlicet, regnum Francorum eiusdem sancte Trinitatis imitando vestigium patet pre regnis aliis a longis retro temporibus claruisse, in strenuitate militum potens, in clero litterarum scientia predito sapiens, et in clementi principum bonitate benignum, quorum medio si duo destituantur extrema in vitia convertentur. Quoniam potentia nisi fuerit sapientia temperata, in presumptionem luxuriat se in arrogantiam extollendo; benignitas vero si eadem suffulta non fuerit, in dissolutionem degenerat et efficitur fatuitati cognata. Igitur sapientia necessaria est utrique, sine qua neutra illarum nomen virtutis obtinet vel effectum."

[35] "Antichristus se esse simulabit regem et pontificem et prophetam." Herbert Grundmann, *Neue Forschungen über Joachim von Fiore* (Marburg, 1950), p. 49.

[36] *Chartularium*, I, No. 230, pp. 252–253.

[37] This is an occasional medieval variant of *gymnasium;* but the allusion to *gigno* is inescapable and with it the implication that, though begetting was the physical occasion of the Fall, the generation of learning under the tutelage of faith may well be the spiritual means whereby Paradise will be restored.

[38] "Excelsi dextera paradisum voluptatis olym plantavit Parisius venerandum gignasium litterarum, unde sapientie fons ascendit, qui in quatuor facultates, videlicet theologiam, jurisperitiam, medicinam, necnon rationalem, naturalem, moralem philosophiam quasi quatuor paradysi flumina distributus per quatuor mundi climata derivatus

Here, "associated by a bond of special law obtained from king and Pope," the university had in peace brought forth abundant "flowers" and "fruits" of scholarship, "knowing that the waters of Siloam[39] flow in silence and in peace." After this introduction the university went on corporately to protest against the intrusion of the friars, particularly the Dominicans, who had impaired the integrity and the autonomy of the university by failing to reciprocate any sense of the scholarly solidarity in the spirit of which they had first been accepted by the academic community in Paris.

Another example of the conflation of the biblical and the classical motifs—a mingling this time of the paradisic and the military themes—appeared in the bold appropriation by the sponsors of the recently organized University of Toulouse of the language of Christian warfare in speaking of the *philosophiae milites,* who, under the joint patronage of the count and the papal legate and drawn to Toulouse by the rays of the Holy Spirit, might study all that Paris had to offer and in addition the new works of Aristotle forbidden on the Seine. In this letter of general invitation and announcement, the philosophical soldiery were recruited with the promise that in the worldly peace now established in the Midi they could sharpen their spiritual swords.[40]

As the cathedral and monastic schools took the lead, and as the University of Paris under the protection of Pope and king emerged as the principal *studium generale* of Christendom, it was natural that Frenchmen should look back to Charlemagne, famed with Alcuin for the rebirth of learning in his age, as the founder of the University of Paris. As early as about 1164, the general pride of Frenchmen in the learning of Paris had been reflected in passages of the popular *Cligès*[41] by Chrestien de Troyes, who picked up the theme of the *translatio studii* from Greece through Rome to France, placing knighthood and the learned clergy on the same level as peers. In the *roman* he acknowledged having gotten his idea from Beauvais.[42] Around 1210 the Cistercian chronicler Hélinand of Froidmont in the diocese of Beauvais was apparently the first to connect the *translatio studii* specifically with Paris, by way of

universam terram irrigat et infundit, ex quo quam multifarios, spirituales ac temporales profectus christiana professio experitur, luce clarius patet cunctis."

[39] Siloam (Isaiah 8:6 and John 9:7) is the body of water into which Jesus sent the young man blind from birth that he might see again. We may have here an allusion to the New Testament restoration of what was lost at the Fall, when, after disobedience, Adam and Eve had their eyes opened to their sinful selves.

[40] *Chartularium,* I, No. 72, pp. 129 ff. The date is 1229. The author may have been John of Garland, author of *Morale scolarium* and *De triumphis ecclesiae.*

[41] Ed. Wendelin Foerster (Halle, 1884), vv. 30–39.

[42] V. 2: "Mon seignor saint Pere a Biauveiz."

the British Isles. The idea was in part based upon the *Vita Karoli* of Notker the Stammerer, and it preserved the valid reminiscence of the importance of four pupils of Bede in the Carolingian renaissance. Hélinand merely drew what for him was a natural inference—that Paris was the principal residence of Charlemagne and that hence his famed palace school was the forerunner of the University now become a fixed point of Christendom. Hélinand's *Chronicle* survives only as it was absorbed in the *Speculum historiale* of the Dominican pupil of Albert the Great, Vincent of Beauvais (d. c. 1264).[43] From Chrestien through C. B. du Boulay (the seventeenth-century historian of the University of Paris), up into the early nineteenth century, Charlemagne stood as the founder of the University of Paris.

English-born John of Garland (c. 1195–c. 1272) went beyond Charlemagne, tracing the westward course of *philosophica speculatio* from Egypt, where Abraham demonstrated the science of astronomy (cf. Josephus), to Athens, from Athens to Rome, and from Rome to Paris.[44]

Some thirteenth-century writers saw in Dionysius the Areopagite, the suppositious founder of the royal Abbey of St. Denis, the actual bearer of wisdom from East to West, by-passing Rome. St. Dionysius of Athens was understood to have brought to Gaul, not only the apostolic faith, but also in his train the Greek ideal of knighthood and the Greek ideal of science. It was Giles of Rheims, writing about 1230, who thus elaborated the theme of the knighthood and the learned clergy derived from Greece—a theme already encountered in Chrestien de Troyes—by connecting it with Dionysius.

Then, about 1270, William of Nangis introduced the theme in both his *Gesta Ludovici IX* and his *Chronicle* of St. Denis.[45] In the royal Abbey of St. Denis, William of Nangis gave to the fleur-de-lis of the *rex christianissimus* the character of a symbol both of the Triune God and of the three co-ordinate orders of France. According to this view, Jesus Christ had especially blessed and endowed France above all realms with the three graces represented by *fides, sapientia,* and *militia.* All three had been brought from Greece by Dionysius and his retinue, that

[43] *Lib.* xxiii, *cap.* clxxiii; *lib.* xxx, *cap.* cxxxvii.

[44] In the Prologue to his *Epithalamium,* ed. by Louis J. Paetow, *Morale Scolarium* in *Memoirs of the University of California,* IV: 2 (= *History,* 1:2) (Berkeley, 1927), p. 100, n. 87.

[45] Bouquet, *Recueil des historiens de France,* XX, 320, 546. Herbert Grundmann has conflated these two slightly variant texts in an effort to approximate the now lost text of Giles. "*Sacerdotium Regnum Studium:* Zur Wertung der Wissenschaft im 13. Jahrhundert," *Archiv für Kulturgeschichte,* XXXIV (1951–1952), 15, n. 21. This study by Grundmann is invaluable for the thirteenth- and fourteenth-century history of the triadic theme.

the apostolic faith might be guided by science and defended by knighthood. Each was symbolically represented by one of the three petals of the royal lily. In the middle was the largest petal, faith; on either side the other two stood guard in the floral array. As long as the royal lily with its balanced parts should hold together, the kingdom would endure:

For as long as the mentioned three remain equal, co-ordinate, and interrelated one with the other in the realm of France, the kingdom will stand. If, however, either of the two should become separated or plucked from faith, the whole kingdom will become desolate and fall.[46]

Under St. Louis, the three orders were thus felt to be in balance—(1) the knighthood, (2) the parochial clergy and episcopate, (3) the learned clergy of the University of Paris. The king held them together in peace because, as the *rex christianissimus,* he was himself by virtue of his liturgical anointment at the coronation an "epiphany" of Solomon (*rex pacificus*). And behind the royal *christus* was the sanction of the eternal Christ.

The climax of this triadic christological theme was reached by a German clerical publicist reflecting on the concentration of political as well as scholastic leadership in France under Louis and his successor. The publicist was Alexander of Roes, and his principal tracts were the *Memoriale de prerogativa Romani imperii* (1281) and the *Noticia seculi* (1288).[47] Distressed, while in the environs of Rome, to discover in the missals available to him for the daily performance of his clerical duties that the prayer for the emperor was omitted, this German patriot addressed a spirited and original treatise to Jacob Cardinal Colonna. In it he embodied an earlier treatise on the prerogatives of the Roman Empire written by a fellow countryman, Jordan of Osnabrück.[48] Alexander's concern was to show that the peace and order of Christendom depended on the concert of the three powers—the Papacy, the Empire, and the University. And to this end, going beyond imperial Bishop Otto of Freising's three (implied) *civitates,* he elaborated in a first and

---

[46] Bouquet, *Recueil,* XX, 320.

[47] These were edited critically by Herbert Grundmann and Hermann Heimpel, *Die Schriften des Alexander von Roes,* Deutsches Mittelalter, 4 (Weimar, 1949). Some of the textual apparatus is in Grundmann's earlier edition, *Alexander von Roes . . . und Jordanus von Osnabrück,* Quellen zur Geistesgeschichte des Mittelalters und der Renaissance, II (Leipzig, 1930). On the subsequent influence of Alexander, see Grundmann, "Über die Schriften des Alexander von Roes," in *Deutsches Archiv für Erforschung des Mittelalters,* VIII (1950–1951), 154. See also Grundmann's synoptic essay, *Vom Ursprung der Universität im Mittelalter* (Berlin, 1957).

[48] Jordan is documented as canon of the cathedral between 1251 and 1283 and was *scholasticus* in charge of the cathedral school around 1255.

second treatise a comprehensive theory of European Christian universalism. Though mixed with legend and imaginative chronicle, the theory as a whole contains valuable insight into what might today be called "critical pluralism"—the constitutional preservation of centers of relative autonomy in order to secure Christian society from aberrations in the name of piety or patriotism.

Alexander took for granted the widely familiar *translatio studii,* and programmatically declared that Charlemagne had given to his heirs and successors in France, "by way of compensating for truncating the kingdom, the *studium* of philosophy and the liberal arts, which he himself had transplanted from Rome to Paris."[49] With the translation of the *studium* from Rome to France, and the translation of the Roman Empire from Rome to Germany, Italy was still left with the Papacy.[50] And this diversification of regional responsibility, according to Alexander, strengthened Christendom, which thus rested upon a tripod of complementary but separate powers. This image of a tripod was not his; but Alexander gave many other examples of threeness in the world to indicate the divine preference for a tripartite ordering of society.[51] Particularly interesting for the line of development we have been following was his appeal both to the Triune God and to the tripartite human personality, made up of body, soul, and mind. Holding "that Christendom [*fides christiana*], i.e., the Roman Church, is the highest representative of mankind," Alexander went on to point out that within Christendom there are likewise three principal bearers of a corporate and universal Christian mission for the good of the whole *corpus Christianum:*

For Father, Son, and Holy Spirit, one God, has so arranged it that *sacerdotium, regnum,* and *studium* should constitute one Christian society (*ecclesia*). Since, then, the faith of Christ is ruled by these three principals, the clergy, magistracy, and scholarship—the Papacy in Italy maintaining

---

[49] *Memoriale, cap.* xxiv (*Schriften,* p. 48).

[50] *Memoriale, cap.* xxv: "And worthy of note is that a meaningful and necessary order requires that upon the Romans as the older people should devolve the Papacy (*sacerdotium*), upon the Germans or [East] Franks as the younger people, the Empire, and similarly upon the French (*Francigene*) as the more perspicacious race should fall the responsibility for the University (*studium*)."

[51] He mentions, for example, the three ages (the periods of natural law, of the Law, and of the Gospel), which correspond to the three main divisions of the human race (Gentiles, Jews, and Christians); also the three continents (Asia, Africa, and Europe). *Noticia, capp.* iii, iv (*Schriften,* p. 70). Some of this threefold scheme derives from *De semine scripturarum* (1204–1205), quoted in Alexander's text. This as yet unedited manuscript was at the time ascribed to Joachim of Flora. Joachimite and other prophetic works were widely read in the circle around Cardinal Colonna, who emerged as the powerful protector of the Spiritual Franciscans.

the faith, and royalty in Germany securing the protection of the same, and scholarship in France so teaching that faith may be sustained—it is clear that the commonwealth of Christian faith has here in these three provinces its principal supports.[52]

Or, to change the image:

If [co-ordinated] in these three—namely, the *sacerdotium,* the *imperium,* and the *studium*—then the Christian body politic and ecclesiastical (*sancta ecclesia catholica*) is spiritually vitalized, enlarged, and guided as is the individual by the integration of his three component parts: soul, body, and mind.[53]

Up to this point we have drawn indifferently upon both of Alexander's two principal works. But in passing over to his prophetic criticism of all arrogations whereby one of the three powers of Christendom encroaches upon the proper domain of another, we shall draw entirely upon his *Noticia.* For between the composition of the *Memoriale* and of the *Noticia,* the Aragonese had defeated the French (the Sicilian Vespers of March 31, 1282), and the European balance of powers had been perilously disturbed. Thereupon, Simon de Brion—formerly chancellor of Louis IX and now Pope Martin IV—had urged upon the French king, Philip III, a crusade against the Aragonese to restore Charles of Anjou; and this had collapsed with tremendous French losses. Since, in the eyes of Alexander, Christendom was the highest representative of mankind, "changes within it might well be considered as symptomatic of pending changes throughout the world."[54] To facilitate his prophetic calculations, Alexander made the observation that, although within each of the three main peoples of Christendom representatives of all three classes or estates or orders were to be found, nevertheless each nation as a whole seemed to have the characteristics of one class—the Italians, the masses; the Germans, the fighting nobility; the French, the spiritual estate. Alexander located a major reason for the disasters being suffered by Christendom in the inordinate love of class and nation. And he warned that, just as a small people, the Aragonese, had overcome the French nation in Sicily, so the Friars Minor and other mendicants might soon take over the University.[55] Never-

---

[52] *Noticia, cap.* xii (*Schriften,* p. 84).

[53] *Memoriale, cap.* xxv (*Schriften,* p. 48): "His siquidem tribus, scilicet sacerdotio imperio et studio, tamquam tribus virtutibus, videlicet vitali naturali et animali, sancta ecclesia catholica spiritualiter vivificatur augmentatur et regitur."

[54] *Noticia, cap.* xii (*Schriften,* p. 84).

[55] *Ibid., cap.* xv (*Schriften,* pp. 86–87). In his attitude toward the Mendicants, Alexander changes noticeably between the *Memoriale* and the *Noticia,* where he is more

theless, like a prophet of an earlier age, Alexander tried to recall Europe from its aberrations and urged Church, State, and University to reassume their proper and co-ordinate functions in Christendom:

... Antichrist will never come as long as the Church has the Roman Empire as a defender in things temporal and the University of the Gauls as an adjutant in things spiritual. But when these are destroyed, when the Church, after the destruction of the Empire and the secular militia in Germany, shall wish to defend itself aginst tyrants, and when, after the University has been wrecked and the spiritual militia in France impaired, she shall prove incapable of defending herself against heretics, then ... that son of Perdition [II Thessalonians 2:3] will come and with impunity wreak havoc on Christendom. Let the Pope therefore beware lest the Empire be destroyed, and let the king of France beware lest the University be broken up, because with the connivance of the devil the destruction of both is now in progress—all under a plausible disguise. Just as Christ did not come until the kingdom of the Jews had been destroyed, so Antichrist will not come unless the kingdom of the Romans be first destroyed. The high priests once declared: We have no king but Caesar [John 19:15];[56] and in the same manner our prelates say: We have no king but the Pope. And just as the secular clergy are affecting the prerogatives of secular authority, so also the regular clergy are presuming to be authorities in natural science. And just as the secular clergy by their manner of life seem to be putting aside the strictures of religion, so the monks and friars by their disputations and studies seem to be neglecting theological science. As a consequence the power of the Empire is being converted into impotence and the science of the University into heresy. And these developments are the forerunners of Antichrist.[57]

Here, and indeed throughout Alexander's whole tract, one observes that the German publicist is discharging the prophetic office of rebuke with the hope that amendment may come before the European catastrophe is intensified. He predicts disaster as a way of sharpening his analysis of the woes of Christendom rather than as a certain prognostication of inevitable judgment. In fact, in several places he expresses some doubts as to whether all of the predictions upon which he has himself based his eschatological thinking should be taken literally; but he does insist upon the seriousness of his analysis of what is wrong with the Christian body politic and ecclesiastical. The sacerdotal, the royal, and the doctoral functions should not be discharged by the same race or

---

favorable to them as possible divine avengers, symbolized in the whip of cords by which Jesus cleansed the Temple.

[56] Cf. *Memoriale*, cap. ii.

[57] *Noticia, cap.* xx (*Schriften*, p. 98). Drawing upon *De semine scripturarum*, Alexander gives the basis for holding that 1415 is the year of Antichrist.

order without their incurring divine chastisement for disturbing a God-willed constitutional distinction among the three powers within the unity of Christendom.

It is interesting to find how a near-contemporary of Alexander of Roes, Ptolemy of Lucca (d. 1326), reworked the conception of three co-ordinate powers. Unlike the more universalist Alexander, he insisted that they should be integrated in the hands of the anointed king. Such a view is all the more remarkable and unexpected in Ptolemy for the reason that it is to be found in his continuation of the *De regimine principum* begun by Thomas Aquinas, a proponent of separation.[58]

Ptolemy, picking up the christological theme long associated with liturgical kingship, declared afresh that the anointed king, as a *christus* for his people, was more than a priest-king; like Christ, he discharged the threefold role of prophet (teacher), priest, and king in imitation of Solomon.[59] For Solomon, a type of Christ, was the embodiment of wisdom and also a priest-king, the *rex pacificus,* who by virtue of his anointment could bring temporal peace just as Jesus Christ would establish a millennial peace. Thus, according to Ptolemy, it was entirely proper that every anointed Christian king should exercise the three functions of Solomon. After pointing out in Israel's history the privileges of the royal *christi,* Saul and David, and in Roman history those of the emperor, who was also *pontifex maximus,* and in Christian history those of the anointed king of the Franks, Clovis, Ptolemy went on to nationalize or regalize the universal or ecumenical tripartite theory we have found in Alexander of Roes:

Thus even the histories teach us that with sovereignty (*monarchia*), regardless of time or space, there have always been three interrelated functions which have followed each other in succession, namely, divine worship (*divinus cultus*), the pursuit of wisdom (*sapientia scholastica*), and the exercise of wordly power (*saecularis potentia*). These follow each other in order, and this sequence is indeed preserved for us in the meritorious actions of King Solomon, for when in reverence for the divine he descended to Hebron (the place of prayer), there to be elevated to the kingship, he

[58] Aquinas wrote only *lib.* i, and *lib.* ii to the middle of *cap.* iv. It was begun by Aquinas for the instruction of the youthful Hugh II of Lusignan, on whose premature death (1267) it was allowed to languish, until completed by Ptolemy in a sense which Thomas would surely not have approved. For the clear distinction drawn by Thomas (in contrast to Augustine) between the proper competence of reason and faith had enabled the Angelic Doctor elsewhere to distinguish rather clearly between the realms proper to Church and State.

[59] I do not find that Ptolemy made reference directly to the threefold office of Christ, a concept that goes back to Eusebius of Caesarea. Ptolemy confines himself to the analogy of Solomon.

pursued wisdom; and by virtue of these two (reverence and wisdom) he later achieved superiority over all the kings of his time in royal power. When, however, he turned from the true worship of God, he suffered an unhappy end.[60]

By appealing to Solomon as the type of Christ and as the embodiment of wisdom, Ptolemy and others were able to find a biblical counterpart for the Platonic philosopher-king. Along such a line of thought, the University of Paris could be eventually constrained to abandon something of her universal mission, as worked out by Alexander of Roes, and through progressive nationalization or regalization be hailed as the daughter of the king (of France)—*filia regis*.

But this nationalization was not completed even by the time of the Reformation. And it should not be overlooked that throughout the last two centuries of the Middle Ages even in France this proud Gallican boast of the University to be *filia regis* also provided a basis for the appeal of the academic community, turmoiled by the vacillating policy of the earthly king, to the heavenly Sovereign Jesus Christ, at once prophet, priest, and king. If the Church as a whole could be thought of as the Bride of Christ, the differentiated community of the learned clergy, the University, could be thought of as the daughter of the eternal Logos. But nationalization was the more obvious emphasis.

This nationalization of the University of Paris was well described in partly legendary, partly theological terms by the poet Philip of Vitry, later bishop of Meaux (d. 1361). Son of the secretary of Philip IV the Fair, he was very close to Philip VI Valois. At the announcement of a crusade sanctioned by the Avignon Pope, John XXII, Philip of Vitry began the composition of the famed *Chapel des trois fleurs de lis* (c. 1335), wherein the triadic theme is emphasized in diverse ways. The Solomonic imagery is prominent. The three royal lilies[61] correspond at once to the Trinity and to the three estates of France—the people, the clergy, and knighthood (*chevalerie, milites*). Knighthood defends the other two estates.[62] But since within the clergy the sacerdotal and the doctoral function can be clearly distinguished, Philip also stresses another triad—*science, foy,* and *chevalerie*. All three came to Paris from Athens in the company of St. Denis. The Areopagite was par-

---

[60] Thomas Aquinas, *Opera omnia*, ed. P. Fiaccadori (Parma, 1852 ff.), XVI, 250.

[61] In William of Nangis, the floral imagery was based upon the three petals of each fleur-de-lis. By Philip of Vitry's time, the royal coat of arms is fixed and the reference is to the three blossoms in the royal device. See Prinet, "Les variations du nombre des fleurs de lis dans les armes de France," in *Bulletin monumental*, LXXV (1911), 469 ff.

[62] Strophes 83–84, in Arthur Piaget, ed., *Romania*, XXVII (1898), 80.

ticularly responsible for knowledge, St. Rusticus for faith, and St. Eleutherius for knighthood. Jesus Christ had the welfare of France peculiarly in mind in dispatching this threefold mission; and, as long as the three endure, France in great power will rule—all her enemies despised.[63]

The close relationship between chivalry and scholarship suggested by Chrestien de Troyes and De Vitry, among others, is illuminated from another angle by the jurisconsult Baldo degli Ubaldi (1319?–1400) who gives evidence that in his period the degrees of aristocracy, the hierarchy, and of scholarship were being brought into rough correspondence and specifically that participation in a doctoral knighthood (*militia doctoralis*) was open to non-jousting scholars, not to the manor born. Commenting on that portion of the Justinian Code directed against a soldier fighting with deceptive insignia, he applies the ancient stricture against Jews and other non-Christians "qui ingerunt se militiae doctorali."[64] Participation in the aristocracy of learning is thus for Baldo theoretically as well as practically limited to Christians. For Dante, in contrast, who had a Christian idea of a truly universal monarchy, there was a full recognition of the place of non-Christian Scythians and Garmantes in the *civiltà umana;* and, had he written expressly on the university, he would conceivably have held that all men are eligible for participation in the *studium,* the purely intellectual perfection of the terrestrial paradise wherein the world intellect is actualized.[65]

During the Avignonese Captivity of the Papacy, when the *sacerdotium* as well as the *studium* were increasingly dependent upon the king of France, and in the Great Western Schism which followed, the University of Paris in particular and all the *studia* of Christendom in general found in the conciliar movement an instrument for the corporate expression of the essentially universal mission of the *studium*—one of the three co-ordinate universal authorities within Christendom—upon which fell with peculiar urgency the assignment of restoring order to the *corpus christianum,* distraught and stricken under the conflicting orders of two and then three papal heads. The practice of voting by nations at the reforming councils was an adaptation of university practice; and the concept of the Holy Spirit as the informing power of

[63] Strophe 159: "Pour ce que Dieu et sainte eglise/Mieulx serviz y sont, et justise/Mieulx faite qu'en autre païs./Et tant comme ce durera/France en grant pouvoir regnera;/Ses anemies seront haïs."
[64] Gloss on Codex VII, 38, 1; *Commentaria in Corpus iuris civilis* (Venice, 1572), VII, 262.
[65] Cf. *De Monarchia,* I, 14, and Ernst Kantorowicz, *The Problem of Medieval Unity* (1944), and now *The King's Two Bodies* (Princeton, 1959). See also above, Part One, Chapter II, sec. 3, at n. 58.

a valid council comported well with the University's own sense of being in tutelage to the Holy Spirit. Three leading conciliarists may be cited as exponents of the late medieval theological elaboration of the nature and function of the University in relation to Church and State. The three are Francis Zabarella (d. 1417), Peter d'Ailly (d. 1420), and John Gerson (d. 1429).

Of Cardinal Zabarella it need only be mentioned that in his *Lectura super Clementinas* he found a place to recount the *translatio studii,* the elaboration of which we have been tracing. He was familiar with Alcuin's letters to Charlemagne and with Notker's *Vita Karoli.* In showing how "the Franks became the equals of the Romans and Athenians in the glory of their studies in the liberal arts," Zabarella attached special importance to the providential role of the Irish (and Anglo-Saxon) monks, whom "God through the instrumentality of Charlemagne employed as the golden head" in the restoration of the multi-metallic statue of Daniel 2, to the end that the *studia litterarum* and the proper *cultus Dei,* which had fallen into desuetude, might make whole the body politic of the Empire of the Franks.[66]

Peter d'Ailly, sometime chancellor of the University of Paris, likewise made use of the familiar theme of the transfer of studies. In 1385, in his defense of the University, before the Avignonese Pope Clement VII, against the chancellor of the archidiocese of Paris and titular head of the whole University, D'Ailly had the Pope addressed by the University as by "thy humble, devout daughter, firstborn of all the Universities" (*primogenita studiorum*). He then had her, speaking in the first person, recount her passage from Egypt to Greece, to Rome, and finally to Paris.[67] Having called upon her to trace her proud lineage, D'Ailly thereupon defended her directly from interference in her interior life at the hands of the chancellor of the cathedral, who threatened her with unfair regulations in violation of her "liberties, privileges, and statues." D'Ailly clearly implied that there were three powers—the Empire, the Church (in the sense of the secular hierarchy), and the University (the learned clergy). He warned that Antichrist was near because of "the destitution of the Empire," "the Schism in the Papacy," and "the destruction of the University."[68] The previous year, in connection with

---

[66] The *translatio* is discussed in Zabarella's commentary on *Clementina, lib.* iv, *tit.* i, wherein Clement V urges instruction in Semitic languages. *Corpus juris canonici,* ed. E. Friedberg (2nd ed., Leipzig, 1879). Zabarella's *Lectura super Clementinas* (Venice, 1481) is not paginated. For Gerson's use, see below, at n. 81. A good account of the originality and daring of the religio-political thought of Zabarella is that of W. Ullmann, *The Origins of the Great Schism* (2nd ed., London, 1948), Appendix, pp. 191–231.

[67] *Chartularium,* III, No. 1519, p. 399.

[68] *Ibid.,* p. 400: "Prout quodam loco scriptum legi, tunc adventus antichristi propin-

the litigation between the faculty of law and the cathedral chapter, the familiar doctrine of transfer of studies had been used to assert a measure of autonomy of the faculties of arts and medicine over against ecclesiastical supervision. It was argued in their behalf that even before the incarnation these two disciplines had been taught.[69] But in another mood the University addressed (1383) all "the faithful sons and alumni" with the reminder that the *primogenita studiorum* had been founded upon the tetragon of one God, one Lord, one faith, a single baptism— these together, by implication, corresponding to the four rivers of the Garden and constituting the University a paradise in which faith and reason might work in harmony.[70]

Of the three conciliarists, by far the most important for the themes we have been tracing was John Gerson, another chancellor of the University of Paris. In one brief paragraph of his, a number of these motifs were brought together in a speech he puts on the lips of the University:

The daughter of the king in particular and all the clergy in general [presents her plea against violence]: . . . "Alas! I am she who was first breathed into Adam; and in his posterity I was established and renewed in Egypt, by Abraham and other sons of Noah. Then I was taken to Athens and named Pallas or Minerva, and then I went to Rome when knighthood was there in the ascendancy. Then I was planted by Charlemagne at great expense in France, in the city of Paris. And so much was I loved and esteemed that the very noble kings of France have desired that I be named the daughter of the king by civil adoption."[71]

We shall take up in succession these several phrases as they are elsewhere and separately elaborated in Gerson.

The filial image seems to be quite new in the development we are tracing. Actually it is a Parisian variant of our christological theme. The University is the eldest daughter of Christ, the celestial Solomon (*rex pacificus*). Although it is very clear that the filial image is pressed in Gerson's time in the language of eulogy and supplication with the hope of gaining royal favor and protection, it is equally clear that behind the seemingly quite Gallican concept of *filia regis* or *fille ainée du*

---

quus erit, cum Romani imperii destitucio, scismatis ecclesiastice desolacio et Parisiensis studii destructio precesseri[n]t, quia spiritualis et temporalis fidei deffensio maxime tunc deerit."

[69] *Chartularium*, III, No. 1486, p. 320 (French); No. 1488, p. 328.

[70] *Declaratio Universitatis Parisiensis pro Clemente VII*, in *Chartularium*, III, No. 1650, p. 589.

[71] In the sermon "Estote misericordes," July 19, 1404, in *Opera omnia*, ed. L. du Pin (Antwerp, 1706), IV, 573. In the dating of the sermons, I am following Louis Mourin, *Jean Gerson: Prédicateur français* (Bruges, 1952).

roi—which sometimes becomes the festive and even preferred locution for the University—shimmers a theological reality and divine sanction, which the imbecility, vacillation, or opposition of a given sovereign sharpens in our view. Moreover, the Pope is also addressed by the University as by a daughter.[72] The two usages are supposedly reconcilable in that the Church is the mother of the University, and the king is the father.[73] But above the Pope as the Vicar of Christ, and above the king as the liturgical *christus* is the celestial Christ himself. And the University, as the aggregation of the learned clergy, is the daughter of this heavenly Bridegroom, even as the Church as a whole is the Bride. As a daughter of the *rex pacificus,* the University is concerned with peace in the Church and peace in the realm.[74] As daughter of the divine Wisdom, she teaches and she imparts peace.[75] As a daughter of Solomon (at once the philosopher-king and the type of Christ), the University is the mother of sciences and may forthrightly speak by authority of the wisdom of Solomon in the interest of preserving or securing spiritual or temporal peace.[76] She is the *veritatis doctrix,*[77] who imparts the truth instituted by Jesus Christ, *Souverain Docteur et Maistre.*[78] She is the *defensatrix fidei,* the light of the Church imparting the Light of the world.[79]

Although Gerson speaks of Christ as *doctor* and *magister* in the founding of the School of Theology, he does not develop the full christological or trinitarian sanction which we have noted elsewhere. He does, however, have a tripartite scheme of society integrated in the headship of the anointed king. The *rex christianissimus* is considered to be "miraculously consecrated" in such a way that he is both a "spiritual" and a "sacerdotal" king.[80] In addition to his kingship over him-

---

[72] See above at n. 67.

[73] E. Pasquier finds the first use of the filial image in 1366. *Les Recherches de la France* (Paris, 1621), pp. 850 ff.

[74] "Veniat pax," November 4, 1408 (*Opera,* IV, 625). The identification of Solomon as *rex pacificus* is, of course, based upon I Chronicles 22:9–10.

[75] This is a reference to the Wisdom that is above (James 3:7).

[76] "Diligite justitiam," 1408, in *Opera,* IV, 642: "Ad exponendum, inquam, ex parte filiae Regni [here, then, daughter of the Realm], scientiae, Studiorum Matris, Universitatis Parisiensis Matris meae; exordior per verbum sapientis Regis Solomonis, qui secundum nomen suum, et interpretationem, significat qualis esse debeat unusquisque: debet enim esse pacificus."

[77] "Veniat pax," p. 625.

[78] "Estote misericordes," p. 572.

[79] "Pax hominibus," December, 1409, in J. Monnoyeur, ed., *Irenikon,* VI (1929), 725. In this same sermon Gerson compares the University to the woman of Revelation 12:1 clothed with the sun and the moon under her feet (p. 732). Elsewhere he speaks of the University festively as "pulcher et clarus Sol Franciae, imo vero totius Christianitatis." "Vivat rex," 1405, in *Opera,* IV, 583.

[80] "Sermo in die Epiphaniae coram rege Carolo VI," January 6, 1391 (*Opera,* III, 980 ff.). Here the three Magi and the three royal lilies are used.

self, he is the head of three estates—the people, the knights and the *spirituales*. Elsewhere he calls the three classes the *bourgeoisie*, the *chevalerie*, and the *clergie*. These three estates are united in the king as the golden head of the multi-metallic statue in the dream interpreted by Daniel. In this view, the knights are represented by the silver arms and chest, the burghers by the legs and feet, the clergy by the brazen middle parts of the body politic—which like a bell made of the same metal sound forth resonantly with the truth![81] Within the clergy, Gerson distinguishes the learned clergy of the University from the parochial clergy and the episcopate. But his social schematization is never very clear. Elsewhere he insists that for the making of peace three things are necessary—*posse, scire,* and *velle*, which in turn find expression in power, knowledge, and benevolence. Roughly, these three would correspond to the institutional concern of magistrates, masters, and ministers in devotion respectively to *aequitas, veritas,* and *charitas*.[82] But Gerson never makes the institutional correlation quite so symmetrical as this because of his reluctance to differentiate the clerical university completely from the clerical estate. Nevertheless, Gerson is quite conscious of the constitutional uniqueness of the University.

The University, recruited from all parts of the world, quite naturally has a responsibility for seeking "the unity and peace in the whole mystical body of men."[83] And within France, drawn from all estates, she is the representative and spokesman for the whole of France.[84] Within the University are situated "the chair and the throne of faith, i.e., the knowledge of sacred Scripture and of divine Wisdom." The task of the University is to make it possible for reason to show clearly what constitutes faith; "for if there were no theological science, the faith would not be known; if it were not understood, it could not be protected; and, after that, without too much of an interval, it would perish and cease to be."[85]

With the authority of Solomon, the University may speak out prophetically on matters affecting the commonweal. And if someone should ask, Gerson continues, "What concern is this of the University, which rather should be engaged in study and devoted to books?" let

---

[81] "Rex in sempiternum vive," September 4, 1413 (*Opera,* IV, 663). This is Gerson's moral interpretation of the Danielic passage. His mystical interpretation refers to the four ages of the world (Ovid), and his literal interpretation, of course, to the four empires, of which the Roman would be the last (Orosius).

[82] "Pax hominibus," p. 764. As a synonym for *charitas* Gerson gives *pietas*. Compare the triad with an almost identical scheme of Gregory IX (above at n. 34) and the similar scheme (*Militia, sapientia, fides*) of William of Nangis (above at n. 46).

[83] "Pax hominibus," p. 735.

[84] "Vivat rex," p. 590.

[85] "Sermo in die Epiphaniae," p. 988.

the answer be emphatic that scholars apply themselves to their studies, "not only in order that we may know but that we may instruct and also act." After giving examples from Ezekiel and Plutarch, Gerson asks, ". . . may not, nay ought not, the Mistress of Truth freely proclaim similar words [of caution or rebuke] before her King and Lord?"[86] The University is under a divine compulsion to proclaim the truth and uphold the faith.[87] And if a king heeds instead the critics of the University, he may imperil the truth and thus become a tyrant. But "the kingdom of France is not governed by a tyrant when she is devoted to scholarship."[88]

So much for the critical, martial, and christological themes as they find full or partial expression in Gerson. Turning back to our initial quotation from his works,[89] we find also the restatement of the paradisic theme in the reference to the University as present in the Spirit breathed into Adam. Gerson is elsewhere quite explicit and imaginative in developing this image. In a sermon before the Avignonese Pope Benedict XIII, he rhetorically appeals for the benediction of spiritual dew and temporal fatness upon that rich field which is the University. He continues:

. . . nor will I err if I should call her the Paradise of delights, in which is to be found the tree of knowledge of good and evil and the fountain of knowledge, divided into the four streams of the faculties, irrigating the whole surface of the earth.[90]

As we noted in the initial quotation from Gerson, the Parisian chancellor also elaborated the theme of transfer of studies. Besides this passage, he made at least three other references to the theme.[91]

Gerson seems to have been the first to combine the Carolingian and the Hieronymic links in the chain of transmission of knowledge in such a way as to establish a continuity of wisdom from Paradise to Paris. Jerome had shown how the knowledge lost with the Fall was recovered in a succession of prophetic schools and disciplined monastic cells; and the Carolingians had paralleled the transfer of empire with the transfer of studies from Athens through Rome to the palace school of Charle-

---

[86] "Vivat rex," p. 589.
[87] "Vivat rex," p. 620; "Pax hominibus," p. 750. In this office, he says, Paris has been more successful than Oxford or Prague.
[88] "Pax hominibus," p. 751.
[89] See above, at n. 71.
[90] "Sermo," November 9, 1403 (*Opera,* II, 51). Gerson goes on to Aristotle, Virgil, and Palladius on agriculture and the four kinds of husbandry—comparing theology, for example, to bee culture.
[91] "Vivat rex," p. 583 (the most important); "Veniat pax," p. 636; "Pax hominibus," p. 758.

magne; Abbot Philip of Harvengt and Abelard, among others, had used links from both these chains. It now remained for Gerson to bring the whole development together as a work of God's providence. In the making of this connection, Josephus was for the first time mentioned as a source. Comparing the University of Paris with the "University" (*sapientes*, Daniel 2) of Babylon, whence the wise men came to counsel Nebuchadnezzar, Gerson wrote:

. . . besides acquired and natural sciences whereby that University distinguished itself, this Parisian University is the first and the foremost in respect to the inspired sciences [known] to the first man in the terrestrial Paradise from the beginning of the world—sciences which, by succession, passed to the Hebrews, and by Abraham (as Josephus writes)[92] to the Egyptians; from Egypt to Athens [thus far, Josephus]; from Athens to Rome, and then from Rome to Paris. This University, I say, has a much more distinguished perception of the true faith and of eternal life than the other.[93]

So much for the reflections on the theological nature and function of the University on the part of the conciliarists Zabarella, D'Ailly, and Gerson.

We may now continue with the theme of the *translatio studii* in the works of another triumvirate, whose chance reflections will bring us to the Reformation era and the Protestant conception of the university and academy. These three had little in common except their testimony to the continuity of a great theme. They were Jacobus Magnus, Robert Goulet, and Theodore Beza.

Jacobus Magnus (d. between 1415 and 1422), a Toulousan, traced the history of study in his *Sophologium*.[94] He pointed to the succession of the three main centers of learning in the rise and transfer of scholarship from Athens to Rome and from Rome to Paris. He cited Notker's *Vita Karoli* on the coming of the Anglo-Saxon scholars and was everywhere at pains to make his account more than a bare schematization of history. He was familiar with Augustine's version of the feminine vote whereby Minerva was barely elected as patron goddess of Athenian learning.[95] More than most of the writers thus far considered, he made specific in what respect Rome was really a center of learning, and again placed Augustine, this time as rhetorician, in the setting of Roman learning, in succession to Cato, Cicero, Virgil.

---

[92] In *Antiquitates*, i, 8, 2. See on Josephus above at n. 21.
[93] "Vivat rex," p. 583.
[94] I have been able to get at his work only to the extent that *lib.* i, *cap.* xv is quoted *in extenso* by Robert Goulet. See below.
[95] *De civitate Dei*, xviii, 9.

Robert Goulet's work is especially interesting for its date, 1517. On the threshold of the Reformation he composed his handbook entitled *Compendium . . . de multiplici Parisiensis universitatis magnificentia.* Herein he gives a very clear idea of how the members of the academic community in Paris thought of themselves and their place in Christendom in the very year from which we date the beginning of its fragmentation under the impact of Luther's reform.[96] Goulet opens his *Compendium* with a prayer to Christ by Thomas Aquinas for the daily use of scholars. Very near the beginning he retraces the history of the university in terms of the now quite familiar *translatio studii.* More significant than its presence in this *Compendium,* however, is the fact that Goulet feels it necessary to quote three authorities, and that the selected testimonies should be of such recent date—namely, the above-mentioned Jacobus Magnus and Cardinal Zabarella and also Robert Gaguin (d. 1501).[97]

[96] The *Compendium* has been translated by Robert B. Burke (Philadelphia, 1928).

[97] Gaguin was minister general of the Order of the Holy Trinity. It is his *Rerum Gallicarum annales* which is quoted. Cf. Du Boulay, *Historia,* V, 916.

Chapter III. The Survival and Restatement of the University Themes in Calvinism

The testimony of Theodore Beza, John Calvin's associate and successor in Geneva, as to the survival of medieval conceptions of the university in a Protestant context, is especially interesting.

John Calvin had from the beginning, like Martin Luther, been interested in popular education as a means of furthering biblical reform; but he was strangely slow about the organization of a higher center of Protestant scholarship in Geneva. It was not until 1559 that the Academy of Geneva was founded.

Beza, elected rector, delivered his inaugural address in St. Peter's in the presence of the ministers, including Calvin, and of the magistrates. He took it as his task, among other things, to relate faith to profane knowledge, and in this connection briefly traced the history of learning from Paradise to Protestantism. After dismissing the testimony of Josephus on the two *stelae* erected by Seth[1] as doubtless untenable, Beza went on to adapt the now familiar *translatio* theme into its theologically and, as he thought, historically most valid form:

I consider the homes of the patriarchs to have been from the beginning schools of true and substantial instruction, in which that image of God, though effaced in men through sin, had nevertheless been restored by their faith, the beneficence of God, of course, succoring them. . . . And it is also probable that the colleges of the prophets were so many schools in which that celestial wisdom prevailed even beyond measure and which far surpassed all human capacity.[2]

Beza did not find it necessary, in his Protestant-humanist adaptation of the transferential theme, to insist that the patriarch Abraham had brought wisdom to the Egyptians. In fact, he dismissed Josephus on this point as "ridiculous"; but Beza did preserve the conception of a transfer of learning from Egypt to Greece. Then, leaving out Rome, he went on to show how, after the barbarian irruption into the empire, God had raised up Charlemagne and "other Caesars, founders of those academies by which today Europe flourishes." Toward the end of the discourse, Beza enjoined the students, as members of "this sacred mili-

---

[1] See above, at n. 71.
[2] Calvin, *Opera omnia*, ed. W. Baum *et al.*, XVII, 545. The academic laws promulgated at this time are in Vol. X, cols. 65 ff.

tia," to be mindful of their responsibility toward the *summus imperator* (Christ).

In the academic laws promulgated in Geneva we find, incidentally, the title *gymnasiarch*—reminding us of the same unusual designation in Increase Mather's praise of President Chauncy. All told, there were in Beza's inaugural address four of our five university themes woven together. Missing was the idea of the co-ordinate authority of magistrates, ministers, and masters. Beza as a matter of policy ignored the papally chartered universities of the Middle Ages and ascribed the foundation of the *studia* to Charlemagne and "the other Caesars," and seemed to be more than dutiful in his deference to the Genevan magistrates.

Protestantism, in fact, as represented by the Lutherans and the Anglicans, seemed forced to break with the universal and clerical medieval constitution of the university. To be sure, both Henry VIII and Luther sought the consensus of the universal community of learning, the one concerned with his divorce, the other with justification by faith; but, in the end, the English and the German Reformations accelerated the nationalization of the university and increased the dependence of the university upon the prince. The magisterial control of the university was essential for the success of the Reformation. The programmatic abandonment of clerical celibacy by professors, moreover, facilitated the integration of the Protestant university into the confessional state. The paradisic motif in the maintenance of learned celibacy dropped away. The royal foundations (Regius professorships) were an indication not only of the sixteenth-century interest in but also of the encroachment of the royal power upon the interior life of the universities, new and ancient. (Needless to say, Catholic institutions were not immune to the nationalizing trend.) It was in this new mood that Beza, addressing the assembled magistrates, disparaged the influence of monasticism and the Papacy in the rise of medieval learning, and deferred to the Genevan Senate as heir to the high policy of the medieval "Caesars."

Calvin, among Beza's auditors, was of a different mind. Calvin's prayer opening the inaugural ceremonies is not preserved; but there is considerable evidence that Calvin—once again more catholic in his ecumenicity than either the Lutherans or the Henricians—endeavored to find a fresh basis for interrelating Church, State, and Academy, while safeguarding a *relative* independence in the theological education of children and older students. It was, in fact, through Calvin, alumnus of Paris, that certain ideas, which had culminated in the medieval University of Paris, reached—by way of the Genevan Academy and the University of Cambridge—the Kirjath-Sepher of Increase and Cotton Mather in the New World.

We must see Calvin's fresh effort to interpret the school and the teacher theologically as an aspect of the *pietas litterata,* the late medieval and early Protestant attempt to adapt the disciplines of Humanism in the cause of piety. Desiderius Erasmus in his several pedagogical works, John Colet in St. Paul's in London, Philip Melanchthon in the two faculties of arts and theology at Wittenberg, John Sturm in the reorganized Protestant *gymnasium* in Strassburg, and Maturin Cordier at Lausanne were major spokesmen of the effort to combine classicism and biblicism in moral tutelage.[3]

Calvin, who no doubt composed the *Ordre du Collège de Genève,* modeling it apparently in part on Cordier's *Leges Scholae Lausannensis,* was of all the exponents of *pietas litterata* the most concerned to place religious, moral, and humanistic studies under the order of teachers and at the same time perhaps the most disposed to allow pagan philosophers and authors to speak in their own pre-Christian accents without glosses.

To secure the relative independence of the Collège from the magistrates, Calvin divided the higher school under its rector (Beza) from the lower or secondary school (*schola privata*) under its principal and placed the appointment of these two administrative officers and all other teachers and regents in the hands of the Venerable Company of pastors and elders. Calvin himself taught theology in the upper school. The Academy or Collège, instituted for the training of ministers and magistrates, gave instruction in Hebrew, Greek, and Latin. For Genevan children not qualified or in a position to have this classical instruction, Calvin insisted, in the *Ordre,* that once a week these less privileged children be conducted from their several lesser schools oper-

---

[3] See V. W. C. Hamlyn, *The Universities of Europe at the Period of the Reformation* (Oxford, 1867). Hanns Rückert, *Die Stellung der Reformation zur mittelalterlichen: Universität* (1933). See also Elmore Harbison, *The Christian Scholar in the Age of the Reformation* (New York, 1956); R. R. Bolgar, *The Classical Heritage and its Beneficiaries* (Cambridge, 1954), esp. "Pietas littera," pp. 329–379; and Jules Le Coultre, *Maturin Cordier et les origines de la pédagogie protestante dans les pays de langue française* (1530–1564) (Neuchâtel, 1926).

Within the Reformation traditions our survey is limited to the survival and mutation of medieval ideas of the university within Calvinism. The role of Anglican Cambridge and Oxford, as well as that of the Scotch and Dutch universities in the transfer of medieval university law and lore to Harvard, has been fully traced by Samuel Morison, *The Founding of Harvard College* (Cambridge, 1935). Robert Waugh Henderson has worked on this problem in his "The Ministry in the Reformed Tradition: A Study of History of the Second [the Doctor] of the Four Ministries Recognized by John Calvin," Harvard Ph.D. thesis, Cambridge, 1959.

ated by the magistrates to join in the instruction given at the Collège by the duly approved teachers. We must see in this provision Calvin's earnestness in implementing the theory that education was primarily a Christian function and as such, even on the lower levels, more closely related to the work of the pastor than to that of the Christian magistrate.

Under the influence of Bucer, Sturm, and Cordier, Calvin worked away at his theory of the office of the Christian teacher or professor as one of the three or four permanent ministries ordained by Christ.

Between the first edition of the *Institutes* in 1536 and the inauguration of Beza as rector of the new Academy of Geneva in 1559, Calvin had been slowly evolving his christological basis for sustaining a tripartite schematization of society analogous to the trinitarian and christological theories of Alexander of Roes and John Gerson. In the process of re-forming a Protestant *corpus christianum*, Calvin seized upon the ancient concept of the threefold office of Christ as prophet (teacher), priest, and king to provide the divine sanction for the ordering of the relationship among Academy, Church, and State. We have seen this schematization in the Middle Ages in incomplete forms. The great emphasis laid upon this concept since the Reformation is due to Calvin.

The schematization is not directly biblical; the three offices are nowhere in the Bible grouped triadically. Among the Reformers it was Martin Bucer who apparently first used the triadic formula, when in commenting on the Messianic title in the Gospels he wrote: "As once kings, priests, and prophets were anointed in order that they might enter upon their several offices, so [as, the anointed,] Christ is king of kings, high priest, and head of the prophets."[4]

Before proceeding with Calvin's development of the triadic scheme, presumably influenced by Bucer, we may at this point go back into ancient history to summarize the earlier reflections leading to this formula.

In Christian literature the triadic scheme comes from Eusebius of Caesarea. In his *Ecclesiastical History*, he adduced the numerous and diverse anointments of the Old Testament as typological references to Jesus Christ, "the divine and heavenly Word, who is the only High *Priest* of the universe, the only *King* of all creation, and the only supreme *Prophet* among the Father's prophets."[5] In the earlier *Demon-*

---

[4] *In sacra quatuor evangelia enarrationes* (Basel, 1536), p. 606 *bis*. First noted by François Wendel, *Jean Calvin* (Paris, 1950), p. 169, n. 125.

[5] *Ecclesiastical History*, I, iii, 8. A recent work on Jesus as prophet is that of Félix Gils, *Jésus Prophète d'après les Évangiles Synoptiques* (Louvain, 1957).

stration of the Gospel Eusebius, writing somewhat more diffusely, referred to his Jewish source vaguely as "another writer, you will remember."[6] Three Jewish writers who might have influenced Eusebius may be mentioned: Josephus, Philo, and the author of *The Testaments of the Twelve Patriarchs.*

The unique assumption of royal, priestly, and prophetic authority by the Maccabean John Hyrcanus (134-104 B.C.) was the original occasion for the theological speculation concerning the threefold office of the Messiah. Of John Hyrcanus, Josephus wrote: "He was the only man to unite in his person three of the highest privileges: the supreme command of the nation, the high priesthood, and the gift of prophecy."[7] Writing in the reign of John Hyrcanus, the author of *The Testaments of the Twelve Patriarchs* provided testimony of John's assumption of the threefold dignity in the form of a promise to the descendants of Levi.[8] Philo Judaeus ascribed the same functions to Moses but, distinguishing king from lawgiver, differentiated altogether four offices.[9] It is not certain from which among the possible Jewish writers Eusebius drew his material. It is clear, however, that though he saw in the assumption of the three offices a confirmation of Jesus' Messiahship, Eusebius was no less inclined to glory in Constantine's threefold role as Christian emperor, as "bishop of those outside,"[10] and as teacher or formulator of doctrine in summoning the Council of Nicaea. Beginning with Eusebius and Constantine, indeed, the combination of the royal, sacerdotal, and doctoral functions was characteristic of the Byzantine imperial dignity. Emperor Marcian was hailed by the Fathers at the Council of Chalcedon in 451 as king, priest, and *didaskalos pisteōs.*[11] It was the Eastern counterpart of the Davidic or Solomonic kingship we have already noted in France.

For the most part the West—or at least the Popes—looked with alarm upon the Eastern imperial attempt to combine the royal, the sacerdotal, and the magisterial functions. Popes Gelasius I and Gregory II were especially eloquent and theologically discerning in their denunciation of the merging of the three kinds of power in the hands of one man.

---

[6] *Demonstration of the Gospel,* iv, 15; I. Heikel, ed., Berlin Corpus, XXIII, 173; W. Ferrar, ed., I, 191 ff.

[7] *Jewish Wars,* i, 68; *Antiquities,* xiii, 299.

[8] *Levi,* 11-15. For a fairly early application of the threefold office to every baptized Christian, see above, Part One, Chapter II, sec. 1 at n. 11 (the Persian sage, Aphrahat).

[9] *De vita Mosis,* ii, i, 3: "For Moses, through God's providence, became king and lawgiver and high priest and prophet."

[10] That is, as *pontifex maximus* in respect to his pagan subjects and as *episkopos tōn ektos* in respect to his Christian subjects. *Vita,* iv, 24.

[11] Mansi, *Concilia,* VII, col. 177.

Gelasius, for example, in 496 pointed out that, though spiritual and temporal power were indeed combined among the Gentiles and even among the people of the Old Covenant, Jesus Christ combined these three offices not only for the eternal salvation of mankind but also for man's earthly welfare; only he who was fully God as well as fully man could hold all this power safely; and to save sinful men from the worst ravages of unchecked power over body, mind, and soul he—"mindful of human frailty"—ordained that these functions should ever thereafter be placed in different hands until the end of time.[12] The high-medieval successors of Gelasius and Gregory overlooked this wholesome instruction in extending the temporal authority of the Papacy.

From this *excursus* we return to Calvin, to whom fell the task of restoring to the eternal Christ what had, from the Protestant point of view, come to be usurped by the papal Vicar of Christ.

In making increased use of the Eusebian threefold office of Christ in ordering the Genevan Christocracy, Calvin was reproducing on a fresh christological foundation the medieval effort to give a new unity to Christian society, while preserving or, better, restoring the relative autonomy of ministers, masters, and magistrates under the eternal Christ, at once priest, prophet, and king. It would be an overstatement to say that Calvin set out programmatically to find a fresh christological sanction for his ordering of society, or that the correlation between the three offices of Christ and the three public institutions of Geneva—Church, Academy, and Magistracy—emerges unequivocally from the pages of his voluminous writings. The outlines are there. The tripartite scheme was to be further elaborated by Calvin's successors. The concept of the threefold office of Christ would eventually win a place in Lutheranism and at length regain its place in Catholicism.[13]

By reaffirming in his massive new cultural ethic the sovereignty of Christ over body, mind, and soul, Calvin was as much concerned as a Gelasius I or a Gregory II to protect the Church (and the School) from improper encroachments on the part of the State—encroachments that were the great bane of the Protestant reform elsewhere in view of its dependence upon princes and patricians for its spread and consolidation in territory and town. On the issue of the independence of the interior life of the Church from the State, Calvin fought many battles, once

---

[12] *Tractatus* IV, in *Epistolae Romanorum Pontificum*, ed. A. Thiel, I, 568.

[13] The fullest historical treatment of the threefold office is that of Karl Müller, "Jesu dreifacher Amt," *Protestantische Realenzyklopädie*, 3rd ed., VIII, 733–741. See also my article "The Role of the Laymen in the Ancient Church," *Greek [Roman] and Byzantine Studies*, I (1958) where, however, no mention is made of the dual and triple messianic expectations in sectarian Judaism, notably in Qumran.

being even obliged to withdraw from Geneva altogether because of his ecclesiastical zeal.

It thus turned out that Calvin was much more definite about the independence of the ministry from the magistracy than he was about the freedom of the masters of the Academy from the Church. In fact, his *doctores* were, like the university clerics of the Middle Ages, only a differentiated or specialized clergy; and, accomplished humanist though he was, Calvin was never able to concede to the academicians any area of knowledge in which they might be regarded as autonomously competent, independent of biblical tutelage. But he was in any case clear that doctrine and ethics were to be determined by the Church and the Academy rather than by the State.

Despite Beza's conspicuous deference to the magistracy in his inaugural address, the rector of the Collège or Academy was in fact elected by the ministers, while the laws of the Genevan Academy were not submitted to the Council of the Two Hundred or to the Council of the whole citizenry but were instead solemnly promulgated in the course of the service of worship in St. Peter's, which was opened and closed with a prayer by Calvin.[14] It was the Reformed Church and not the State which created the Collège destined to become the University of Geneva. The emendations by the magistracy of the section on *docteurs* in the *Ordonnances ecclésiastiques* of 1541 show that Calvin purposed to perpetuate in a new climate the "papal" idea of a school; the magistracy, the "imperial" conception of a proper charter.[15] In respect to higher education, then, Calvinism was much closer to Catholicism than was Lutheranism,[16] or even Anglicanism.

To understand Calvin's conception of the Academy, it is helpful to note that Calvin developed both a threefold and a fourfold ministry. In the *Institutes*[17] he stressed a threefold ministry of the Word (pastors), of discipline (presbyters), and of charity (deacons), the latter two subordinate to the pastor as *praeses* of the presbyterate. In the

[14] Charles Borgeaud, *Histoire de l'Université de Génève* (Geneva, 1900), I, 48. Of a similar view is F. Kampschulte, *Johann Calvin: seine Kirche und sein Staat in Genf* (Leipzig, 1899), II, 320 ff.

[15] In the following, the italicized words were added to Calvin's by the magistracy: "Que nul [docteur] ne soit receu s'il n'est apprové par les ministres, *l'ayant première-ment faict scavoir à la seigneurie, et alors derechef qu'il soit présenté au conseil,* avec leur tesmoignage, de peur des inconvéniens. Toutesfois l'examen debvre estre faict présent deux des seigneurs du petit conseil." *Opera omnia,* X, col. 22. Cf. Borgeaud, *Histoire,* p. 30. Borgeaud restores to Calvin his very important role in the conception of the Academy.

[16] On the university concept of the *praeceptor Germaniae,* Philip Melanchthon, see Friedrich Paulsen, *Geschichte des gelehrten Unterrichts* (2nd ed., Leipzig, 1896), pp. 200, 223 ff.

[17] *Lib.* iv, 3, 4–9; iv, II.

Ecclesiastical Ordinances (1541, 1561) a fourfold ministry of pastors, *docteurs*, presbyters, and deacons became more clearly indicated. In Strassburg, where Bucer prevailed who so greatly influenced Calvin, the local synod as early as 1533 recognized the four ministries, the fourth being lecturers in languages and the liberal arts, all masters of schools, and regents.[18]

The doctorate became increasingly important as Calvin, after his return from Strassburg in 1541, moved toward the establishment of the Academy in 1559. In the revision of the *Ordinances* of 1561, two years after Beza's rectoral address, the doctorate is said to constitute *l'Ordre des écoles*, functioning in a *collège* for the purpose of training for the ministry and for civil government.[19] Ordinarily in Calvinist congregations, as they became organized, not much practical distinction could be drawn between the minister who held the title of pastor and his colleague who held the title of teacher. This was surely true in New England usage apart from the one college it could boast (for 175 years) —although the teacher was theoretically more qualified to expound the Scriptures and the pastor more gifted in sermonic application. But in Calvin's own writings it is clear that something institutionally more significant was being striven for in a schematic way.

Though their functions were often undifferentiated, still Calvin was inclined to place the *doctor* much closer than the *pastor* to the prophet. Of the three New Testament offices—that of apostle, that of evangelist, and that of prophet—Calvin was certain that the first two had become extinguished. But he was unwilling to admit that the prophetic office had completely lapsed. God had diminished prophecy in punishment for the world's ingratitude, "Mais . . . il nous en donne petite portion."[20] By extension, at least, *doctor* and *propheta* might be used as synonyms.[21] In the *Institutes* of 1543 (and again in 1559) Calvin expressly connected the doctorate with the prophetic office of both the Old Testament and the Apostolic Age:

For our pastors bear the same resemblance to the apostles as our teachers do to the ancient prophets (*veteribus prophetis*). The office of the prophets was more excellent on account of the special gift of revelation, by which they were distinguished; but the office of teacher is executed in a similar manner and has precisely the same end.[22]

---

[18] F. Wendel, *L'Église de Strasbourg . . . 1532–1535* (Paris, 1942), p. 63.
[19] *Opera omnia*, X, col. 100.
[20] *Ibid.*, LI, col. 556.
[21] *In Acta apostolorum*, in *Opera omnia*, XLVIII, col. 278.
[22] *Corpus Reformatorum*, I, 564; II, 780.

Elsewhere he speaks of Jesus himself as a *doctor* and goes on to generalize that no one may be legitimately counted a *doctor* "unless he has proceeded from God."[23] It is specifically from Christ as *prophet* (teacher), priest, and king that the academician, the professor and schoolmaster, in the Calvinist system may be said to derive his authority.

It has already been indicated that Calvin only gradually developed his conception of the threefold office of Christ[24] and, by implication, that its elaboration was related to his comparably slow development of an academy in Geneva, where the *docteurs* taught apart from the parish churches and St. Peter's (formerly the cathedral). But in the fully revised edition of the *Institutes* of 1559, the year of Beza's rectoral address, Calvin could write definitely that Christ

. . . was given as a prophet, a king, and a priest; though we should derive but little benefit from an acquaintance with these names, unaccompanied with a knowledge of their end and use. For they are likewise pronounced among the Papists. . . .

Now it is to be observed that the appellation of "Christ" belongs to these three offices. For we know that under the law not only priests and kings, but prophets also, were anointed with holy oil. Hence the celebrated title of "Messiah" was given to the promised Mediator. But though I confess that he was called the Messiah with particular reference to his kingdom . . . , yet the prophetic and sacerdotal unctions have their respective places.[25]

He went on to observe that Jesus received the unction of the Spirit, "not only for himself that he might perform the office of *doctor,* but for his whole Body, that the preaching of the Gospel might continually be attended with the power of the Spirit."[26]

Though Calvin came gradually to his conception of the threefold office of Christ, his formulation was quickly appropriated and elaborated as a characteristic emphasis wherever Calvinism penetrated.[27] He

---

[23] *In Evangelium Ioannis,* in *Opera omnia,* XLVI, col. 52. "Atque ab hoc principio pendet omnis doctorum auctoritas in ecclesia."

[24] The threefold office is not mentioned in the *Institutes* of 1536. Christ's role as priest-king was introduced for the first time in the French Catechism of 1538; *Opera omnia,* XXII, col. 53. It is repeated in the *Institutes* of 1539. Only subsequently was the prophetic role added to the royal and priestly offices, at first perfunctorily. See the composite of the editions from 1543 to 1554, *Opera omnia,* I, cols. 513 ff.

[25] *Institutes,* ii, 15, 1–2. Elisha is the only prophet specifically recorded as having been anointed.

[26] *Ibid.*

[27] For example, in Poland his doctrine of the tripartite office of Christ was taken

himself gave an indication of the way in which this tripartite scheme might be developed when, in his commentary on Malachi, he indicated that unless mutually checked the kings and the priests, and the *doctores* of the Old Covenant—and presumably also of the New Dispensation—tend to regard themselves as exempt from their order, seek to release themselves from the laws and customs of their office, and thereupon, having been "blinded by that grace of God," come to think of themselves as "demigods." He specifically mentioned the Papacy as having incurred the divine wrath because the sacerdotal *pastores* had in their *hybris* converted ecclesiastical government into tyranny.[28]

On the subsequent development of the tripartite scheme of Calvinism, we shall confine our discussion to those writers who are known to have influenced the formulations of Increase and Cotton Mather and their associates in the transmission of Old World ideas about University and Academy to the New World.

Suffice it to say that the Calvinist conception of the doctorate as a kind of ministry and of the school (grammar school, academy, or university) as a concern of church and synod no less than of prince or parliament found fullest expression in the pre-Revocation Huguenot Churches of France and in the *First Book of Discipline* (1560) of the Kirk of Scotland. In the latter the whole of Chapter VIII is devoted to the teacher and the school from village schoolmaster to university professor.[29]

As a result of the Independent influence in the discussion of the teaching office during the Westminster Assembly the doctorate was regrettably *parochialized*. Since the professorships of the two historic universities could not easily be subsumed under the Calvinist doctorate, a *doctor* or teacher in each parish was all that could be contended for; and thus Calvin's supra-parochial teaching ministry became largely nominal or vestigial, except in the New World where Puritan Congregationalists, alumni of old Cambridge, could at some remove establish a university doctorate in combining the medieval tradition of Cambridge and the newer theories of Calvin. In colonial Harvard the medieval *magister* and the Calvinist *doctor-propheta* were one.

The first divine to be mentioned in this development is William Ames (1576-1633), from whom, by no means incidentally, the Matherian seal of Harvard University, *Christo et Ecclesiae*, was ultimately

over by the pre-Socinians, and it became the theoretical basis for the prominence of the catechetical school and Academy in Raków.

[28] *Opera omnia*, XLIV, col. 431.

[29] Alexander Peterkin, *A Compendium of the Laws of the Church of Scotland* (2nd ed., Edinburgh, 1837), I, 45 ff.

derived.[30] In his *Medulla theologiae,* a basic text in the development of the New England mind, Ames clearly restated Calvin's conception of the threefold office of Christ.[31] In his clarification of the three functions he was at pains to show that in his royal and sacerdotal capacities —that is, in the atonement and in his governance of the world—Christ is unique, but that in his prophetic function he has predecessors and successors, for the burden of the prophet, apostle, or *doctor* is "the declaration of the divine will among men."

John Henry Alsted (1588–1638), the teacher of John Comenius,[32] made explicit in his *Triumphus bibliorum sacrorum*[33] that Christ, the eternal prophet, priest, and king, "exercises his [doctoral] function today partly in the triumphant Church, partly in the Church militant." In his *Synopsis theologiae*[34] he elaborated this point by distinguishing within Christ's prophetic office the external promulgation of the Gospel and the internal illumination of the heart. In the Old Covenant, Christ taught ordinarily through the priests and his other servants, extraordinarily in his appearances to the Fathers; in his earthly ministry he taught directly as one having authority; today he again teaches "through his servants." Alsted did not at this point distinguish *doctores* from *pastores;* but it is clear from another work, *Theologia didactica,*[35] written at the same time, that he was quite conscious of a *scholastic* estate or order as distinguished from a *hieratic* (or priestly) and a political order, all dependent upon the basic economic order. Although he was here writing about the constitution of biblical Israel, he was apparently prompted by a contemporary interest in the place of the school in a covenantal society to insist upon the importance of the scholastic estate as one of the orders under the Old Covenant. In his *Synopsis,* as in so many comparable works of the age, he devoted a whole *locus*[36] to schools.

Alsted, as we might expect from our survey, held that there had been *in populo Dei* an orderly scholastic succession from Paradise to the present. From Adam to Moses and Aaron the school was domestic or private. Thereafter it became public, with a specialized doctorate. Moses and Aaron were thus the first *doctores publici.* Alsted regarded the prophets and their schools as extraordinary enterprises called forth by

[30] Samuel Eliot Morison, *Harvard in the Seventeenth Century* (Cambridge, 1936), II, 493.
[31] *Medulla,* i, *cap.* xix.
[32] Alsted is mentioned as a source by Cotton Mather, *Magnalia,* iv, pt. 1, § 1 (II, 8).
[33] Frankfurt, 1625, p. 332.
[34] Hanover, 1627, pp. 74–75.
[35] Hanover, 1627, pp. 426–432.
[36] *Synopsis, loc.* xxvii, p. 69.

God when the ordinary means of public instruction failed. As in Beza's discussion, the *translatio studii* loses at this point some of its links, largely no doubt because of the improved knowledge of the history of education. But Charlemagne still has his place in the succession.

Jacob Alting, already mentioned as one of the Mathèrian sources on the history of universities, likewise counted Moses among the *doctores,* while Adam was "the first and unique *Doctor* on earth in his time."[37] Alting also saw in the mantle of Elijah, shed upon the anointed prophet Elisha, the Old Testament equivalent of the doctoral or magisterial gown (*toga*).[38]

With the mention of Jacob Alting, we are brought back to our point of departure—the Harvard of Charles Chauncy, "our Charlemagne," the New England "Cadmus," the commander of the learned militia of Christ; the Harvard of Increase Mather, unique rector and first recipient of a doctorate from the first "American University"; the "School of the Prophets" dedicated to the eternal "Christ and the Church" and encamped in the new Kirjath-Sepher.

We first identified five basic university themes in the formative period of Harvard's history: the critical, the christological, the transferential, the paradisic, and the martial motifs. Within the framework of the book as a whole, we can now say further by way of conclusion that the martial motif, going back as it does to the monks and the early Christian martyrs, may be assimilated to the paradisic cycle and that the transferential theme, the moment the line of transmission was extended to Adam before the Fall (Gerson), may likewise be subsumed under the paradisic theme. Our five university themes may then be reduced to two: the paradise-wilderness cycle and the trinitarian-christological pattern of the three intersecting institutions of faith, learning, and commonwealth.

---

[37] Alting, *Hebraeorum respublica scholastica* (Amsterdam, 1652), pp. 62–63; see also above, notes 30 and 32, Chap. I of this essay. Itter, also known to the Mathers, quotes Alting on these points, *De honoribus . . . academicis* (Frankfurt, 1698), pp. 74–76.

[38] See Itter, *De gradibus,* p. 76. Itter, it may be remarked here for the sake of completeness, developed an interesting variant of the transferential theme, according to which Protestant Germany rather than France represented the culmination. He is here dependent upon Georg Christopher Walther: "Altius adhuc originem Academicorum Graduum repetit Waltherus, cap. 3., tractatus sui, *tria* corum principia constituens, *inchoantia* scilicet, *crescentia,* et *perficientia.* Ad inchoantia refert mores Judaeorum et Graecorum. Ad crescentia consuetudines Romanorum. Ad perficientia denique instituta Germanorum." Among the latter, of course, he would include Charlemagne and Lothair II. *De gradibus,* p. 73.

Chapter IV. Surviving Traces of the Five Themes in the
Conflicts Between College, Church, and Commonwealth After
Increase and Cotton Mather

We have now completed our survey of the interrelationship and mutual reinforcement of these five themes in the millennial development
of the Western conception of what constitutes the universal community
of scholarship, with its mission as a third force between Church and
State. We have traced the rise of this self-consciousness and increasing
autonomy of the community of learning from its monastic beginnings
in Alcuin, Anselm, and Abelard to its Calvinist reformulation in Ames,
Alsted, and Alting, upon whom early Harvardians drew for guidance
and instruction in defining the nature and function of their university.

In the nineteenth century, much of the discussion of the "theology"
of the university and the perpetuation of the five "university themes"
in attentuated strength centered at Harvard in the succession of controversies over the University seals and over the relationship of the
Divinity School, founded in 1811, to the College and in the Commonwealth which at the time supported Harvard financially.

1. College, Church, and Commonwealth

Harvard College had, of course, been founded to train ministers and
magistrates of a godly Commonwealth. The collegiate requirements for
a learned clergy were emphasized. Nevertheless, studies in colonial Harvard were not conspicuously clerical. In fact, they scarcely differed from
those in Oxford and old Cambridge except for the greater prominence
in Harvard of Hebrew—and this linguistic emphasis could be explained
as much by the widespread humanist theory that Hebrew was the primal language as by the needs of ministerial training. Thus, prospective
ministers, magistrates, and merchants submitted to the same classical
discipline. They enjoyed the same general education. After receiving
the bachelor's degree at the end of four years (which in the medieval
tradition had not been regarded as terminal), prospective ministers tar-
ried in Cambridge or its environs to read on their own in the College
library, or with the president, or with some established minister. At
the end of three additional years, having completed in this more casual
fashion the medieval *septennium,* they were qualified as Masters of

Arts and ready for ordination. For the seventeenth- and eighteenth-century New England divine, there was no professional degree.

The traditional right of the graduate of the Harvard (as also of the Yale) Divinity School to wear the "doctoral" gown (actually the "magisterial" gown) is an indirect survival of the days when a graduate of the Divinity School had presumably already spent seven years in the university and was thus a Master of Arts with all the rights and privileges appertaining to the degree. The *academic* gown—as distinguished from the *Geneva* gown—is a fairly late introduction in the United States; but the magisterial dignity was clearly defined. Only in the nineteenth century, under Continental influence, was a Master of Arts differentiated from a Doctor of Philosophy. All this is to say that the professionally undifferentiated, classical education of Harvard College in the seventeenth and eighteenth centuries survived into the nineteenth, and that even when the Divinity School was separated, in 1816, for more specialized training, breadth of instruction remained the ideal.

It was undoubtedly easier for the Harvard Divinity School, being Unitarian and classical, to continue in the broad rational channel than for Andover Theological Seminary, which had been organized in 1808 expressly in protest against the rationalist emphasis at Harvard. But an unexpected consequence of Andover's concern for ministerial and missionary training under proper theological auspices was the setting of a sectarian pattern in American education. Commenting on this educational isolation as a consequence of theological schism in Massachusetts, William Adams Brown wrote: "The example set by the Congregationalists at Andover was speedily followed by other denominations, and soon a score of denominational seminaries were in existence, each designated to perpetuate the special teaching of the sect it represented."[1]

The movement thus initiated had far-reaching consequences for the American educational system. It was the first step on the long road which led to the weakening of the college as a school of liberal arts and the professional isolation of theology from the academic centers of debate. Church, State, and University were constitutionally linked in Mas-

---

[1] *The Case for Theology in the University* (Chicago, 1938), pp. 34–35. He continues: "Even those colleges, like Harvard and Yale, which still remained true to their original purpose of educating ministers, followed the denominational model and set up departments of theology which became in time distinct professional schools. The story of this change in the methods of professional education can be read in the biography of President Eliot." On the pre-eminence of Andover in the rise of American seminaries, see Frank Dixon McCloy, "The Founding of Protestant Theological Seminaries in the United States of America 1784–1840," Harvard Ph.D thesis, Cambridge, 1959.

sachusetts until 1833, when the first two were separated, and 1865, when the last two were likewise disjoined. Thus in the early nineteenth century Harvard was subject to the severe strains imposed by the schism within the Standing Order (Congregationalism) and the subsequent tension between the Unitarian congregationalists of the eastern part of the Commonwealth and the trinitarian Congregationalists and other evangelical parties.

Before the virtual "disestablishment" of the University by the Act of 1865, Harvard was subject to numerous attacks upon its corporate liberties. Only the more notable episodes need to be recalled. They are all part of a succession of controversies over clerical and political influence and possible interference in the interior life of the College on the part of the Board of Overseers.

The State Constitution of 1780, confirming the ancient charter of "the Republic of Letters" in Cambridge, had been content to declare the successors of the magistrates and "teaching elders" therein named as constituting the Honourable and Reverend the Board of Overseers. The elders were interpreted to be the several Congregational ministers of the adjacent six towns. Then, in 1810 (and again, after the act had been repealed, in 1814), the legislature, with the consent of the Harvard Corporation and Board of Overseers, determined that the clerical representation on the Board should consist of fifteen Massachusetts Congregational ministers without regard to local habitation. But by 1820 the problem of clerical representation was again to the fore. For the withdrawal of Maine as a separate state disturbed the political balance, and a new constitution was deemed necessary. Chapter V on Harvard, and particularly the clerical composition of its Board of Overseers, was up for review.

In vituperative preparation for the Constitutional Convention, the Boston *Patriot* in 1819 ran a series attacking the University because of its alleged aristocracy and atheism (Unitarianism), and demanding "a people's University." This was the year of the decision of the Dartmouth College case, argued before Chief Justice John Marshall. Feeling ran high as to whether a pre-Revolutionary charter granted to an educational institution, once confirmed, should ever thereafter be free from legislative curtailment, and this in turn depended on whether a college was construed as a private or as a public corporation. Daniel Webster, who had movingly defended the royal charter of Dartmouth College, was a delegate from Boston to this convention, which in its turn, under his guidance, had occasion to think through the corporate liberties of Harvard.[2]

The presence of magistrates *ex officiis* (responsive to the will of the people) on the highest governing Board of the University, public support of the University, and its established place in Chapter V of the Constitution were all interpreted as clear evidence that Harvard was a public corporation and therefore subject to recurrent legislative supervision. On the other hand, the presence on this same Board of Congregational ministers (whether Unitarian or orthodox) seemed to some to argue for the essentially private character of the corporation. And for this very reason there were some, both within and without the Standing Order, who acknowledged or even urged that the clerical representation on the Board should be open to ministers of all denominations. One such delegate to the convention, the Rev. Joseph Richardson from Hingham (a Unitarian congregationalist), expressed alarm, indeed, lest a Board in which there were exclusively Congregational ministers might "place the University above the control of the State government" and that there might thus emerge "a powerful institution, built up by the State, and independent of the State."[3]

---

[2] *Report upon the Constitutional Rights and Privileges of Harvard College,* by order of the Convention, 1821. Although the case of Dartmouth College against the Legislature of New Hampshire was argued and decided primarily in terms of the inviolability of a charter granted to a *private* corporation (with the consequence that commercial as well as eleemosynary corporations were thereafter put beyond the supervision of the state in the spirit of laissez-faire), it is pertinent to remember that Webster himself, both in Washington and then in Boston, was expressly concerned with the freedom of colleges as such; he cited several instances in English history of the impropriety of royal or parliamentary interference in their interior life. He closed his plea for Dartmouth with words pregnant with meaning for educational institutions today:

"They [the people] have, most wisely, chosen to take the risk of occasional inconvenience from the want of power, in order that there might be a settled limit to its exercise, and a permanent security against its abuse. . . . No legislature in this country is able, and may the time never come when it shall be able, to apply to itself the memorable expression of a Roman pontiff: 'Licet hoc *de jure* non possumus, volumus tamen *de plenitudine potestatis.*'

"The case before the court is not of ordinary importance, nor of every-day occurrence. It affects not this college only, but every college, and all the literary institutions of the country. . . . It will be a dangerous, a most dangerous experiment, to hold these institutions subject to the rise and fall of popular parties, and the fluctuations of political opinions. If the franchise may be at any time taken away or impaired, the property also may be taken away, or its use perverted. Benefactors will have no certainty of effecting the object of their bounty; and learned men will be deterred from devoting themselves to the service of such institutions, from the precarious title of their offices. Colleges and halls will be deserted by all better spirits, and become a theatre for the contention of politics. Party and faction will be cherished in the places consecrated to piety and learning."

The Writings and Speeches of Daniel Webster (Boston, National Edition, 1903), X, 232–233.

[3] *Journal of Debates and Proceedings in the Convention of Delegates Chosen to Re-*

Other delegates with equal urgency argued that to tamper with an original provision of the charter was to encroach upon the liberties of the College and the rights of the original donors. They would prefer to suffer a manifest sectarianism in the composition of the Overseers in order to preserve the chartered liberties of the College. Still others, more concerned with orthodoxy, likewise defended the denominational restrictions of the old charter in order to secure the possibility of eventually regaining evangelical control of Harvard. Popular and evangelical charges against the University had in any event to be taken into cognizance by the convention, which was at first disposed to let Chapter V of the Constitution as modified by the acts of 1810 and 1814 stand unaltered. Thanks to Daniel Webster, the University was cleared of the charges, with the salutary recommendation, however, that the ministers of all denominations be eligible for the *clerical* seats on the Honourable and *Reverend* the Board of Overseers. For some of the reasons given the recommendation was not ratified. Denominational diversification on the Board was not realized until the Act of 1843.

In controversy and reorganization of the Divinity School in 1830 the basic issue politically was whether "the President of the University of the Commonwealth" could be legitimately the head of what was, in effect, a sectarian divinity school. The Rev. Dr. John Codman of Dorchester, orthodox Congregationalist member of the Board of Overseers, in a speech before them on February 3, 1831, asked ironically whether the president was "to be officially and publicly the Head—I will not say of the Church—the Defender of the Faith—but I must say, the Head of a Unitarian Theological School."[4]

In 1851 the ministerial section on the Board was eliminated entirely; thenceforth clergymen were eligible on the same basis as others without regard to status. And the same act greatly reduced the magisterial representation *ex officiis;* only the governor, the lieutenant governor, the president of the Senate, the speaker of the House, and the secretary of the Board of Education survived as magistrates *ex officiis* on the Board. But this measure of University autonomy was secured only after a major crisis, during which the Democratic leader, George S. Boutwell, as spokesman for the rural Calvinists and the urban Catholics, had pushed a bill that would have made the president and fellows of Harvard Col-

---

vise the Constitution of Massachusetts (Boston; new edition, 1853), p. 71. The principal portions devoted to the Harvard Overseers are pp. 69–87; 491–493; 527–532; 542–551. For a vigorous anti-Unitarian voice outside the Convention, see paid letter in the *Massachusetts Spy,* April 4, 1821.

[4] On the background of the issue, see further Conrad Wright in *The Harvard Divinity School* (Boston, 1954), p. 35.

lege elective by the legislature for six-year terms, would have made professorial salaries dependent upon course registration, and would have thus made the University subject to the will of the people of the Commonwealth in respect to theology, professional training, and Free Soil.[5]

Harvard seemed for a moment to have narrowly escaped becoming a state university proliferating in trade-school courses, with its theology, its politics, and entire curriculum subject to the recurrent scrutiny of the electoral majority. Though the University was freed from its last official connections with the state in 1865, the same religious, political, and utilitarian arguments were never far below the surface in recurrent threats to the corporate autonomy of the University. At the same time the venerable constitutional—and ultimately theological—undergirding of the University's claim to certain corporate freedoms dropped out of the general consciousness of the academic community as it faced fresh perils.

2. *Veritas and Ecclesia: The Sphragistic Controversy at Harvard*

President Increase Mather had not been conscious of breaking with venerable usage of the College when the Corporation during his rectorship ordered the cutting of a "Common Seale" in accordance with the provisions of the College Charter of 1692. There had been, to be sure, an earlier seal, that of 1650, with the legend *In Christi Gloriam*. And, earlier still, the so-called Overseers' Seal of 1643 had been imperfectly projected with the simple legend *Veritas*. We have indicated some of the motives that may have prompted Increase Mather to adopt the wording of a third seal: *Christo et Ecclesiae*.[6]

As the 200th anniversary of the College approached in 1836, President Josiah Quincy, deep in his researches into the history of Harvard, discovered the *Veritas* design in the surviving archives.[7] Finding it a more acceptable motto of the College over which he presided than the Matherian dedication to Christ and the Church, Quincy programmatically had it reproduced on a large banner for the bicentennial procession.

[5] That the later leader in the impeachment proceedings against President Andrew Johnson had, nevertheless, his own very clear conception of the role of education in the preservation of freedom is amply evident in his address "Liberty and Learning" (1857), printed in *Educational Topics and Institutions* (Boston, 1859), p. 274.

[6] The fullest sphragistic and heraldic account is that of Samuel Eliot Morison, "Harvard Seals and Arms," *Harvard Graduates' Magazine*, XLII (1933), 1 ff.

[7] The seal is reproduced in his *History of Harvard College* (Cambridge, 1840), I, facing p. 48. Here also he gives his constitutional and theological reasons for "restoring" the first seal.

What Quincy countenanced, the treasurer of the College, Samuel A. Eliot, vigorously defended in an intense epistolary interchange in the fall of 1846 between himself and Quincy's successor, President Edward Everett.[8] At the beginning of this year, a committee of the Board of Overseers had brought in one of the periodic reports on the proper relationship of the Divinity School to the University as a whole. Though it had dealt inconclusively with the problem of "sectarian" preaching in the chapel of a "state" institution, it had been quite emphatic "That the College Government . . . have no power, in law or equity, to transfer property" that had been originally given to "the College for the promotion of Theological Science as a Branch of University Education."[9] With the problem of the proper relationship of the College to Commonwealth and Church very much to the fore at the beginning of his presidential administration, Everett discovered that as early as 1843 the Matherian seal of the University had been quietly replaced (in the *detur* book plates awarded to deserving students) by the *Veritas* seal, redesigned by President Quincy.

At the outset of the correspondence with Eliot, it turned out that the treasurer himself had ordered the change and was, moreover, eager to defend it. Everett, in the opening letter, took cognizance of the difference between an "academical" or "literary" as distinguished from a "theological" and hence "professional" school; but he argued that the dedication of the College as a whole to Christ and the Church was entirely appropriate. Besides advancing artistic and constitutional reasons against the unauthorized substitution, Everett made it his chief argument that ". . . if it had been the name of a human benefactor we should not readily in his life time have struck it from our seal; how much less the name of him 'who ever liveth to make intercession' for us."[10] Eliot, in reply, renounced any intention of permitting the Matherian seal to be *quietly laid away*. He would in fact insist upon a "requiem" to draw attention to its sepulture. He was not so certain as we have since become that the seal was in fact Matherian, but on internal evidence Eliot was convinced that he could detect the hand "of the worldly-minded, aspiring and bold Increase Mather." Taking up Everett's argument, he reproached Mather precisely "for forgetting his immortal benefactor" by putting the *Ecclesia* "on an equality with its head." He continued:

[8] The correspondence is unpublished; Harvard College Papers, 2nd series, XIV (1846–1847), folios 136 ff.

[9] Lemuel Shaw, *Report of the Committee of the Board of Overseers of Harvard College in Relation to the Theological Department* (Boston, 1846), pp. 10–14.

[10] Harvard College Papers, XIV, folio 139 *verso*.

. . . if ever the cloven foot of the arch fiend, ambition, were betrayed to the stander by, it is in the claim which was made, in this motto, to the possession of the College, body and soul, by "the church." The first [used] motto [*In Christi gloriam*] contained one falsehood, this conveys two in the briefest compass. This is enough to disgust me with its use. But I object, as a Christian, and as a republican against the use of the word "church" in any such connexion. The primitive Christian idea of a church, in my belief, is any separate congregation of believers; and I can hardly conceive of greater evils than have befallen the world by the abandonment of this simple idea, and conveying power to, or suffering power to accumulate in, the hands of the representatives of churches, or of those who claimed to be such. The church, in the idea of Mather, was the reverend board of teaching and especially *ruling* Elders, and to any such church as that I know the College was never dedicated, and it should not, therefore, profess to be.[11]

Eliot denied "that the College was originally instituted as a theological school" and rejoiced in the original *Veritas* seal as at once derived from "the highest authority ever known to the College"—namely, the Overseers appointed by the General Court—and as the most appropriate in view of its comprehensive simplicity:

There is nothing exclusive [about it], nothing limited, nothing which fetters, nothing which pretends to control the free search after truth, no worldly ambition, no temporary purpose. . . . Will any one say, you have ceased to dedicate your institution to your Saviour? I answer, not so, for he has declared himself to be "the truth," and we seek it through him still; and by changing [the seal] we merely mean to say that religious truth is not the only truth which is sought after in the College, as is so strongly implied in the other mottos, and that we give no countenance to the arrogance which claims for the church the power which belongs only to its master and head.[12]

In a later communication, Eliot made the further point that nothing better than truth in the sense thus defined could be the proper object "in education by public institutions" and insisted that the original intent of the Matherian seal was dedication to the ecclesiology of the Cambridge Platform of 1648.[13]

In the meantime, Everett had composed his principal letter in defense of the Matherian seal.[14] He reminded Eliot that the authors of the

---

[11] *Ibid.*, Folio 140 *recto*.

[12] *Ibid.*, Eliot to Everett, October 10, 1846; folio 142 *recto*.

[13] *Ibid.*, Eliot to Everett, November 25, 1846; folio 149 *verso*.

[14] *Ibid.*, Everett to Eliot, November 24, 1846; folios 145 ff. Whether the seal had been actually created by Mather, Everett, too, was not sure.

Veritas seal "were men who thought all political power ought to be monopolized by church members," while in contrast Increase Mather was responsible for the more liberal Provincial Charter "under which the exclusive privileges of church members were taken away." But his principal argument was that the Matherian seal "implies the great truth that the education we aim to impart, like all modern civilization, is founded on Christianity." Everett continued:

The "church" referred to . . . I conceive to be not any separate communion of worshippers nor any ecclesiastical organization existing in any country; but that "holy church throughout the world." . . . I do certainly regard it as the ultimate object of our Institution to train up educated young men to be worthy members of that body and worthy disciples of its Head.

Everett thereupon moved decisively to restore the *Christo et Ecclesiae* seal.

Before passing to the next phase of Harvard's extended sphragistic controversy, we should take note of another aspect of the recurrent struggle among ministers, masters, and magistrates. Everett's successor by one, President James Walker, expressed himself clearly on the proper relationship of Church, College, and Commonwealth. It was on the occasion of the induction of the Rev. Frederic D. Huntington as Preacher to the University, on September 4, 1855. On this occasion Walker asserted that the College was "pre-eminently a child of the Church." After tracing briefly the history of the community of clerical scholarship from the sixth century until it emerged as "a distinct and independent organization under the name of University," he pointed out that "it was independence from local jurisdiction," political and diocesan, for which it strove, and "not from the Church." He continued:

The first university was the University of Paris; and its title was, "The First School of the Church." At the Reformation the English Universities were lost to the Church of Rome by one of those high-handed measures of social and state necessity, which make but small account of parchment and precedents. But, true to their original destination as belonging to the religion of the country, they passed into the hands of the Church of England. Down to the present day, the government and instruction of these institutions are to all intents and purposes in the hands of Churchmen. Our fathers brought over with them the same general feelings and convictions on this subject, in consequence of which Harvard College was dedicated, as its corporate seal testifies, "to Christ and the Church."[15]

[15] *A Discourse at the Induction of the Rev. Frederic D. Huntington, D.D.* (Cambridge, 1855), pp. 11-12. For other pertinent portions of this *Discourse*, see *Harvard Divinity School*, Chap. III, n. 20.

Walker, true to the Calvinist tradition in distinguishing between the pastoral and doctoral functions among the several ministries of the Church, declared in the same *Discourse* that "the Christian life is not a development of human nature, but something superinduced upon it, and wholly the work of Grace" and that the College "must make the obvious distinction between Christianity considered as a means of enlightening and civilizing men in their relations to each other and the world, and Christianity considered as a means of eternal salvation to individuals"—"both legitimate functions of Christianity,—the first as truly as the last." Walker was at the same time alert to the complexity of the problem of supplying the religious dimension in university instruction because of the disparate claims and needs of the diverse denominations; and he was also aware that any favoritism might force the detachment of the Divinity School from the College on separationist principles. Nor did he desire that the College become a church. At the same time, he vigorously denounced the facile solution of secularization. "Before Harvard College does this," he said, "she ought at least, for consistency's sake, to break her seal, and blot out and forget, if she can, her whole history."[16]

The Plummer professor, in accepting the challenge of the president, outlined his own somewhat variant conception of the role of theology in the University, concluding with words reminiscent of the tripartite theme we have been noting throughout these pages: "Then we shall do something cheerfully and harmoniously together for the perpetual re-dedication of those ancient honored halls to Christ and the Church, and the *scholars* of human learning shall be *kings* and *priests* unto God."[17]

A few years later Huntington developed this idea in a sermon on "Christ our Prophet, Priest, and King," wherein he defined the prophetic office in the largest sense as "the communication of religious wisdom." He quoted Eusebius (not Calvin!) and indicated familiarity with an unsigned, substantial article on the other historical sources of the threefold office in *The American Theological Review*, I (1859).

Walker's successor, President Cornelius Conway Felton, was sustained by similar convictions. In an *Annual Report*[18] he stated emphat-

---

[16] *Ibid.*, p. 23. Walker (A.B. 1814), significantly, headed the list of convenanting signatories of "The Form of Admission to the Church in Harvard University," which was gathered "within the walls" on November 1, 1814. See Harvard College Papers, 2nd series, VII (1811–1815).

[17] *Christian Believing and Living* (Boston, 1860), p. 323.

[18] *Annual Report*, 1860–1861, pp. 7 f. See further in *Harvard Divinity School*, pp. 102 f.

ically that a "Theological Faculty is an essential part of a University," which without it "can lay no claim to the rank of a University."

A sometime member of the Divinity faculty itself, Frederic Henry Hedge, had a different view, when in 1866 he declared that "the secularization of the College is in violation of its motto, *Christo et Ecclesiae.*" The occasion was an address to the alumni at their triennial festival the summer after the General Court had by the Act of 1865 "disestablished" the University by providing for the election of the Overseers by the alumni and holders of honorary degrees. "This act," he told the alumni, "indicates a radical change in the organization of this University. It establishes for one of its legislative houses a new electorate."[19] Hedge was thinking in political and national terms in the aftermath of the Civil War, which had convulsed the nation for four years. He was understandably drawn to compare the defeated forces of the South with the divisive feudal nobility of medieval France and took satisfaction in what he interpreted as the complete nationalization of the University of Paris under John Gerson:

The faithful ally of the sovereigns of France against the ambitions of the nobles and against the usurpations of Papal Rome, she bore the proud title of "The eldest Daughter of the King. . . ." She upheld the Oriflamme against the feudal gonfalons, and was largely instrumental in establishing the central power of the crown.[20]

Then, after evoking the memory of Harvard during the Revolution and alluding to the war just ended, he did not scruple to stress the "patriotic" and specifically the "political duty" of the University and warned in an intensely Unionist mood: "Better the College should be disbanded than be a nursery of treason." Thus the universal mission of the University sank momentarily from view—but Hedge had not completely forgotten the "ecumenical consciousness" of the *studium generale*. He knew that "Time was when universities were joint estates of the realms they enlightened." Christian Transcendentalist that he was, he found no difficulty in asseverating that a secularized university with academic leisure defined as "command of one's time for voluntary study" and with the privilege of free inquiry for all professors and elec-

[19] "University Reform: An Address to the Alumni of Harvard, July 19, 1866," *Atlantic Monthly*, XVIII (1866), 301; see also Samuel Eliot Morison, *Three Centuries of Harvard 1636–1936* (Cambridge, 1936), p. 309.

[20] "University Reform," p. 305. Hedge's immediate sources for the history of universities were Eugene Dubarle, *Histoire de l'Université*, 2 vols. (Paris, 1829); Karl von Raumer, *History of German Universities* (German ed., 1854), tr. Frederic B. Perkins (New York, 1859); and John Henry Newman, *The Office and Work of Universities* (1856).

tive courses for the students was in its profoundest sense still dedicated to Christ and the Church:

> For, as I interpret those sacred ideas, the cause of Christ and the Church is advanced by whatever liberalizes and enriches and enlarges the mind. All study, scientifically pursued, is at bottom a study of theology, for all scientific study is the study of Law; and "of Law nothing less can be acknowledged than that her seat is in the bosom of God."[21]

The Transcendentalist professor of ecclesiastical history and German literature could thus reconcile faith and reason and solve the millennial problem of the University by identifying law and revelation. The Fall had been forgotten; and the paradisic motif, in the long evolution of the Christian conception of a self-disciplined community of scholars, had been extinguished.

Quite unexpectedly Oliver Wendell Holmes evoked its memory in once-famous sonnets read at the Harvard Club banquet in New York a dozen years later. With two sonnets[22] devoted respectively to the Matherian seal and the Overseers' (or Quincy) seal, Holmes opened the next phase of Harvard's sphragistic controversy. Referring disparagingly to Increase Mather and his "black-robed conclave," he declared that the narrow door of their church

> Shut out the many, who if over bold
> Like hunted wolves were driven from the fold,
> Bruised with the flails these godly zealots bore,
> Mindful that Israel's altar stood of old
> Where echoed once Araunah's threshing-floor.[23]

Concluding thus, he moved in confidence to his glorying in the simpler, earlier, and—as he strangely supposed—more confident seal: *Veritas.* Oblivious of the millennial effort of the historic community of scholarship which had endeavored to vindicate Christian learning and strengthen reason despite the Fall through intensified obedience to the God who had exiled disobedient Adam from Paradise, Holmes wrote with impish glee:

> 1643 "Veritas" 1878
> *Truth:* So the frontlet's older legend ran,
> On the brief records opening page displayed;
> Not yet those clear-eyed scholars were afraid
> Lest the fair fruit that wrought the woe of man

[21] "University Reform," p. 301.
[22] *Poetical Works* (Boston, 1900), III, 77–78.
[23] II Samuel 24:16–25.

By far Euphrates—where our sire began
His *search for truth,* and, seeking, was betrayed—
Might work new treason in their forest shade,
Doubling the curse that brought life's shortened span.
Nurse of the future, daughter of the past,
That stern phylactery best becomes thee now:
Lift to the morning star thy marble brow!
Cast thy brave truth on every warning blast!
Stretch thy white hand to that *forbidden bough,*
And let thine earliest symbol be thy last!

The controversy which issued from Holmes's reading of his two sonnets on the seals divided the liberals from the evangelicals among the alumni and engaged the University itself in extended deliberations. In 1885, in anticipation of the 250th anniversary, a compromise seal, embodying both legends, was adopted, the familiar Appleton Seal.[24]

In the course of the discussions on the relation of *Veritas* and *Ecclesia* in the life of the University, William Chauncy Langdon, sometime rector of Christ Church in Cambridge, drew very close to the heart of the problem as he wrote on "The Future of Harvard Divinity School."[25] Herein Langdon, mindful of the uniqueness of Harvard's storied motto, *Christo et Ecclesiae,* but with his attention directed primarily to the Divinity School recently reorganized under President Charles W. Eliot (1869–1909) and Dean Charles C. Everett, pressed the claims of the Church as the unitive principle in the curriculum of the enlarged School. "Harvard Divinity School," he wrote, "will be eventually transformed into an American Academy of Ecclesiology and Theological Philosophy." The divinity school of the oldest university of the land, he felt, should make possible an irenic, philosophical, and sociological study of the *ecclesia* and thus help the several competing churches find their way to the fulfillment of their mission. He looked forward to the establishment of a "pioneer chair for the scientific study of comparative ecclesiology." Proponent of both an ecumenical and a sociological approach to sectarianism under the auspices of a university, he was alert to the fact that the scholar in this new field can never be a sectarian or a controversialist—"but as little can he be found among those who hold that the questions which divide the churches and sects of Christen-

---

[24] In connection with the tercentenary in 1936, still another arrangement was worked out whereby the *Veritas* shield as a heraldic and decorative device was distinguished from the official seal reserved for the Corporation.

[25] *Atlantic Monthly,* XLVIII (1881), 377. On Langdon's rectorship in Cambridge, see Gardiner Day, *The Biography of a Church* (Cambridge, 1951), p. vi and Appendix H.

dom are matters of indifference." Episcopalian Langdon, a watchful ally of Unitarian Eliot, rejoiced in what seemed to be the general tendency of Eliot's reform. Langdon was confident that a new emphasis upon an "exhaustive" and "oecumenical" ecclesiology would, in bringing about the constructive interchange of conservative and liberal, "appear not only a logical development of the past history of this school, but also a profoundly philosophic interpretation of the obligations of such an institution as Harvard University to the present and coming age."

Church historian Ephraim Emerton, appointed in 1881 as part of the Eliot-Everett program of enlarging the scope of the Divinity faculty, took his turn in defining the provinces of faith and reason in the University and declared: "If we say that the historian must be 'objective,' as free as possible from 'subjectivity,' we have to admit that the theologian must be permitted just the opposite standard. If his conclusions are to have any value whatever, they must be his conclusions, and not those of anyone else."[26] He foresaw a time, however, when "the prevailing contempt for theological study" might change. Then rightly interpreted, theology would "reassert its claim to be in the true sense a 'science,' perhaps even in due time to take its place as the *regina scientiarum* of the Erasmian age."

With this final echo from the nineteenth century, we may bring to a close our account of the *translatio studii* and all its lore to the New World as illustrated in the annals of the oldest American university. Much more significant than to carry the account any further in the development of one institution would be to offer a few concluding generalizations as to the relation of religion to American higher education as a whole. The divinity faculty[27] or school of every university is now a focal point at which converge new concerns and problems of the Church, the university, and society at large, groping for some larger dimension and for redirection of American life.

The university or college in America today, fortunate in the ample scope of the immunity it has won from religious and political criticism on the outside and in the freedom from ecclesiastical and partisan interference it has both demanded and been granted in its interior life in the process of secularization, should nevertheless from time to time acknowledge not only by ceremonial gestures but also by other ways

---

[26] Emerton, *Living and Learning* (Cambridge, 1921), pp. 298 f.

[27] A long but not always unambiguous usage at Harvard has tended to distinguish between the professional and academic assignments of the theological professors in terms of "Divinity School" and "The Faculty of Divinity" whose courses have in the past been open alike to seminarians and undergraduates and graduates of the College.

appropriate to the Republic of Letters that it remains ever indebted to certain theological and constitutional principles of great antiquity in the long evolution of our ideal of a free university. On some of these principles and themes the university or college may again have occasion to draw for a valid restatement of that critical pluralism which recognizes the mutual obligations of Church, School, and Commonwealth— while preserving each from the improper interference of the other.

Chapter V. Epilogue: The Christian Heritage and a Theory of American Higher Education[1]

In the foregoing survey with seventeenth-century Harvard as the point of departure, we were able to distinguish five recurrent themes which have been historical components of the theological idea of higher education. We saw these themes in turn grouping themselves into two: the Paradise-Wilderness Cycle and the Tripartite Trinitarian-Christological Pattern.

It is within the Paradise Cycle that the college or university has at its center a *green*, symbol of Paradise restored amidst the wilderness; its *campus* for the training of the spiritual militia of Christ; and its *wall*, library, and commons the practical means and the symbols too of the autonomy of the university in the transfer of its law, its learning, and its lore. It is in accordance with the Tripartite Pattern that the ongoing Republic of Letters has also its *chapel*, symbol of the presence of Christ as priest, prophet, and king and an *aula* where, in the exercise of the judicial (or critical) role of the university, honorary degrees are granted for outstanding achievement in Church, State, and Academy.

Inextricably bound up with biblical myth and medieval tradition, do the constitutional and cultural impulses behind these symbols survive in any significant strength into the modern institutions of higher learning? Even if here and there the old terms persist, are they not rather part of the lore of the university rather than of the law of its being?

For clearly, the proportionate strength of the traditional three orders and the sanctions in modern society are so different even from what obtained in the nineteenth century that the material assembled in the foregoing pages may well appear to many as unsalvageable antiquarian-

[1] The substance of this Epilogue is adapted from an article "The Christian College" in *The Christian Scholar*, XLI (1958), 193–209. The article was originally delivered as an address at the Second Quadrennial Convocation of Christian Colleges, Drake University, June 23, 1958. The article was carefully analyzed and theologically criticized, along with other recent studies, by Cornelius Van Til, "The Christian Scholar," *The Westminster Theological Journal*, XXI (1950), 147–148. The basic criticism was that the "Christian scholar" of the mid-twentieth century is in effect Emerson's "American scholar" brought up to date. In the larger context in which the essay is here reprinted others may draw a different conclusion. See, for example, the extensive treatment of the problem by the Editorial Associate, "Notes on Contingency," *The Christian Scholar*, XLIII (1960), 83–90.

ism, even to professing Christians interested in some restatement of the Christian character of higher education.

Though it has not been the purpose of the writer to conclude his historical essay on the theological idea of the university with the outlines of a new theory of higher education from a Christian point of view, he no doubt owes it to those of his concerned readers who have examined with interest and attention the half-theological, half-mythical material strewn over the pages of the history of the Christian community of scholarship, to make for their benefit some final observations about the possible significance of these themes in the contemporary situation. In fact, in placing the present revision of this study of the theological idea of the university in the larger framework of a book on the Paradise-Wilderness Cycle at the base of so much that has been historically creative in Christian civilization, he would in fact like to take the occasion to set down some supplementary reflections growing out of this chronicle as to the vitality of these historic Christian ingredients in the idea of a university for American education.

We must begin by acknowledging the programmatically sectarian and confessional origins of a very large percentage of American institutions of higher learning, many of them among the most distinguished.

Denominational seminaries and colleges created, indeed, the basic patterns of American higher education from colonial times until the founding of the great private and state universities after the Civil War. The profusion of Christian colleges, both those pregnant with a future and those weak from conception and destined to an early demise, is a major fact in the cultural history of the United States. Unfortunately, in their confessional zeal—and, one must add, in their overweening ambition—many of them, especially in their initial phase, competed with each other in costly internecine strife and in consequence left considerable institutional debris and many casualties upon the battlefield. It often happened, moreover, that a regionally powerful denomination failing to acquire control or predominant influence over a newly formed state university, turned upon it as godless and defiantly set up a rival, confessional college, sometimes in an adjacent town.

In the meantime, the primary and the secondary schools were obliged by the increasing heterogeneity of the religious and cultural backgrounds of their pupils to become as religiously neutral as the state universities which had come to arouse denominational fears, while somewhat more gradually many of the Christian colleges themselves in varying degrees reasoned their way to a severing of their connections with their sponsoring denominations.

These same secular influences are flowing, but today a countercurrent has also set in. Many of the emancipated colleges are joining with others still under denominational control or influence in re-appraising their Christian heritage and in re-examining their Christian vocation.

But while these colleges are trying to reconceive their Christian character and their academic responsibility to their sponsoring denominations, the churches might well ask for their part the question whether they should not be turning their major attention and support to the larger group of American youth below the collegiate level. It is now in the high schools that the increasingly sophisticated and ethically bewildered young people are facing, largely without benefit of adequate Christian tutelage in their churches and during the most crucial and perhaps most vulnerable period of their lives, those intellectual, moral, and social temptations and challenges which formerly were thought by the churches to be concentrated in the college years; hence the past concentration on and the present vested interest in the denominational college.[2]

The Christian colleges must therefore redouble their efforts to justify denominational support at the very moment in American cultural and social history when the churches are increasingly baffled by the spread of juvenile delinquency and are following with close attention the important changes going on in educational theory and practice in the public schools below the level of the college; at a moment also when, above the colleges, the universities and the graduate professional schools are raising new and challenging questions about vocation and professional responsibility in a Christian perspective—even state universities, which have hitherto been prevented on constitutional grounds from giving anything more than respectful attention to formal religious instruction and activity on the margins of their tax-supported precincts.

1. Toward a "Sectarian"-Protestant Theory of Higher Education

Any so-called Protestant theological clarification of the structure and purpose of higher education emerging out of the American experience

[2] Only the Roman Catholics and some of the Lutherans and a few others insisted in the nineteenth century on developing their own parochial schools at a time when most Christian bodies were taking for granted the communication of a basically Protestant ethos in the public school system.

I have dealt with the religious problems in and presuppositions of American secondary education elsewhere: "Religious Education in a Pluralistic Democracy," *Religious Education*, L (1955), 38 ff.; "Church-State Separation and Religion in the Schools of Our Democracy," *ibid.*, LI (1956), 369 ff.; and "The Seminary in the Wilderness," *Harvard Library Bulletin*, XIII (1959), with special reference to the rise of the early academies.

of divided Protestantism and sectarianism should be on its guard against laying claim to a purely Protestant genealogy. Most Americans who count themselves Protestant are not purely Protestant in the normative, classical sense; for the sectarian impulse, deriving from the Radical Reformation, has already entered strongly even into American denominations of the classical Protestant heritage. And, while almost all main-line American denominations have at length abandoned their sectarianism in the sense of moralistic exclusiveness and doctrinal bigotry, they are still directly or indirectly heirs or beneficiaries of the sectarian ideal of the gathered church of committed believers living in the fellowship of mutual correction, support, and abiding hope. An emergent Christian theory of higher education from the Protestant side should not conceal this dual heritage, but should seek rather to re-interpret the significance, at its origins, of the frankly sectarian and confessional character of much of American higher education. Doing so, it may also proceed to lay claim as well to the medieval Catholic tradition, embodying those university motifs which have persisted, by way of Anglicanism and sectarian Protestantism, in the educational presupposition of the founders of our oldest colleges.[3]

To be more specific, the sectarian principle, when transposed to the realm of education, can be understood as a means of mitigating the strenuousness of the normative Protestant posture of being continuously provisional and contextual in affirmations about faith and ethics. Moreover, by way of providing a theological foundation for a mutually supportive togetherness of discipline, aspiration, and loving comradeship in the often hazardous pursuit of truth (not only for the immature, but

[3] The author is not prepared to discuss the extent to which the medieval Christian university motifs may also have persisted into Tridentine and modern Catholicism. It was, to be sure, the Council of Trent which, in making provisions for the recruiting and training of priests in each diocese, gave widespread prominence to the word *seminary*, featured as a metaphor in our essay. But he is disposed by casual observation to infer that the orderly rationalism of modern Catholic educational theory would probably have allowed the medieval themes to expire without comment. Consequently, in this Epilogue we are implicitly contrasting medieval (Catholic) usage and (post-Tridentine) Catholic usage. Among several factors which would have tended to obliterate the vestiges of the medieval university themes which have largely survived in "sectarian" guise were the fact that the Catholic Church was obliged to abandon many of the old seats of learning as a consequence first of the Reformation, then of the Enlightenment, and finally of the French Revolution and its sequels; the fact also that the new schools were for the most part sponsored by the newer teaching orders filled with the spirit of the Counter-Reformation, which much preferred new types of schools to the old and in some cases demonstrably unreliable universities; and finally the fact that in the nineteenth century Thomism, with its clear delimitation of the realms of faith and reason, grace and nature, was elevated to the rank of virtually the official philosophy of the Church. All this had the consequence of placing the majority of university disciplines directly under the purview of reason and observation without reference to those biblical and theological presuppositions so evident in sectarian Protestant curricula.

also for those exploring on the brinks of knowledge), the sectarian principle is a perhaps needed compensation for the lack of those securities which in Catholic higher education and research are provided by the solid framework of ecclesiastical dogma, the Church's international scope and solidarity, and the rational precision of Thomist philosophy.

The extraordinary sense of belonging developed by American college students, their intense involvement in self-government for four collegiate years, and the loyalty of the alumni returning to their beloved haunts for reunion and in financial support of their *alma mater* are, so to speak, voluntarist or "sectarian" aspects of American higher education that are distinctive, precious, and never to be neglected in the reworking of any contemporary theory of the institutions of higher learning in American society from a Christian point of view.

i. The Paradise-Wilderness Cycle

Of our five venerable university themes, the transferential motif no doubt has today the least significance. It reflected a basically conservative conception of education. The American sectarian colleges, denominational seminaries, or Bible colleges at their inception were preoccupied with the handing down of correct doctrines and, at the beginning, often admitted only as much or as many of the secular disciplines as could be safely fitted into a biblical or confessional curriculum. But the transferential theme, though fully Christianized, could never be divested of its abiding significance, that of pointing to the origins of the ongoing community of learning, *as distinct from the church or sect,* back beyond the beginnings of Christianity itself.

The *transferential theme,* it will be recalled, was the notion that in the providence of God a community of seekers and custodians of the truth was to be recruited in each generation into that intellectual encampment which is the university, charged with the great responsibility of transferring to each generation the accumulated arts and sciences of the ages. The archaic notions of the *translatio studii* schematized the history of education as a succession of schools in which the torch of knowledge was handed down from the schools of the prophets in ancient Israel, through the Academy in Athens, the palace school of Charlemagne that evolved in Paris into the fostering mother of the medieval universities, all the way to the colonial colleges of our own eastern seaboard.

Since we have thus far drawn largely upon the tradition of the oldest seaboard college, let the Rev. LeRoy Jones Halsey, addressing the alumni of the University of Nashville, Tennessee, restate the transferential theme in a southern accent:

> . . . we can now trace back [he wrote in 1841] in the bosom of classical and theological literature, the whole course of our learning and our religion; first, from our American shores to the states of Europe, thence back to the shores of Greece and Italy, from these again to the land of the Patriarchs and Prophets, and from that chosen land up to the top of old Ararat and the ark of Noah, thence back to the Garden of Eden, and thence again to heaven and to the throne of God.[4]

Better informed about the history of education than our forebears, and much more disposed than were they to explore and to experiment, rather than to conserve and transmit, contemporary Christians, aware of the storied account of the millennial transfer of knowledge from conscientious teacher to devout scholar, still speak of the college or university as the beloved community of memory and hope. For its officers, students, and alumni it is a diminutive but venerable Republic of Letters, which, by way of the archaic wording of its charter and academic custom, can trace its constitution and privileges back to the beginnings of civilization, a *Res publica,* indeed, with its own laws and liberties antedating not only the state conferring its charter but also the denomination which may have sponsored it.

Today, precisely because the prevailing mood of the modern university is created by the extraordinary new findings in every field of research, it is perhaps appropriate for the institution of higher learning by way of compensation to rehabilitate its role in the transfer of basic human wisdom. When successful business executives return to our universities, at company expense, it is more often than not that even in the graduate schools of business they are looking not for new skills and methods but for some replenishment from the store of reflective human wisdom in order to be able to return refreshed for the tremendous burden they bear in the world of affairs.

There is another realm in which the duty to transmit wisdom as the principal function of the university has relevance. The afore-cited address at the University of Nashville in 1841 was directed to the alumni, as it happens, in connection with their theological library. It is appropriate therefore to remark that learned librarians, fully as much as the professors, are agents or stewards in the transfer of knowledge.

---

[4] *Address to the Alumni Society of the University of Nashville, on the Study of Theology as a Part of Science, Literature and Religion* (Nashville, 1841), p. 288; quoted by Frank Dixon McCloy, "The Founding of Protestant Theological Seminaries in the United States of America 1784-1840," Harvard Ph.D thesis, Cambridge, 1959, p. 303.

The university is in fact a reliable community of memory and hope in the measure that its library conserves in its corridors and archives the muted voices of the past, which from time to time are awakened to speak, sometimes indeed even more movingly than to their own age and generation. It will be recalled that Cotton Mather (drawing upon cabalistic lore) imagined that God, in driving Adam from Paradise, entrusted him, as an act of grace, with a book of wisdom to be handed down from generation to generation.

The quotation from the alumni address at the University of Nashville with its reference to the Garden of Eden encourages us to take up next the most important of the five university themes and in some ways the most difficult to make relevant in the modern educational situation.

This basic theme within what we have now enlarged and named the Paradise-Wilderness Cycle is the conflict between *sapientia* and *scientia*. It is that complex of theories, notions, and legends about the relationship between human *scientia,* which is arrived at by means of sensory data arranged according to the categories of frail reason corrupted by the Fall of primal man in disobedience to the divine command not to eat of the paradisic tree of the knowledge of good and evil, and the divine *sapientia,* which Christian man may possess through baptismal regeneration, sacramental incorporation into the second Adam, and sustained inspiration from the Holy Spirit in the community of self-discipline and the fellowship of Christian grace or love. It was the awesome sense of the precariousness of the quest of knowledge that gave the medieval Christian university its élan in the rise of the western European conception of the nature and function of licit knowledge. The *paradisic motif* was at the very origin of the constitution and ceremonial of the university and remains to this day the hidden background of its grave gestures and august sense of mission. We have seen that a notable variant of the theme, especially in America, was the conviction that the seminary of the remnant or the biblical college was thought of eschatologically as the "garden" in the protective wilderness marked out by Providence in the New World. In this view, the seminary green was a walled garden in which the fruit of knowledge might once again be savored, thanks to the disciplines of the spirit made possible by Christ's atoning work and to the effects of the revivals of the Holy Spirit in the restoration of the clouded image of the divine in man and in the redirection of his disordered will.

More than any of our themes, it is precisely the contrasting symbols of paradise and wilderness which, inextricably bound up with biblical myth, seem to flout the basic ideals of the present-day community of scholarship, namely, the sober quest of truth and the patient, unbiased search for solid facts. If taken seriously, these symbols might seem to countenance either a phantom claim to a plenitude of wisdom to be recovered merely by piety or an expeditionary evasion of the toils of scholarship. More seriously still, the paradise motif involves the Christian scholar and the Christian student at the very outset of the academic enterprise in the dilemma of trying to clarify by means of fallen, i.e., fragmented, reason a faith once for all delivered to the saints. His consistently secular colleagues usually have no such lack of confidence in man's rational competence and repudiate on principle any formulation of a body of truth that would exempt it from continuous testing and revision.

The fact is, of course, that the Christian scholar himself does not today willingly subscribe to any ecclesiastical stricture that would mark off any portion of knowledge—say, biblical and ecclesiastical history and theological formulation—as inaccessible to the same methods of inquiry applicable in other fields. Moreover, today's Christian scholar, unlike generations of Church Fathers, Schoolmen, and Reformers, knowing as he does much more than they about history, the transmission of texts, and the evolution of life, can no longer accept the account of the Fall as an historic narrative.

At the same time, as a professing Christian scholar, he is vaguely aware—the professional theologian more keenly—that he is not free to ignore the doctrine of the Fall as it affects the pursuit of knowledge, since the doctrine of the beclouded reason is inextricably linked with the doctrine of the corruption of the will and, in the end, with the whole concept of the solidarity of mankind both in the fall of the first Adam and in the atonement through the obedience of the second Adam. If there was no historic act of disobedience, there is less plausibility in a unique historic and universally redemptive act of fulfillment of the Law in the utter obedience of Jesus Christ in knowing and willing one thing. The whole structure of Christian theology is involved in the paradisic theme.

Thus, since both the medieval university in respect to the limits of fallen reason and the Church in every age in respect to the corrupt will and man's mortality have been alike grounded in the biblical narrative about Paradise, the theologian, if not the ordinary Christian scholar, must systematically come to grips with the fact that the central dogma of the Church, the atonement—with all its doctrinal, sacramental, and constitutional explication—is ultimately implicated in any casual or accommodative decision that is made about the paradisic motif in the realm of epistemology, or more generally, the pursuit of knowledge. Both the redeeming Church and the Christian university have been genetically linked to a specific conception of Creation and the Fall; and the Christian scholar must be aware of its implications for his activity as scholar in library and laboratory no less than as a dutiful worshiper in the college chapel or as sponsor of the Christian action group on campus.

The Christian scholar, accepting all the criteria and canons of research and exposition of his secular colleague on the faculty, is aware that something else is involved which cannot be covered or more than pointed to by such terms as "inspiration," "depth," "dimension," "context," "concern," "existential," "committed." He is called upon as a Christian scholar to be epistemologically more precise than this. On closer inspection he may indeed discover that, for all its phantom fragility, the paradisic element in the traditional theory of corporate education may well have an unexpected pertinence in the atomic age, when we are again reminded of the moral ambiguity of knowledge and the corporate hazards of the pursuit of knowledge in a new kind of eschatological setting. Perhaps greater precision and an enhanced sense of relevance to the central enterprise of the academic community may be gained by interpreting fallen reason, for example, in terms of the universally predatory exploitation and even parasitical character of life as it comes into the purview of the biologist; the irrationality and the subtle rationalizations exposed by the modern psychologist; the disfigurations of reality perceived by the modern painter; the incongruities and vagaries now coming into view under the intent gaze of the atomic physicist and the astro-physicist; and the fragmentation or fatuousness of many philosophical and theological constructs disclosed by the scrutiny of the logical positivist or linguistic analyst.

It is pertinent to recall that it was never the contention of the monkish scholars, the medieval Schoolmen, and their sectarian continuators into New England Puritanism, that they were angelic or Adamic in their mastery of knowledge, but rather that, set in the midst of the wilderness of the world, they were, in Christ, permitted by God to cultivate the garden of knowledge and to pursue wisdom so long as, mutually reinforced by the ministries of grace, they heeded those wise restraints by which the university maintained its corporate being and eschewed methods inconsonant with its divine charter or in contravention of the traditional oaths of its masters of arts, of medicine, of law, and of theology. There was always, moreover, a strong futuristic, progressivistic, or eschatological impulse in the paradisic motif, presupposing, as in the medieval university, that so long as scholars were in fact obedient within their creaturely bounds they might, with God's sanction in Christ, surpass primal man in the plenitude of their wisdom.

The medieval stress on the oath and on obedience suggests the militia of Christ. Instrumental to the realization of paradisic yearning in the rise of Christian education was our third, the *martial motif*. This military theme is the tradition according to which learning is a kind of warfare that calls upon all the resources of bodily and spiritual discipline in order to withstand the onslaughts of Satan in the form of sloth, carnal temptation, and spiritual pride including heresy. In this view the Christian campus was, as in the original Latin sense of the word, the training ground of a Christian militia determined to engage in combat with error in the surrounding world.

If there was one of the medieval themes that the Lutheran Reformation university perpetuated and made its own, it was no doubt this conception of the university as a spiritual militia. Not only was the territorial, princely university a major instrument of international policy in the parlous age of the Reformation of religion, but also the individual German professor himself, in a manner different from that of any other national tradition, came to exemplify the virtues and disciplines of intense intellectual warfare. Especially after the founding of the University of Berlin amidst the debris of the Napoleonic wars, the German scholar set the standard for the learned world in the accuracy and plenitude of his footnotes and in the relentlessness of his critiques of academic foes and allies alike. No clarification of the American ideal of higher education can neglect the tremendous influence of Germany and the German Protestant repristination of the medieval ideal of the *militia Christi*. But for all the achievement of German scholarship, it is nevertheless a basic postulate of this essay that an expressly or distinctively Protestant theory of the university was never fully and clearly enunciated in Germany or elsewhere.

A Protestant principle would in general place the work of reason and also the rational schematizations of faith under the continuous judgment of Christ rather than of the Church, of an abstract *Veritas* rather than of dogma, and held all institutions—alike the University, the Church, and the State—under the divine judgment mediated by the preached and written Word. An expressly Protestant theory of the university (the community of rational clarification, research, and transmission) might also have been worked out in relation to the basic Protestant postulate or experience of salvation by faith or grace alone (solafideism) in a context always critical of law, constitution, tradition, sacrament, and sacred myth. Such an expressly "Protestant" theory of the university would have been admittedly ill at ease with most of our sectarian-medieval motifs.

Since it was Luther who most clearly enunciated the Protestant principle of salvation *sola fide,* one would expect to find in Lutheran Germany or Scandinavia the earliest formulations of the relationship of this regent principle of Protestantism to the realm of reason, research, and pedagogy. To be sure, beginning with Philip Melanchthon there were great German educators and reorganizers of university education, but there emerged no fresh, positively Protestant conception of the university as a corporation.

In Reformation Germany, beginning with the new foundation of Philip of Hesse in Marburg, universities multiplied, partly as a consequence of the ambition of princes to establish, in their diminutive territories, those coveted centers of higher learning which before had been chartered solely by pope or emperor. But no distinctively Protestant theory of the university or academy emerged. Protestant attempts in the seventeenth century (cf. Chapter III of this essay) represented rather a reappropriation of the old medieval and sectarian themes, sometimes with a pansophistic, cabalistic, or scholastic ingredient, in any case without giving due prominence to the distinctively Protestant principle. To be sure, in the nineteenth century the German universities with their renowned *Lehr-* and *Lernfreiheit* became the paradigms of the learned world. But their virtues were never construed as expressly Protestant or in any theological sense Christian. These universities had their great faculties of theology, but methodology within them and without was much the same. Friedrich Schleiermacher's important *Kurze Darstellung des theologischen Studiums* (1811) was concerned with the training of theologians in the university. It was not a Protestant theory of the university.

There was, of course, an effort to develop a nonsectarian Calvinist theory of higher education in Holland, which eventuated in the establishment of the Free University of Amsterdam, and there were other attempts in the Reformed tradition, but the major effort at a Christian theory of the university in modern times came from the Catholic side as the Church after the French Revolution endeavored to cope with the rising tide of anticlericalism. John Henry Newman's *The Idea of the University* (1852) was one among several such formulations.

Sir Walter Moberly's now almost classic *The Crisis in the University* (1949) stands out among the more recent Protestant analyses of the problem. In later years there has been indeed a great stirring as to the theory of what constitutes a university.[5] But the abiding biblical-theological problem of fallen reason and *scientia* has not been central to the discussion since the seventeenth century, and what would appear to be the distinctively Protestant problem of solafideism and science has not been taken up as it would affect the theory of the university as a community.

The Protestant principle of solafideism is perhaps most significant for the individual Christian as scholar. Douglas Horton made a useful contribution in this direction[6] when he drew upon Martin Luther's famous dictum in the ethical realm, that characterized the Christian justified by faith as *simul justus et peccator,* and fashioned his own academic dictum, by characterizing each Protestant Christian in the context of the university as *simul certus et dubitator.* Luther himself not only pointed to the regrettable persistence of sin in the Christian justified by faith but also acknowledged his own occasional doubt, which he pilloried as a sin. We are properly reminded of this latter fact when we deal in the university with the role of faith or theology as organized belief. In this view faith is the armor and the sword of the individual scholar, while systematic theology is most usefully present in the academic community, not as a would-be queen of the sciences, but as a servant, by which is meant primarily a loyal critic of the other disciplines.

One may carry further the rephrasing of Luther. The Christian scholar is also *simul praescitus et scrutator.* In Romans 8:29 Paul writes of those whom God *foreknew,* that he *predestined* them to be conformed to the image of his Son. In Paul's sense in this particular text, one could say that the Christian teacher or student is at once foreknown of God (*praescitus*) and a researcher (*scrutator*) of God's ways among men and in creation at large.[7] All who feel called or destined by tutelage, the church, or a personal sense of mission to work and witness as Christians in the community of learning are seekers on the same level as the secular scholars and researchers, using the same methods. Just as

[5] Recent works include *Towards a Christian Philosophy of Higher Education,* ed. John Paul von Grueningen (Philadelphia 1957) and Alexander Miller's *Faith and Learning* (New York, 1960). The Commission for Higher Education of the National Council of Churches, under the direction of Hubert C. Noble, is currently at work on "A Christian Theory of Higher Education, with Special Relation to the Protestant Churches."

[6] *The Meaning of Worship* (New York, 1959).

[7] As early as Hippolytus, there is a suggestion of this meaning, *Philosophoumena,* X, 32–34, 4 f. In the history of theology those foreknown of God, the *praesciti,* unfortunately became differentiated as the reprobate from the *praedestinati,* those predestined to salvation! But there is nothing in Paul's original phrasing to justify this distinction.

Luther's believer *justificatus sola fide* remains a *peccator* but released from the toils of guilt and anxiety in the joyful fulfillment of his vocation in a fallen and fragmented world, so by the same token it may be said in the more specialized realm of the life of the mind that the Christian scholar, foreknown of God, assured of a truth which is at the same time God's love (humanized in a historic figure who called men even before they knew him), remains nonetheless a *scrutator*, like any other scholar. Released from inhibitions about probing forthrightly even into the historic sources of his own faith, such a scholar may be confident in the prosecution of his researches and tentative constructions amid the fragmentation, the incompleteness, and notably the ambiguities of the ever expanding realms of knowledge.

The conscientious Christian scholar or student *simul praescitus et scrutator* is placed upon the same level as the agnostic or secularist colleague with no invidious comparisons from either side, although it may be useful to remind the Christian himself that just as it was not the righteous Pharisee but the *peccator* on the Temple steps whom Jesus saw going down justified in the sight of God, so it is frequently not the professed Christian member of the faculty or student body but the researcher openly despairing of ever coming close to God who may go down the steps of the Temple of wisdom strangely illumined in his darkness. There are many earnest, magnanimous, but unbelieving scholars who, without knowing it, have discharged a kind of secular apostolate on the campus. The work of the Lord is not infrequently accomplished by those who are reverently slow to say "Lord, Lord."

ii. The Tripartite Pattern

The Protestant scholar today fights as a member of a spiritual militia that is no longer for the most part even nominally under Christ, except in the strictly denominational college. Receiving the same orders and carrying out the same missions as his secular colleagues, he may in our fourth theme find the recourse for interpreting his role in the community of learning. This is the *christological sanction* for the authority of the (Christian) teacher as prophet, discharging in relative autonomy one of the functions of Christ the eternal prophet, priest, and king. In this christological sanction was grounded the relative independence of a Christian faculty from undue interference on the part either of the Christian or secular magistrate or of the diocese, the sponsoring church, or the supporting denomination. John Calvin, it will be recalled, and the educational theorists in the Reformed tradition were from the sixteenth through the eighteenth centuries particularly significant in defining the office of the professor or teacher (*doctor ecclesiae*) as distinct from that of the three other ministers of the Church: the pastor, the deacon, and the ruling elder.

Unfortunately for the academic independence of the professor in the Christian college in the American nineteenth century, the faculty came more and more under the control of lay trustees, that is, lay trustees in the sense of being nonacademic or nonprofessorial though in denominational colleges they might well have been clergymen. The American college president, traditionally an ordained minister with tenure, with ever enlarged executive powers, and with an overriding concern for financial support from the business community preponderantly represented on the college board of trustees, emerged as a distinctively American academic figure, with whom the often largely honorific rector of a typical European university, elected or appointed sometimes for a single year, could scarcely be compared. The emergence of lay control and the pre-eminence of the ministerial but often nonacademic president were in part a consequence of the influence of the separation of Church and State on American collegiate education and in part a consequence of the transfer of the congregational type of sectarian churchmanship (with its lay call and dismissal of the preacher) to the college constitutions even of denominations not in the tradition of congregational polity and lay control. In smaller colleges in the Reformed tradition and, by cultural osmosis and by explicit imitation, in later collegiate foundations of a non-Calvinist background the ministerial college president tended to monopolize the "prophetic" office, as indeed Increase Mather did in the days when Harvard had but a few tutors, while the status of the ordinary teaching members of the faculty came close to being assimilated to that of the employees of a commercial board of trustees. Thus, despite the rather high conception of the office of the teacher inherited from Calvinism, the theological theory of the American college professor as a prophet called of God to be bold in his asseveration of truth ceased to be a living memory even in colleges of Reformed background. In fact it was the most Calvinist of the American colleges and seminaries (Andover and Princeton) that introduced the confessional oath as distinguished from the medieval university oath of corporate solidarity.[8] Thus it has worked out as a matter of historic record that the increasingly large measure of academic freedom enjoyed by the American professor is more readily traced to the influ-

[8] On the oath, see McCloy, *op. cit.*, and my "Seminary in the Wilderness."

ence of the *Lehrfreiheit* of the nineteenth-century faculties of the German universities than to the more remote Calvinist idea of the *doctor* as *propheta*.

Nevertheless, the christological sanction of the freedom of the professor as prophet and, indirectly, of the university as a third force constitute a well-documented strand in the long theological history of the university idea, and though it is not directly appropriable by American professors of the state universities, it could be useful in arguing for academic freedom in small Christian colleges where "lay" control,[9] especially when it is "ecclesiastical," still makes improper demands upon its professors and encroaches upon their Christian vocation of instruction and research.

In this view the Christian professor, clear about his calling, is a minister or officer in the larger Kingdom of Christ, and for him, in contrast to the pastor or priest, it is precisely *his* vocation to deal forthrightly with faith in the context of reason, experimentation, hypothesis, and academic dialogue with colleagues who may not share his Christian convictions. In this valid ministry under Christ, the Truth, he should not be trammeled by ecclesiastical ties. So long as Christ is the avowed Lord of his life, he properly insists that he be free in the pursuit of his vocation of verification and transmission.

This view also has it that the college itself and particularly the university is, as it were, a replica of Jerusalem—not Jerusalem the golden which is above, but the teeming city of man with all its vested religious interests, its bustling bazaars, its untutored rabble. The academician who is committed to the Christian faith must witness before its multitudes and on some occasion traverse its streets burdened by the scandalous cross of irrationality, destined perhaps to be subjected to mockery, to be adjudged pretentious and marked out for proscription because of the inveterate divisiveness of religion. In this broken world, the explicitly Christian teacher does not presume to have the whole truth. But whoever feels in himself the inheritance of the *doctor* as prophet will not shrink from the ideal of trying to safeguard the wholeness of truth.

Passing from this christological motif, which largely concerns the freedom and the responsibility of the Christian professor in his vocation as scholar, we turn to the modern relevance of the fifth university theme, the *critical or judicial* function of the university as a whole in the midst of the world. We recall the prophetic words of a medieval

---

[9] That is, lay in contrast to academic.

Pope who eloquently summed up the millennial evolution of the corporate self-consciousness of a relatively independent university when he confirmed the critical function of the University over against both Church and State in declaring that

if of the middle [i.e., the University] the other two are deprived, they fall into extreme corruption, because power [in the State] unless it is tempered by wisdom, luxuriates in presumption and gives itself over to arrogance, while [the] benignity [of the Church], too, if it is unsupported by knowledge, becomes amorphously degenerate and rendered akin to fatuousness.[10]

It is of significance that this sense of the corporate liberty of the university, to be sure in a nationalized context, was all through the Reformation era safeguarded in England and that the two ancient universities conserved even during the seventeenth century much of their medieval character and constitution, including the faculty control over the interior life of the colleges, and the immunities of the colleges in the universities from royal (which in time came to mean parliamentary) intervention. The vigor of this tradition in England persisted into the nineteenth century. The quaint language of our university themes, for example, resounded again in the debates in the House of Lords and the Privy Council in connection with the strong Anglican opposition to the establishment of the new University of London, where there would, to be sure, be an adequate supply of cadavers and diverse diseases for the proposed medical faculty but where theology (of the Church of England) would be expressly extruded.[11]

In the theory of the critical role of the corporation of scholarship in the Christian commonwealth, the center of the university, it will be recalled, was the *aula,* where at convocation or commencement the university bestowed its honorific hoods upon selected leaders of Church, State, and Academy. It was the ceremonial courtroom where, as it were, spiritual men judged all things but were themselves judged by none save by *Veritas* itself. Unfortunately, for all their safeguards, the world has not been spared the treason of the intellectuals against humanity.

German academicians recall with intellectual anguish the Nazi ceremony in the *aula* of the oldest German university, in which the statue of Minerva, symbol of universal reason, was replaced with an image symbolic of German wisdom. The academic community is today keenly aware of the recurrent danger that some new idol—no less of an abom-

[10] See above, Part Two, Chap. II, at n. 34.
[11] George Elives Carrie, ed., *Brief Historical Notices of the Interference of the Crown with the Affairs of English Universities* (Cambridge, 1839).

ination for being invisible—could be again installed in our universities. For the true academician knows the harm wrought by encumbering any pursuit or field of knowledge with a nationalist, a dialectical materialist, or a confessional label. It was precisely a German theologian— one once in the clutches of the Nazis—who after the war in the *aula* of that same university, Heidelberg, gave eloquent expression to the independence of the community of all learning and did so in the mythopoeic language of our critical theme. Edmund Schlink, in his rectoral address,[12] drew attention to the medieval ceremonial mace of the University of Heidelberg, which portrays the four faculties, including theology, represented by four scholars, none pre-eminent over the others, all sitting equally under the judgment of Christ above them.

It is with this image of *Veritas* as the Supreme Judge over university, church, and state at the Great Assize that we bring this essay to its conclusion.

There is a remnant of the tripartite ordering of society even in the United States, where the gowns of the justices of the court, the ministers of religion, and the professors at commencement suggest the co-ordinate dignity of magistrates, clerics, and scholars. It was only a generation ago, near the climax of public emotion over the capital case of two immigrant Italian anarchists, that the president of Harvard was asked for an impartial judgment; and the fact that in the end he confirmed the findings of the supreme court of the commonwealth, detracts but does not destroy the significance of this precedent of a latter-day revival of the role of the university as arbiter. To be sure, we may well ask whether an efficaciously critical role of the university as a third force in society does not presuppose the survival of a pervasive sense of the medieval *corpus christianum,* even if in our day that might mean no more than a common assent to Judaeo-Christian values. And precisely this consensus can no longer be taken for granted in universities at work in the context of a world culture. The members of the university community themselves no longer, like their medieval forebears, construe scholarship as a semi-autonomous and authoritative order, separate from, but also in Christ related to, the ministries of religion and government. When the dean of the federated faculty of theology of the University of Chicago not long ago sought to serve as spokesman for the whole University in making a major appeal before the chief executive of the nation in a criminal case involving sedition and science, he found that there was scarcely any residue among

---

[12] "Das Szepter der Universität," *Studium Generale,* II (1949), 439–448.

his colleagues of the medieval sense of the university's having a corporate voice in the realm of public righteousness even though, to the dean's credit, he persisted in his mission.

In the future the abiding significance of the ancient Tripartite Pattern must be asserted as when Gelasius first pointed out the hazard of combining in the same hand or in the same organization the power of the commonwealth, the pursuit of truth, and the sanction of faith.

2. Conclusion

The medieval-Protestant-sectarian impulses clearly live on in the present day. A Christian conception of higher education can bring out the practical meanings of these motifs, as it concentrates for the pedagogical task of tutelage and transmission on the small homogeneous, denominational college; and it will fully accredit, for the scientific task of fearless research and clarification, the mixed and often incorrectly styled "secular" university where the Christian scholar with his colleagues is reverently and painstakingly at work amidst the provisional and fragmentary state of knowledge. Wherever he is at work on the frontiers of knowledge the Church should give him its blessing and sanction so long as the whole of his *scientia* be seen within the epic and the cosmic perspective of that biblical vision of the truth which begins with the created order; which is mindful that men are but dust, yet made little lower than the angels, a conception of man in creation that prompts the search for a meaning in human history; which declares that it was precisely in a man—a Person with one nature consubstantial with humanity—not in some impersonal force, that God was most clearly manifest in his reconciliatory action within creation; and which, finally, holds ever before him the quest of that invisible goal toward which we hasten.

It is in the current conflict over professional specialization and liberal education that our venerable medieval-Protestant-sectarian motifs may prove to have a fresh social context in which to be again significant.

Like the classical humanist on the faculty, the professing Christian is aware of rational man's frailties and pretensions. The swift-paced secular scholar, in contrast, has no such qualms about the limits or goals. He is best represented today perhaps in the recently decolonialized states without a high indigenous culture, and in the Soviet Union, but also in the United States wherever a purely functional view of the university prevails or where governmental and commercial research now proceeds outside the fostering matrix of the university altogether. But while the classical humanist and the Christian humanist differ from the instrumental secularist in their kindred reserve, precaution, and restraint, the two differ from each other in that the latter goes beyond the former in holding that grace may operate not only in the realm of behavior and redemption but also in the realm of knowledge, as at once a check upon rational pretension, irrational distortion, and ideological disfiguration, and occasionally in intuitive anticipation or confirmation of the findings of reason and experimentation.

The relative merits of humanistic, classical, or liberal education over against the urgency of academic specialization and professional concentration are being much discussed as the American and western European educational systems face the challenge of the enormously successful secular specialization and hence impressive professional competence being achieved in the Soviet Union and more recently in Marxist China. In the struggle going on among American educators, the defenders of classical Humanism and those also who more recently are stressing the humanistic significance of the natural sciences should find allies in the Christian humanists in the defense of the traditional missions of the university, not of course to the neglect of its new and equally pressing applied scientific and national-defense assignments. To be sure, the temptation has already been largely resisted so to stress professional and applied scientific specialization in a crash program that our traditional liberal arts and sciences would be scrapped or undercut; but the temptation will be ever before us. It is no doubt at this very juncture in the development of American higher education that the so-called Christian denominational college acquires a renewed charter of responsibility and the old motifs, too, acquire a new significance in the vast cultural pluralism of American life.

Coherence in ultimate meaning, as distinguished from comprehensiveness in the realms progressively subjected to the specialist's onslaught, can never again, of course, become, as once it was in the Middle Ages, the regnant principle of the modern university—often for that reason disparagingly called a "multiversity"—because of the overriding needs of this practical specialization. But as the process is accelerated, the Christian colleges and the colleges within these great universities can also refurbish their conceptions of classical or general or Christian education and moral tutelage in keeping with their traditional stress upon full collegiate life in the disciplined community of knowledge, centered in the college green, the campus, the commons, the *aula*, and the chapel—to recall in conclusion the paradisic, the martial, the transferential, the critical, and the christological motifs in the history of the theological idea of learning.

In our medieval-Protestant-sectarian traditions of Christian education in a pluralistic democracy, we can be helped to a fresh understanding of the role of our denominational colleges if we think of them as a congeries of semi-autonomous centers of regional, personal, and denominational attachment but spiritually united in their relationship in a way roughly comparable to the schools under the various Roman Catholic orders—with just that amount of rivalry and local pride to keep them ever poised for fresh experimentation and solid achievement but never again so divided, as was once alas the case, that they withstand each other more vigorously than they stand together against the vast wilderness about them of ignorance and misshapen concepts which ever threatens to overrun the academic grounds. The faculties of Christian colleges might, incidentally, find a special mission during these difficult days for the staffs of the public schools in helping to re-establish a sense of solidarity with them as fellow citizens of the Republic of Letters, jointly engaged in transferring knowledge from generation to generation.[13]

Christian theology and the churches and the colleges of these churches must do all that can be done to maintain and strengthen rational discourse among all men of good will and guard against contributing inadvertently to the relativism and to the bewilderment of the age by a failure as Christians to agree on certain basic postulates. Christian scholars must seek to reach a consensus among themselves. They have a special charge laid upon them in this age of automation, atomic energy, and astronauts, with man taking full control of himself and human destiny through the manipulation of everything from the atom and the gene to the minds and motives of his fellow men, to foster wisdom, to replenish the reserves of the human spirit, and to reconsider in the modern idiom those wise restraints by which the aboriginal search for truth was hedged.

Lest, like primal man in the Garden, in the quest for the full fruit of knowledge, with the control of genetic and cosmic law hanging now

---

[13] In earlier days the college was often called the academy, while in living memory many of our high schools went by the same name. Christian professors and high school instructors should find occasions to come together academically to help especially the latter renew their sense of membership in the ancient guild of tutors and scholars and to reconceive and sharpen their sense of vocation within and conformable to the constitutional limitations of our religiously neutral public school system.

almost within the grasp, modern man be tempted to violate the very law of good and evil implanted in his being, the communities of faith and science must in a freshly relevant way reinterpret the moral aspect of knowing inherent in the biblical account both of the fall of the mind and of its restitution in the Logos incarnate. The university must exert itself to descry the manifold and serpentine distortions of *scientia,* of which unregenerate man so often proves himself guilty. For the academic world has been amply alerted to the fact that it enjoys no special immunity to irrational contagions. It has been warned by the ghastly example of those universities, long the paradigms throughout the learned world, which in a convulsion of the spirit gave reign to a satanic pseudo-science of manipulation and experimentation and which presumed in the laboratories and the law books of the medical and the legal faculties to pluck at the very souls of men in violation of all the professional and academic oaths.

With a christologically sanctioned sense of freedom, humane judgment, and corporate responsibility and with a renewed sense of the solidarity and the universality of citizenship in the Republic of Letters, the Christian scholars with the Christian colleges may contribute decisively to preventing the recurrence of a frantic utilitarianism which would again transform into a wilderness of ethically bewildered specialists the cultivated garden of the mind.

Though some Christian and humanist theorists of the university may be attracted by the refurbishment and adaptation of the Thomist conception of an overarching system of revelation and reason, a distinctively Protestant and yet venerably Catholic theory is already part of the American heritage, an inchoate theory of the interconfessional, "secular" community of scholarship which conserves precisely those concepts and procedures that are consonant with the provisional pluralism of our empirical grasp of truth and at the same time undergirds our modern concern to perpetuate and cultivate the fellowship and the international solidarity of all scholars and technicians who are being called upon to gaze into what is at once a terrifying and a luring wilderness at the frontiers of space, and at the very interior of the heart and of the mind of man.

Related GHW Bibliography

"Wilderness and Paradise in the History of the Church," *Church History* 28 (1959), 3-24.
"The Seminary in the Wilderness: A Representative Episode in the Cultural History of Northern New England," *Harvard Library Bulletin* 13 (1959), 27-58.
Wilderness and Paradise in Christian Thought: The Biblical Experience of the Desert in the History of Christianity and the Paradise Theme in the Theological Idea of the University (New York: Harper & Brothers, 1962).
"Christian Attitudes Toward Nature," *Christian Scholar's Review* 2 (1971-72), 3-35, 112-126. Expansion of article in *Colloquy* 3 (1970), 12-15.
"Ecology and Abortion," *New England Sierran* 3, 6 (1972), 2, 6.
"Creatures of a Creator, Members of a Body, Subjects of a Kingdom," *To God be the Glory: Sermons in Honor of George Arthur Buttrick*, ed. Theodore Gill (Nashville: Abingdon, 1973), 98-108.
"The Idea of the Wilderness of the New World in Cotton Mather's *Magnalia Christi Americana*," *Magnalia Christi Americana* I, eds. Kenneth Murdock and Elizabeth Miller (Cambridge: Harvard UP, 1977), 49-58.

GHW Festschrifts

Continuity and Discontinuity in Church History: Essays Presented to George Huntston Williams on the Occasion of His 65th Birthday, ed. F. Forrester Church and Timothy George (Leiden: Brill, 1979).
The Contentious Triangle: Church, State and University. A Festschrift in Honor of Professor George Huntston Williams, ed. Rodney L. Peterson and Calvin Augustine Pater (Kirksville, MO: Truman State University Press, 1999).

Selective Ecotheology Bibliography

Berry, R. J., ed. *Environmental Stewardship: Critical Perspectives – Past and Present.* (London: T. & T. Clark, 2006).
Berry, Thomas. *The Dream of the Earth.* (San Francisco: Sierra Club Books, 1988).
Berry, Wendell. *The Art of the Commonplace: The Agrarian Essays of Wendell Berry.* Ed. Norman Wirzba. (Berkeley, CA: Counterpoint, 2002).
Bouma-Prediger, Steven. *For the Beauty of the Earth: A Christian Vision for Creation Care*, 2d. ed. (Grand Rapids: Baker, 2010).
Carson, Rachel. 1962. *Silent Spring.* (Boston: Houghton Mifflin, 1962).
DeWitt, Calvin B. *Caring for Creation: Responsible Stewardship of God's Handiwork.* (Grand Rapids: Baker, 1998).
Houghton, John. *Global Warming: the Complete Briefing*, 4th ed. (Cambridge: Cambridge University Press, 2009).
McKibbon, Bill. *The End of Nature.* 2d ed. (New York: Random House, 2006).

Rasmussen, Larry. *Earth Honoring Faith: Religious Ethics in a New Key* (New York: Oxford UP, 2012).

Santmire, H. Paul. *The Travail of Nature: The Ambiguous Ecological Promise of Christian Theology*. (Philadelphia: Fortress Press, 1985).

Sittler, Joseph. *Evocations of Grace: The Writings of Joseph Sittler on Ecology, Theology, and Ethics*. Ed. Steven Bouma-Prediger & Peter Bakken (Grand Rapids: Eerdmans, 2000).

Stoll, Mark., *Inherit the Holy Mountain: Religion and the Rise of American Environmentalism* (Oxford Univ Press, 2015).

White, Lynn. "The historical roots of our ecologic crisis." *Science* 155, no. 3767 (10 March, 1967): 1203-7.

Wilkinson, Katherine. Between God and Green (New York: Oxford UP, 2012).

INDEX

This index includes major topics, keywords, catchwords, and the names of all secondary writers whose works are cited in the notes. Where the same topic appears in the text and the notes, reference to the latter is not made. Attention is drawn to two especially useful analytical entries, "University Themes" and "Wilderness," literal and religious senses. A segregated index of scriptural passages follows.

Aaron, 194
Abbo of Fleury, 161, 167
Abelard, 162, 163, 182
Abraham, 35, 66, 67, 164, 169, 178, 184; cave of, 37
Academy, as forerunner of high school, 125, 126 n., 213 n., 230 n.; undifferentiated as high school and college, 144, 145, 149, 150, 153 n., 154, 156, 159, 211, 221, 226; *Academiae*, distinguished from *collegia*, 154; see also Genevan Academy and Harvard
Accidie, 94
Acumen, City of, 145
Adam, 29, 30, 43, 46, 50, 71, 80, 140, 148, 150, 181, 194, 195; Book of, 150, 217; first *doctor*, 195; Second Adam, 26, 28, 29, 34, 44, 50; see also Jesus Christ; Adam, the American, 128, 129; the new, 140
Adamites, 62, 81, 82
Aequitas, 180
Afrikaaners, 95, 96, 97
Agricola, 59, 66, 161
Albert the Great, 169
Albigensians, 75
Alcuin, 159, 160, 177
Alexander I, Tsar of Russia, 94
Alexander IV, Pope, 165 n.
Alexander VI, Pope, 64
Alexander of Roes, 104, 170–171, 172–173, 174, 175
Alexanderwohl, 95
Allen, William Francis, 121 n.
Alsted, John Henry, 194
Alting, Jacob, 150, 151
Alton, Ill., 3
Ambrose, bishop of Milan, 44, 45
America, land of rebirth, 99, 128, 129; Revolution, 112
American Board of Commissioners of Foreign Missions, 128; American Home Missionary Society, 127
Ames, William, 114, 193
Anabaptists, 67, 68, 69, 83, 87, 90, 122
Anastos, Milton, 101 n.
Anderson, John M., 134
Andover Theological Seminary, 127, 197, 224

Androcles, 42
Anglicans (Church of England), 86, 93, 107, 110, 112, 152, 154, 185, 190, 204, 214
Animals, allegorical meaning of, 47, 69, 71, 92, 96, 145; covenant with, xi; demonic or hostile, 4, 13, 14 n., 21, 27, 29, 31, 33, 39, 41, 42, 43, 47, 48, 60, 63, 78, 83, 84, 92 n., 105, 108, 109, 115, 123, 131, 133, 136, 137; friendly, 13, 15, 27, 33, 34, 42, 60, 104, 115, 116, 137; harmony with, 2, 42, 46, 60, 78, 92 n., 115, 117, 136; salvation of, 46, 83, 84, 94; at once satanic and paradisic, 46
Anne (Queen of England), 87
Anointment, unction, 31, 45, 162, 167, 170, 187, 192
Anselm of Canterbury, 161
Anselm of Laon, 164
Anthony the Hermit, 38, 41
Antichrist, 108, 173, 177; see also Satan
Aphrahat, Sage of Persia, 31
Apollyon, 85
Apple, 43, 117, 123, 159
Appleseed, Johnny, 117
Appleton Seal, 208
Aquinas, Thomas, see Thomas
Arabah, 12 n.
Aragonese, 172
Ararat, 216
Arena, desert as, 14; martyr in, 23, 38, 65
Aristotle, 168, 181 n.
Arius, 105
Arlington, Mass., 112
Armstrong, M. F., 120 n.
Arndt, Johann, 87, 109
Arrowsmith, John, 149
Ashmun, Jehudi, 126
Asp, 21, 34
Asperges, 140
Ass, 27, 60
Astronauts, 219, 230
Asylum, right of, 47
Athens, 144, 159, 160, 161, 169, 175, 178, 182
Atomic bomb, 132, 136, 230
Auden, W. H., 133 n.

Auerbach, Elias, 10 n.
Augustine, 47, 97, 162 n., 182
Aula, see University symbols
Automation, xi, 230
Ayer, Ildefonse, 28 n.
Azazel, 13, 14

Baal Haddad, 12
Babcock, Rufus, 3 n.
Babylonia, 146, 164
Baker, Samuel, 4 n.
Baldo degli Ubaldi, 176
Baldwin, Alice, 111 n.
Bale, John, 75
Bangor Seminary, 126
Baptism, 5, 20, 22, 23, 24, 25, 28, 29, 32, 36, 40, 43, 44, 45, 67, 71, 72, 84, 104, 106, 107, 113, 140 159, 162 n., 178
Baptists, 80, 82, 106, 124
Barge, Hermann, 66
Barnabas, 29
Barrett, Richard, 82 n.
Bartsch, Franz, 95 n.
Basil the Great, 39, 51
Baxter, Richard, 74, 149 n.
Bears, 116, 137
Beasts, 21, 23, 33, 46 n., 112; *see also* Animals
Beauvais, Vincent of, 168
Beck, Edmund, 45 n.
Bede, the Venerable, 46
Beecher, Lyman, 127
Beissel, Conrad, 114
Benedict XIII, Pope, 181
Benedict of Nursia, 159
Benignitas, 166
Benz, Ernst, 36 n., 38 n., 99 n., 145 n.
Berengar of Tours, 164
Bernard of Clairvaux, 163, 164
Berthold the Carmelite, 55
Bethany, cave of, 37
Beza, Theodore, 157, 182, 185, 186, 187, 190
Birds, 33, 60, 82, 83, 84, 103
Bison, 137
Blakney, Raymond B., 53 n.
Blanche, queen of France, 166
Boas, George, 101 n.
Boehm, Anthony William, 87, 88, 94, 109
Boethius, 160
Boismard, M. E., 10 n.
Bole, John A., 115 n.
Bolgar, R. R., 186 n.
Borgeaud, Charles, 190
Bonaventure, 61
Bonnard, Pierre, 22 n.
Book of Common Prayer, 73, 90
Borman, Robert, 149 n.
Bosco, Giovanni, the Salesian, 133
Boulay, C. B. du, 169
Boutwell, George S., 200
Boyes, Michael, 22 n.

Bradford, John, 83, 84
Brakel, William à., 96
Brasilia, 133
Braun, R. P., 26 n.
Bread of Heaven, *see* Eucharist
Bride of Christ, 28, 32, 114, 120, 121, 175, 179
Brousson, Claude, 92
Brown, William Adams, 197
Brownlee, W. H., 22 n.
Brueghel, Jan, 92 n.
Bruyne, Lucien de, 30 n.
Bucer, Martin, 187, 191
Budge, E. A. Wallis, 41 n.
Bugbee, Henry G., Jr., 133, 134, 135
Bulldozer, x, 135, 230
Bultmann, Rudolf, 23 n.
Bunyan, John, 84, 107 n., 119
Buonaiuti, Ernesto, 59 n.
Burial places, 13, 24, 53 n.; cemeteries, 13; sepulchre, 10, 162 n.; Sheol, 13, 18 n.; tomb, 36
Betrothal and nuptial imagery, 15, 16, 18, 28, 32 n., 54 n., 56, 67, 68, 91, 106, 114, 119, 179
Burroughs, John, 130
Bushman, Richard L., 118 n.

Cadbury, Henry Joel, 151 n.
Cadmus, 145, 164, 165
Caleb, 165 n.
Calues, 33
Calvin, John, 65, 184, 185–187, 189–190, 191, 192, 223–224
Calvinism, 75, 99, 100, 186 n., 190, 192, 193
Cambridge, Mass., 144, 148; England, 149, 193; Platform, 203
Cameronians, 92, 95
Camisards, 92, 95
Canaanites, 40, 72
Caritas, 49, 55, 180
Carlstadt, Andreas Bodenstein von, 66, 67
Carmelites, 52, 55, 75
Carrie, George Elives, 226 n.
Cassian, John, 41, 46, 51
Catholicism, 30, 58 n., 65, 111, 189, 214 n.
Cato, 182
Cavarnos, John, 39 n.
Caves and dens, 36, 37, 38 n., 45, 55, 78, 85, 93, 108; as stable, 37; as Paradise, 37, 38; as Womb of Mary, 37
Celestine V, 61
Celibacy, Continence, 43, 44, 46, 114, 162, 185
Cerchi, Eugenio, 133
Chaos, 12 n., 14, 15
Chapel des trois fleurs de lis, 175
Chapman, John, 117
Charlemagne, 143, 144, 159, 160, 168, 169, 171, 177, 178, 181–182, 184, 195 n.

Charles, R. H., 21 n.
Charles I, 80
Charles of Anjou, 172
Charles the Bald, 160
Chase, symbolism of, 33
Chauncy, Charles, 143, 144, 145, 148,
  149, 185, 195
Childs, Brevard S., 11 n.
Chorbah, 12 n.
Chrestien de Troyes, 176
Christ, *see* Jesus Christ
Christendom, 172, 173
Christmas tree, 49, 50
Christo et Ecclesiae (Harvard University
  seal), 143, 150, 152, 193, 201, 204,
  206, 208
Christological theme, 147, 157, 162, 171,
  174, 178, 223
Church, the, 8, 20, 22, 24, 32 n., 73, 83,
  104, 107, 109, 110, 112, 113, 122, 126,
  128, 133, 141, 154, 156, 161, 163, 167,
  171, 172, 173, 177, 202, 208, 211, 212,
  213, 215, 218, 219, 220, 222, 226, 227,
  228, 230; as bride, 112, 120, 121, 175,
  179; as enclosed garden, 99, 100, 105,
  106, 136; immigrant, 98; as paradise, ix,
  6, 27, 28, 30, 32, 35, 44, 45 n., 63, 64,
  106, 148, 158, 166; primitive (apostolic), as ideal, 69, 71, 118, 157, 158;
  as Promised Land, 29; as sect (conventicles), 114, 214, 215; spiritual
  (*Ecclesia Spiritualis*), 52, 58; as woman
  of wilderness, 25, 47, 57 ff., 58, 67, 69,
  70, 75, 76, 84, 94, 107, 108, 113, 117,
  120, 121, 122, 124, 126; as Zion, 63, 64,
  92, 93, 119, 123
Church of England, *see* Anglicans
Church of Galilee, 24
Church of Jerusalem, 24
Church of Jesus Christ of Latter Day
  Saints, 118, 119
Cicero, 182
Claudel, Paul, 140
Claxton, Lawrence, 81
Cleveland, John, 111
Clement V, Pope, 61, 158, 177 n.
Clement VII, Pope, 177
Clergie, 180
Clovis, 174
Codman, John, 200
Cohn, Norman, 81 n.
Colonna, Cardinal, 170, 171 n.
Cole, Thomas, 129
Colet, John, 186
College, *see* University Academy
Colman, Benjamin, 146, 147 n., 151, 156
Columbanus, 51
Columbus, Christopher, 100
Comenius, John, 194
Communio Sanctorum, 8
Community of goods, communism, 48,
  57, 68, 69

Condor, 136
Confirmation, 162 n.
Congregationalism, 82, 125, 148, 154,
  155, 198
Conring, Hermann, 151
Cooke, Samuel, 112, 113
Conservation, xi, 130, 131, 136, 137, 140
Constantine, 33, 34, 36, 188; basilicas, 47
Contemplation, 4, 5, 17, 18, 26, 41, 55 n.,
  57, 161 n.
Cordier, Maturin, 186, 187
Corpus Christianum, 167, 171, 176, 187,
  227
Cotton, John, 99, 100, 105–106
Council of Chalcedon, 188; Council of
  Nicaea, 71, 188; Council of Trent, 214
  n.
Covenant (Testament), 7, 17, 18, 20, 25,
  98, 107; with animals, xi; Covenanters,
  92
Cow, 116
Cowdery, Oliver, 118
Cranmer, Thomas, 73, 86
Crandon, John, 149 n.
Creatures (creation), xi, 8, 14, 23, 83,
  84, 136, 137, 140, 228, 229; *see also*
  Animals, Nature
Crisp, Stephen, 82 n.
Critical Pluralism, 171, 210
Critical theme, 157, 161, 170, 171, 180,
  181
Crocodiles, 42
Cromwell, Oliver, 149
Cromwell, Thomas, 149 n.
Cross, Frank, 19, 20 n.
Crows, 137
Cupiditas, 49
Curtius, Ernst Robert, 160 n.
Cuthbert, 46, 51
Cyprian, bishop of Carthage, 32–33
Czechowic, Martin, 73

Dahl, N. H., 29 n.
D'Ailly, Pierre, 100, 177, 182
Damascus, desert of, 17, 19
Damian, Peter, 47 n.
Daniel, 180
Daniélou, Jean, 22 n., 28 n.
Dante, 48, 176
"Dark night of soul," 56
Dartmouth College, 122, 198, 199 n.
"Das Weib der Wüste," 114
D'Asbeck, Melline, 54 n.
David, 40, 156, 162 n., 174
Daws, 60
Day, Gardiner, 208
Death, 11, 13, 14, 15, 18 n., 29, 56, 131,
  137
Debir, 145
Deer, 15, 103
Defensatrix fidei, 179
Deferrai, Roy J., 39 n.

Delamare, Roger B., 161
Dell, William, 149 n.
Demons, 13, 38, 41, 43, 46, 93, 94 n.,
    108, 131, 149
Desert retreats, 55
Desert, *see* Wilderness
Desertum, 50, 52, 53, 57, 66, 67, 80
Devils, *see* Satan, Demons, Evil Spirits
Dickenson, Edmond, 145 n.
Didaskalos pisteōs, 188
Diggers, 80
Diman, Lewis, 104 n.
Diognetus, 31
Dionysius (Denis) the Areopagite, 53 n.
    54 n., 163, 169, 175
Disert (or *Disart*), 46
Doctor, see Professor
Dölger, Franz-Joseph, 30
Dorn, C. A. Wynschenk, 55 n.
Douglas, William O., x
Doves, 5, 63, 92, 104
Downey, Glanville, 158 n.
Dragons, 13, 21, 27, 34, 38, 43, 63, 69,
    86, 112 n., 145
Drought (dryness), 4, 5, 12, 14
Dubarle, Eugene, 206 n.
Dudley, Thomas, 155
Dunster, Henry, 143, 155
Du Plessis, J., 96 n.
Duss, John S., 115 n.
Dwight, Timothy, 124, 125

Eagles, 33
Ecclesiology, *see* Church
Eckhart, Meister, 52, 53, 67, 135, 136
Eden, Garden of, 11, 12, 20, 26, 43, 44,
    49, 60, 71, 72, 159, 182; New Eden,
    4, 10, 32
Edict of Nantes, 92
Edin, 12 n.
Edmonds, H., 161 n.
Education, ix, 141, 148, 160, 211, 212,
    213, 214, 215, 216, 217, 219, 220, 221,
    224, 228, 229, 230, 231; opposition to,
    for clergy, 76, 78, 79, 148, 149; *see
    also* Academy (high school), School,
    Seminary, University (college)
Edwards, F. H., 119 n.
Edwards, Jonathan, 110–111
Egypt, 27, 29, 51, 146, 164, 169, 177,
    178, 182, 184
Eleutherius, 176
Eliade, Mircea, 11 n.
Elijah, 17, 24 n., 39, 46, 55, 121, 146,
    147, 155, 162, 195; cave of, 37
Eliot, Charles W., 208, 209
Eliot, John, 101, 102
Eliot, Samuel A., 202–203
Eliot, T. S., 133 n.
Elisha, 17, 55, 106, 123, 146, 147, 148,
    162, 192, 195
Ellis, John, 4 n.

Emerson, Ralph Waldo, 130
Emerton, Ephraim, 209
England, 76, 77, 87, 185
Engnell, Ivan, 11 n.
Ephraem, 45 n.
Epiphanius, 28 n.
Episcopalians, 107
Episkopos ton ektos, 188 n.
Epp, Claasz, Jr., 95
Erasmus, Desiderius, 186
Eremos, eremia, 12 n.
Eschatology, 6, 20, 21, 22, 24, 26, 27, 98,
    105, 109, 123, 125, 127, 136, 219
Essenes, 19, 20, 25
Eucharist (bread of heaven), 25, 28 n.,
    32, 36, 62 n., 66, 140; eucharistic wafer,
    50; *agape*, 24, 62
Eucherius, 45
Eusebius, bishop of Caesarea, 33, 34, 35–
    36, 66, 174 n., 187, 188
Everett, Charles W., 208
Everett, Edward, 202, 203–204
Evil Spirits, 13, 14 n.; jinn, 13; demons,
    13, 14, 38, 93, 109; devils, 38, 41,
    108, 131, 149; ghouls, 13
Evlogius, metropolitan, 132
Exodus, (I) from Egypt, 15, 25, 33; II,
    return from Babylon, 15; III, flight to
    Qumran, 19; IV, flight of Christians from
    Judaism, 22, 25; V, flight from "Chris-
    tianized" Empire, 38, 39; VI, mystical
    and other uses of the image, 33, 51, 97,
    98, 110, 117, 118, 120, 124
Extreme unction, 162 n.
Ezekiel, 15, 181

Fall, the, 6, 218, 222; of creation, 84, 103,
    129, 140, 219; of man (Adam), 10, 11,
    20, 26, 44, 65, 71, 74, 82, 83, 84, 129,
    136, 148, 150, 158, 159, 167 n., 168 n.,
    217, 218; of reason, 30, 47, 72, 148,
    150, 157, 217, 218, 219, 222, 231
Faulkner, William, 121 n.
Fawcett, John, 87, 89
Fayetteville, N.Y., 118
Felix Culpa, 11 n., 71, 74
Felton, Cornelius Conway, 205
Fertile Crescent, 15
Fiesole, Giovanni da, 60 n.
Filial image, 178–179; *Filia regis*, 175, 178
Fire, 12, 21 n., 22, 121, 123; *see also*
    Wilderness
Fish, 82
Fisher, Miles, 119 n.
Fitzgerald, Margaret, 89 n.
FitzRalph, Richard, 61
Flight, John, 10 n.
Flood, 29, 135
Florence, 63–64
Florovsky, Georges, 38 n.
Forests (woods), 21, 40, 66, 73, 84, 85,

92, 120, 123, 126, 130, 131, 132, 136, 137, 140
Fox, George, 82, 104
Foxes, 63
France, 92, 175, 176, 181; Franks, French, 160, 172, 177; *see also* Gauls
Francis of Assisi, 59, 60, 137
Franck, Sebastian, 66
Fraticelli, 61
Frederick I, Emperor, 153
Free University of Amsterdam, 221
Friends of God, 35, 52, 66
Frontier, 3, 4, 101 n., 117, 118, 122, 126, 131, 134, 231
Froom, LeRoy Edwin, 112 n.
Fuller, Andrew, 87 n.
Funk, Robert, 22 n.

Gaguin, Robert, 183
Gallanta, Nicholas, 121 n.
Gamaliel, 149
Garden, 132; precariousness of, 6, 8, 12, 30, 98, 103, 105, 231; good and bad sense of, 49; *see also* Paradise, Eden
Garden of Eden, *see* Eden
Gaster, Theodore H., 20 n.
Gatry, Raymond, 136 n.
Gauls, 160, 163, 164, 169; *see also* France
Gelassenheit (yieldedness), 54, 67, 68
Gelasius I, Pope, 188, 189
Genevan Academy, College, University, 155, 184, 186, 187, 190
Georgia (Asiatic), 94
Gerasimus, 42, 43
Germany, 94, 195 n., 220–221; German Pietism, 94, 109, 113–115, 145 n., 148; German Reformation, 185
Gerson, John, 177, 178, 179, 180–181, 182
Gethsemane, 44
Ghouls, 13
Giet, Stanislas, 25 n.
Gignasium (*gymnasium*), 167, 186
Giles, John D., 118 n.
Giles of Rheims, 169
Gils, Felix, 187 n.
Gnostics, 30
Gnu, 137
Goats, 13
Godhead, barren, 53
Godwyn, Thomas, 151 n.
Goldammer, Kurt, 62
Golden age, 2, 27, 30, 33, 63
Golder, Harold, 85 n.
Goodykoontz, Collin B., 128 n.
Gospel, eternal, 58, 87; of all creatures, xi
Gothoniel, 165
Goulet, Robert, 182, 183
Gown, Academic, *see* Professor
Grabar, André, 35 n.
Grant, Frederick, 23 n.
Great Awakening, in New England, 122
Greccio, 60

Greece, 145, 177, 184
Greek Orthodox Church, 100, 110, 132
Greeks, 145, 146, 164
Gregory II, Pope, 188
Gregory IX, Pope, 60, 165, 166, 167, 180 n.
Gregory of Nyssa, 39, 40, 46, 80
Grimold, Abbot, 159
Grottoes, *see* Caves
Grueningen, von, John Paul, 222 n.
Grundmann, Herbert, 167, 169 n.
Guillet, Jacques, 10 n.
Gunkel, Hermann, 10 n.
Gurley, Ralph R., 126
Guyon, Madame, 89, 91, 114
Gymnasiarch, 143, 185

Halder, Alfred, 10 n., 12
Halsey, LeRoy Jones, 215
Hamlyn, V. W. C., 186 n.
Harbison, Elmore, 186 n.
Harmony, Pa., 114, 118
Harvard College, university, ix, 141, 142, 148, 149, 152, 154, 155, 157, 193, 196; corporate freedoms, 198–201; charter, 151, 153, 154, 155; degrees, 152, 153, 155, 201, 204; sphragistic controversy, 201–209; 193; *see also* under various seals; church in, 202, 205 n.; overseers, 146, 200, 202, 206; disestablishment, 206
Harvard Divinity School, 128, 141, 197, 200, 208, 209
Hassinger, Kurt, 47 n.
Hawks, 33
Hawthorne, Nathaniel, 129
Hayne, Coe, 3 n.
Heath, 163
Heaviness, distinguished from wilderness state, 90, 91
Hebrews, 145 n., 146
Hebron, 145, 174
Hedge, Frederick Henry, 206–207
Heimert, Alan, 101
Heiric of Auxerre, 160
Helen, mother of Constantine, 36
Hélinand of Froidmont, 168, 169
Hellenes, *see* Greeks
Héloise, 162
Henderson, Robert Waugh, 186 n.
Henry VIII, king of England, 185
Herdt, René, 50 n.
Hicks, Edward, 115, 116; "The Peaceable Kingdom," 115
Higginson, John, 110
Highway in desert, 15, 19, 20, 22, 34, 107
Hildegard of Bingen, 51
Hilkiah, 149
Hippolytus, 32
Hirelings, 123
Hirsch, Elizabeth, 106 n.
Hivite, 145

Hofmann, Melchior, 67, 68, 75, 90
Hofstadter, Richard, 130
Holland, 221
Hollanda, Sergio Buarque de, 100 n.
Holmes, Oliver Wendell, 207, 208
Holy Alliance, 94
Holy Land, 36, 37
Holy Sepulchre, 36, 47
Holy Spirit, 8, 27, 30, 105, 125, 126, 147, 150, 159, 160, 163, 164, 166, 168, 181, 231
Holzmeister, Urban, S.J., 23 n.
Honorius of "Autun," 161
Honorius III, Pope, 165
Horace, 160 n.
Horebites, 62
Horton, Douglas, 106 n., 222
Hospinian, Rudolph, 151
Hound, 33
Hugh of Besançon, 166 n.
Hugh of Lusignan, 174 n.
Hugolinus, 153
Huguenots, 92, 95
Huldah, 149
Hunting lodge, as symbol of church, 85
Huntington, Frederic D., 204, 205
Hutchinson, Anne, 154
Hutchinson, Thomas, 111
Hutter, Jacob, 69
Hutterites, 65, 69, 70
Hybris, 193
Hyenas, 13
Hyrcanus, John, 188

Iberian mysticism, 52
Icon, displayed by Constantine, 33
Ignatius, bishop of Antioch, 38
In Christi Gloriam, 201, 203
In hoc signo, 34
In populo Dei, 194
Indians as either Israelites or demonic savages, 4, 102, 103, 108, 112, 114, 117, 122
Innocent III, Pope, 57
Ipswich, Mass., 106
Irenaeus of Lyons, 28 n., 30
Ishmael, 34 n.
Ishtar, 12 n.
Isidore, 165
Israel (church as), 16, 17, 29, 74, 92, 95, 97, 109, 145 n., 146, 147, 160
Israelites, 89, 96, 102, 107, 145
Italians, 172
Itter, Johann Wilhelm, 150, 151, 195 n.

Jaarsveld, F. A. van, 95 n.
Jackson, John, 81, 87
Jacob, 16, 39
Jaeger, Werner, 40 n.
Jaguar, 133
James I, king of England, 109
Jameson, J. F., 107 n.

Jehoshaphat, 106
Jehu, "Wilderness" king, 17
Jeremias, Joachim, 23 n.
Jerome, 43, 51, 158, 159, 162, 181
Jerusalem, 27, 65, 149, 161, 164
Jesus Christ, xi, 22, 23, 26, 27, 28, 29 n., 30, 34, 36, 39, 43, 44, 68, 69, 77, 78, 79, 92 n., 121, 149, 150, 157, 162, 163, 167, 169, 170, 174, 176, 179, 187, 189, 192; as Prophet, 147; *see also* Christological theme; as Hermit, 78
Jews, 26, 102, 162, 171
Jinn, 13
Joachim of Flora, 57, 58, 59, 61, 62, 66, 167, 171 n.
Johannes in Eremo, 111
John, disciple of Jesus, 28
John of Garland, 168 n., 169
John of Parma, 61
John the Baptist, 20, 22, 24 n., 39, 43, 65, 107, 118
John XXII, Pope, 61, 175
Johnson, Edward, 107
Jonadab, 17
Jordan River, 5, 23, 44, 54, 120, 121
Joshua, 145
Julian the Apostate, 45, 148
Jung-Stilling, Johann Heinrich, 94, 95
Juvenile delinquency, 213

Kamlah, Wilhelm, 57
Kampschulte, F., 190 n.
Kantorowicz, Ernest, 34 n., 48 n., 162, 176 n.
Käsemann, Ernst, 25 n.
Kedron, 45
Kelpius, Johann, 113, 114
Keyes, Sidney, 133
Kid, 116
Kirchberger, Clare, 51 n.
Kirjath-Sepher (Debir), 145, 146, 148, 164, 165, 195
Kirtland, Ohio, Mormon Temple, 117
Kittel, Rudolph, 22 n.
Klein, Walter C., 113 n.
Klingender, F. D., 60 n.
Knighthood, 161, 168, 169, 170, 175, 176, 178, 180
Koch, Robert A., 55 n.
Kopp, Clemens, 55 n.
Kraeling, C. H., 22 n.
Kruger, D. W., 95 n.
Kuckhoff, Joseph, 54 n.

Lactantius, 32, 33, 35; *Divine Institutes*, 33
Ladner, Gerhart B., 28 n., 31 n.
Lambs, 60, 116
Langdon, William Chauncy, 208, 209
Langerbeck, Hermann, 40 n.
Lanko, Tatjana, 94 n.
Latin America, 100

Laubenstein, Paul F., 120 n.
Laud, William, 145 n.
Lausanne, 186
Lavater, Johann Casper, 94
Lawrence, Matthew, 3 n.
Lazarus, cave of resurrection of, 37
Lebanon, 40, 85, 86
Lebanon, N.H., 123
Le Coultre, Jules, 186 n.
Lefftz, J., 50 n.
Lehrfreiheit, 221, 225
Leigh, Edward, 151
Leopards, 27, 108, 116
Leverett, John, 146, 147, *Discourse on John Harvard*, 151 n.
Levi, 188
Leviathan, 14 n.
Levie, J., 23 n.
Lewis, R. W. B., 129
Lexington, Mass., 112
Liber Pontificalis, 48
Libertines, Spiritual, 81, 82
Libido sciendi, sentiendi, 150
Lichtensteyn, Petrus, 53 n.
Lilith, 13, 38
Lily, fleur-de-lis, xi, 40, 169, 170, 175 n., 179 n.
Lions, 27, 33, 34, 42, 78, 108, 116
Locusts, 39, 43
Lollards, 74
Lombard, Peter, 153 n.
Lopez, Gregory, 89
Lord's Supper, *see* Eucharist
Lothair II, Holy Roman Emperor, 153, 195
Louis IX, king of France, 166
Louis XI, 166 n.
Louis the Pious, 161
Lowrie, Donald A., 133 n.
Lundberg, Per, 29 n.
Luther, Martin, 74, 86, 157, 184, 185, 221, 222
Lutheranism, 99, 185, 189, 190, 213 n., 220
Lyttle, Charles, 141 n.

McCloy, Frank Dixon, 197
M'Clure, David, 122 n.
Magisterial (classical Protestant) Reformation, 86
Magnasco, Alessandro, 92 n.
Magnus, Jacobus, 182, 183
Maine, 126
Major, R. H., 101 n.
Maltby, John, 128 n.
Mamre, oak of, 39
Manegold of Lautenbach, 164
Marcel, Gabriel, 134
Marcian, Byzantine Emperor, 188
Marriage, 11 n., 16 n., 39, 68, 114
Marrou, H. I., 31 n.
Marshall, Charles, 82

Marshall, Chief Justice John, 198
Martial motif, 143, 160, 161, 168, 220; *see also* Spiritual warfare
Martin IV, Pope, 172
Martyr, as prototype of the monk, scholar, missionary, and patriot, 19, 38, 67, 112, 113, 160; *see also* Arena, Warfare, spiritual
Mary the Mother of Jesus, 26, 37, 121
Mather, Cotton, 107, 109, 141, 144, 145, 146, 148, 149, 150, 151; *The Devil Discovered*, 108; *Magnalia*, 108, 110, 143, 153 n., 154 n., 156; *Parentator*, 152, 153 n.
Mather, Increase, 143, 144, 146, 150, 151, 152, 154, 155, 195, 201, 202, 224; *Elijah's Mantle*, 148 n.
Matherian seal, 201, 202, 203, 207
Maxentius, 33
Maximus the Confessor, 46
Mayhew, Jonathan, 111
Mechthild of Magdeburg, 51
Meecham, Henry G., 31 n.
Meek, Theophile James, 16 n.
Meir, Gabriel, 160 n.
Melanchthon, Philip, 186, 221
Melchizedek priesthoods, 118
Melville, Herman, 129
Mendicants, 172 n.
Mennonites, 65, 95
Messiah(s), 19, 20, 188, 192
Methodists, 91, 120, 124
Methodius of Olympus, 35 n.
Metzger, Dunster, 141 n.
Meyer, Carl S., 115 n.
Midbar, 12 n.
Middendorp, Jacob, 151
Midian, wilderness of, 22
Military, *see* Martial motif
Milites Christi, 46 n., 144, 166, 175
Militia Christi, 29, 144, 169, 180 n.; *see also* Martial motif
Millennium, 33, 125
Miller, Alexander, 129
Miller, Johannes Leonard, 16 n.
Miller, Perry, 101 n., 103 n., 129, 152 n.
Milton, John, 76–77, 79, 87; *Areopagitica*, 77; *Defensio*, 80; *Eikonoklastes*, 80; *Paradise Lost*, 11 n., 77, 78; *Paradise Regained*, 77, 78, 79
Minerva, 178, 182, 226
Missions, missionary, 6, 7, 8, 9, 24 n., 46, 70, 87, 88, 109, 122, 123, 124, 125, 126, 127, 149 n., 222, 230
Missouri Compromise, 126
Mitchell, Jonathan, 146, 146 n., 147 n.
Mithraism, 36 n., 37
Moab, 13
Moberly, Sir Walter, 221
Monachus, 43
Monastery as paradise, ix, 6, 38, 40, 42, 43

Monasticism, 7, 39, 57, 106, 114, 122, 158, 159, 161, 162, 163, 164, 168, 173, 219
Monks, Irish, 46, 177
Monod, Albert, 92 n.
Monsters, 13, 41
Montanists of Asia Minor, 28
Monte Cassino, 158 n.
Montgomery, James A., 10 n.
Moravia, Hutterites, 70
Moravian Brethren, 90
Moreland, Samuel, 62 n., 75, 76
Morino, C., 44 n.
Morison, Samuel Eliot, 141 n., 148 n., 151 n., 152 n., 155 n., 186 n., 201 n., 206 n.
Mormonism, *see* Church of Latter Day Saints
Morrone, Peter, 61
Moses, 20, 21, 22, 33, 43, 44, 79, 156, 188, 194, 195
Mosse, George L., 83 n.
Mount Carmel, 37, 39, 55
Mount Horeb, 17
Mount of Olives, 36, 39, 44
Mourin, Louis, 178
Müller, Karl, 189
Münsterites, 68, 69
Müir, John, 130, 131
Murdock, Kenneth B., 101, 144 n., 152 n.
Murray, Andrew, 96
Mysticism, 7, 35 n., 39, 40, 41, 47, 50, 51, 52, 53, 54, 56, 67, 81, 89, 98, 114, 115 n., 137 n.

Naboth, 44
Napoleonic age, 94
Nations with distinctive missions, 170–173
Nature, 6, 79, 83, 111, 129, 130, 135, 136, 137, 140, 231
Nayler, James, 82
Nazareth, cave at, 37
Nazirites, 162
Nebuchadnezzar, 182
Negroes, 120–121
Nephi, 119 n.
New Church, 93
New England, 109, 125
New Englanders, 109, 110, 123, 148
Newman, John Henry, 206 n., 221
Nicklas, Anna, 54 n.
Nicodemus, 162
Nieper, Friedrich, 113 n.
Noah, xi, 178; ark, 29, 216
Noble, Hubert C., 222 n.
Non-Conformists, 152
North America, 100, 109
Norton, John, *The Answer to Apollonius*, 106
Noth, M., 11 n.
Notker the Stammerer, 160, 169, 177, 182
Novus dux, 59
Novus, populus, 59

Nuptial imagery, 15, 54 n.
Nystrom, Samuel, 10 n.

Oath, *see* University
Oberlin, Johann Friedrich, 94
O'Connor, W. V., 121 n.
Olschki, Leonardo, 101 n.
Ong, Walter S., S.J., 134 n.
Optatus of Mileve, 35
Otto, bishop of Freising, 170
Ovid, 180 n.
Oxen, 136

Palestine, 10, 28, 72, 145
Palladius, 41, 181 n.
Palmyra, N.Y., 121
Papacy, 171–172, 176, 177
Paradeisos, 50
Paradise, 11, 26–27; architectural sense, 47, 48; Believer as, 80; Christ as, 23; Church as, ix, 6, 27, 28, 30, 32, 35, 44, 45 n., 63, 64, 106, 148, 158, 166; future, 4, 9, 21, 26, 44; heavenly, 26, 33, 39, 65; terrestrial, 26, 48, 72, 100, 140; monastery as, ix, 6, 38, 40, 42, 43, 159; as mystical staff, 40; primordial, *see* Eden; wilderness as, 23; *see also* Garden, Eden, *and* Seminary
Paradise-wilderness cycle, 92 n., 195, 211, 212, 215–223
Paradise motif, problem of knowledge, 20, 30, 31, 32, 60 n., 71, 72, 80 n., 83, 100, 148, 157, 162 n., 169, 217, 218, 219; a university theme, 148, 157, 159, 162, 167, 168, 181
Paran, wilderness of, 34 n.
Paris, university of, 153, 164, 165, 166, 168, 169, 175, 177, 178–183, 185, 186, 204, 206
Parish, Elijah, 122 n.
Pasquier, E., 179 n.
Passover, 29
Pastores, 193, 194
Patrick, Symeon, 147
Patmos, 26
Patriot (Boston), 198
Paul, the Apostle, x, 24, 26, 34, 44, 68, 81, 102, 116, 136, 149, 160
Paulicians, 75
Paulinus, bishop of Nola, 48
Paulsen, Friedrich, 190 n.
Peaceable kingdom, xi, 2, 27, 28, 33, 39, 82, 83, 115, 116, 117
Peccator, 223
Peck, John Mason, 3, 4, 9
Peden, Alexander, 92
Pedersen, Johannes, 10 n., 14 n.
Peers, Allison, 56 n.
Pelasgians, 145 n.
Peleg, 145 n.
Pentateuch, 79

Pentecost, 24 n., 163
Pepuza, 28
Perkins, Frederic B., 206 n.
Perkins, William, 107 n., 114
Perrin, Jean, 75
Persia, 11, 146
Peterkin, Alexander, 193 n.
Peterson, E., 35 n.
Pfeiffer, F., 53 n.
Pfleger, A., 50 n.
Phoenicians, 144, 145
Philadelphia, Penn., 114
Philanthropy, eschatologically motivated, 76
Philip Augustus, 59 n.
Philip de Harvengt, 164, 182
Philip of Hesse, 221
Philip of Vitry, 175
Philip III, king of France, 172
Philip IV, the Fair, 175
Philip VI, Valois, 175
Philips, Dietrich, 68, 69
Philo, 39 n., 188
Philosophiae milites, 168
Philosophica speculatio, 169
Pietas litterata, 186
Pierce, Edith Lovejoy, 2
Pietism, 87, 90, 94; *see also* Wesley, German Pietism, etc.
Pilgrimage, 21, 25, 45, 46, 50, 58, 75, 81, 82 n., 84, 94, 96, 98, 99, 101 n., 114, 127
Plato, 162 n.
Plummer, Charles, 46 n.
Plutarch, 181
Polycarp, 143, 144
Pontifex maximus, 174, 188 n.
Pool, 14, 15, 21, 105, 120, 124, 127, 128
Pope, 154, 179
Portuguese, 100
Posse, 180
Postumianus, 42, 51
Potentia, 166
Poverty, 60, 61; of desert, 57
Praedestinati, 222 n.
Praesciti, 222 n.
Praeses, 190
Pratum spirituale, 42
President (rector), *see* University
Pretorius, Andries, 95
Pretorius, H. S., 95 n.
Price, Robert, 117 n.
Primogenita studiorum, 177, 178
Princeton University, 224
Principes, 161, 166
Professor, as apostle, 46; as *doctor ecclesiae*, 58, 146, 153, 158, 179, 190, 191, 192, 193, 194, 195, 224; gown of, 195, 197, 227; as prophet, 146, 147, 156, 192, 223, 224, 225; rank of, 186, 187; as teacher, 216, 218, 219, 220, 222, 223, 224, 225, 227, 228, 230, 231;

constituting teaching order, 147, 157 n., 194; doctoral knighthood of, 176
Promised Land, 5, 19, 26, 27, 28, 29, 40, 50, 51, 54 n., 69, 98, 101, n., 108, 111, 133
Prophets, 6, 8, 15, 17, 99, 130, 147, 159, 162, 163, 165, 191, 193, 216, 225; professor as, 146, 147, 156, 223, 224, 225; *see also individual prophets by name*
Protestantism, 65, 185, 214
Pseudo-Clement, 27
Pseudo-Dionysius, *see* Dionysius
Ptolemy of Lucca, 174, 175
Puma, 136
Puritanism, 80, 154
Puritans, 74, 76, 99, 101, 104, 144, 148
Pythagoras, 162 n.
Pytho, 145

Quakers, 80, 82, 115
Quebec, Treaty of, 111
Queen of Sheba, 164
Quietism, 91 n.
Quincy, Josiah, 201

Racovian Catechism, 73
Radical (Left-Wing) Reformation, 65, 87, 214
Rains (showers), 12, 123, 124; "Rain follows the plough," 130
Raków, 73, 193 n.
Ranters, 80, 81, 82
Rapp, Johann George, 114, 118
Rashdall, Hastings, 153 n.
Raumer, Karl von, 206 n.
Rechabites, 17
Red dragon, 47, 69
Red Sea, 5, 29, 43, 69, 81; wilderness, 54 n.
Reformation, "reforming of," 77, 78, 110
Reformed Church, 154, 190
Refuge, 4, 6, 10; for the Church, 5, 66, 69, 70, 107, 112; for the contemplative, 17, 18, 78; for protection, 25; for wildlife, x, xi
Regina scientiarum, 209
Regnum, 171
Republic of Letters, name of university, 140
Res publica, 216
Restoration of all things, 22, 46, 69, 70, 71, 99, 129; *see also* Animals, friendly
Rex christianissimus, 169, 170, 179
Rex pacificus, 161 n., 170, 174, 178, 179
Richard of St. Victor, 50
Richard the Lion-Hearted, 59 n.
Richardson, Joseph, 199
Ridolfi, Roberto, 64 n.
Rivers (and streams) of Paradise, 14, 15, 32, 33, 40, 47, 72, 127, 140, 167, 178, 181; rivers as four faculties, 167, 178, 181; *see also* Pools

Roberts, B. H., 118 n.
Robertson, D. R., Jr., 49 n.
Robinson, James M., 24 n.
Robinson, J. A. T., 22
Robinson, John, 99
Roger of Hoveden, 59 n.
Roman Catholics, 213 n.
Roman Church, 171
Romans, 146
Rome, 160, 164, 169, 177, 178
Rose, blossom as, 8, 36, 87, 89, 124, 132
Rotmar, Valentin, 151, 154
Rückert, Hanns, 186 n.
Rufinus of Aquileia, 41
Rupert of Deutz, 57
Russia, 94, 95, 132, 228
Rusticus, 176
Rutherford, Samuel, 92
Ruthwell Cross, 34 n., 46 n.
Ruysbroeck the Admirable, 54
Ryan, John, 46 n.

Sacerdotium, 171, 172, 176
Sachse, Julius Friedrich, 113 n.
St. Denis, Abbey of, 163, 169, 175; *see also* Dionysius
St. Gall, 159, 160
St. John of the Cross, Carmelite mystic, 55, 65
St. John the Baptist of Flora, monastery of, 59
St. Martin's, 160
St. Mihiel-sur-Meuse, 159
St. Peter's, Rome, 47
St. Sophia, mother of the arts, 159
Sair, 13
Sainte Croix, Benoit Marie de la, 55 n.
Salesians, 133
Salles, A., 29 n.
Samarkand, 94
Samivel, xi
Samuel, 146
Sapientia, 47, 49, 162 n., 166, 169, 180 n., 217
Sartre, Jean Paul, 135
Satan, 5, 14, 29, 41, 44, 69, 78, 79, 89, 108, 109, 112, 113, 118, 120, 130, 131, 157, 173, 231; as Antichrist, 69, 75, 93, 108, 120, 167, 173, 177, 220
Satyr, 13
Saul, 174
Savery, Roelant, 92 n.
Savonarola, Girolamo, 62, 63–64
Scandinavia, 221
Schaff, Philip, 33 n.
Schapiro, Meyer, 34 n., 38 n.
Schlatter, Richard, 149 n.
Schlee, Ernst, 47 n.
Schleiermacher, Friedrich, 221
Schlink, Edmund, 227
Schlosser, Julius von, 160 n.
Schmauch, Werner, 21 n.

Schneider, Artur, 53 n.
Schoff, Wilfred H. 16 n.
Schools, 6, 122, 144, 148, 149 n., 151 n., 159, 169, 186, 194, 215, 230; high school, 213; parochial, 213 n.; public, 212, 213, 230; of the prophets, ix, 123, 144, 147, 148, 150, 155, 156, 215; *see also* Sons of
Schultz, Howard, 80, 149 n.
Schuze, W. A., 23 n.
Schwenckfeld, Caspar, 65, 66, 67
Scientia, 47, 49, 79, 162 n., 217, 222, 228, 231
Scire, 180
Scorpions, 43
Scotland, 74, 92, 193
Scott, Nathan, 133 n.
Scott, Walter, 93
Sea monster, 29
Seals, *see* Harvard, sphragistic controversy, etc.
Second Church of Boston, 156
Seedbed, 4, 6, 115, 117, 122, 123, 124, 149 n.; control plot, xi
Seekers, 80, 81, 102, 103
Sélestat, 50
Seminary, 4, 8, 121, 122, 123, 124, 125, 126, 127, 128, 153 n., 154, 197 n., 212, 214 n., 215, 217, 224; as seedbed, 4, 6
Senza glossa, 60
Separatists, 122
Separation of Church, State, and University, *see* Threefold office, Tripartite society
Septennium, 196
Sepulchre, 37; *see also* Burial places
Sergius, Russian saint, 132
Serpent, 14 n., 29, 31, 33, 34, 43, 71, 78, 105, 108, 109
Servetus, Michael, 65, 70, 71
Seth, children of, 164 n.
Shaw, Lemuel, 202
Shed (storm devil), 13
Sheep, 33
Sheol, 13
Shepard, Thomas, 102
Sherwood, Samuel, 112
Sicilian Vespers, 172
Siloam, 168 n.
Simon, Maurice, 151 n.
Simon de Brion, 172
Simons, Menno, 65, 69
Simpson, Sydrach, 149 n.
Sinai, 29
Singleton, Charles S., 48 n.
Sisters of Ephrata, 114
Sjodahl, James M., 119 n.
Smaragdus, 159
Smith, Edward D., 132
Smith, Elizabeth Abbot, 112 n.
Smith, Henry Nash, 129–130
Smith, Hyrum H., 119 n.

Smith, 117; *The Book of Mormon*, 118, 119; *Commandments*, 118, 119; *Doctrines and Covenants*, 119
Socinianism, 73, 193 n.
Solafideism, 220, 221, 222
Soli Deo gloria, 97
Solitary Brethren, 114
Solitudo, 50, 57
Sollicitudo, 57
Solomon, 85, 159, 161, 164, 174, 175, 179, 180
Sons (Schools) of the Prophets, 146, 147, 159, 162, 165; see also Schools of Soucek, J. B., 11 n.
South Africa, 95
South America, 100
Soviet Union, 228
Sown Land, 10 n., 12
Spain, 164
Spaniards, 100
Sparrows, 60
Spartans, 145 n.
Spectacles, 108
Sperling, Harry, 151 n.
Spirit, (wind) as blasting breath of God or gods, 4, 6, 8, 12, 14, 75, 123; hurricane, 12 n.; storm god, 12, 13; see also Evil Spirits *and* Holy Spirit
Spiritual Franciscans, 59, 61, 62, 171
Spoelstra, C., 96, 97
Springs (pools), 14, 15, 21, 105, 120, 124, 127, 128
Steinmann, Jean, 22 n.
Stelae, 164 n., 184
Stendahl, Krister, 22 n.
Stevens, Wesley M., 211
Stienkamp, Anna, 96 n.
Storm devil, 12, 13
Stoughton, William, 107
Strabo, 145 n.
Strassburg, 49, 50
Streams (and rivers) of Paradise, 14, 15, 32, 33, 40, 47, 72, 127, 167, 178, 181
Studia litterarum, 177
Studium (*studia*), 171, 172, 176, 185; *Studium generale*, 141, 161, 168, 206
Sturm, John, 186
Summus imperator, 185
Suso, Henry, 54
Sweden, 93
Swedenborg, Emanuel, 93, 94, 117
Sweet, William Warren, 3
Syrus, Ephraem, 35

Tabernacle (Mormon), 119
Taborites, 62
Tammuz-Adonis, 12, 37
Tan, tannin (howling dragon and monster), 13
Tauler, John, 54
Taxis, 158
Teacher, office of, 223-224

Temple, 35, 119, 129, 163, 223; Christian (allegorical), 32, 85, 86, 223; Old Testament, 85, 173 n.; tabernacle, 35, 119; Zion, 63, 64, 92, 93, 119, 123
Temptation, of Christ, 2, 5, 22, 23, 24, 26, 34, 38, 44, 65, 77, 78, 89, 108, 109, 120; of man, 5, 16, 17, 19, 23, 25, 43, 45, 68, 71, 73, 93, 102, 109, 220
Tersteegen, Gerhard, 114
Tertullian, 35, 29 n.
Theodore of Mopsuestia, 46
Theophilus of Antioch, 35
Third force, university as, 196; see also Tripartite society
Thode, Henry, 60 n.
Thomas, D. Winton, 11 n.
Thomas Aquinas, 174, 183
Thomism, 214 n., 215
Thoreau, David, 130
Thorowgood, Thomas, 102 n.
Three-fold office (priest, prophet, and king), of Christ, 147, 156, 157, 162, 167, 174, 175, 176, 187, 188, 189, 192, 194, 205, 211, 223; of baptized Christians, 32, 188 n., 205
Tiger, 78, 137
Tohu, 12 n., 14
Tombs, see Burial places
Transferential theme, iv, ix, 140, 143, 144, 146, 150, 157, 160, 162 n., 168, 171, 177, 182, 183, 184, 195, 209, 215, 216
Translatio studii, see Transferential theme
Treaty of Quebec, 111
Trees, 31, 40, 106, 123; Christmas, 49, 50 n.; fruit, 123; olive, 14, 30, 31, 32; cedar, 59; orchards, 4, 12; paradisic, 15, 20, 27, 29, 30, 116; see also Forests
Trent, 214 n.
Trinitarian-christological pattern, 195, 223
Trinity, 53, 71, 165, 169, 170, 171
Tripartite society, pattern of, 164, 167, 172, 173, 174, 179-180, 187, 189, 193, 211, 223, 227; Ariadic theme, 167, 169-170, 175, 187
Trocmé, Étienne, 24 n.
Troyes, Chrestien de, 168, 169
Turkestan, 95
Tuttle, Julius Herbert, 151 n.

Ullmann, W., 177 n.
Uminità, 48
Underhill, Evelyn, 55 n.
Unitarianism, 70, 73, 124, 128, 198
Universalists, 124
University and college, ix, 122, 124, 130, 141-145, 148, 149, 150, 151, 154, 155, 156, 157, 158, 161, 167, 168, 169, 170, 173, 175, 176, 177, 179, 185, 186, 211, 212, 213, 214, 215, 216, 217, 218, 219, 220, 221, 222, 223, 224, 225, 226, 227, 228, 229, 230, 231; as paradise, ix, 6;

of Palestine, 145; seals, 143, 150, 152, 193, 201, 203 n., 204, 206, 208; as Republic of Leters, 140; charter and freedoms, 151, 152, 153, 154, 155, 184, 186, 190 n., 199 n., 216, 217, 219, 221, 225, 226, 227, 229; 231; officers, 153 n., 162 n., 216; dean, 227; overseer, 200 n., overseer Elisha, 146; faculties, 167 n., 178 n., 181, 219, 221, 223, 225, 226, 227, 228, 230, 231; immunities and privileges, 153 n., 166 n., 199, 226, 231; oaths, 162 n., 166, 219, 220, 224, 231; degrees (doctorate), 146, 152, 153, 154, 155, 157, 195 n., (Master of Arts), 196–197; alumni, 166, 178, 215, 216; president, 146, 152, 154, 155, 224; rector, 143, 144, 151, 152, 166 n., 224; *see also* Professor
University, symbols: *aula*, 211, 226 n., 230; campus, 144, 211, 219, 220, 223, 230; chapel, 205 n., 211, 219, 230; commons, 230; green, yard, 211, 217, 230; library, 211, 216, 217, 219; wall, 205 n., 211, 217
University Themes, 156 f., 195, 211; *see under special headings and esp.*:
A. Paradisic-Wilderness Cycle, 195, 214
1. Paradisic Theme, 217
2. Transferential Theme, 215
3. Martial (military) Theme, 220; *see also* Warfare, spiritual
B. Trinitarian-Christological Tripartite Pattern, 145, 223
4. Christological-prophetic sanction of teacher, 223; *see also* Professor
5. Critical-judicial-triadic Theme, 225; *see also* Threefold Office
University of: Athens, 158 n., Babylon, 182; Berlin, 220; Bologna, 153; Cambridge, 186; Chicago, 227; Geneva, *see special entry;* Harvard, *see special entry;* Heidelberg, 227; London, 226; Nashville, 216, 217; Oxford, 153; Paris, *see special entry;* Toulouse, 168; the Wilderness, 130
Uzziah (King of Judah), 156

Vane, Henry, 105
Vastitas, 52, 53
Velle, 180
Vendettuoli, James, Jr., 81 n.
Veritas, 144, 146, 148, 152, 180, 201, 203, 204, 207, 208, 220, 226, 227
Veritatis doctrix, 179
Vespasian, 143
Vetter, Ferdinand, 54 n.
Vicar of Christ, 179
Vincent of Beauvais, 169
Vineyard, 6, 34, 44, 51 n., 59, 63, 96, 97, 114
Virgil, 181

Vita monastica, 161
Voetius, 154 n.
Voegelin, Eric, 18 n.

Wace, Henry, 33 n.
Wadsworth, John, 23 n.
Waldensians, 62, 63, 74, 75, 92, 109, 112
Waldo, Peter, 57, 62, 75
Walker, James, 204, 205
Walther, Georg Christopher, 195 n.
War of the Sons of Light, 20
Warblers, 137
Warfare, spiritual, 19, 20, 41, 156, 157, 158, 161, 220
Wars of Yahweh, The, 20
Wasteland, 5, 7, 134, 135, 136; *see also* Wilderness, religious sense
Wastity (wastine, wastern), 73
Webster, Daniel, 198, 199 n., 200
Weigel, Valentin, 149
Weisinger, Herbert, 11 n.
Wendel, François, 187 n., 191 n.
Wesley, John, 89, 90, 91, 110, 114
Westminster Assembly, 193
Weston, Jessie, 133
Whales, 136
Wheelock, Eleazar, 122, 123, 124
White, Henry, 23 n.
White, Morton, 141 n.
Wild beasts, *see* Animals
Wilderness (desert), literal sense, 132
dry desert, 4, 5, 24; *see also* Drought
the wilds, 66
the unsown, 10 n., 15, 113
natural area to be protected, x, xi, 130, 131, 136, 137, 140
nature, 6; *see also separate entry*
part of a formal garden, 74 n.
as distinguished from:
desert, 66
forest, *see separate entry*
Wilderness (desert), religious and moral meanings, 18, 73, 110, 132, 135, 231
ambiguity of, 8, 23, 74, 102, 103, 104, 129, 137
as wasteland, weary land, 8, 13, 65, 88, 103, 104, 111, 113, 115, 134
as the unredeemed world, 28, 59, 63, 69, 84
as realm of demons, death and darkness, 12, 14, 41, 85, 108, 112
as wickedness, 40, 91, 104, 120
as moral waste but potential garden, 4, 8, 14, 15, 39, 40, 42, 44, 45, 78, 92, 122, 124, 126, 129, 134, 211; Paradise-Wilderness Cycle, 195, 212, 215
as natural park, 130, 136
as place of refuge and redemption, 6, 17, 21, 25, 26, 29, 57, 58, 70, 71, 76, 94, 95, 96, 98, 99, 103, 106, 107, 108, 109, 112, 119, 120; "our

true home," 134; *see also* Refuge; Church, woman of the Wilderness; Israel, church as
  of tutelage, 15, 43, 46, 73, 77, 81
  of election and prophetic or royal anointment, 17, 22, 147
  of temptation, 16, 17, 25, 44, 68, 73, 79, 102, 109
  of combat, 41, 120; as arena, *see separate entry*
  of darkness (mortification), 55, 56
  of nuptial, covenantal bliss, 10, 15, 16, 54, 67, 113, 118
  of purification, 7
  of contemplation, 17, 26, 41, 56, 77, 106
  of the restoration of all things: covenant, communism, paradise, harmony, 22, 46, 84 *and separate entries*
  of wanting property, 44; *see also* communism
  of knowing, 135
  as state of mind; soul at leisure from self, 53, 54, 67, 70; "wilderness state," 5, 66, 86, 89, 90, 114; negative sense (wilderness), 91, 116
  as mystical stage, 40, 51, 52, 114
  as ground of being, 52
  as ground of divine being (*adyton*), 52, 53
  as reality perceived no longer as wasteland, 59, 132, 134, 136
  as unfallen, 82; *see also* Nature
  as "university," 130
  water as:
    primal abyss as, 14
    ocean as, 14, 29, 135
    swamp as, 135
  "wilderness of nations," 18, 19, 20, 31, 105
heathen cults, 32
church as, 35, 76, 80, 87, 91, 93, 103
  nationalism in church as, 87
  sectarianism as, 80 ff., 88, 124
materialism as, 128
civilization as, 132
  as misshapen concepts, 230
  distinguished from heaviness, *see*

special entry
  distinguished from desert, 134
  bewilderment, 84; fire in the wilderness, 12, 22, 121; heath, 163; "fruitful wilderness," 114; "progress in," libertinism, 81, 82; three stages of, 113, cf. 45; "wild stranger land," 114; "wilderness assemblies," 120; wilderness frugality, 101, 102, *see also* Highway; Damascus, desert of; etc.
William, king of England, 152
William of Nangis, 169, 175 n., 180 n.
Williams, Aaron, 94
Williams, George H., 122 n., 153 n., 158 n., 189 n., 213 n.
Wind, 8, 12, 14, 46, 75, 123; *see also* Spirit; Storm god, *and* Hurricane
Windsor, Vermont, 125, 126
Winslow, Edward, 99
Winstanley, Gerrard, 80
Wittenberg, 99
Wolfe, Linnie Marsh, 131 n.
Wolfson, Harry, 151 n.
Wolves, 4, 33, 42, 48, 60, 116
Woman in the Wilderness, *see* Church
Women, as spiritual, 162
Wordsworth, William, 89
Workman, Herbert, 42 n.
Worm, 78
Württembergers, 94, 114
Wüste, 52, 53, 67
Wright, Conrad, 200 n.
Wyclif, John, 61, 77

Yahad, 19
Yeshimon, 12 n.
Yieldedness, *see Gelassenheit*

Zabarella, Cardinal Francis, 177, 182, 183
Zadokite Documents, 19
Zeno of Verona, 35 n.
Zimmerman, Benedict, 56 n.
Zimmerman, Johann Jakob, 113
Zieglschmid, A. J. F., 70
Ziegler, Caspar, 151
Zion, 25, 26, 27, 63, 64, 72, 92, 117, 119, 123
Zwingli, Ulrich, 86

SCRIPTURAL INDEX

Old Testament

Genesis *1:2*, 14; *2:8*, 100, 115; *2:15*, 115; *2:16*, 30; *:323–24*, 115; *5:1*, 150; *10:25*, 145 n.; *11:16*, 145 n.; *37:9*, 25
Exodus *16:15*, 56; *24:18*, 22; *34*, 62
Leviticus 20, 62
Deuteronomy 8, 102; *8:2 f.*, 16, 22, 110; *32:10* f., 16; *36:17*, 13
Joshua *9:7–17*, 145; *15:16–17*, 165, 165 n
Judges *9:10*, 165 n.
I Kings 7:2, 85; *19:16*, 17, 22, 147, 192 (implied); *19:48*, 17
II Kings *2:25*, 55 n.; *3:12*, 106; *4:38 f.*, 17, 43; *6:1–7*, 43, 123, 165; *10:15*, 23, 17; *22:14*, 149
I Chronicles *22:9–10*, 179 n.
II Chronicles *26:16–17*, 156
Job *3:5*, 85; *10:22*, 85; *26:7*, 14
Psalms 26, 162 n.; *42:1*, 63; *78:40 f.*, 16; *80:13*, 40; *91:4–13*, 23; *91:13*, 34; *95: 7*, 90; *105:15*, 35; *106:13 f.*, 17; *106:26*, 17; *144:6*, 40
Song of Solomon (Canticle of Canticles) *1:7*, 55 n.; *3:6*, 87, 88, 106; *3:16*, 32; *4:8*, 108; *4:12*, 16, 80; 5, 105; *6:2*, 99; *6:10*, 86; 119; *6:43*, 119; *8:5 ff.*, 16, 32, 45, 51, 54, 55, 87, 88, 106; *8:8*, 102
Isaiah *1–3*, 60; *3:18–21*, 127; 5, 96; *8:6*, 168 n.; *10:1–13*, 112; *25:1 ff.*, 127; 5, *27:1*, 34; *33:16*, 36, 38; *33:20*, 119; *34:13*, 13; *35:1 ff.*, 14, 40, 41, 42, 75, 89, 128; *35:1–7*, 36; *40:3*, 20, 22, 119; *41:18 f.*, 14; *42:11–16*, 81; *43: 18–21*, 32; *43:19 f.*, 94; *44:3*, 72; *48:21*, 32; *51:3*, 9, 72, 94; *54:2*, 119; *55:1*, 72; *58:11*, 72, 80; *61:4*, 107; *64:4*, 94; *65:8*, 31; *66:8*, 9
Jeremiah *2:2*, 15, 54, 55, 67, 113; *2:3*, 21, 110; *2:21*, 110; *2:6*, 85; *5:6*, 48 n.; *6:7 f.*, 13; *7:34*, 13; *9:2*, 17; *25:38*, 12; *35:6 f.*, 17; *43:50*, 62
Ezekiel, *20:10*, 63; *20:33–36*, 18; *20:34 f.*, 20; *20:35 ff.*, 19, 85; *36:35*, 72; *37:1–6*, 14; *46:12*, 75, 127
Daniel *2:45*, 37; *12:1 f.*, 71
Hosea *2:12*, 53; *2:14 f.*, 15, 54, 55, 68; *2:16*, 51; *12:9 f.*, 17
Joel *2:3*, 12, 72
Amos *5:25–27*, 19; *5:26 f.*, 18, 25 n.
Zechariah *13:5*, 59, 66
Malachi, *3:1*, 22; *4:5* 22, 46

New Testament

Matthew *3:11*, 22; *12:1 ff.*, 45; *18:20*, 39;

24, 36 n.; *24:16*, 25 n.; *24:26* 104, 26, 44; *26:23*, 166 n.
Mark *1:13*, 2, 23, 34; *14*, 44; *16:15*, xi; *16:19*, 36 n.
Luke *3:1–13*, 45 n.; *3:16*, 45 n.; *4:1*, 73; *14:26*, 54; 22, 44; *23:42 f.*, 27; *23:43*, 26, 45; *24:50 n.*, 36 n.
John *9:7*, 168 n.; *15:14*, 35; *18:1*, 45; *19:15*, 173; *21:15–19*, 112
Acts *1:1*, 36 n.; *2:7 f.*, 70; *3:21*, 46, 84; *7:29 f.*, 22, 43; *7:38*, 86, 107; *13:33*, 23; *21:38*, 21 n.
Romans *5:14*, 71; *8:22*, xi, 84; *11:14*, 102; *11:17 ff.*, 30; *12:3*, 30; *14:14*, 81
I Corinthians *3:6–9*, 40; *6:17 ff.*, 163; *10*, 69; *10:1 ff.*, 24, 44, *10:5–10*, 84; *11:1*, 67; *15:45*, 26
II Corinthians *11:2*, 68; *12:2 ff.*, 27, 39; *12:4*, 26
Ephesians, *1:22*, 34; *2:6*, 72
Colossians *1:13*, 72; *3:3*, 53 n.
II Thessalonians *2:3*, 173
II Timothy *2:3*, 144
Titus *1:15*, 81 n.
Hebrews *3:7–18*, 25; *11:13 f.*, 111
James *2:23*, 35; *3:7*, 179 n.
Revelation *1:9*, 26; *2:7*, 26, 27; *4:4*, 68; *6:9–11*, 112; *6:19*, 104; *11:3*, 58; *11:5*, 86; *11:7*, 86; 12, 71, 85, 105, 108, 124; *12:1 f.*, 25, 175 n.; *12:6*, 25, 57, 58, 68, 70, 92, 93, 95, 112 n., 113, 119, 119 n.; *12:12*, 108; *12:14*, 86; *13*, 105; *14:1 ff.*, 68; *14:6*, 58; *15:2–4*, 25; *17:3*, 12, 96; *17:3*, 12, 26, 96; *17:11*, 106; 18, 62; *18:6*, 107; *21:2*, 106, 119; *21:6*, 127; *22:2*, 27

Baruch *21*, 28; *24:5*, 28 n.; *58:6*, 23; *71: 4–7*, 8 n.
Apocalypse of Baruch *29:8; 73:6; 77:13 f.*, 21
Enoch, First and Second 21
IV Esdras *14:37 f.*, 39
Judith *6:15*, 165 n.
I Maccabees *2:29–35*, 21; *6:9*, 145 n.; *12:6–7*, 145 n.
II Maccabees *5:27*, 21
Psalms of Solomon *14:2*, 31 n.
Vita Adae et Evae, 21; *6:1*, 23; *8:3*, 23
Testament of the Twelve Patriarchs 188
Levi *18:10–13*, 31
Wisdom *16:2*, 56
Pseudo-Barnabas *6:8–19*, 28; *11:9*, 36
Proto-evangelium of James *21:3*, 26
Pseudo-Matthew 27
Gospel according to Thomas *1–4*, xi; *77–79*, xi